Inessa Armand was the first Director of the Women's Section of the Russian Communist Party (the Zhenotdel). She was one of the most important women in the pre-revolutionary Bolshevik Party, and second only to Aleksandra Kollontai in the ranks of early Soviet feminists. Yet if Armand is mentioned at all in Western literature, it is solely as Lenin's protégée and probable mistress.

In this political biography of Armand, the first to appear in English, Professor R. C. Elwood seeks to correct this picture by portraying her as an accomplished revolutionary propagandist and Bolshevik organizer before 1917 and as a feminist who devoted much of her life to defending women's interests in the home, in the workplace and in society. Based on unpublished police reports, memoirs, Armand's letters to her five children and two husbands, and Lenin's 118 published letters to her, this study provides new and revealing information on Inessa's up-bringing in the wealthy Armand family, on the revolutionary sympathies of many members of that family, on their subsequent and controversial financial support of the Bolshevik Party, and on her career as a Tolstoyan and feminist long before she became a revolutionary. The author also examines Armand's stormy relations with Lenin and casts doubt on the veracity of earlier evidence that they had an extended love affair.

Nonetheless Armand was a close friend of Lenin from 1909 to her death from cholera in 1920 and this biography also provides insights into the private life of the first Soviet leader – a man who was often patronizing, inconsiderate, rude and prudish and from whose tutelage Armand spent many of her last years trying to escape.

INESSA ARMAND

INESSA ARMAND

Revolutionary and feminist

R. C. ELWOOD

Carleton University, Ottawa

CAMBRIDGE
UNIVERSITY PRESS

Published by the Press Syndicate of the University of Cambridge
The Pitt Building, Trumpington Street, Cambridge CB2 1RP
40 West 20th Street, New York, NY 10011–4211, USA
10 Stamford Road, Oakleigh, Victoria 3166, Australia

First published 1992

Printed in Great Britain at the University Press, Cambridge

A catalogue record for this book is available from the British Library

Library of Congress cataloguing in publication data
Elwood, Ralph Carter, 1936–
Inessa Armand: revolutionary and feminist / R. C. Elwood.
p.   cm.
Includes bibliographical references and index.
ISBN 0–521–41486–5 (hardback)
1. Armand, I. F. (Inessa Fedorovna), 1874–1920.
2. Women communists – Soviet Union – Biography.
3. Feminists – Soviet Union – Biography.
I. Title.
HX313.8 .A75E48   1992
305.42′092–dc20
[B]   91–33752   CIP

ISBN 0 521 41486 5 hardback

47

CONTENTS

ILLUSTRATIONS

PREFACE

Inessa Armand, if she is mentioned at all in Western textbooks of Russian history or in popular biographies of V. I. Lenin, is usually portrayed as a beautiful woman with a talent for playing the piano and for speaking in four languages. She is rarely seen as a person of revolutionary significance other than allegedly being Lenin's mistress for most of the decade before he came to power. The first time I had reason to question this view was twenty years ago when working on Lenin's troubled relations with the pre-revolutionary *Pravda*. I was struck by the fact that in 1912 the Bolshevik leader sent Armand to St Petersburg to try to bring the recalcitrant editors into line. I wondered then (but not sufficiently to put my doubts into print) why he would dispatch a political neophyte, who supposedly was his lover, on a difficult and dangerous revolutionary mission that predictably ended with her arrest. Several years later, my preconceptions about Armand were again challenged when studying another event of revolutionary significance: the Brussels 'Unity' Conference of 1914. Once again Lenin chose her for a politically sensitive mission – this time to defend his untenable position on party unity before the leaders of European social democracy in Brussels. I was particularly intrigued by the nuances of their extensive correspondence at the time of this conference: by the way Lenin implored her to represent the Bolshevik faction, by his insensitive and condescending comments to her during the meeting, and by her show of independence in refusing to bow to his demands after Brussels. The impression conveyed was certainly not the conventional one of a loyal, docile and mindless protégée.

I was fortunate that in 1981 Janet Hyer, then an undergraduate at Carleton University, was looking around for a topic on which to write her honours research essay. I suggested that the prevailing view of Armand might bear re-examination. Her excellent essay and subsequent Master's thesis on *Rabotnitsa* focussed on Inessa's contributions to the women's movement in late Imperial and early Soviet Russia – another facet of her life which has largely been ignored by Western and

Soviet commentators. On the basis of Ms Hyer's work and my suspicions, I decided to look at Armand's entire life, not just at her relations
with Lenin, and to attempt a biography that would concentrate on her
overlooked roles as a revolutionary and as a feminist. As a summer
research assistant, Ms Hyer has called my attention to many of the
sources on which this book is based; as a person with a sharply focussed
feminist perspective, she challenged an old-fashioned political historian's view of the world and forced me to rethink many of my own
stereotypes; as a friend, she read a draft of this manuscript and made
many helpful criticisms – some of which I have taken to heart. I would
like to acknowledge my very great debt to Janet Hyer for the assistance
which she has given me and to absolve of blame in those areas where
critics may still find me too old fashioned.

Most of my research was done in various hospitable libraries in
London and in the marvellous archives of the Hoover Institution in
Stanford, California. Like most Canadian scholars, I am indebted to the
Social Sciences and Humanities Research Council of Canada which has
generously supported my research. I also wish to thank Peter Redda-
way, then of the London School of Economics, who provided me with a
conducive work space while I was on sabbatical leave at LSE in
1984–5; Jacques Galley and Pierre-Alain Crausaz who loaned me their
foresters' hut near Ecuvillens so that I might collate material gathered in
London while gazing at the Swiss Alps; and Ronald M. Butaloff, archi-
vist at the Hoover Institution, who patiently answered my queries
before, during and after my visit to Stanford in 1986. The writing of this
biography was done in Ottawa thanks to a Marston LaFrance Fellowship which relieved me of teaching duties at Carleton University for a
year. I hope that both the then Dean of Arts, Naomi Griffiths, who
administered this unique fellowship, and the former Dean of Social
Sciences, Dennis Forcese, who provided me with a quiet hideaway in
which to write, will realize how much they have contributed to the
completion of this project. I doubt if any historian working in North
America and especially in Canada could function without the services of
local Inter-Library Loan offices. I am grateful that Doris Cole and her
efficient associates at Carleton were able to acquire all but one of the
many items I requested.

My thickest research file contains correspondence with friends, colleagues and other scholars known to me only through their published
work who have generously answered my questions, sent me material I
had overlooked or, in a couple of cases, gone to archives I could not
visit. To them, and to others closer to home who have helped me with

problems either of translation or of an unfriendly computer, I wish to express my sincerest appreciation. I hope that the following people will see reflections of their assistance at different points in Inessa's biography and will accept this simple expression of thanks: Andrei Belykh, Laurie Bernstein, John Bushnell, Barbara Clements, John Channon, Fred Corney, David Doughan, Linda Edmondson, Hasmik Egian, Ben Eklof, Marjorie Elwood, Beate Fieseler, Carl Jacobsen, Samuel Kassow, John Keep, Peter King, Ronnie Kowalski, George Melnikoff, Egor Nazarenko, Iuri Orlov, Elizabeth Popoff-Böcker, Teresa Rakowska-Harmstone, Steve Sampson, Joseph Sanders, Gregory Smolnyec, Mikhailova Svetlana, Edward Swiderski, Michael Sydenham and Tova Yedlin.

To Robert H. McNeal – friend, scholar, tiller of the same vineyard – who for twenty-five years answered my questions, encouraged my efforts, and commented in a constructive fashion on my work – I owe a most profound debt. While we argued on occasion about Lenin's relations with Inessa Armand, I was greatly looking forward to Bob's reading of this manuscript before it went to press and to his usual insightful criticism. It certainly would have been a better book for it. Tragically, the profession was deprived of an excellent historian and I lost a good friend when Robert McNeal was killed in a car accident in June 1988. This book is dedicated to his memory.

To my wife, Jill St. Germain, who listened patiently as I tried to work out seeming contradictions in Inessa's life, who put my illegible scrawl onto readable computer disks, and who criticized my style and questioned my logic to good effect, I can only repeat that old bromide of other over-indulged author-husbands: without you this book would never have been written.

* * *

The dates used herein have been expressed in the form used by the participants themselves at the time and place in question. This means that all events in western Europe or in Soviet Russia after February 1918 are dated according to the 'new-style' Gregorian calendar. When dates refer to publications or occurrences in tsarist Russia or during the 1917 revolutions, I have used the 'old style' Julian calendar. When the distinction is unclear or confusion seems possible, I have sought to provide both dates.

INTRODUCTION

At 3 a.m. in the early morning of 11 October 1920 Polina Vinogradskaia was awakened by the ringing of her telephone. The hour of
the call and the fact that the Moscow telephone system was working at
all must have surprised her but not as much as the identity of her caller.
The high-pitched voice at the other end of the line belonged to the head
of the new Soviet state, V. I. Lenin. He was calling to tell Vinogradskaia
that the body of their mutual friend, Inessa Armand, was just arriving
at the Kazan Station. Was she ready? Could she meet them on the train
platform?[1] He did not have to say that Armand had died of cholera at
the age of forty-six while on a vacation in the Caucasus he insisted she
take. Vinogradskaia knew since she also had been there and was well
aware that her caller's hectoring telegrams to local officials to make
sure Armand was properly cared for and protected from counter-
revolutionary irregulars[2] had contributed to her unnecessary evacuation from Kislovodsk. After five days of being shunted from one dirty
train station to another and six nights of sleeping in a crowded railway
car, their friend had contracted the dread disease and died in the small
town of Nal'chik on 24 September 1920.

It was still dark when Vinogradskaia arrived at the nearly deserted
Kazan Station. Standing quietly on the platform with Lenin and his wife
Nadezhda Krupskaia were Armand's five children, ranging in age from
sixteen to twenty-five, her estranged husband Alexander Armand, and
several women from Zhenotdel, the Women's Section of the Central
Committee of the Russian Communist Party which Inessa directed at the
time of her death. By 8 a.m. the cortège was on its way through the
gloomy cobblestone streets of a city still suffering from the effects of
more than six years of world war, mass revolution and civil war. Lenin
insisted on walking behind the horse-drawn catafalque as it made the 3

---

[1] P. S. Vinogradskaia, *Sobytiia i pamiatnye vstrechi* (Moscow, 1968), pp. 227–8.
[2] *Leninskii sbornik*, vol. XXXVII (Moscow, 1970), p. 233; V. I. Lenin, *Polnoe sobranie
sochinenii*, 55 vols. (Moscow, 1958–65), vol. LI, pp. 261, 262, 265, 273 (hereafter
PSS).

kilometre trip down Kalanchevkaia and Miasnitskaia, past the headquarters of the Cheka in Liubianskaia Square, to the House of Unions
where the body was to lie in state. To Alexander Armand, once a
wealthy textile manufacturer before being expropriated by his fellow
mourners, the choice of this impressive eighteenth-century building
must have seemed ironic. He had visited it on occasion when it had
served as a club for the Moscow aristocracy and he had sat in its Hall of
Columns as a liberal deputy to the Moscow City Duma fifteen years
earlier. Now his wife's body was to lie on a dais in the Small Hall
surrounded by an honour guard of four women from Zhenotdel. The
walls were already decorated with revolutionary banners while around
the unopened casket were put a score of wreaths, including a large one
of white hyacinths with the inscription 'To Comrade Inessa – from
V. I. Lenin'.[3]

At noon the next day, the zinc-lined coffin was carried through
Theatre Square and the Square of the Revolution past the hideous
Historical Museum to the walls of the Kremlin in Red Square. The
mourners on that clear, sunny fall day included what *Izvestiia* called an
'endless flow of women workers'[4] paying their last respects to a person
who had quietly but effectively championed the equality of women in
the workplace, in trade unions, in the party and in the home. If they
were near the freshly dug grave they would have heard V. I. Nevskii,
speaking in the name of the party's Central Committee, praise Armand
as a revolutionary leader and Old Bolshevik who joined the party before
the 1905 Revolution. S. I. Polidorov spoke for the Moscow Soviet in
lauding the deceased's work as head of the Moscow Guberniia Sovnarkhoz (Economic Council) where, 'thanks to her knowledge of economics
and her experience, she successfully put the economic construction of
Moscow Guberniia on a firm foundation'.[5] Aleksandra Kollontai, her
colleague and sometime rival in the women's movement, gave an
'especially impassioned speech'[6] about Inessa's role in 1914 in establishing and editing *Rabotnitsa*, the first Bolshevik paper for women
workers, and about her subsequent efforts to attract women to party
and soviet work. Anna Kalygina, speaking for the Moscow section of
Zhenotdel, noted that these accomplishments were all the more impres-

---

[3] Vinogradskaia, pp. 231–2; *Izvestiia*, 12 October 1920, p. 4; *Pravda*, 12 October 1920,
p. 1; *Lenin v Moskve: mesta prebyvaniia, daty i sobytiia* (Moscow, 1959), p. 166. See also
photograph of Armand's coffin lying in state in *Kommunistka*, 1920, no. 5, p. 19.

[4] *Izvestiia*, 13 October 1920, p. 2. See also a photograph of the many women in the
funeral procession in Pavel Podliashuk, *Tovarishch Inessa: dokumental'naia povest'*, 4th
edn (Moscow, 1984).

[5] *Pravda*, 13 October 1920, p. 2.   [6] *Izvestiia*, 13 October 1920, p. 2.

sive since Armand had had to rise above her 'rich bourgeois background'.[7] There followed three more speeches by representatives of working women in Petrograd, the Far East and the Caucasus. Finally, after the firing of a military salute and the singing of the 'Internationale', the body of Inessa Armand was laid to rest in the 'Red Graveyard'.

It may have seemed curious to some that Lenin, who had known Armand well for over eleven years and had shown such personal concern about her funeral arrangements, was not among the speakers in Red Square. One of those present, who saw him standing with his crying wife by the side of the grave, felt that he would have been physically unable to do so.

I never saw such torment. I never saw any human being so completely absorbed by sorrow ... Not only his face but his whole body expressed so much sorrow that I dared not greet him ... It was clear that he wanted to be alone with his grief. He seemed to have shrunk ... his eyes seemed drowned in tears held back with effort ...[8]

*   *   *

Within a decade, the contributions of Inessa Armand to the revolutionary and women's movements in Russia which had been so praised by her funeral orators in Red Square had been forgotten or suppressed. Six months after her death, the New Economic Policy brought to an end the Sovnarkhoz experiment in economic centralization and nationalization; in 1930 Zhenotdel was closed down by a male-dominated party no longer interested in paying lip service to female equality and family reform; and, in the 1930s, Old Bolsheviks, especially those from rich bourgeois backgrounds, disappeared from the history books as well as from the party itself. Biographies of Lenin and histories of the party, whether written in the Soviet Union or the West, almost without exception failed to mention the name of Inessa Armand during the last quarter-century of Stalin's life, let alone her leading role as a revolutionary and a feminist in Lenin's time.[9]

Ironically, if the funeral orations had been forgotten in the Soviet Union by the time of Stalin's death, Lenin's conduct at the funeral was being recalled at the same time in the West and offered up as evidence of

[7] *Pravda*, 13 October 1920, p. 2.
[8] Angelica Balabanoff, *Impressions of Lenin* (Ann Arbor, 1964), pp. 14–15.
[9] See, for instance, the early biographies of Lenin by Valeriu Marcu (1928), Christopher Hollis (1938) and David Shub (1948); the party histories of N. N. Popov (1926) and Em. Iaroslavskii (1929); and Stalin's *Short Course* (1938).

3

yet another reason for Soviet reticence concerning Inessa Armand. In 1952, a disgruntled French Communist remembered a conversation he had had many years earlier with Aleksandra Kollontai in Oslo which touched on Lenin's behaviour in October 1920. The Bolshevik leader 'was unrecognizable' at the funeral, Kollontai told Marcel Body. 'He walked with his eyes closed and every moment we thought he might fall to the ground.'[10] Her explanation for his distraught state and inferentially for his great personal interest in the funeral arrangements was that Lenin had been in love with Armand for many years before the revolution. The affair had been so intense, she said, that Krupskaia offered to leave her husband in 1911 to facilitate his happiness with the 'other woman'.[11] This undocumented revelation was picked up by Bertram Wolfe who received confirmation of its supposed accuracy from Angelica Balabanoff, once an important figure in the communist movement but now an elderly and disillusioned woman, who had also been present at the funeral. While Wolfe discounted Balabanoff's assertion that Armand had had a child by Lenin, he felt that there was other evidence to support the conclusion that the two had probably been lovers from 1910 to 1916. He was particularly struck by Soviet reluctance to publish Lenin's voluminous correspondence with Armand and by his highly unusual use of the familiar form of address in the few edited letters that appeared in Stalin's lifetime.[12]

Western biographers were overjoyed that Wolfe had found a human element in Lenin and many rushed off to discover other loves in his life.[13] Few bothered to question the veracity of his evidence[14] and none showed much interest in Inessa Armand beyond portraying her as a Paris-born woman of striking beauty who had a talent for foreign languages and for playing the piano. In all other respects, she was simply Lenin's close comrade-in-arms and of no particular consequence in her own right as a revolutionary. During the last decade, some

10 Quoted by Marcel Body, 'Alexandra Kollontai', *Preuves* (Paris), vol. II, no. 14 (April 1952), p. 17.
11 *Ibid.*
12 Bertram D. Wolfe, 'Lenin and Inessa Armand', *Slavic Review*, vol. XXII, no. 1 (March 1963), pp. 96–114.
13 See, for example, Louis Fischer, *The Life of Lenin* (New York, 1964); Robert Payne, *The Life and Death of Lenin* (New York, 1964); Stefan T. Possony, *Lenin: The Compulsive Revolutionary* (Chicago, 1964); Robert H. McNeal, *Bride of the Revolution: Krupskaya and Lenin* (Ann Arbor, 1972); Ladislaus Singer, *Korrekturen zu Lenin* (Stuttgart, 1980); M. C. Morgan, *Lenin* (London, 1971).
14 Among those who did were Adam B. Ulam, *The Bolsheviks: The Intellectual and Political History of the Triumph of Communism in Russia* (New York, 1965) and Neil Harding, *Lenin's Political Thought*, vol. I: *Theory and Practice in the Democratic Revolution* (New York, 1977).

Western scholars of the Russian women's movement, most notably Richard Stites and Barbara Clements, have been less flippant and more willing to acknowledge Armand's contributions to post-revolutionary Soviet feminism.[15] Even they, however, have paid little attention to her pre-war interest in women's issues or to her decisive role in establishing *Rabotnitsa*.[16]

Following Stalin's death, Soviet and Soviet-approved writers also rediscovered Inessa Armand. In 1957 Jean Fréville, a French poet and communist with the cooperation of Inessa's daughter Inna, wrote an authorized biography of his compatriot[17] which has generously been described as 'thin and pious'.[18] Poetic licence is the least of the faults of his misleading exercise in hagiography. Six years later, at the same time that Bertram Wolfe's account was appearing in the *Slavic Review*, the first Soviet biography of her was published by Pavel Podliashuk.[19] Now in its fourth edition, *Tovarishch Inessa* is a popular account designed to make Armand into a role model for sixteen-year-old Russian girls. With

---

[15] Richard Stites, *The Women's Liberation Movement in Russia: Feminism, Nihilism, and Bolshevism, 1860–1930* (Princeton, 1977) and Barbara Evans Clements, *Bolshevik Feminist: The Life of Aleksandra Kollontai* (Bloomington, 1979). See also Beatrice Farnsworth, *Alexandra Kollontai: Socialism, Feminism and the Russian Revolution* (Stanford, 1980). Like the less flamboyant Armand, Kollontai's importance as a political leader and feminist was for many decades dismissed by male historians fascinated only by her theories about 'free love' and her libertine lifestyle. Unlike Armand, Kollontai is now generally accepted as the preeminent figure in the communist women's movement and indeed is often given credit for some of Armand's accomplishments.

[16] It is indicative that two recent and important studies of pre-revolutionary Russian feminism virtually ignore Armand's contributions to the women's movement. See Linda Harriet Edmondson, *Feminism in Russia, 1900–1917* (Stanford, 1984) and Rochelle Lois Goldberg, 'The Russian Women's Movement: 1859–1917' (unpublished Ph.D. dissertation, University of Rochester, 1976).

[17] Jean Fréville, *Une grand figure de la Révolution russe: Inessa Armand* (Paris, 1957). See also review by L. M. Egorova in *Istoriia SSSR*, 1958, no. 4, p. 188.

[18] Richard Stites, 'Kollontai, Inessa, and Krupskaia: A Review of Recent Literature', *Canadian-American Slavic Studies*, vol. IX, no. 1 (Spring 1975), p. 87.

[19] Pavel Podliashuk, *Tovarishch Inessa: dokumental'naia povest'*, 1st edn (Moscow, 1963). The *New York Times* speculated that the renewed Soviet interest in Armand was an attempt to counteract recent Western fascination with Lenin's love life. This was reflected, the paper said, in commemorative articles praising Armand's virtues that had appeared in *Pravda* and *Izvestiia* on her ninetieth birthday and in the concurrent closing of *Time* magazine's Moscow bureau for 'touching with dirty fingers the memory of the founder of the Soviet state' in its 24 April 1964 issue (*New York Times*, 17 May 1964, p. 23; see also *Pravda*, 8 May 1964, p. 4, and *Izvestiia*, 8 May 1964, p. 4). An equally plausible explanation for Podliashuk's biography was the imminent appearance of Lenin's hitherto unpublished correspondence to Armand in volumes XLVIII and XLIX of his *Polnoe sobranie sochinenii*. Someone had to tell inquisitive Soviet readers something about this obscure woman to whom their leader had written over one hundred letters and whose body lay in the hallowed precincts behind his mausoleum.

5

far more attention to historical accuracy than Fréville, Podliashuk portrays Armand as a good mother, as a dedicated revolutionary who endured five arrests and several years in tsarist detention and, above all, as a loyal and efficient disciple of Lenin. Little of consequence is said about her early life in the 'nest of gentlefolk', about the way in which she became a revolutionary, about her work as an underground propagandist long before she met Lenin, about the role of the Armand family in financing the Bolshevik cause, or about her work as a feminist after the revolution. Needless to say, even less is said about her willingness to contradict and oppose Lenin on the numerous occasions when she felt he was wrong in political matters or inconsiderate in personal relations.

These unanswered questions are some of the issues which the present biography seeks to address. Inessa Armand will be viewed primarily as a revolutionary: first as a Social Democratic propagandist in Moscow from 1904 to 1907, then as a Bolshevik organizer and spokeswoman for Lenin in emigration from 1910 to 1917, and finally as a Communist administrator from 1918 to 1920. She also will be seen as a feminist – a term which she herself would have rejected – working to rehabilitate prostitutes before the 1905 Revolution, trying to organize women workers on the eve of the war, and seeking to achieve female equality in the new Soviet state. Insofar as the sources permit, an attempt will be made to illuminate both her personal qualities which so impressed many of her revolutionary colleagues and also her personal relationship with Lenin which has so intrigued recent Western writers to the detriment of serious study of other aspects of her life.

While I disagree with many of Bertram Wolfe's conclusions, I am indebted to him for having aroused my interest in Inessa Armand and for having raised some of the important issues in her life. I also recognize that Mr Wolfe did not have at his disposal many of the sources on which this biography is based. The veil of obscurity over her revolutionary career before 1909 and her family life, for example, has been partially lifted with the recent publication of more than sixty of Inessa's letters to her children, her husband Alexander and his brother Vladimir.[20] While heavily edited and obviously incomplete, these letters offer the best

---

[20] The largest number of these letters appear in I. F. Armand, *Stat'i, rechi, pis'ma* (Moscow, 1975), pp. 179–257. Somewhat more complete versions of many of these are to be found in 'Pis'ma Inessy Armand', *Novyi mir*, 1970, no. 6, pp. 196–218. Portions of twelve other letters not found in either of these collections are included in the fourth edition of Podliashuk (Moscow, 1984) and in Vladimir Sanov, 'Mezenskaia ballada', *Sever*, 1971, no. 12, pp. 82–96. The most recent compilation, S. Vinogradov's *Sokrovishcha dushevnoi krasoty* (Moscow, 1984), offers nothing which has not already been published.

insight available into her personality and the evolution of her early political thinking. Since 1964 ninety-five new letters from Lenin to Armand have appeared in the fifth edition of his collected works and in recent volumes of the *Leninskii sbornik* in addition to more complete versions of the twenty-three that were belatedly published in the fourth edition.[21] This correspondence, which is concentrated in the period from December 1913 to April 1917, reveals much not only about Lenin but also about Armand's party activities in emigration and her often troubled relations with the Bolshevik leader. The period from 1909 to 1917 is also covered by the twenty-two police reports found in the Okhrana Archives of the Hoover Institution. These reports, which were first made available to scholars in 1964, are neither sensational nor unique in their revelations but they do add useful confirmation and detail to published memoir literature. Scholars have long been aware of the reminiscences of Armand's contemporaries collected by Krupskaia and published in 1926.[22] Very little attention has been paid, however, either to the host of other and often obscure memoirs that appeared in Soviet journals in the 1920s[23] or to the few brief but interesting accounts which started to reappear in the 1960s.[24] A study of Armand's short post-revolutionary career has been facilitated by the re-publication in 1975 of thirty-five of her journalistic articles and three short brochures.[25] While this corpus falls short of the one hundred articles two Soviet scholars claim she wrote,[26] I have found references to only five pieces not in this collection. Finally, it should be noted that persons interested in Armand's activity in the women's movement

---

[21] Lenin, *PSS*, vols. XLVIII and XLIX; *Leninskii sbornik*, vols. XXXV (1945), pp. 108–9, XXXVII (1970), pp. 35–8, 52–8, 233, XL (1985), pp. 49–50; 'Novye dokumenty V. I. Lenina', *Izvestiia TsK KPSS*, 1989, no. 1, pp. 215–16.

[22] N. K. Krupskaia (ed.), *Pamiati Inessy Armand* (Moscow, 1926). Krupskaia's own *Reminiscences of Lenin* (Moscow, 1959), which first appeared in Russian in 1926, also contain interesting if somewhat sanitized and occasionally misleading information about her good friend Inessa.

[23] An invaluable bibliography of early Soviet historical literature pertaining to Armand will be found in V. I. Nevskii (ed.), *Deiateli revoliutsionnogo dvizheniia v Rossii: Bio-biblio-graficheskii slovar'*, vol. V: *Sotsial-demokraty, 1880–1904*, vyp. 1 (A–B) (Moscow, 1931), pp. 128–9.

[24] See, among others, the Vinogradskaia and Sanov items already cited as well as A. E. Margarian, 'Novoe ob Inesse Armand', *Voprosy istorii*, 1962, no. 3, pp. 213–15, and N. M. Druzhinin, 'O trekh uchastnitsakh revoliutsionnoi bor'by', *Voprosy istorii*, 1983, no. 1, pp. 85–9.

[25] Armand, *Stat'i*, pp. 23–176. While occasional ellipses appear in these versions, those that I have been able to check against the originals do not appear to involve the omission of extensive or significant material.

[26] Iu. Rusakov and V. Solov'ev, 'Stanovlius' bol'shevichkoi ... ', *V mire knig*, 1978, no. 8, p. 79.

especially and also as a Soviet administrator have been aided immeasurably by recent doctoral research done in the United States and Great Britain. One cannot help but be impressed by the quality of this research, much of which remains unpublished. While none of it deals extensively with Inessa Armand, in toto it provides the social and economic background which was absent from Western scholarship at the time Bertram Wolfe was writing.[27]

Despite the wealth of material that has become available since 1963, certain periods in Armand's life remain poorly documented and valuable sources of information still remain inaccessible in Russian archives. The background of the Armand family, details about their comfortable life in Pushkino, and information about the revolutionary activity of Inessa's in-laws remain scarce. Unfortunately, Armand was very reluctant to talk about this period of her life with friends in the party or to write about it herself.[28] Several manuscripts which are important for an understanding of her intellectual maturation – a draft of her first major but unpublished article, a prospectus for a brochure on marriage and the family, and a very brief autobiography – appear to exist in Russian archives but have not been published in their entirety.[29] The most important lacuna, however, has resulted from the failure of Soviet authorities to publish almost any of Armand's extensive correspondence with Lenin.[30] It is frustrating in the extreme to hear only one side of an argument, especially when that point of view is expressed by a

---

[27] See, for example, the following unpublished Ph.D. dissertations on aspects of the women's movement: Laurie Bernstein, 'Sonia's Daughters: Prostitution and Society in Russia' (University of California, Berkeley, 1987); Anne Louise Bobroff, 'Working Women, Bonding Patterns, and the Politics of Daily Life: Russia at the End of the Old Regime', 2 vols. (University of Michigan, 1982); Carol Eubanks Hayden, 'Feminism and Bolshevism: The *Zhenotdel* and the Politics of Women's Emancipation in Russia, 1917–1930' (University of California, Berkeley, 1979); Amy W. Knight, 'The Participation of Women in the Revolutionary Movement in Russia, 1890–1914' (University of London, 1977). Other theses which I found particularly useful include Herbert Ray Buchanan, 'Soviet Economic Policy for the Transition Period: The Supreme Council of the National Economy, 1917–20' (Indiana University, 1972) and J. L. West, 'The Moscow Progressists: Russian Industrialists in Liberal Politics, 1905–1914' (Princeton University, 1975).

[28] Vinogradskaia, p. 208; Rusakov and Solov'ev, 'Stanovlius' bol'shevichkoi', p. 77.

[29] Her four-page 'autobiography', which was written in 1918, was discovered in 1964. Excerpts from it have appeared in recent editions of Podliashuk's biography.

[30] To my knowledge only a couple of letters written to Lenin in 1916 have ever been published. See *Blizhe vsekh: Lenin i iunye internatsionalisty (sbornik dokumentov i materialov)* (Moscow, 1968), pp. 152–7; Krupskaia, *Pamiati*, pp. 18–22. The rest of this correspondence would appear to be in *fonds* 17 and 127 of the Central Party Archives in the Institute of Marxism-Leninism. According to the *New York Times* (22 January 1992, p. A5), some of these are to be released in the fall of 1992 for eventual publication abroad.

supposedly unquestionable source such as Lenin. A biographer would also like to see the seventeen unpublished letters he wrote to her, which are acknowledged to exist in the Central Party Archives of the Institute of Marxism-Leninism,[31] as well as Inessa's correspondence with Alexander after 1910 which remains in family hands.[32]

Until these documents are published or scholars are given better access to Russian archives, this account of Inessa Armand and her activities as a revolutionary and a feminist must remain incomplete in some of its detail and tentative in many of its conclusions.

[31] References to the contents of these letters are made in Institut marksizma-leninizma pri TsK KPSS, *Vladimir Il'ich Lenin: biograficheskaia khronika*, 12 vols. (Moscow, 1970–82) (hereafter *Biog. khr.*). See Chapter 8, below, for a fuller discussion of this correspondence and reasons for its suppression.

[32] See comments by Inna Armand in her introduction to 'Pis'ma Inessy Armand', p. 197.

CHAPTER 1

IN THE NEST OF GENTLEFOLK

In the early nineteenth century the Russian textile industry was ailing. Begun by Peter the Great, it depended on government orders and serf labour to survive. The Russian nobility was either uninterested or unable to invest the capital necessary to acquire the technology needed to make the industry efficient, productive and competitive. Then in 1812 Napoleon's army completed what Alexander I's scorched-earth policy had begun by destroying many of the textile mills and noble estates around Moscow.[1]

This may have been a blessing in disguise. During the decades that followed, new and more innovative non-noble entrepreneurs entered the field. Many were Old Believers such as the Guchkovs, Riabushinskiis, Alekseevs, Morozovs and Konovalovs who had bought their way out of serfdom and then used the financial reserves of their religious communities to set up mills and to hire more productive free labour.[2] They were attracted at first to the weaving of rough wool cloth not only by its being a logical outgrowth of earlier cottage industries but also by the fact that the Russian government offered a guaranteed market for their wares. To clothe its large armed forces, the state allocated sixteen rubles per soldier a year, or as much as 11 per cent of its military budget, for the purchase of wool uniforms.[3] The government, in addition, guaranteed through a policy of high tariffs that these infant industries would be protected from undue foreign competition.

The War of 1812 also provided a unique source of technological

---

[1] On the problems of the early Russian textile industry, see William L. Blackwell, *The Industrialization of Russia: An Historical Perspective*, 2nd edn (Arlington Heights, Ill., 1982), pp. 39, 47–51; M. I. Tugan-Baranovsky, *The Russian Factory in the Nineteenth Century*, trans. by Arthur and C. S. Levin (Homewood, Ill., 1970), pp. 22–3, 47, 54, 58–60; Peter I. Lyashchenko, *History of the National Economy of Russia to the 1917 Revolution*, trans. by L. H. Herman (New York, 1949), pp. 332–3.

[2] William L. Blackwell, 'The Old Believers and the Rise of Private Industrial Enterprise in Early Nineteenth-Century Moscow', in William L. Blackwell (ed.), *Russian Economic Development from Peter the Great to Stalin* (New York, 1974), pp. 139–58.

[3] Walter M. Pintner, 'The Burden of Defense in Imperial Russia, 1725–1914', *Russian Review*, vol. XLIII, no. 3 (July 1984), p. 239.

expertise for the Russian textile industry in the form of French prisoners-of-war or soldiers who had been left behind as Napoleon retreated from Russia. Some of these soldiers had had considerable experience with wool weaving and dyeing in France, particularly in the Alsace, and were often persuaded to seek new careers as advisors, technicians or managers in the backward Russian textile industry.[4] In time a few came to own their own mills and their success attracted other French specialists to settle in Russia. Among the French expatriates who prospered during the half-century following Napoleon's defeat were an Alsatian by the name of Steinbach who set up a mechanized textile mill in Moscow in 1825; A. O. Hubner, also from the Alsace, who by 1846 owned a mill outside of Moscow;[5] and Evgenii Armand.

Evgenii Evgen'evich Armand was the third generation of his family to live in Russia. His grandfather had settled in the Moscow area even before the War of 1812, perhaps attracted by the special privileges Catherine the Great offered to prospective foreign colonists.[6] His own profession is unknown but his descendants, like many others in Moscow's growing French colony, recognized the opportunities offered by textile manufacture. By 1861 E. Armand and Sons owned several wool-weaving and dyeing factories in Pushkino, 28 kilometres northeast of Moscow. Located at the confluence of the Ucha and Serebrianka Rivers, Pushkino offered all the ingredients needed for a successful textile mill: water power, nearby forests and peat bogs to provide convenient fuel, a ready supply of cheap labour in the form of emancipated serfs and reasonably good transportation for raw materials or finished products by river or by the rail line that ran through Pushkino from Moscow to Iaroslavl.[7] Unlike Steinbach, Hubner and most of his Old Believer competitors, Evgenii Armand did not branch out into cotton textiles in an effort to satisfy the huge new peasant demand for calico or to take advantage of better machinery which now

---

[4] Ralph M. Odell, *Cotton Goods in Russia* (Washington, 1912), pp. 7 and 32; M. O. Gately, 'The Development of the Russian Cotton Textile Industry in the Pre-Revolutionary Years, 1861–1913' (unpublished Ph.D. dissertation, University of Kansas, 1968), pp. 18 and 23.

[5] William L. Blackwell, *Beginnings of Russian Industrialization, 1800–1860* (Princeton, 1968), p. 250; Odell, pp. 32–3.

[6] I. V. Got'e, *Time of Troubles: The Diary of Iurii Vladimirovich Got'e (Moscow, July 8, 1917 to July 23, 1922)*, ed. and trans. by Terence Emmons (Princeton, 1988), pp. 10, 73n.

[7] Margaret Miller, *The Economic Development of Russia, 1905–1914*, 2nd edn (London, 1967), p. 251; Gately, pp. 198, 230; Walter C. Hanchett, 'Moscow in the Late Nineteenth Century: A Study in Municipal Self-Government' (unpublished Ph.D. dissertation, University of Chicago, 1964), pp. 11–13.

could be imported from England.[8] There were still enough orders for rough wool, particularly by the army at the time of the Russo-Turkish War of 1877–78, to ensure 900,000 rubles of business a year and to provide employment for 1200 workers.[9] By 1912 E. Armand and Sons had two thousand employees and was one of the largest firms of its kind in Russia.[10]

Evgenii Armand and his wife Varvara Karlovna Demonets also had a very large family. The first of their six daughters, Anna, was born in 1866 followed three years later, by the eldest of their five sons, Alexander.[11] As children of an hereditary 'honorary citizen' (*pochetnyi grazhdanin*) and councillor, they and their siblings lived a very comfortable existence. In addition to the manor at Pushkino, which was looked after by forty-five servants, the family owned extensive real estate, including a house or apartment in Moscow, and was in a position to take annual vacations in the Crimea, along the Volga or in Finland.[12] One of the perquisites of money was that it allowed the Armands to hire governesses and tutors to help bring up and educate their children at home. Following a well-established Russian tradition, they looked abroad for this help and, not surprisingly, to France in particular. Around 1880 a new governess and piano teacher from Paris was engaged and she brought with her her young niece, Elizabeth Stéphane. Elizabeth, or Inès, as her new family called her, was raised with the rest of the eleven Armand children. More than two decades later, after marrying Alexander Armand and becoming involved in revolutionary politics, she came to be known as Inessa. Later still, after the revolution had swept away the Armand fortune, she dropped her husband's name, used 'Elena Blonina' as her *nom de plume*, and usually was referred to as simply 'Comrade Inessa' in party circles.

*　　　*　　　*

8　JoAnn Ruckman, *Moscow Business Elite: A Social and Cultural Portrait of Two Generations, 1840–1905* (DeKalb, Ill., 1984), p. 61; Roger Portal, 'Muscovite Industrialists: The Cotton Sector (1861–1914)', in Blackwell (ed.), pp. 161–96.

9　Pavel Podliashuk, *Tovarishch Inessa: dokumental'naia povest'*, 4th edn (Moscow, 1984), p. 12 (hereafter all citations will be to this edition unless otherwise indicated). As is the case throughout his biography, Podliashuk does not provide sources for his information or precise dates. By implication, these figures apply to the period around 1880.

10　K. A. Pazhitnov, *Ocherki istorii tekstil'noi promyshlennosti dorevoliutsionnoi Rossii: sherstianaia promyshlennost'* (Moscow, 1955), pp. 194–5.

11　I am indebted to Egor Nazarenko, a great grandson of one of Evgenii Armand's brothers, for helping me straighten out the intricacies of the Armand family tree (correspondence with the author, 19 February 1991).

12　Podliashuk, pp. 12–13.

1. Inessa's parents, Nathalie Wild and Théodore Stéphane, in operatic costume (1870s).

Elizabeth – Inès – Inessa Armand was born on 8 May 1874 at number 63 rue de la Chapelle. This working-class area, which is surrounded by the railway switching yards of northern Paris, was an appropriate birthplace for the only prominent Russian communist of French origin. Until her birth registry was located in 1964, the precise date of her birth was in dispute.[13] Armand contributed to this confusion by telling the Russian police after one of her early arrests that she was born on 16 June 1879.[14] A few years later, when she registered at the Université Nouvelle in Brussels, she gave her birthdate as 16 June 1876.[15] When applying for a residence permit to live in Switzerland in 1915, she

[13] *Pravda*, 8 May 1964, p. 4; Jean Fréville, *Lénine à Paris* (Paris, 1968), p. 105.
[14] Okhrana Archives (Hoover Institution), file XIIIf, folder 2, item 12206, and incoming dispatch 608 (22 March 1912), file XVIIa, folder 1B (hereafter OA).
[15] Bulletin d'Inscription, no. 42, Université Nouvelle de Bruxelles.

13

decided that the real date was 16 June 1877.[16] And, a year later, a French agent of the Russian secret police in Paris reported that she was born on 16 June 1881.[17] There is even less agreement on the nationality of her mother, Nathalie Wild, which is variously given by Western writers as French, English, Scottish, Russian or a combination of these. According to Krupskaia, who had the advantage of knowing Armand well, Inessa's mother was half English, half French.[18] She made a modest living as an actress and sometime voice teacher in Paris.

Inessa's father, Théodore Pécheux d'Herbenville, was French by nationality and an opera singer by profession. He also has confused the historical record by being widely known under his stage name of Théodore Stéphane. Inessa's memories of her father, which were understandably 'vague', were of a 'handsome, joyful man'[19] who sometimes scared her out of her wits by wearing his operatic costumes at home.[20] Her French biographer suggests that he was somewhat bohemian in nature and that he was forced by his profession to travel a great deal.[21] There is no evidence to support the assertion that his travels took him to Russia or that the French police considered him to be 'politically suspect'.[22] Success on the stage eluded him until well into middle age and even then he was neither an 'outstanding artist'[23] nor 'well-known' as an opera singer.[24] Stéphane made his debut at the Opéra Comique in November 1875 singing the role of Haydée in one of Jacques Offenbach's least successful operas, La Créole. The critic for Le Temps was not impressed: 'All that can be said in his favour is that he has a good supporting-role voice but his projection is unsure and often gutteral, and he is lacking in style. There is a sluggishness in the acting and in the diction.'[25] Two years later, the same reviewer was only marginally better disposed to the tenor's efforts in Halévy's comic opera

16 Bern Staatsarchiv, BB4. 1. 946. Akten der Polizei-Direktion. 1914, file 4352/14, f. 1.
17 OA, report of 30 May 1916, file XVIIa, folder 5. Several other dates between 1874 and 1881 have also been suggested by Soviet and Western writers with even less evidence to support them. Her tombstone next to the Kremlin Wall still lists her birthdate as 1875.
18 N. K. Krupskaia, 'Inessa Armand', in Krupskaia (ed.), Pamiati, p. 5.   19 Ibid.
20 I. Fel'dman, 'Inessa Armand – revoliutsionerka i mat'', Doshkol'noe vospitanie, 1966, no. 4, p. 72. See Plate 1 for a photograph of Inessa's parents in costume.
21 Jean Fréville, 'Portrait d'Inessa Armand, révolutionnaire', La nouvelle critique, nos. 87–8 (1957), p. 85.
22 As suggested by G. Dolinov, 'Inessa Armand', Rabotnitsa i Krest'ianka, no. 9, May 1941, p. 18.
23 Podliashuk, p. 9.   24 Fischer, p. 74.
25 J. Weber in Le Temps, 16 November 1875, p. 1.

L'Eclair: 'This singer portrays the role of Lionel with feeling and assurance but he exaggerates and dulls the interpretation.'[26]
Very soon after this performance, Théodore Stéphane died, leaving his wife penniless and with three young daughters to support.[27] Two years later Nathalie Wild also passed away.[28] Relatives of the couple apparently came to the conclusion that maintenance costs dictated the splitting up of the three orphans. Inessa, being the oldest, and her English maternal grandmother who perhaps had come to Paris to help out after Stéphane's death, left for Russia sometime around 1880 in the care of Nathalie's sister. Even though Inessa did not return to the city of her birth for almost thirty years and did not maintain contact with her few French relatives and siblings,[29] she nevertheless always retained a fondness for the French capital. In the decade before her own death, during which time she lived intermittently in Paris, she served as the Bolsheviks' liaison with the French Socialist Party and as their expert on all matters relating to France. Perhaps her early upbringing in the bilingual and musical Stéphane household also helps to explain her lifelong interest in music and her proficiency in English and French – qualities which Lenin, among others, was to admire in the years to come. To Krupskaia, Inessa's unique background was reflected in her party work which she approached with French 'fervor and passion' and English 'persistence and self-control'.[30]

*   *   *

Evgenii Armand was not the exception among upper-class nineteenth-century Russians in having a large family. Nor was he unique in hiring a foreign governess to manage the upbringing of his children. A mother, such as Varvara Karlovna, would bear her children but typically would not rear them and would re-enter their lives only when her daughters reached marriageable age. According to E. Vodovozova, 'every

---

[26] *Ibid.*, 2 October 1877, p. 1.
[27] Henry Lyonnet, *Dictionnaire des Comédiens Français* (Geneva, 1969), vol. II, p. 513, lists an actor named Etienne Pécheux d'Herbenville who was born in 1839 and died in 1904. Wolfe ('Lenin and Inessa Armand', p. 97n) assumes this is Inessa's father whereas in fact he would appear to be her uncle.
[28] Fel'dman, 'Inessa Armand', p. 72. In 1907 Armand engaged in a bit of disinformation when she told her police interrogators that her mother was still alive and living in Moscow (OA, file XIIIf, folder 2, item 12206). This has led some Western writers to the mistaken conclusion that Nathalie Wild was in fact Russian (see, for example, Possony, p. 120).
[29] Outside of the fact that one of Inessa's sisters was named Renée (Sanov, 'Mezenskaia ballada', p. 96), I have come across no information concerning her surviving French family and no indications of future contact with them.
[30] N.K. [Krupskaia], 'Inessa Armand', *Kommunistka*, 1920, no. 5, p. 17.

governess spent most of her time trying to keep the children, as much as possible, from bothering the parents'.[31] It was also not unusual that upper-class children would be educated at home. In the case of boys, they would receive a home education until they reached gymnasium age and, in the case of girls, until marriage or their late teens. In the Armand household, the new governess did double duty as tutor in her native French and in piano. What set the Armands apart was Evgenii Evgen'evich's decision not to be bound by the traditional restraints of his class in allowing the young orphaned niece of their governess to be reared as part of his own family. As a result of his generosity, Inessa received an excellent home education, acquired many of the manners and interests of the privileged class, and experienced a happy childhood. Very possibly the roots of her subsequent feminism and Marxism are also to be found in the comfortable years she spent in the Armand family.

Elizabeth-Inès Fedorovna Stéphane fitted in nicely with her new family. Anna and Alexander Armand were slightly older than she, while Vladimir (born in 1875), Evgeniia (1876) and Boris (1878) were somewhat younger. She, like the daughters of many rich merchants, was trained primarily in the arts.[32] Almost as soon as she arrived in Pushkino, her aunt began giving her piano instruction. For at least the next six years she was taught in what Krupskaia later described as 'the English spirit' which demanded many hours of memorizing musical scores.[33] This rigorous training produced results for, in later years, Inessa would find great enjoyment in playing the piano and would impress many of her non-musical revolutionary friends with her skills. She also received formal instruction from her aunt in French, from her grandmother in English and from assorted other tutors in German and Russian. Very often these tutors would be wandering students or friends of the older Armand children to whom Evgenii Evgen'evich offered temporary room and board in return for instruction in appropriate subjects. On occasion, however, the radical orientation of some of these tutors was deemed inappropriate, even by a relatively liberal father, and the tutors would be released. While this was the fate of one of Inessa's teachers in 1888,[34] she and the Armand children were certainly exposed through them to the ideas of the Enlightenment, German

---

[31] As cited by Barbara Alpern Engel, 'Mothers and Daughters: Family Patterns and the Female Intelligentsia', in David L. Ransel (ed.), *The Family in Imperial Russia: New Lines of Historical Research* (Urbana, Ill., 1978), p. 48.

[32] Thomas C. Owen, *Capitalism and Politics in Russia: A Social History of Moscow Merchants, 1855–1905* (Cambridge, 1981), p. 155.

[33] Krupskaia in Krupskaia (ed.), *Pamiati*, p. 5.   [34] *Ibid.*, p. 6.

Romanticism, and the nineteenth-century Russian intelligentsia – ideas which called into question their own class privileges, the backwardness of Russian society and the anachronism of tsarist autocracy.

Some of this incipient social awareness also came from perusal of books in Evgenii Armand's large personal library. By the time she was sixteen, Inessa had supposedly read most of his books pertaining to philosophy, history and Russian literature. The Russian classics, she felt, provided an ideal way of learning about her adoptive country.[35] If this were the case, then her views of Russian society were shaped by writers like Nekrasov, Uspenskii, Dostoevskii, Tolstoy and Chernyshevskii.[36] The latter two authors are of particular interest in light of Inessa's own subsequent development.

Her reaction to Tolstoy was mixed. She considered him to be a great artist and, above all, one who made his readers think about the meaning of life. She was moved by his faith in the Russian *narod* and by his commitment to improving the condition of the peasantry. Indeed, her first personal philosophy, like that of a number of other Russian women who later became Marxists, was that of a Tolstoyan.[37] But, at the same time, she was appalled by his conception of women. Many years later she wrote to her teenage daughter that

there is one phrase in *War and Peace* which I first read when I was 15, which had an enormous influence on me. He said that Natasha, having married, became a complete woman [*samka*] ... this phrase seemed terribly insulting to me; it hit me like a whip; and it produced in me a firm resolve never to become a *samka* but to be a person instead.[38]

The heroine of Chernyshevskii's atrocious utopian novel *What is to be Done?* was anything but a *samka*. Vera Pavlovna excited the imagination of many late-nineteenth-century Russian girls and served as a prototype of a true emancipated woman. Vera refused to accept an arranged marriage; she insisted on living unconventionally and on equal terms with her two husbands; and she led a socially useful life as

[35] Fel'dman, 'Inessa Armand', p. 72; Inna Armand, 'Inessa Armand' in E. D. Stasova (ed.), *Slavnye bol'shevichki* (Moscow, 1958), p. 75.

[36] Rusakov and Solov'ev, 'Stanovlius' bol'shevichkoi', pp. 79–80.

[37] Krupskaia, Konkordiia Samoilova, Vera Bonch-Bruevich and Mariia Ul'ianova were among the other female Marxists who initially were attracted to Tolstoyism. Mark Chapin Scott, 'Her Brother's Keeper: The Evolution of Women Bolsheviks' (unpublished Ph.D. dissertation, University of Kansas, 1980), p. 207.

[38] Letter to Inna Armand (fall 1916), in Armand, *Stat'i*, p. 247. Armand's faulty reading of *War and Peace* allowed her to take the term *samka* out of context and to give it an unintended pejorative and sexual twist. Cf. Leo Tolstoy, *War and Peace*, 2 vols., trans. by Rosemary Edmonds (London, 1957), vol. II, p. 1369.

2. Inès Stéphane (Inessa Armand) as a teenager in Pushkino (late 1880s).

the director of a women's sewing co-operative. Inessa's own life – which goes through a Tolstoyan phase, shows great concern for the plight of women, and mirrors some of Vera Pavlovna's least plausible experiences – would seem to provide evidence of the long-range influence these two novelists had on her.[39]

Inessa's teenage years, however, were patterned neither after the spoiled and aristocratic Natasha nor after the repressed and bourgeois Vera Pavlovna. Instead, she grew up in an atmosphere which her Soviet biographer describes as 'hospitable, radically minded and intellectual'[40] but with many of the advantages which only money can bring. Every year she and the Armand children were driven to a photographer in Moscow to have their portraits taken.[41] Every summer there were vacations along the Volga. And every holiday and nameday there were parties on the veranda or in the manor with friends and relatives.[42] Among the frequent guests were acquaintances from Moscow's French colony, such as the family of Iurii Vladimirovich Got'e (Gautier),[43] as well as Evgenii Evgen'evich's brothers, Emil and Adolf Armand, who also had estates in Pushkino. Emil's children, Lev and Natalia, were close to Inessa in age and shared many of her childhood experiences and subsequently travelled along a similar revolutionary path. It was on festive occasions such as these with aristocratic friends and relatives that Inessa acquired the social graces that later impressed so many of her revolutionary colleagues and set her apart from them.

Soviet writers liked to mention that she also started to acquire a Marxian class consciousness during these comfortable years spent in the nest of gentlefolk when she supposedly observed the vast economic distance between the Armands residing in their manor houses and the textile workers living in hovels around Pushkino.[44] They can produce little evidence to support this assertion, however, other than an incident when at the age of fifteen she allegedly spoke up in defence of a servant criticized for preparing a poor meal.[45] What Soviet historians do not mention is that the Armands themselves may have been the victims of

---

[39] While many Western writers assert the importance of Chernyshevskii's work on Armand, I have found no mention of *What is to be Done?* in Inessa's letters to her daughters, which touch extensively on her literary tastes, or in her short autobiography.

[40] Pavel Podliashuk, 'Prekrasnaia zhizn' (I. F. Armand)' in L. P. Zhak and A. M. Itkina (eds.), *Zhenshchiny russkoi revoliutsii* (Moscow, 1968), p. 29.

[41] See Plate 2. Other examples are reproduced in Armand's *Stat'i* and in the various editions of Podliashuk's biography.

[42] Podliashuk, p. 10.   [43] Got'e, p. 73n.

[44] See, for example, Elena Stasova's comments in *Pravda*, 8 May 1964, p. 4.

[45] N.K. [Krupskaia], 'Inessa Armand', p. 17.

social alienation and that this influenced the subsequent revolutionary orientation not only of Inessa but also of almost all of her adopted siblings. One is struck when reading the few reminiscences of this period by the lack of social contact and intermarriage between the Armands and either the local landed gentry or their fellow textile manufacturers of Old Believer origin.[46] Both groups in the late nineteenth century tended to be close-knit, conservative, nationalistic and opposed to foreign influences in Russia. People of foreign ancestry are conspicuously absent from later political groups such as the Moscow-based, gentry-dominated Beseda Circle[47] and from the various professional associations formed by the Moscow merchantry.[48] One would have thought that by virtue of inclination, money and profession the Armands would have been part of these groups. Perhaps this apparent social, political and professional ostracism helped to cause wealthy but liberal families such as the Shmidts and the Armands to turn against the local establishment and to look for reform solutions outside those offered by their own economic class. While firm evidence to support such a hypothesis is lacking, the revolutionary activities of almost all of the children of Evgenii and Emil Armand during the early years of the twentieth century would seem to warrant speculation along these lines.

*   *   *

In 1891, at the age of seventeen, Inessa's education at Pushkino came to an end when she received a certificate qualifying her to be a tutor or home teacher – one of the few professions open to educated women in late Imperial Russian society. Two years later she had an opportunity to use her new teaching skills and also to fulfil some of her Tolstoyan dreams when she married Alexander Armand, the oldest of Evgenii's sons, on 3 October 1893. As a wedding present from his parents,

---

46 No Armands are to be found in the numerous Moscow family trees published in Ruckman, pp. 212–19, and Owen, pp. 222–7. The patronymics of Evgenii Evgen'e-vich's wife (Karlovna) and of the spouses of several of his children and relatives would seem to indicate that the Armands often married other persons of foreign ancestry. Inessa's later correspondence to members of her family includes virtually no reference to friends of this period who might be considered ethnically Russian.

47 Terence Emmons, 'The Beseda Circle, 1899–1905', Slavic Review, vol. XXXII, no. 3 (September 1973), pp. 461–90.

48 In recent years several extensive studies have been made of the Moscow business elite and particularly of those in the textile industry. These merchants were also often involved in joint banking and publishing ventures. The Armands do not appear on the membership lists of any of these associations. See, for example, the unpublished dissertations of Michael Gately, Walter Hanchett and J. L. West as well as the books of Thomas Owen, JoAnn Ruckman and Alfred Rieber (Merchants and Entrepreneurs in Imperial Russia [Chapel Hill, 1982]).

3. Inessa and Alexander Armand two years after their marriage (1895).

Alexander was given a small estate at Eldigino, ten kilometres northwest of Pushkino. In this pleasant, two-storey house set in a grove of
trees and surrounded by cultivated fields, Inessa spent the next five
years.[49] According to Krupskaia, early 'married life turned out to be

---

[49] Vinogradskaia, p. 226; Krupskaia in Krupskaia (ed.), *Pamiati*, p. 6. There is a picture
  of the house, which in 1977 was turned into a museum in Inessa's honour, in Rusakov
  and Solov'ev, 'Stanovlius' bol'shevichkoi', p. 79.

happy' for Inessa.[50] Her husband was a 'gentle and charming man'[51] whom she valued for 'his culture and great kindness'.[52] Inessa assiduously studied works on agrarian economics so that she could help him reorganize and run their estate.[53] They also jointly set up a school for local peasant children. Perhaps modelled after the one which Tolstoy established at Iasnaia Poliana in 1849, Inessa taught in this school and served as its official trustee.[54]

She, in addition, was busy during these years having children. A son, Alexander, was born in 1894, followed in short order by Fedor (1896), Inna (1898) and Varvara (1901). The birth of her first child also occasioned a religious crisis for her. As a teenager she had been very devout and carefully followed all of the rites of her faith.[55] There is considerable disagreement, however, over the nature of her faith. Even the Okhrana was confused. At the time her police biographical card was compiled in 1909, probably on the basis of information or disinformation supplied by Inessa herself, she was considered to be Orthodox[56] like her husband and the rest of the Armands. A few years later, an Okhrana agent reported that she was Jewish.[57] According to Vinogradskaia, she was Roman Catholic (which one would assume was her father's faith) and the crisis was provoked when a Roman Catholic priest refused to admit her to his church because she was pregnant and thus 'unclean'.[58] And yet the registry book of marriages, births and deaths of the church in which she was married noted her faith as Anglican.[59] One would surmise that Théodore Stéphane was not a particularly religious man, that his wife and her relatives raised Inessa in the Church of England, and that since Anglican churches were rare in Russia she attended the rather similar services offered by a Roman Catholic church in Moscow until the superstitions of that faith shook her belief in God and in all religions.

Several years later, after the birth of her third child, she underwent

50 N. K. Krupskaia, 'Inessa Armand' in F. Kon (ed.), *Pamiati pogibshikh vozhdei* (Moscow, 1927), p. 63.
51 Podliashuk in Zhak and Itkina (eds.), p. 30. See Plate 3 for a photograph of Inessa and Alexander Armand taken shortly after their marriage.
52 Inna Armand in her introduction to 'Pis'ma Inessy Armand', p. 197.
53 Krupskaia in Krupskaia (ed.), *Pamiati*, p. 6.
54 Podliashuk, p. 14.
55 Vinogradskaia, p. 209; N.K. [Krupskaia], 'Inessa Armand', p. 17.
56 OA, file XIIIf, folder 2, item 12206. This has been accepted by Wolfe, Possony and a number of other Western writers.
57 Report of 29 August 1911 in M. A. Tsiavlovskii (ed.), *Bol'sheviki: dokumenty po istorii bol'shevizma s 1903 po 1916 g. byvsh. Moskovskago Okhrannago Otdeleniia* (Moscow, 1918), p. 67.
58 Vinogradskaia, pp. 209–10.   59 Podliashuk, p. 11.

another crisis but one which is more familiar to contemporary married women. The raising of three children and a ward,[60] even if she had help, took time and energy and soon lost much of its initial appeal. Moreover, Alexander was increasingly involved in interests of his own – he was a member of the Moscow Guberniia Zemstvo and of the Moscow Forest Protection Committee – with the result that he was frequently away from Eldigino, thus leaving Inessa to run the estate and to manage its school. The attractions of the latter may also have begun to fade. Many young women teachers of this period found teaching in village schools and dealing with local authorities to be difficult, unrewarding and ultimately disillusioning.[61] As a woman in her mid-twenties whose expectations for the future had been raised through a liberal home education, life as a mother on an isolated rural estate had its drawbacks. The extended Armand family no longer offered compensations for her isolation. As she wrote to her daughter many years later, 'I felt very lonely among the Pushkino-ites. I was always a foreigner who had entered the family, but still with my own rules . . .'[62]

One obvious solution was to get away from Eldigino more often. In 1898 she stopped teaching and took her children on a lengthy holiday in the Crimea. She also took with her Peter Lavrov's recently published *Zadachi pominaniia istorii* (The Problems of Understanding History). From Lavrov, who was one of Russia's most respected agrarian socialists, she derived ideas about more radical ways of solving the peasant problem than just teaching in a village school. 'It has been a long time', she wrote Alexander, 'since I read a book which more closely conforms with my own opinions.'[63] She spent the spring of the next year in Montreux so that one of her sons could receive foreign medical attention. Her letters to Alexander reflect her new-found love of the Swiss mountains, her joy at hearing Verdi's 'Requiem' performed in Vevey, and her impressions of various books on social issues which she was reading.[64] As much as she liked Switzerland, she assured Alexander 'I will be happy only when I am in Eldigino with you.'[65] Her real feelings of the time are perhaps better reflected in her further observation that

---

[60] Vladimir Afanas'ev grew up with Inessa's children. He is variously described as her foster son, adopted son (*priemnyi syn*) or ward (*vospitannik*). See, for example, Sanov, 'Mezenskaia ballada', p. 92; 'Pis'ma Inessy Armand', p. 205n.
[61] Knight, pp. 49–50. [62] Quoted in Podliashuk, p. 16.
[63] Quoted in *ibid.*, p. 22.
[64] Letters of late April and early May 1899 to A. E. Armand, 'Pis'ma Inessy Armand', pp. 197–8.
[65] Letter of late April 1899 to A. E. Armand, *ibid.*, p. 198.

she knew 'only two, or at most three [people] who are content with their situation and their lives, and they are probably pretending'.[66]

It is obvious that she was not 'content' with her present position in life. After her return to Eldigino in the summer of 1899 she and her husband started to make frequent trips to Moscow to attend concerts, the theatre and art exhibits.[67] Her energies and personal aspirations also found a new outlet in Moscow as she became involved in philanthropic work and in issues of special concern to women.

[66] *Ibid.*   [67] Podliashuk, p. 14.

CHAPTER 2

FROM FEMINISM TO MARXISM

The growth of the intelligentsia during the second quarter of the nineteenth century brought with it a new awareness of the subordinate position occupied by Russian women in the home, in education and in employment. According to Article 107 of the Imperial Code of Civil Laws, a 'wife must obey her husband as the head of the family, live with him in love and treat him with esteem, utmost respect, obedience and humility due to him as master of the house'.[1] She could not get a passport without his permission and needed his approval to work, to travel or to establish a separate residence. While she could own property, she had limited rights of inheritance. To obtain a divorce was extremely difficult, expensive and often degrading. Education was restricted to upper-class finishing schools and home tutors with the result that illiteracy was even higher among Russian women than among men.[2] And most professions – including the civil service and law – were closed to women.

During the 1840s some of these inequities were recognized for the first time by the Russian followers of Charles Fourier, as were theories concerning sexual freedom advocated by George Sand. A decade later N. I. Pirogov and M. L. Mikhailov gave more focus to the 'woman question' by arguing that it was the social conditioning of women that led to their sense of inferiority and to their subordinate position. The solution lay, Mikhailov said, in better education which, in turn, would lead to greater professional opportunities and thus to a degree of financial independence. While hundreds of radical Russian women found temporary personal equality in a revolutionary movement seeking the total transformation of Russian society in the 1870s, others achieved modest but more lasting gains through expanded educational

---

[1] Quoted in Yelena Yemelyanova, *Revolution in Women's Life* (Moscow, 1985), p. 9.
[2] In 1897, 71 per cent of the Russian men were illiterate and 87 per cent of the women. B. G. Rosenthal, 'Love on the Tractor: Women in the Russian Revolution and After' in Claudia Koonz and Renate Bridenthal (eds.), *Becoming Visible: Women in European History* (Boston, 1977), p. 373.

opportunities at universities abroad, in women's gymnasia and 'higher courses for women' at home, and ultimately by auditing selected subjects in Russian universities.[3] For many women this education, limited as it was, opened doors for employment in medicine and teaching which previously had been closed to their sex.

Upper-class women, in addition to seeking self-realization and self-emancipation, also started to engage in philanthropic activities designed to improve the conditions of the urban poor. One such venture was the 'Society to Provide Cheap Lodgings and Other Assistance to the Needy Population of St. Petersburg' formed in 1861. For twenty years the society offered temporary accommodation for the poor, ran workshops and operated communal kitchens. Equally important, this activity brought women together and provided them with experience as administrators, a sense of self-respect and a belief that they were doing something worthwhile. Like the concurrent gains in women's education, philanthropic work of this nature was curtailed during the reactionary reign of Alexander III. In 1894, however, Anna Filosofova, who had been one of the major figures in the Society to Provide Cheap Lodgings, put new life into the women's movement by helping establish the Russian Women's Mutual Philanthropic Society in St Petersburg. This group, which has been called 'by far the most important feminist institution prior to 1905',[4] functioned both as a women's club and as a provider of accommodation, meals and childcare for their less fortunate sisters. As its organizers soon found out, any attempt to go beyond these charitable and educational activities, such as by pursuing broader issues relating to the political and legal equality of women, met with resolute government opposition. Nor were the authorities keen to see similar societies grow up elsewhere in Russia. In 1895, for instance, the Ministry of the Interior rejected the draft statute for a philanthropic group submitted by some upper-class women in Moscow. Four years later, however, permission was granted to set up a Moscow Society for Improving the Lot of Women (*Obshchestva uluchsheniia uchasti zhenshchin*). One of the persons actively involved in the establishment of this society was Inessa Armand.

---

[3] More information on the gradual expansion of education for Russian women can be found in Hayden, pp. 8–13; L. D. Filippova, 'Iz istorii zhenskogo obrazovaniia v Rossii', *Voprosy istorii*, 1963, no. 2, pp. 211–15; Ruth A. Dudgeon, 'The Forgotten Minority: Women Students in Imperial Russia, 1872–1917', *Russian History*, vol. IX, pt. 1 (1982), pp. 1–26.

[4] Stites, *Women's Liberation Movement*, p. 195. For an excellent summary of nineteenth-century Russian feminism, see *ibid.*, pp. 29–198. Also Edmondson, pp. 1–26, and Knight, pp. 11–56.

Someone looking for early manifestations of Armand's interest in feminist issues might note her teenage rebellion at Tolstoy's notion of women finding fulfilment solely through bearing children or her serving as godparent for an illegitimate child when Varvara Karlovna refused to participate in its christening.[5] More concrete examples can be found in her reading interests at Eldigino. Her library contained a well-annotated copy of *House for Working Girls in London* (London, 1898) and she requested that her husband get for her M. K. Gorbunova-Kablukova's *Zhenskie promysly v Moskovskoi gubernii* (Women's Work in Moscow Guberniia). Inessa had met Gorbunova, a leading advocate of women's professional education, on one of her trips to Moscow and soon started to attend her Sunday soirées, renowned for their wide-ranging discussions of social issues.[6] Perhaps as a result of this association she entered into correspondence with Adrienne Veigelé, the secretary of the Women's International Progressive Union, who invited her to London and suggested that she establish a branch of the Union in Moscow.[7] While she did not go to England, the Progressive Union named her its Russian vice-president in 1899 and in that same year claimed to have a Moscow branch.[8] This undoubtedly was the Moscow Society for Improving the Lot of Women set up in July of that year. After a brief spell as chair of its 'Educational Commission', Armand was chosen in 1900 to be president of the Moscow Society – a post she was to hold for more than three years.[9]

According to its constitution, the Moscow Society wanted to go beyond the purely self-enlightenment activities of the Progressive Union.[10] Its goals were much closer to those of the Mutual Philanthropic Society in that it sought 'to fight against depravity and the drunkenness which is closely associated with it'. To this end, it intended

---

[5] Krupskaia in Krupskaia (ed.), *Pamiati*, p. 6; Iu. Neiman, 'Inessa Armand', *Smena*, 1941, no. 5, p. 11.

[6] Rusakov and Solov'ev, 'Stanovlius' bol'shevichkoi', pp. 77–8.

[7] S. V. Karavashkova, *Publitsistika A. M. Kollontai, I. F. Armand, L. N. Stal', A. I. Ul'ianovoi-Elizarovoi v bor'be za ukreplenie mezhdunarodnogo rabochego dvizheniia* (Moscow, 1973), p. 6.

[8] *Englishwoman's Year Book, 1899* (London, 1899), p. 193. The Union had been formed by Melle. Veigelé in 1896 along 'strictly non-party and non-sectarian lines' (*ibid.*). It appears to have ceased operations after 1904.

[9] Z. L. Peregudova and V. V. Khmeleva, 'Dokumenty ob Inesse Armand', *Sovetskie arkhivy*, 1967, no. 6, p. 104. See Plate 4 for a photograph of Armand taken at Eldigino during the period when she was president of the Moscow Society.

[10] The Union had as its professed aim 'to arouse the interest of women in all subjects that tend to progress, and to their own advancement and elevation, also to create and bring forward new workers in the cause of justice and equality'. This was to be done

to render women moral and material support, to promote the spread of women's education and technical training; to establish . . . shelters and refuges for fallen women, and for juveniles who have sunk into the vice of depravity; and to set up canteens, hostels and temporary accommodations [for working women].[11]

To achieve these objectives, the society's 643 members – most of whom, like Armand, were women from professional, manufacturing and noble families – gave both money and volunteer labour. Their endeavours often suffered from the same bureaucratic obstructionism which frustrated earlier efforts by the Mutual Philanthropic Society. Despite the Moscow Society's charitable objectives and its privileged composition, the ever-suspicious police had doubts about the 'political trustworthiness' of 120 of its members and noted that 'unreliable elements had made persistent efforts of late to penetrate all kinds of legal organizations and to use them as a means of spreading anti-governmental ideas'.[12]

'To promote the spread of women's education and technical training' Armand, in the name of her society, applied for permission in 1900 to open a Sunday school. Similar schools, which offered basic education to often illiterate workers on non-working days and in the evenings, had been functioning in Moscow since 1874. By 1886, over 1300 young men – two-thirds of them fresh from the countryside – were enrolled in sixteen of these schools.[13] Russian radicals soon realized that Sunday schools offered a good place for the intelligentsia and workers to meet and for the surreptitious discussion of socialist texts under the guise of teaching workers how to read.[14] What made the school proposed by the Moscow Society different was its intention to offer instruction to young women rather than men. The police, not unaware of the hidden curricula of some of these schools, required that each of the fifteen potential teachers receive a 'Certificate of Political Reliability'. In reviewing Armand's own application, the authorities decided it would be 'awkward' to deny the society's president permission to teach even

through 'frequent meetings, lectures, debates, social gatherings, etc.' *Englishwoman's Year Book, 1899*, p. 193.
[11] Cited in Margarian, 'Novoe ob Inesse Armand', p. 213.
[12] Peregudova and Khmeleva, 'Dokumenty', pp. 104–5. One of the members of the Moscow Society at this time whom the police probably considered 'unreliable' was Lenin's sister Anna Elizarova (*ibid.*, p. 104).
[13] Hanchett, pp. 451–3.
[14] Robert Jean Burch, 'Social Unrest in Imperial Russia: The Student Movement at Moscow University, 1887–1905' (unpublished Ph.D. dissertation, University of Washington, 1972), p. 424, n. 39; Knight, pp. 45–9.

4. Inessa Armand in her study at Eldigino (1902).

though she had some 'undesirable acquaintances', but then, in contradictory fashion, they refused to allow the school itself to function.[15]

Undeterred, Armand decided the Moscow Society needed broader support and should be addressing a wider audience. She therefore suggested that the group publish a periodic leaflet that would eventually become a full-fledged women's newspaper. The paper, which she proposed to call the *Izvestiia* of the Moscow Society for Improving the Lot of Women, would print articles on social questions, summaries of press reports concerning what other societies in Russia and abroad were doing to help women, a calendar of events of interest to women, and accounts about the work of the Moscow Society. On 19 February 1901 an application was submitted to the Chief Directorate for Publishing Affairs for permission to publish such a paper with Inessa Armand listed as its editor-designate. The Chief Directorate responded by asking for Armand's passport and for a copy of the society's constitution as well as seeking police clearance of the proposed editor. Despite the fact that she was found to be 'financially secure and morally upright', her application was denied on 12 February 1902.[16] The result was essentially the same when she attempted to set up a free library which would concentrate on books of interest to women: the authorities asked for more documentation and then delayed giving approval until the fall of 1905[17] by which time Armand had long since given up on philanthropic work.

In 1902 Armand applied for permission to open a 'Shelter for Downtrodden Women'.[18] This represented part of her society's major effort to help rehabilitate prostitutes and to keep young girls from entering the 'oldest profession'. Prostitution was undeniably a serious problem in late Imperial Russia. As in other countries, it was a product of increasing industrialization, urbanization and general social instability. In Moscow, there were ten men for every seven women.[19] Women factory workers and domestic servants were paid appallingly low wages which they frequently were forced to supplement through other means in order to support themselves or their families. There also was a constant stream of peasant girls coming into the city looking for a more exciting and financially rewarding life than their villages could offer. The result was that prostitution flourished. In 1890 Moscow had 105 brothels and 1178 registered prostitutes[20] with perhaps ten times that number of

---

[15] Podliashuk, p. 19. See also Peregudova and Khmeleva, 'Dokumenty', p. 105.
[16] Margarian, 'Novoe ob Inesse Armand', p. 214; see also Karavashkova, p. 7.
[17] Podliashuk, p. 20.   [18] Peregudova and Khmeleva, 'Dokumenty', p. 105.
[19] Hanchett, pp. 29 and 42.   [20] *Ibid.*, p. 42.

women working on a casual unregistered basis.[21] Over half came from peasant households and a very large percentage were under the age of twenty.[22] The brothels that sprang up in the Sretenskaia district of Moscow soon became nests of crime, white slavery and syphilis.

The government's response was to legalize the profession in an ineffectual attempt to deal with the spread of venereal disease. Starting in 1843 prostitutes had to register with the local police, receive a 'yellow ticket' in place of their passports, and undergo a weekly and humiliating medical inspection.[23] The response of philanthropic groups was different. In 1833 the Magdalena Shelter was set up in St Petersburg 'to promote the return of repentant public women to the path of honest labor' through a 'strict regimen of hard work and religious devotion'.[24] Similar shelters were established in Moscow in the 1860s and in 1900 the Russian Society for the Defence of Women was created to coordinate and promote attempts to rehabilitiate Russia's large prostitute population throughout the empire.

The Shelter for Downtrodden Women established by the Moscow Society was a product of this feminist philanthropic enthusiasm. There is no evidence that Armand, as the moving force behind it, at this early date felt that prostitutes were the victims of 'bourgeois hypocrisy and a double standard of morality'.[25] The Moscow Shelter undoubtedly shared many of the characteristics of shelters established elsewhere in Russia.[26] To recruit girls to be saved, women volunteers either would attend meetings of the medical-police committee where would-be prostitutes had to register or they would meet trains coming in from the countryside to enrol peasant girls before pimps could get to them. The girls were expected to rehabilitate themselves through long hours of hard work but often the 'skills' they were taught – cooking, cleaning and sewing – were just those they were attempting to escape. They also were subject

---

[21] This is Richard Stites' conclusion based on statistics from St Petersburg on the eve of the war. He implies the same rate applies for Moscow. Richard Stites, 'Prostitution and Society in Pre-Revolutionary Russia', *Jahrbucher für Geschichte Osteuropas*, vol. XXXI, no. 3 (1983), pp. 350–1.

[22] Hanchett, p. 43. According to Stites, 44 per cent of the St Petersburg prostitutes in the early twentieth century were between sixteen and twenty years of age ('Prostitution and Society', p. 352).

[23] Goldberg, pp. 13–14.   [24] Bernstein, p. 189.

[25] As suggested by Gail Warshofsky Lapidus, *Women in Soviet Society: Equality, Development and Social Change* (Berkeley, 1978), p. 47.

[26] The following account is based on Laurie Bernstein's excellent description of the work of similar shelters in St Petersburg and Moscow at the turn of the century (Bernstein, pp. 189–236). While I have found very little information on the Shelter for Downtrodden Women, *per se*, I see no reason why Dr Bernstein's observations and conclusions should not apply to it as well.

to interminable lectures by well-meaning society ladies about the virtues of temperance, religion and chastity. Discipline was strict and amusements were few. Not surprisingly, these half-way houses for prostitutes were often only half full and the recidivism rate ran between 50 and 75 per cent as inmates of the shelters returned to the more exciting and profitable life on the streets. As Laurie Bernstein has concluded, the lady philanthropists who ran these shelters failed to provide 'downtrodden women' with 'viable intellectual and economic tools' for use in the outside world. 'By relying on that dull mixture of prayers, drab gowns and sewing machines, salvationists underestimated the complexity of the problem of prostitution and betrayed their own confusion and self-righteousness'.[27] In an attempt to end their own confusion, one of the members of the Moscow Society wrote to Tolstoy for advice on how to deal with the evils of prostitution. His response probably cured Armand of any lingering Tolstoyism she may have had. 'Nothing will come of your work', he answered. 'It was thus before Moses. It was thus after Moses. Thus it was ... thus it will be.'[28]

As a consequence of these discouraging results, feminists increasingly turned away from philanthropic work after 1904. Rather than trying to help their downtrodden sisters through good deeds, many started to seek political rights and particularly the right to vote for themselves. Through political pressure from within the system they thought they could ameliorate the condition of less fortunate women. Others, such as Armand, came to the conclusion that the entire economic and political system had to be changed before lasting improvement for women could be realized. In the summer of 1903 she stopped working in the Moscow Society. The four years she spent doing charitable work in Moscow were by no means wasted. To be sure, bureaucratic obstructionism and government fear of any independent social action undermined almost all of her efforts to improve the education of women and to increase the general understanding of women's problems. This response to moderate attempts at legal change convinced her and many like her that more radical solutions to Russia's problems were the only alternative. It is also true that the patronizing approach of the philanthropists to the problem of prostitution was probably doomed to failure. The social distance between the society ladies and the 'fallen women' was simply too great and the ladies' understanding of the root causes of prostitution was clearly wrong. Nevertheless, Armand's study of prostitution

[27] *Ibid.*, pp. 231–2.   [28] Quoted by Krupskaia, in Krupskaia (ed.), *Pamiati*, p. 7.

broadened her social perspective. She gained during these years in Moscow a first-hand knowledge of the social and economic problems besetting Russia's urban poor. And she developed an interest in women's issues which was to last the rest of her life.

*   *   *

The year 1903 marked the first of three turning points in Inessa's life. Not only was she disillusioned with charitable work but also she experienced a crisis in her personal life. Her active involvement in the Moscow Society required that she spend much of her time after 1899 in Moscow. Alexander, while also engaged in some philanthropic work in the city[29] and, after 1901, as an elected deputy in the Moscow City Duma, had to be in Eldigino much of the time looking after the estate, taking care of his provincial zemstvo commitments, and assisting his father in the family textile business. Husband and wife, separated by their work, started to grow apart in other ways as well.

When Inessa was in Moscow, she often stayed in one of the Armands' apartments in or near the Arbat district – the 'centre of the Moscow intelligentsia' before the war.[30] She spent much of her time with her brother-in-law, Vladimir. Vladimir Evgen'evich Armand, who was a year younger than Inessa, was a student at the University of Moscow. According to Inessa's daughter, he showed 'great promise as a future biologist'.[31] A friend of the family described him as 'a rare individual, remarkably well educated, with a profound outlook on life, and at the same time he had an uncommon ... [almost] apostolic simplicity about him'.[32] Of all the brothers, he was the most intellectual and with the widest-ranging interests.

According to Vinogradskaia, Vladimir was 'close' to Inessa 'in temperament, a like-minded individual'.[33] To a greater extent than Alexander, he shared her artistic tastes and growing social concerns. In later years they corresponded at length about Symbolist poetry, plays at

---

[29] One of the volunteer committees he sat on dealt with the Care of Beggars in Moscow. Podliashuk, p. 12.

[30] M. M. Novikov, *Ot Moskvy do N'iu Iorka* (New York, 1952), p. 152. Of Inessa's six pre-revolutionary Moscow addresses that I have been able to track down, four were in or near the Arbat.

[31] Inna Armand, introduction to 'Pis'ma Inessy Armand', p. 197. In 1904, however, Vladimir enrolled in the Faculty of Law at the University of Moscow (M. T. Beliavskii and V. V. Sorokin, 'Neizvestnye stranitsy zhizni soratnikov V. I. Lenina', *Vestnik Moskovskogo Universiteta*, series VIII: *Istoriia*, 1979, no. 6, p. 55). The reason for this change in programme of study is unclear.

[32] Quoted in Sanov, 'Mezenskaia ballada', p. 87.   [33] Vinogradskaia, p. 212.

33

the Moscow Arts Theatre, and books which they had read.[34] Unlike Alexander, who Podliashuk described as a man simply of 'advanced liberal views',[35] Vladimir's political outlook was more radical. He was involved in left-wing student organizations at the University of Moscow and, one would assume, in the various student demonstrations which unsettled the university in 1901 and 1902.[36] Through him, the students' Executive Committee met several times during 1901 in Inessa's apartment[37] on Spiridonovskaia (now Aleksei Tolstoi) Ulitsa which she apparently shared with Vladimir when she was in Moscow. In February 1901, in an unsuccessful attempt to head off student protests planned for that month, the police raided one of these meetings. While Inessa was not among those arrested, she clearly came into contact with 'revolutionary-minded students' and with revolutionary literature through Vladimir.[38] At a time when she was discouraged with her feminist philanthropic work, he offered more radical alternatives and, as she later acknowledged, was instrumental in her gradual evolution from feminism to Marxism.[39]

The intellectual and political affinity which Vladimir and Inessa shared in time became an emotional and personal bond. In January 1903, while on a holiday with Vladimir in Italy, Inessa became pregnant.[40] The Armands' solution to this potentially disruptive family

[34] See, for example, letters to V. E. Armand of 13 August, 22 November and late November/early December 1908 in 'Pis'ma Inessy Armand', pp. 212–16.
[35] Podliashuk, p. 12.
[36] Burch, pp. 106–8, 119; Samuel D. Kassow, *Students, Professors and the State in Tsarist Russia* (Berkeley, 1989), pp. 133–62. Neither author, in their extensive discussions of student unrest in Moscow during these years, makes mention of Vladimir Armand.
[37] Peregudova and Khmeleva, 'Dokumenty', p. 105; Beliavskii and Sorokin, 'Neizvestnye stranitsy', p. 55.
[38] *Pravda*, 7 May 1964, p. 4; Inna Armand in Stasova (ed.), p. 76; Karavashkova, p. 7.
[39] See letter to V. E. Armand (20 December 1908), 'Pis'ma Inessy Armand', p. 217. Vladimir's personal commitment to Marxism appears to have been more cerebral than organizational. Inessa's daughter, Inna, hints at this when she said he was a 'Social Democrat by conviction' (introduction to *ibid.*, p. 197). A student friend of theirs confirmed that Vladimir had 'ties with revolutionaries' and gave Inessa 'ideological support' and answers to many of her political questions (Druzhinin, 'O trekh uchast-nitsakh', p. 85).
[40] Singer, p. 184. Podliashuk, while acknowledging that Inessa was in Italy at the time, reflects Soviet reticence to discuss the affair: it was 'a loving relationship that had nothing in common with secret betrayals, with banal adultery. There was a sense of reciprocity, of openness' (pp. 33–4). Inna Armand simply said her mother 'tied her life with Vladimir Evgen'evich Armand from 1903 on' (introduction to 'Pis'ma Inessy Armand', p. 197). For conflicting accounts on the parentage of Inessa's fifth child, see Vinogradov (ed.), p. 16, and Alexander Solzhenitsyn, *Lenin in Zurich* (New York, 1976), p. 224. Subsequent generations of the Armand family accept the fact that it was Vladimir's child (letter to author from Egor Nazarenko, 19 February 1991).

34

imbroglio was straight out of Chernyshevskii. Alexander accepted that his wife was in love with his younger brother and that the two of them should henceforth live together in free union without bothering about a tedious bourgeois divorce and another marriage. Jealousy and anger were demeaning emotions to those who followed Chernyshevksii's code. Unlike Dmitri Lopuklov in *What is to be Done?*, Alexander did not simply disappear but instead supported Inessa and many of her socialist causes with the profits from his textile mills until the time of the revolution. Except for a period in 1904 and 1905, when he was in the Far East administering medical supplies donated by the Moscow City Duma to the Imperial forces in the Russo-Japanese War,[41] he raised all five children and made sure that they visited their mother abroad whenever possible. Her daughters later recalled that 'father was kind and gentle; he felt sorry for us and spoiled the children. Mother was strict, severe. We were rather afraid of her.'[42] Alexander also made sure Pushkino was always available to Inessa as a haven or a hide-a-way during her years in the underground. For the rest of her life Inessa corresponded regularly with her estranged husband and not without reason expressed wonder at his 'devoted and selfless friendship . . . What a good relationship we have established' she wrote in the early summer of 1905. 'What a good feeling our friendship has! Honour and glory to you'.[43] Alexander was indeed an 'uncommon man' whose generosity and kindness made it easier for Inessa to be an 'emancipated woman'.

*   *   *

In late July, after winding up her affairs with the Moscow Society, Inessa left Russia for another extended stay in Switzerland[44] accompanied only by her four children. Three months later, in October 1903, her third son Andre, was born. She stayed on until late the next spring hiking in the Alps which she had come to love, taking mule rides on Swiss glaciers (Plate 5), and reading widely on social issues, political economy and pedagogy.[45] One of the books she read was Lenin's *Development of Capitalism in Russia*.[46]

---

[41] N. I. Astrov, *Vospominaniia* (Paris, 1940), p. 280.
[42] Quoted by Podliashuk in Zhak and Itkina (eds.), p. 43.
[43] 'Pis'ma Inessy Armand', p. 203.
[44] One of the persistent myths in Western literature, perhaps begun by Bertram Wolfe ('Lenin and Inessa Armand', p. 101), is that Inessa went to Sweden rather than Switzerland in order to study with the feminist scholar Ellen Key. There is no question that she went to Switzerland in 1903–4 and no evidence that she ever stayed in Sweden for an extended period of time.   [45] Podliashuk, p. 30.
[46] According to Jean Fréville ('Portrait d'Inessa Armand', p. 90), Inessa met Lenin for the

5. Inessa Armand on holiday in the Swiss Alps (1904).

Fifteen years later, after the success of the October Revolution had put her life in a different perspective, she recalled the great impact this book supposedly had on her. 'In 1903', she wrote in her brief auto-biography, 'while abroad in Switzerland and after some vacillation between the Socialist Revolutionaries and the Social Democrats over the agrarian question, I came under the influence of Il'in's [i.e., Lenin's] *Development of Capitalism in Russia* ... and I became a Bolshevik.'[47] This unique explanation of her conversion, if indeed she became a Bolshevik in 1903, was simple, convenient and the answer to an agit-prop official's dream in 1918. But is it really credible that anyone would be converted almost overnight by Lenin's turgid and tedious tome? The explanation which Inessa chose to avoid is more complex and less fashionable in that it concerns her upbringing in the privileged Armand household, her own experiences as a Tolstoyan and a feminist, and factors influencing the political orientation of her adoptive siblings. In some respects, she was the product of the same forces which shaped other Russian revolutionaries; in other ways, her path was unique but followed a course which neither she nor subsequent Soviet historians wished to illuminate.

Most of the prominent women Bolsheviks came from comfortable upper- or middle-class families rather than from lives of personal poverty and class oppression. One of the explanations why women such as Krupskaia, Kollontai, Evgeniia Adamovich, Sofia Smidovich, Liud-mila Stal' and Armand became Bolsheviks is that their families were able to provide them with the necessary education and with opportuni-ties for personal freedom which their less fortunate sisters often lack-ed.[48] Within this privileged environment, Armand received as a child the type of support from her surrogate family which facilitated her subsequent development as a revolutionary. She shared several of the characteristics which Marie Mullaney has identified as being common to five leading women revolutionaries: she was given a feeling of specialness within the Armand household which later endowed her

---

first time in Switzerland in 1904. This is possible, since the Bolshevik leader was then living in Geneva, but unlikely and unconfirmed by any other source. Indeed, N. Valen-tinov (N. V. Vol'skii), who knew Lenin well during this period and later enthusiasti-cally supported the idea of an affair between the two, makes no mention of such a meeting until 1910 (*Vstrechi s Leninym* [New York, 1953], p. 98).

[47] Quoted by Podliashuk, in Zhak and Itkina (eds.), pp. 31–2.

[48] Barbara Evans Clements, 'Baba and Bolshevik: Russian Women and Revolutionary Change', *Soviet Union/Union Soviétique*, vol. XII, pt. 2 (1985), pp. 166–7; Scott, pp. 23–5.

37

with a sense of self-confidence; her adoptive father raised her in a politically conscious atmosphere; and she acquired an urge to do something meaningful with her life.[49]

What set Armand apart from many of her future revolutionary colleagues was the way in which this growing social awareness was manifested. As she herself admitted, 'Marxism for me was not a youthful enthusiasm but the culmination of a long evolution from right to left.'[50] She started as a Tolstoyan trying to educate peasant children. When this proved unproductive, she attempted to rehabilitate prostitutes as a feminist. In each instance, she was frustrated in her efforts by bureaucratic obstructionism and by the lack of quick results. Not surprisingly, she looked for more radical alternatives in the works of Lavrov and Marx. In her autobiography she indirectly acknowledged the role played by Vladimir Armand and his student friends in this evolution: 'From 1901 on I was attracted to revolutionary organizations and in 1902 I became familiar with several SDs and SRs who rendered me some assistance and provided me with illegal literature.'[51] As L. B. Kamevev later recalled, 'she came to Bolshevism in her own unique way, after a long search,'[52] with the result that she was almost thirty – older than most of her revolutionary associates[53] – before she supposedly found the final answer in *The Development of Capitalism in Russia*.

Any explanation of Inessa's evolution to Marxism must also take into account that almost all of the younger Armands – the sons and daughters of Evgenii and Emil Armand – became revolutionaries in the early twentieth century. Since the scions of wealthy industrialists were not

---

[49] Mullaney drew her conclusions from studying the early lives of Rosa Luxemburg, Kollontai, Balabanoff, Eleanor Marx and Louise Michel. There is not enough information to determine whether Inessa shared a fourth characteristic: close contact as a child with a role model of a strong and independent woman (Marie Marmo Mullaney, 'Gender and the Socialist Revolutionary Role, 1871–1921: A General Theory of the Female Revolutionary Personality', *Historical Reflections/ Réflexions historiques*, vol. XI, no. 1 [Summer 1984], pp. 122–3). Little is known about the personality of Varvara Karlovna except that she was supportive and on surprisingly good terms with her daughter-in-law and was rather conservative in her political outlook (see Inessa's 1915 letter to her daughter, in Armand, *Stat'i*, p. 237).

[50] Letter to V. E. Armand (20 December 1908), 'Pis'ma Inessy Armand', p. 218.

[51] Quoted by Podliashuk, in Zhak and Itkina (eds.), p. 31. Inessa was not unique in having her 'brother' play an important role in her conversion to Marxism. In a survey of 255 female Bolsheviks, Barbara Clements found that of those who reported the person who introduced them to radical ideas, 40 per cent identified siblings ('Baba and Bolshevik', p. 177).

[52] L. B. Kamenev, 'Tovarishch Inessa Armand', in Krupskaia (ed.), *Pamiati*, p. 36.

[53] According to Barbara Clements' survey, only 15 per cent of her sample joined the party after the age of 29 ('Baba and Bolshevik', p. 175).

supposed to seek the overthrow of their own class, this fact has been conveniently ignored by Soviet historians.[54]

The first of the Armands to attract the attention of the Okhrana was Evgenii Evgen'evich's third son Boris. In the summer of 1896 Evgenii had engaged E. E. Kammer to serve as Boris's tutor and coach. Kammer, who was involved in a revolutionary group at the University of Moscow, received the family's permission to hide at least four mimeograph machines and a large quantity of Social Democratic literature on the Armand estates in Pushkino and Eldigino. The police were aware of the subterfuge and in April 1897 seized the propaganda material as well as Kammer and Boris Armand. The latter apparently served one month in jail for his youthful transgression. Nine years later he worked as an underground Social Democratic propagandist in Pushkino and in January 1908 was once again arrested after the police found fifty Menshevik brochures in his Moscow apartment.[55] Vladimir Armand, as already mentioned, was actively involved in student groups in 1901 and 1902 as well as being Inessa's tutor in Marxism. Like most student radicals, who were interested primarily in academic reform, he initially eschewed identification with a formal revolutionary party. In time, however, the amorphous, unfocussed and disorganized nature of the student movement drove him and other Moscow student leaders to seek more revolutionary and structured solutions outside the confines of the university.[56] Early in 1904, while Inessa was still in Switzerland, Vladimir joined a Social Democratic propaganda group in Moscow and by July of that year was under police surveillance.[57] Eight months later he was arrested and briefly imprisoned for Social Democratic activity.[58] His sister, Anna Evgen'evna, helped finance party organizations around

54 One of the few to acknowledge it, however obliquely, was K. Tarasenko: 'all members of the [Armand] family were notable for their critical minds and the youngest branch ... fought tsarist despotism and helped the revolution' ('Inessa Armand, 1874–1920', *Agitator*, 1974, no. 9, pp. 47–8).

55 Material on Boris Armand can be found in Nevskii (ed.), *Deiateli*, p. 23; L. P. Men'shikov, *Okhrana i revoliutsiia*, vol. I (Moscow, 1923), pp. 359–60; 'Sudebnaia khronika', *Russkie vedomosti*, no. 293 (18 December 1908), pp. 5–6. Wolfe, Valentinov and other Western commentators assert that Boris introduced Inessa to Social Democratic ideas. Inessa herself, however, as already noted, gives Vladimir credit for this and has some rather harsh things to say about the depth of Boris's revolutionary convictions (letter to V. E. Armand [20 December 1908], 'Pis'ma Inessy Armand', p. 218).

56 For the frustration and growing radicalism of the Moscow student leadership, see Kassow, pp. 143–51, 191. Among the Moscow student leaders who shared Vladimir's sentiments and also gravitated toward Social Democracy were G. I. Chulkov, Iracli Tseretelli and Mark Vishniak.

57 Police report 7916 of 2 September 1904 in N. Miliutina, *Nakanune pervoi revoliutsii v Moskve* (Moscow, 1926), p. 63.

58 See Chapter 3, below.

Pushkino before and after the 1905 Revolution, was arrested and exiled to Vologda Guberniia in 1908, formally joined the Bolsheviks in 1913 and, together with Lenin, Inessa and sixteen other Bolsheviks rode on the famous 'sealed train' back to Petrograd in April 1917.[59] Alexander Armand was primarily involved in legal political activity, first in the provincial zemstvo and then in the Moscow City Duma. He did, however, lend a hand in spreading Social Democratic ideas in his Pushkino factories in 1906, was arrested in November 1907 for his lenient treatment of striking factory workers, and from 1911 to 1914 gave considerable sums of money to the Bolsheviks through his estranged wife.[60] Less information is available on the revolutionary involvement of other members of the family: two of Evgenii Armand's daughters, Sofiia and Varvara, married Brilling brothers, Nikolai and Evgenii Romanovich, both of whom were active Social Democrats in 1904;[61] and two of his youngest children, Sergei and Mariia, were identified by the Okhrana as being members of the Socialist Revolutionary Party in 1905.[62] Their cousins, Emil Armand's children, were similarly involved in revolutionary activity: Natalia Emil'evna was a Social Democratic propagandist in Pushkino in 1906[63]; her brother Lev was active in the Socialist Revolutionary Party from 1902 to 1911[64]; while Lev's wife Lidiia Marianovna was a member of the SR's Moscow Committee in 1905 and remained associated with that party until at least 1916.[65]

In other words, Inessa was not the exception in being attracted to revolutionary politics and to Marxism in particular; she belonged to a truly 'revolutionary family'.[66] Part of the explanation for her becoming a Marxist lies in factors which caused her entire family to follow this

[59] N. P. and P. P. Bulanov, 'Dela davno minushikh dnei', *Put' k Oktiabriu: sbornik statei, vospominanii i dokumentov*, vol. IV (Moscow, 1925), p. 75; Lenin, *PSS*, vol. XLIX, p. 641. Anna Evgen'evna Armand is better known in party literature by her married name – Anna Konstantinovich.

[60] P. P. Bulanov, 'Kratkaia istoriia Pushkinskogo revoliutsionnogo dvizheniia', *ibid.*, vol. II (1923), pp. 330–32; Bulanov, *ibid.*, vol. IV, pp. 77–79. For Alexander's financial help to the Bolsheviks, see Chapters 5 and 6, below.

[61] Bulanov, *ibid.*, vol. IV, p. 72.

[62] Report of 30 November 1905. I am indebted to Joseph Sanders, who found this report in TsGAOR, *fond* 102, *opis* 233, ch. 2, 1905, for calling this information to my attention.

[63] Bulanov, *Put' k Oktiabriu*, vol. II, p. 330.   [64] Nevskii (ed.), *Deiateli*, p. 53.

[65] Joseph L. Sanders, *The Moscow Uprising of December 1905: A Background Study* (New York, 1987), p. 391, n. 153; OA, incoming report of 22 January 1916, file IIe, folder 43; 'Organizatsiia i zhizn' okhrannago otdeleniia', *Golos minuvshego*, nos. 9/10, September/October 1917, p. 259.

[66] A. Shestakov, 'Nachalo Moskovskoi "Okruzhki"', *Put' k Oktiabriu*, vol. II (1923), p. 75.

path. The reasons for this revolutionary orientation can only be sur-
mised owing to the lack of reliable evidence. Perhaps, as suggested
earlier, the apparent ostracism of the Armands by the local nobility and
the Old Believer merchantry had an alienating effect. Perhaps the
Armands – like E. D. Miagkov, N. A. Shmidt, Savva Morozov and other
'repentant capitalists' in the Moscow area[67] – assisted the Social Democrats to expiate a sense of guilt for the wealth which they had derived
from their factories.[68] Perhaps the Armands, like other Moscow
industrialists, grew increasingly disenchanted with government policies
in the early twentieth century – Zubotovism, suppression of Zemstvo
reformism, failure to end economic recession and rural hunger – and
joined the extreme wing of a broad opposition movement.[69] Perhaps the
Armands, like many young educated Russians at the turn of the
century, were simply seeking an explanation for the obvious injustices
in Russian society and thought they found an answer in Marxism which
explained industrial exploitation, offered hope for the future, claimed to
be scientific, demanded a personal commitment and was both modern
and European.[70] Any explanation for the revolutionary activity of the
younger Armands after 1900 must take into account the intellectual
milieu, liberal upbringing and enlightened education which Evgenii
Armand provided for his children and for the niece of their governess.
Inessa's conversion to Marxism in 1903, far from being a sudden
transformation in Switzerland caused by reading *The Development of
Capitalism in Russia*, obviously began a decade and a half earlier in
Pushkino.

It is also necessary to question her assertion that she became a
Bolshevik, *per se*, a few months after the founding of Lenin's faction at
the Second Party Congress. Police reports and recollections of persons
who knew her in the underground before 1908 refer to her simply as a

---

67 Robert C. Williams, *The Other Bolsheviks: Lenin and His Critics, 1904–1914* (Bloomington, 1986), pp. 58–61, 69, 78; B. I. Pak, 'Savva Timofeevich Morozov', *Soviet Studies
in History*, vol. XX (Winter 1981–82), pp. 74–95; P. A. Buryshkin, *Moskva kupecheskaia* (New York, 1954), p. 315. Joseph Sanders has concluded that 'the single
most important source of financial support for the [revolutionary] parties in Moscow
appears to have been the more well to do' (p. 310; see also pp. 134–6).

68 The phenomenon of 'repentant capitalists' clearly confounded later Russian émigrés.
Speaking of the Tikhomirnov family from Kazan, which supported some of the same
Bolshevik causes as the Armands, George Denike wondered 'what kind of bourgeoisie
was this? To the extent that they became politically involved and actually revolution-
ary, they joined a party that was antagonistic to the bourgeoisie. This was not unique;
there were a good number of such Bolshevik merchants' (as interviewed by Leopold H.
Haimson, *The Making of Three Russian Revolutionaries: Voices from the Menshevik Past*
[Cambridge, 1987], p. 384).

69 Owen, pp. 164 and 171.   70 Clements, *Bolshevik Feminist*, p. 17.

Social Democrat. When she was in exile north of Archangel in 1908 she specifically requested Menshevik as well as Bolshevik literature.[71] It is safe to assume therefore that she, like most underground operatives, abhorred émigré factionalism and did not identify with either of the two factions until after she settled in western Europe in 1909 and became acquainted with Lenin.

Amy Knight has suggested that for many revolutionary women there was a connection between breaking with a conventional marriage and becoming a revolutionary.

A woman had to be liberated from the chains of bourgeois morality before she could find true happiness in creative work. Thus, if a woman wanted to become a revolutionary, she could not be enslaved in a conventional marriage. In order to seek freedom for others she had to be free.[72]

In the case of Inessa Armand, it would be misleading to see too much of a connection between the two decisive events of her life in 1903 – the termination of her marriage and her conversion to Marxism. Her interest in philanthropic work had been waning over several years just as her interest in Marxism had been increasing. So also her parting with Alexander and committing herself to Vladimir had been a gradual process. After leaving Alexander, she continued to live an apparently monogamous married lifestyle with Vladimir in Moscow and even in exile in northern Russia. Her children lived with them until her arrest in February 1905; she interrupted her revolutionary activity to be with them in Pushkino in 1908 and 1913; and they visited her in western Europe during three summers. Had it not been for the outbreak of the First World War she probably would have left the revolutionary movement at least temporarily to be with her family in Russia. Her commitment to Vladimir when he was ill in 1905 and to Andre when he was sick in 1917 kept her from participating in the revolutionary events of these two years. Inessa was a revolutionary and she may have lived an unconventional private life but the two are not necessarily connected in their origins.

Finally, it is necessary to assert that Inessa Armand did not become a revolutionary because she was a feminist even though her early experiences in the women's movement made her susceptible to Marxism. Her years in the Moscow Society sensitized her to general urban social conditions and convinced her that 'small deeds' and charitable work would not produce meaningful change in Russian conditions. These

---

[71] See letter to V. E. Armand (8 May 1908), 'Pis'ma Inessy Armand', p. 213.
[72] Knight, p. 55.

lessons made Marxism attractive. At the same time, Marxism had little to offer someone specifically interested in women's issues. To orthodox Marxists, the problems of women were the same as those of men and could be resolved only within the framework of the general class struggle. For Marxists, the 'woman question was one of class and economics, not gender itself'.[73] Any attempt to address women on issues of interest to women through organizations run by women was immediately condemned even by female Marxists as both separatism and feminism. Thus, to be a Marxist Inessa Armand had to submerge her new-found interest in women's problems; to accept the premise that they would be solved in some undefined manner after the ultimate socialist revolution; and to devote herself in the meantime to raising the class consciousness of all workers. However, while she was to spend the next decade as an underground propagandist and as Lenin's assistant in emigration, this did not mean she had forsaken her interest in women's issues.

[73] Mullaney, 'Gender and the Socialist Revolutionary Role', p. 148.

CHAPTER 3

UNDERGROUND PROPAGANDIST

In May 1904 Inessa and her five children took the train from Switzer-land back to Moscow. The only exciting part of this long trip was the customs check at the Russian frontier. The fact that she was an upper-class lady travelling in a first-class compartment with a baby in arms kept the inspection to a minimum. This was fortunate since on her person and in the false bottom of one of the children's trunks were hidden large quantities of Social Democratic literature.[1] These illegal brochures were to become the core of a lending library for Social Democratic propagandists which Inessa and Vladimir had planned to set up before her trip abroad.[2]

To safeguard the new library, the brochures and other books col-lected in Moscow were kept in the apartment of an actress who did not belong to the party. Vladimir and Inessa also moved out of their house on Spiridonovskaia, which was well known as a meeting place for student radicals and had been raided at least once by the police, and rented new and more modest accommodations at no. 8 Ostozhenka (now Metrostroevskaia Ulitsa). They were joined in these quarters, which were somewhat further from the Arbat but still in central Moscow, by Inessa's children and a former peasant from the Armand estate, I. I. Nikolaev, who was studying medicine at the University of Moscow at the family's expense.[3] Once a week either N. M. Druzhinin – a student friend of theirs and the brother of the actress – or N. M. Lukin would stop by their new apartment to collect the titles of books Inessa wanted. They would then get the books from Druzhinin's sister and deliver them to various propaganda circles connected with the Moscow Social Democratic Committee.[4] These circles in turn would help develop

---

[1] See her autobiographical account, quoted in Podliashuk, p. 39.
[2] See letter to V. E. Armand (2 August 1903), 'Pis'ma Inessy Armand', p. 198.
[3] Podliashuk, p. 30.
[4] Druzhinin, 'O trekh uchastnitsakh', pp. 85–6; *Vospitanniki Moskovskogo universiteta – Bol'sheviki oktiabr'skogo prizyva* (Moscow, 1977), p. 98; Beliavskii and Sorokin, 'Neiz-vestnye stranitsy', p. 55.

the political consciousness of a new generation of Social Democrats to replenish the badly depleted local party organization.[5]

This work, plus the political discussions she had with Druzhinin and his friends, invigorated Armand. To supplement her income from Alexander, she started taking in translation work and applied for permission to set up a French-language circle where she might teach a group of adults how to speak her native tongue. When this request was turned down by the authorities, she and Nikolaev explored the possibility of finding students in need of home tutoring.[6] In October 1904 she wrote to Alexander, who was still in the Far East doing medical relief work for the Moscow City Duma, saying that she felt better than she had in two or three years. The only bad news was that she had experienced some difficulty in getting Fedor admitted to an acceptable Moscow gymnasium. She reported that she had taken the older children to the theatre; and that on one of their periodic visits to Pushkino, she and Inna had taken advantage of an early snowfall to have a sleigh ride around Eldigino. She also told him about boring meetings of the Psychological Society which she had attended and relayed current political gossip making the rounds of Moscow.[7] When she wrote again on 7 January 1905 her tone was more serious. This time she told him about recent sessions of the Moscow Zemstvo and the Moscow Duma, some of which she had attended as an observer, where protests to the government and plans for political reform were discussed. She also reported that the street demonstrations had picked up in intensity and that Nikolaev had returned from one of them badly beaten.[8] Two days later, on Bloody Sunday, police in St Petersburg fired on demonstrators in front of the Winter Palace. As Inessa informed Alexander on 14 January, 'We're having something like a revolution! There is an extraordinary animation. All of Petersburg is out on strike, and even Moscow is beginning to go out.'[9]

Less than a month later these early events of the 1905 Revolution

---

[5] According to Burch, 'in Moscow between 1900 and 1904 active Social Democrats at any one time probably would not have numbered more than 100, and many of these would have worked alone, without any ties with the Moscow Committee' (p. 142). The situation was made worse by the arrest of the remaining members of the Moscow Committee in June 1904 (police report 7916 of 2 September 1904 in Miliutina, p. 63). For the weakness of the Moscow Social Democrats on the eve of the 1905 Revolution, see Sanders, pp. 240–5.

[6] See letter to A. E. Armand (October 1904), 'Pis'ma Inessy Armand', p. 199; *Bratskaia mogila: Biograf\u0441heskii slovar' umershikh i pogibshikh chlenov Moskovskoi organizatsii RKP*, vol. I (Moscow, 1922), p. 15.

[7] 'Pis'ma Inessy Armand', pp. 199–200.   [8] *Ibid.*, pp. 200–3.

[9] *Ibid.*, p. 203.

caught up with the Armands. On 4 February a Socialist Revolutionary, Ivan Kaliaev, assassinated the Governor General of Moscow, the Grand Duke Sergei. The response of the police was to round up student radicals and known SRs, among them the Armands' boarder, Ivan Nikolaev. Inna Armand, then six years old, recalled the fright caused by the police knocking on their apartment door on the night of 6 February and turning everything upside down including the children's beds in their search for incriminating evidence.[10] In Nikolaev's room they did indeed find illegal SR literature and conspiratorial correspondence. In Inessa's room they unexpectedly uncovered Social Democratic leaflets and also a revolver and ammunition which she was probably hiding for Nikolaev. After taking Nikolaev, Vladimir and Inessa into custody, the police then set a trap to ensnare all those who came to the apartment on party business. Druzhinin, with a list of books needed from the Social Democratic library, and several of Nikolaev's SR friends were among those seized.[11]

This mixed bag of revolutionaries confused the police at the time and has confused historians ever since. The authorities came to the conclusion that the Social Democrats and the Socialist Revolutionaries were planning joint operations against the regime. Initially they decided that Inessa was an SR, perhaps because of the revolver, and they put her in Butyrsk prison with the other SR prisoners.[12] This fate was duly noted in the SR press[13] which has led some Soviet and Western writers to the mistaken conclusion that she was a member of that party in 1905.[14] Unlike Vladimir and Nikolaev, who were soon released, Inessa was kept in prison for almost four months. Perhaps because of the revolver, she was charged under Article 126 of the Criminal Code with belonging to an organization seeking the 'overthrow of the existing social order'. Isolated in a damp cell, her health soon deteriorated to the point that she had to be placed in the prison hospital. After being returned to the Moscow provincial prison in mid-May, she informed the Procurator that

---

10 Inna Armand in Stasova (ed.), p. 76.
11 Druzhinin, 'O trekh uchastnitsakh', p. 86; Tsiavlovskii (ed.), p. 192; Podliashuk, pp. 42–4; 'Novye dokumenty ob Inesse Armand', *Istoricheskii arkhiv*, 1961, no. 3, p. 281. Because of the other precautions taken, the library itself was not detected and the alternate courier, Lukin, took Inessa's place as its curator. *Vospitanniki Moskovskogo universiteta*, p. 98.
12 Druzhinin, 'O trekh uchastnitsakh', p. 86.
13 'Khronika pov. gonenii', *Revoliutsionnaia Rossiia*, no. 67 (15 May 1905), p. 22; 'Delo o pokushenie 16-ti lits na zhizn' generala Trepova v 1905 godu', *Byloe*, 1907, no. 10 (22), p. 277.
14 See, for example, Possony, p. 120; *Deiateli SSSR i Oktiabr'skoi Revoliutsii (avtobiografii i biografii)*, vol. I (Moscow, 1925), p. 15.

she had 'developed anaemia and [was] in generally poor health'. Her petition to be allowed more fresh air and increased contact with other prisoners, however, was turned down.[15] At the same time, her father-in-law and Alexander, who had returned from the Far East, were attempting to use their influence to get her released on bail. This bothered her. She wrote to Alexander saying that she did not want 'special favours' and 'not to bother so much' about her. 'You see, I feel fine, I am quite healthy, and you see they will probably take a lot of money from you.'[16] She was more concerned that he take their sons on a holiday she had planned for them along the upper Volga and through the Finnish lakes. In her next letter she commented on the Russian naval defeat at Tsushima in May 1905 which she felt 'is useful for the revolution', but at the same time it was the 'people who grow hungry and must pay the price . . . It seems to me that we are indeed heading for disaster. It is necessary to throw off the hated and disastrous yoke as soon as possible – this is the only path to salvation.'[17] She apparently felt that her own freedom was still a long way off for she asked Alexander to send her some books so that she could prepare history lessons 'for our little boys'. In particular, she wanted copies of works by William Ashley, Edward Gibbon, François Guizot and Augustin Thierry which she had in Moscow or Eldigino and asked him to buy 'something good but *not too voluminous*' on German medieval history.[18]

Much to her surprise, the intercession of the Armands must have been successful since she was freed on 3 June 1905. The charges against her, however, were not dropped and she was to remain under police 'supervision' until her trial. Considerable confusion exists over Inessa Armand's role during the rest of the revolutionary year. One Soviet writer claims she immediately returned to the underground;[19] another has her appearing before the Moscow City Duma on 15 October to demand a partial transfer of civil powers to the party's Moscow Committee;[20] and several Western historians claim she played an active

---

[15] See petition of 20 May 1905 in 'Novye dokumenty', p. 282.
[16] Undated letter in 'Pis'ma Inessy Armand', p. 203.
[17] Undated letter in *ibid.*, p. 204.   [18] *Ibid.* (emphasis in the original).
[19] Tarasenko, 'Inessa Armand', p. 48.
[20] *Istoriia Moskvy: kratkii ocherk*, 3rd edn (Moscow, 1978), p. 168. Had she indeed been there, it would have set up an interesting exchange with her ex-husband Alexander. As a member of the Moscow Duma, he had joined S. A. Muromtsev's liberal wing in calling on the tsar shortly after the October Manifesto to erect a memorial 'to those who gave their lives for the cause of Russian freedom'; to grant full amnesty to political prisoners such as Inessa; and to establish a fund to aid the families of striking workers (quoted in Owen, p. 192). He resigned from the Duma in November 1905, apparently

part in the Moscow uprising of December 1905.[21] In fact, shortly after her release from jail and a brief visit to Pushkino, Inessa and Vladimir left Russia and were to remain abroad for the rest of the year. Most of this time was spent near Nice where they hoped the Riviera climate would help Vladimir recuperate from an illness contracted during his short stay in prison.[22] She felt 'cut off' from Russia and greatly regretted missing out on the general strike which paralyzed the country in the fall and on the euphoria which accompanied the granting of the October Manifesto. 'I so wanted to be there', she wrote Alexander on 9 November 1905, 'and also to bring to the great and popular cause at least my modest contribution.'[23] She later rationalized her absence by noting to some friends that 'friction between personal and family interests [on the one hand] and societal interests [on the other] is one of the most serious problems facing the intelligentsia today'.[24]

If in the second half of 1905 personal interests took precedence, then in the first half of the next year she was able to combine her family and societal commitments in what was certainly one of the more enjoyable and perhaps one of the more successful interludes in her revolutionary career. Taking advantage of the general amnesty which eliminated the charges against her, she returned alone to Russia in early 1906 and rejoined her children and other members of the extended Armand family in Pushkino. This was not the first time since her separation from Alexander that she had been to her childhood home. She made brief visits there after her return from Europe in the summer of 1904 and again a year later before leaving for Nice so that her children could visit their grandparents and relatives. These occasions also gave her an opportunity to carry out party activities in familiar surroundings, usually by helping the informal local organization in its propaganda activities.[25] As her Soviet biographer remarks in his abbreviated treatment of her work in Pushkino: she 'used the slightest pretext to carry out revolutionary work there' and at the same time to be with her family.[26]

in protest against the government's handling of the Sevastopol mutiny (information from Joseph Sanders, letter to the author of 29 October 1990).

21 See, for example, Stites, *Women's Liberation Movement*, p. 255. Sanders' extensive treatment of the Moscow uprising makes no mention of Armand.

22 See notes to letter to A. E. Armand (9 November 1905), in 'Pis'ma Inessy Armand', p. 205; and Armand, *Stat'i*, pp. 189 and 271.

23 'Pis'ma Inessy Armand', p. 204.

24 Letter to A. Ia. and V. M. Asknazi (August 1908), *ibid.*, p. 214.

25 See Bulanov, *Put' k Oktiabriu*, vol. IV, pp. 72–3, for comments on her work in Pushkino in 1904.

26 Pavel Podliashuk, *Tovarishch Inessa: documental'naia povest'*, 3rd edn (Moscow, 1973), p. 55. Podliashuk says very little about Inessa's activities between July 1905 and

In 1906 she was able to be in Pushkino for an extended stay and to become fully involved in the local Social Democratic group. In March or April of that year she and a number of other party members decided to set up a formal underground organization which would establish links with the Moscow District Committee and could be used to expand propaganda work in the local textile factories. The principal figures in the organization besides Inessa were A. N. Rodd, who ran the 'Free People's Library and Reading Room of Pushkino'; N. N. Pechkin, a doctor associated with many of the factories; and Boris Armand, who sat on the group's four-person executive. Among the other Armands involved to a lesser degree were Anna Evgen'evna who helped out financially, Natalia Emil'evna, the twin Brilling brothers-in-law and, for a while, Alexander.[27] The group would exchange messages through the library and would meet either in Dr Pechkin's apartment or at the Armands' manor. As one of the participants later recalled, 'it seemed extraordinary that [party affairs were arranged] in the home of the factory owner against whom these arrangements then and later would be used'.[28] These 'arrangements' included using the organization's hectograph machine to print leaflets which would be left at night by the village well for the women to find; holding agitational meetings in the nearby woods with non-party workers; and organizing illegal propaganda circles to familiarize more advanced workers with political and party matters. The latter was Inessa's primary responsibility. With one other colleague, she was able to set up and run three circles in Pushkino and two others in neighbouring villages which had some fifty-five members.[29]

Inessa stayed in Pushkino until July 1906 when she left for Finland either to go on the deferred holiday with her children or to meet Vladimir.[30] The organization which she helped to establish in Pushkino continued to operate sporadically for another year and a half. In 1907 a number of the other key intellectuals departed hurting the propaganda efforts of the group. On 5 July of that year a four-day strike broke out at the Armand factory now run by Alexander. When he agreed to all but

September 1906 and avoids a detailed discussion of her activities in Pushkino (see Podliashuk [4th edn], pp. 52–3, which omits the statement cited above).
27 Bulanov, *Put' k Oktiabriu*, vol. II, pp. 330–1; vol. IV, pp. 72, 75.
28 Shestakov, *ibid.*, vol. II, p. 75.
29 Bulanov, *ibid.*, vol. II, p. 331.
30 See letter sent from Finland in late July 1906 to A. E. Armand, 'Pis'ma Inessy Armand', p. 205. For information about Vladimir's rather imprecise whereabouts between March 1906 and May 1907, see Inessa's letters to him of 11 May 1907 and late November 1908 in *ibid.*, pp. 206 and 216.

one of the strikers' demands, the police were suspicious about where his sympathies lay but restricted themselves to arresting four local party members. On 22 November another strike and demonstration took place at the factory to protest the trial of the Social Democratic deputies to the Second Duma. This time the police arrested twenty-four strikers and, shortly thereafter, Alexander Armand, Boris Armand and A. N. Rodd.[31] Even the manor house in Pushkino was subject to an 'invasion of barbarians' as the police sought more incriminating evidence in what had once been a quiet 'nest of gentlefolk'.[32] These arrests broke the local organization with the result that Social Democratic activity in Pushkino, as in the rest of Imperial Russia, was negligible between 1908 and 1912.

After a brief stay in Finland, Inessa and Vladimir once again settled in Moscow. One of the reasons for staying in the city was to take advantage of a decision by the Council of the University of Moscow in October 1905 to admit women as auditors or external students. In the fall of 1906, at the age of thirty-two, she enrolled in the Faculty of Law.[33] This choice reflected either an optimism that conditions for women would change rapidly in Russia or a commitment on her part to make party work her future vocation. Most women tended to enter the natural sciences or the humanities – an area where she had shown some aptitude – rather than law which prepared students for careers still closed to women in the government bureaucracy or as practising lawyers.[34]

Inessa continued to be heavily involved as an underground propagandist during the year that she studied at the University of Moscow but her attention was focussed on the urban proletariat rather than on her fellow students. The revolutionary student circles, which five years earlier had attracted Vladimir and indirectly Inessa, now were in eclipse. It seemed to her that that the prevailing mood of political indifference and apathy doomed to failure any attempt by the few

---

[31] Information on the 1907 strikes can be found in Bulanov, *Put' k Oktiabriu*, vol. II, pp. 331–2 and vol. IV, pp. 77–9; Inessa's letter to A. E. Armand (16 February 1908) in 'Pis'ma Inessy Armand', p. 211; and Podliashuk, pp. 68–70. Bulanov implies that a third Armand brother or cousin was also arrested in the aftermath of the November strike.

[32] See letter to A. N. Rodd (1 February 1908), 'Pis'ma Inessy Armand', p. 210.

[33] Beliavskii and Sorokin, 'Neizvestnye stranitsy', p. 55.

[34] Dudgeon, 'The Forgotten Minority', pp. 10–14. While two-thirds of the students in the Law Faculty opted to pursue civil law and thus prepare themselves for a legal or government career, it is possible that Armand chose one of the less popular faculty options – political science or economics – which were introduced for the first time in 1906. Kassow, p. 302.

remaining radical student leaders to stir up meaningful short-term unrest at the university.[35] It was better she felt to concentrate her efforts on achieving long-term gains through increasing class consciousness in the working-class sections of Moscow.

In the late summer of 1906 she took over as the chief Social Democratic propagandist in the Lefortovo District. She was given this position, one suspects, partly on the basis of her experience as party librarian in 1904 and as propagandist in Pushkino in 1906 and partly because she was older, well-educated and a woman. The party was short of trained propagandists as the Social Democratic intelligentsia, which had traditionally filled this role, withdrew from the revolutionary movement in large numbers after the failure of the 1905 Revolution.[36] As chief propagandist it was her job to select the proper literature to be studied, to find other and younger students to lead the propaganda circles, and to train them in their duties. On occasion the students she selected would come to her apartment near the Arbat, which she shared with at least two of her children and Vladimir, to discuss study programmes and ways of raising the class consciousness of poorly educated circle members.[37] She also had to travel across the city to find suitable and innocuous places for the circles to meet, such as in the Annengofskii woods or along the banks of the Iauza River which ran through the district. The job obviously required the same blend of energy, initiative and organizational ability which she had shown in her work with the Moscow Society.

Being a woman was usually seen as an asset for a party organizer or propagandist in that a well-dressed lady was less likely in most areas to arouse police suspicions. Moreover, male workers, who often were reluctant to see female workers participate in their circles since politics was 'men's business', were quite prepared to accept a well-educated woman as their circle leader.[38] But work in Lefortovo was difficult. The

[35] See letter of 11 May 1907 to Vladimir Armand ('Pis'ma Inessy Armand', p. 206), which confirms other observations about the growing political apathy of the Moscow students at this time. Also J. D. Morison, 'Political Characteristics of the Student Movement in the Russian Revolution of 1905', in F-X. Coquin and C. Gervois-France-lle (eds.), *1905: La Première Révolution Russe* (Paris, 1986), pp. 72–3; Kassow, pp. 301, 306–7, 321.

[36] This is discussed in more detail in my *Russian Social Democracy in the Underground: A Study of the RSDRP in the Ukraine, 1907–1914* (Assen, 1974), pp. 60–73.

[37] Elena Vlasova, 'Pamiati Inessy Fedorovny Armand' in Krupskaia (ed.), *Pamiati*, pp. 69–70.

[38] Knight, pp. 72 and 76. In areas such as Lefortovo, where there were many women workers, this situation often led to separate circles for male and female workers with women leading the latter. The party was not pleased with this separatist solution and there is no evidence that it was employed during Armand's tenure in Lefortovo.

workers in the district – food processors, bakers, textile workers – were employed in small and dispersed factories. Many were seasonal workers, often close to illiterate, and backward in terms of prior political consciousness. Despite the best of will, it was hard for many members of the intelligentsia to communicate with this type of worker. Armand was surprisingly successful in bridging the gap. She apparently had the ability to simplify, repeat and popularize theoretical arguments without appearing to condescend.[39] On several occasions, many years later, participants in her circles recalled the enthusiasm and optimism which she conveyed in these propaganda sessions.[40]

When winter came the outdoor meeting places she had selected were no longer appropriate for propaganda work and she sensed that she was being followed whenever she visited Lefortovo.[41] She therefore switched her operations to the Railway District and moved into a new and less fashionable apartment on Staraia Basmannaia with a fellow party worker, Elena Vlasova. According to Vlasova, Inessa wanted to isolate herself from her children so as to spare them further trauma of night-time police searches such as they had experienced in February 1905.[42] The move may also have been prompted by Vladimir's decision to return to the healthier wintertime climate of southern France. Freed of family distractions, she turned her attentions to propaganda activity made somewhat easier by the fact the workers in the Railway District had been proletarians longer and thus were already more class conscious. She also became involved, according to her unpublished autobiography, in educational work inside legal trade unions and was a member of the party's 'Lecturers Commission' which served as a pool for experienced propagandists.[43]

In 1907 the government of Prime Minister P. A. Stolypin started to crack down both on legal trade unions and on underground propaganda. The Okhrana's first target was the Socialist Revolutionaries in Moscow and particularly their All-Russian Military Union of Soldiers and Sailors. Apparently operating on mistaken information from two years earlier, the police arrested Inessa Armand on 9 April. When a search of her apartment uncovered only Social Democratic literature and nothing to connect her with the Military Union, she was released

39 Vlasova in Krupskaia (ed.), *Pamiati*, p. 70.
40 See, for example, Krupskaia in Kon (ed.), p. 64; N. Krupskaia, 'Plamennye bortsy za sotsializm', *Sputnik kommunista v derevne*, 1938, no. 4, pp. 16–17.
41 Inna Armand in Stasova (ed.), p. 77.
42 Vlasova in Krupskaia (ed.), *Pamiati*, p. 71.
43 Podliashuk, p. 52.

after several days in jail.[44] In May she was arrested again – this time while attending an unauthorized meeting – and once again freed in short order after paying a fine.[45]

The outcome of her third arrest in 1907, however, was different. In early July the Okhrana decided to terminate Social Democratic operations in the Railway District by seizing the party's printing press, leaflets and key personnel. On the seventh of that month they raided a strike meeting of a Social Democratic railway workers' union, which was being held in the office of an employment agency, and arrested eleven participants. Armand, who arrived late, became the twelfth when the police refused to accept her story that she was in the building simply to hire a cook.[46] Despite the fact that this time they found in her possession nothing more incriminating than a book in English on trade unionism, the authorities felt that they had accumulated sufficient information since her release from prison in June 1905 to warrant another long incarceration.[47] Inessa did not feel particularly cooperative when taken to Prechistenskii jail to be photographed and interrogated. She kept her eyes closed to make her police mug shots less useful (see Plate 6) and she fictionalized her personal data. She told the police she was twenty-eight when she was actually thirty-three, that she was Orthodox by faith, that her mother was alive and living in Moscow, and she supplied the names of her children when asked for those of her siblings. The police noted with more accuracy that she was of medium height with an oval face, grey eyes, very light brown hair, and a sharp-featured nose.[48]

Conditions in the Lefortovo prison, where she was to spend the next three and a half months while the police concluded their investigations, were considerably better in the summer of 1907 than they had been in Butyrsk during the winter of 1905. She informed Vladimir, who had returned to Pushkino, that she and the other women prisoners had formed a 'commune' in which each took a turn preparing meals,

[44] Tsiavlovskii (ed.), p. 192; *Bratskaia mogila*, vol. I, p. 16. I am indebted to John Bushnell for information concerning the raids on the All-Russian Military Union of Soldiers and Sailors.

[45] Podliashuk, p. 56.

[46] *Ibid.*, p. 58. Alexander offered a slightly different excuse for her presence at the meeting when he petitioned for her release (see Sanov, 'Mezenskaia ballada', p. 90).

[47] See police report 3534 of 1 September 1907 in Sanov, p. 90.

[48] OA, file XIIIf, folder 2, card 12206. Some Western writers – in their search for the dramatic and in the absence of coloured photographs to the contrary – have portrayed Armand as having hypnotic green eyes and red, chestnut or 'golden hair'. See, for example, Harrison E. Salisbury, *Black Night: White Snow: Russia's Revolutions, 1905–1917* (New York, 1978), p. 227.

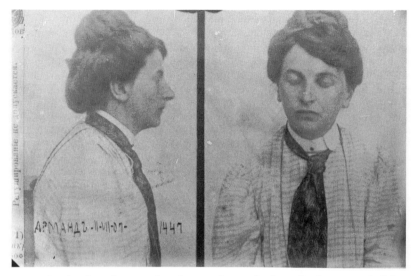

6. Official police photographs of Inessa Armand taken after her arrest in July
1907 (Okhrana Archives, file XIIIf [4] [2], folder 1).

cleaning up, etc. Since her own culinary skills were decidedly limited,
she felt relieved when her first attempts at making soup turned out
satisfactorily. Every day she would read until 2 pm, give a French lesson
and take a walk in the inner courtyard after lunch, and then give two
more French lessons following the evening meal.[49] Prison life nevertheless was monotonous, the police investigation of her activities seemed to
drag on interminably, and she felt cut off from her family. Even visits by
Vladimir and his parents could not eliminate the sense of isolation.[50]
Finally, on 22 October she learned that she was not going to be brought
to trial but was instead to serve two years' administrative banishment
in the north of Russia with the term being made retroactive to 30
September 1907. Alexander immediately appealed, first to the Governor of Moscow and then in person to the Minister of Internal Affairs in
St Petersburg, that she be allowed to spend her exile abroad.[51] Neither
official showed any desire to decide the matter before Inessa's scheduled
departure or to give special consideration to the estranged wife of an

---

[49] Letter to V. E. Armand (July 1907), 'Pis'ma Inessy Armand', p. 206. The portions of
this letter which describe the reasonable jail conditions are omitted from the version
published in her 'collected works'. Cf. Armand, *Stat'i*, p. 191.
[50] Vlasova in Krupskaia (ed.), *Pamiati*, p. 71; Fel'dman, 'Inessa Armand', p. 76.
[51] Sanov, 'Mezenskaia ballada', p. 90.

hereditary honorary citizen. Eventually, in February 1908, the appeal was formally rejected on the grounds that since the appellant was 'unlikely to stop her criminal activity, she would do less harm in Archangel Guberniia than abroad'.[52]

*   *   *

Inessa had in fact departed for Archangel in mid-November 1907 in the company of two guards and Vladimir Armand who, despite his poor health and his studies, had decided to emulate the wives of the Decembrists by following his spouse into exile. She was equally touched by Alexander's unexpected gesture in bringing their children to see her off at the Iaroslavl Station in Moscow.[53] Half an hour later the train passed through Pushkino on its way north.

When Inessa arrived in Archangel on 21 November she was immediately put into solitary confinement in the local jail rather than in one of the holding cells where deportees were usually kept until their final destinations were known. Very likely she was put there for her own protection and not, as one Soviet writer has speculated,[54] out of fear she might escape. Conditions in the jail were the worst she ever experienced. There was only one other political prisoner, an 18-year old woman who had become deranged from nine months in solitary; all the other prisoners were common criminals. During the two weeks she spent isolated in this 'crypt',[55] Vladimir, who was staying in a local furnished apartment, was busy protesting prison conditions to the Social Democratic Duma fraction and appealing to the authorities that Inessa be allowed to stay in Archangel for medical reasons or be sent to a nearby town such as Pinega or Kholmogory.[56]

His appeals, like those of Alexander, fell on deaf ears. On 6 December she was released from solitary confinement and told to leave the following day for her next destination – the small town of Mezen, 360 kilometres to the northeast. This time she and Vladimir had to travel by horse-drawn sledge – an experience which made her 'bless civilization' and 'fully value the railways'.[57] Every dozen kilometres or so they had to compete with other travellers for fresh horses at the way stations,

[52] Peregudova and Khmeleva, 'Dokumenty', p. 106.
[53] See letter to A. E. Armand (mid-December 1907) in 'Pis'ma Inessy Armand', p. 208.
[54] Sanov, 'Mezenskaia ballada', p. 87.
[55] For her account of her stay in this jail, where she acknowledged her 'frame of mind was very bad', see her letter to A. E. Armand (mid-December 1907) in 'Pis'ma Inessy Armand', pp. 207–8.
[56] Sanov, 'Mezenskaia ballada', pp. 87, 90; Podliashuk, p. 60.
[57] Letter to A. E. Armand (mid-December 1907) in 'Pis'ma Inessy Armand', p. 207.

sometimes having to wait up to twenty-four hours before some became available. They also stayed overnight in these stations. Inessa was immensely impressed by the stations' huge Russian stoves, with their provisions for drying winter clothes and warming cold travellers. She was less pleased with the dirty divans or double beds provided for travellers, preferring instead to sleep on the floor. The sun was up for only four hours a day in December but she was struck by the beauty of the countryside on clear days, by the unbroken stretches of forest, and by the vast expanse of snow that looked blue in the pale northern light. At first she found the *malitsa* worn by the coachmen and local people 'very curious' and described them at great length in letters to Alexander. In time she came to appreciate the value in very cold climates of 'these marvellous garments' which were made of fur and put on over the head like a bulky poncho.[58]

When they finally arrived in Mezen, 1 degree south of the Arctic Circle, on 12 December 1907 it was 37 degrees below zero. Much to their surprise, they were told by the local administrator that they had to go another 110 kilometres further north to the even smaller village of Koida on the White Sea. Inessa did not want to leave: Koida had no political prisoners other than a few 'expropriators' whom she felt were probably 'hooligans', and the area was rife with syphilis 'which also is not particularly nice'.[59] Vladimir once again appealed, this time by telegraph to the governor of the province, and this time his request was granted: Inessa was allowed to stay in Mezen where she was to spend the next ten months in exile.

Because of its isolation and extreme climate, Mezen had had a bad reputation among deportees ever since Avvakum had been sent there in the seventeenth century. Inessa agreed that it was 'a mean little town' but initially, at least, 'better than I had expected'.[60] Its 2500 residents lived along two broad parallel streets or on the short lanes connecting them. Contrary to Inessa's rather romanticized preconceptions, they resided in drafty and poorly constructed *izbas* or huts rather than in *iurtas* (tents). To supplement their meagre income from fishing or

---

[58] See letters of mid-December 1907 and mid-January 1908 in *ibid.*, pp. 207 and 209.
[59] Letter to A. E. Armand (mid-December 1907) in *ibid.*, p. 207.
[60] Postcard of late December 1907 to Anna Asknazi quoted in Sanov, 'Mezenskaia ballada', p. 88. All of the information in this chapter about Mezen and the Armands' activity there, unless otherwise indicated, is derived from Inessa's lengthy and informative letters to Alexander, her children or Moscow friends such as Anna Asknazi. The most complete version of these is to be found in 'Pis'ma Inessy Armand', pp. 207–14. Many of her less critical remarks about Mezen and her self-deprecating remarks have been omitted from the same letters in Armand, *Stat'i*, pp. 192–203.

working in the local sawmill, some of the permanent residents rented out rooms to the one hundred political prisoners who were there when the Armands arrived. Mezen also had a four-class school whose teachers were considered the local aristocracy, a hospital, church, police station, post and telegraph office, and a village store with a piano Inessa could play on occasion. She was pleased to find that the town had a newspaper but distressed to learn that reading matter was otherwise very scarce. As she told her children, Mezen resembled the village of Pushkino in size if not in conveniences.[61]

Since Inessa was the wife of an 'honorary citizen' and thus not expected to have a profession, she was given a monthly stipend of twelve and a half rubles, unlike most of the other 'politicals' who received only eight.[62] She used this money to rent a small *izba* with three rooms but without running water for Vladimir and herself. She liked the kitchen, which probably served as a bedroom as well, because it had one of those large stoves that had fascinated her in the way stations. The living room, furnished only with three chairs and a small bench, reminded her of a shed. The pantry or storeroom was too cold to be used in the winter but she thought it might be converted into a bedroom should her children be able to visit during the next summer.

The daily routine called for Vladimir to get up first to stoke the stove, melt the water in the water buckets, and set up the samovar. 'Strictly speaking', Inessa confessed to her children in an un-feminist manner, 'I should set up the samovar, but I am famous for being lazy. I get up late and . . . it always seems the samovar is almost ready.'[63] The time before 4 pm was taken up with housekeeping, cooking and giving lessons. As in Lefortovo prison, cooking was a problem for a woman brought up in a house staffed with servants. Making *bliny* with yeast petrified her but she was optimistic they would be able 'to hack through' the final product.[64] In contrast, she enjoyed giving lessons to her fellow deportees. While Vladimir taught mathematics, she tutored Jewish or Lithuanian exiles in Russian, or Russians in French and, for a while, she offered level four gymnasium lessons. The lack of furniture and books hindered but did not stop their two favourite evening activities – visiting with friends or simply reading. As she informed her children, she loved to curl up in bed at night, 'cozy and warm', with a book. If it were a serious book 'then I fall asleep immediately. I implore you, however, not

[61] Letter of mid-December 1907 in 'Pis'ma Inessy Armand', p. 208.
[62] Sanov, 'Mezenskaia ballada', p. 88.
[63] Letter of mid-December 1907 in 'Pis'ma Inessy Armand', p. 209.
[64] Letter to A. E. Armand (16 February 1908), *ibid.*, p. 211.

to follow my example (only here, in all other areas, as is well known, I am *perfection*).'[65] The wintertime monotony was broken by occasionally going to plays put on by fellow 'politicals', shopping in the periodic village fair, and even taking walks on relatively warm days. As she wrote after a month in Mezen, 'We live a little at a time – certainly it is not lively here but also there is nothing particularly bad.'[66]

Inessa was also involved, though not as much as she would have liked or as much as Soviet writers would like us to believe, in Social Democratic activities in Mezen. On 9 January 1908, within a month of her arrival, some of the 'politicals' held a demonstration to mark the third anniversary of Bloody Sunday. The police must have thought Armand was one of its instigators for she was once again threatened with exile to an even more remote community. With the deepening of Stolypin's repression, the number of deportees in Mezen grew to 200 by late February and was up to 300 by the end of August. This provoked a local 'housing crisis' in that the pressure on the insufficient number of rooms caused rents to go up. When forty political exiles met to discuss the situation on 21 February, the local cossack detachment raided the meeting and beat up many of its participants. Inessa's contribution to this sad affair, other than to care for some of the wounded, was apparently to write an exposé which eventually appeared in the liberal newspaper *Rech'*.[67]

Social Democrats were in a minority among the exiles in Mezen; they were outnumbered by the SRs and by others of indeterminate political persuasion. Those who arrived in 1908 were a 'mixed lot' in Inessa's estimation. Some wanted

nothing more to do with the revolution and even less with socialism and bitterly and loudly complain that they lost two or three years because of the revolution; others drink and carouse – in general hard drinking is very great here – and the majority of these people are anarchists or SRs. I must say without any bias that all of the SDs compare favourably with them in the level of their needs as well as in their way of life.[68]

Armand was instrumental in melding the Social Democrats into a local party organization of sorts. She arranged meetings and lectures

---

[65] Letter of mid-December 1907, *ibid.*, p. 209 (emphasis in the original).

[66] Letter to A. E. Armand (mid-January 1908), *ibid.*, p. 209. See Plate 7 for a photograph taken in 1908 of Armand and some of her fellow exiles in Mezen.

[67] 'Izbrienie ssyl'nykh: Pis'mo iz Arkhangel'ska', *Rech'*, 1908, no. 66. The article was unsigned but, according to one of the participants in the meeting, its author was Armand (Sanov, 'Mezenskaia ballada', p. 95). It was said to have been 'from Archangel' to protect her from reprisal. If she were indeed its author, then this represents her first known publication.

[68] Letter to A. Ia. and V. M. Asknazi (August 1908), in 'Pis'ma Inessy Armand', p. 213.

7. Inessa Armand and exile friends in Mezen (1908).

and laid plans to publish a very unsophisticated leaflet. She also utilized her experience in Pushkino and Moscow to set up a Social Democratic propaganda circle which she led. The major problem she faced was the lack of study material. At first 'one of the best things we had' was Karl Kautsky's *Istoriia obshchestvennykh techenii*.[69] Through a friend she

---

[69] Letter to A. N. Rodd (1 February 1908), *ibid.*, p. 210.

received some five-year-old copies of *Iskra* which only she found to be of any interest.[70] Later she was delighted when Vladimir, who had temporarily left Mezen in the early spring, sent her the protocols of the Fifth Congress of the RSDRP and of the Stuttgart Congress of the Socialist International. 'If more party literature pops up', she urged him in May, 'send it ... send both Menshevik and Bolshevik' literature and especially something on the question of Duma participation.[71] The latter was particularly important in that Social Democratic efforts in Mezen had prompted the SRs to try to organize themselves as well and the two groups were planning a joint discussion where differing attitudes toward the Duma would obviously come up. In late August she once again pleaded with the Asknazis, her friends in Moscow, to 'please send new Social Democratic literature since we have absolutely nothing here'.[72]

And yet, while exile life may have 'picked up' after Inessa's arrival,[73] even she came to the conclusion after eight months in Mezen that 'we try to deceive ourselves' with this party activity.[74] 'Mezen', she wrote to the Asknazis in August,

is a city of the spiritually dead and dying; there is nothing shocking or terrible here, as for example in penal servitude, but there is no life and people grow sickly like a plant without moisture. Civilized people ... cannot get along in a quiet Mezen-like bog and fall into spiritual decay ... There are no interests here, no living ties with the population, there isn't even simple physical work, or if there is it is only temporary and accidental. Muscles forget how to work, the brain how to think intensively. It is sad to see how comrades arrive here cheerful and full of energy and then waste away; it is difficult to ascertain this process in oneself.[75]

The malaise which obviously overtook Inessa Armand in August 1908 was caused by a combination of boredom, isolation and loneliness relieved only by the presence of Vladimir. Like the other 'politicals', she had little or no contact with the permanent residents whom she found to be unsociable and uncommunicative. 'We are getting by as usual', she had written to Alexander,

the same dull life; the days don't pass but somehow imperceptibly slide by like pale bloodless shadows. As much as we can, we deceive ourselves, we try to convince ourselves ... that there is life here. Of course, I am better off than the

[70] Sanov, 'Mezenskaia ballada', p. 94.
[71] Letter of 8 May 1908 in 'Pis'ma Inessy Armand', p. 212.
[72] Quoted in Sanov, 'Mezenskaia ballada', p. 89.
[73] S. M. Zubrovich in *Bratskaia mogila*, vol. II (1923), p. 14.
[74] Letter to A. Ia. and V. M. Asknazi (August 1908), in 'Pis'ma Inessy Armand', p. 213.
[75] *Ibid.*

others because I am not alone. Many others are completely alone and they are having a bad time of it. On the other hand, I am worse off than the others because there, in Moscow, are the children whom I miss and worry about.[76]

She had admitted at the very beginning of her exile that 'I don't know how I shall survive for two years without the children.'[77] She thought wistfully about the happy times everyone was having at Pushkino over Christmas. But at least during the winter months she could write to her children about their studies, their friends, their activities and could receive mail from them twice a week. She could also 'dream about your coming to visit us in the summer' by taking the old steamship *Barty* which plied the White Sea once the ice was out and about how they could pick mushrooms, hunt and fish together.[78] When spring came, however, all communication with the outside world was cut off for six weeks until the frost was out of the ground and the muddy roads became passable once again. By then she had come to the reluctant realization that the hordes of mosquitoes that descended on Mezen each summer made it an unsuitable place for children to visit, let alone go walking in the woods as she had planned. The final blow came when Vladimir left Mezen for good in early September 1908. He had gone to Moscow temporarily just before the roads became impassable, apparently returned during the summer, and then left again when his deteriorating health made another winter in the north inadvisable.

Inessa, now 'completely alone', was determined to leave Mezen, legally if possible, illegally if not. On 5 April 1908 she had once again petitioned the Minister of Internal Affairs to spend the remainder of her term abroad on the grounds that 'the local climate is extremely harmful for my health' and she attached a medical certificate attesting to the fact that as a result of malnutrition she was suffering from 'chronic malaria and chronic gastric catarrh'. The Minister, who was upset that she demanded rather than requested a change in venue and that she did not use his title 'Your high excellency', turned down her petition in late July.[79] On 15 September she appealed for the last time: she asked that she be allowed to live in Archangel so that she could get medical and dental treatment. Unstated but paramount in her thinking was the fact that her young children could live in Archangel. As she had written to Inna the month before, 'further separation is completely

---

[76] Letter of 16 February 1908, *ibid.*, p. 211.
[77] Letter to A. E. Armand (mid-December 1907), *ibid.*, p. 208.
[78] Letter to her children (mid-December 1907), *ibid.*, p. 209.
[79] Quoted in Sanov, 'Mezenskaia ballada', p. 91.

inconceivable'.[80] When this appeal was rejected, she tried other means. Early in the morning of 20 October she simply left Mezen without permission with S. M. Zubrovich, a young Polish worker she had befriended, and some other Poles whose terms of exile were over. For good measure she cloaked herself in a local *malitsa*, one of those 'marvellous garments' she had admired when she first arrived in the north. After a long but uneventful trip over pot-holed dirt roads, she and Zubrovich arrived in Archangel, took one train to Vologda and another to Moscow, arriving in the former Russian capital on 3rd or 4th November 1908.[81] After four arrests and more than twenty months in prison or exile, her four and a half year career as an underground propagandist was over.

[80] Quoted in *ibid.*, p. 94.   [81] *Ibid.*, p. 96.

CHAPTER 4

YEARS OF WANDERING

Inessa stayed in Moscow for a month. Since her forced departure a year earlier, her family circumstances had changed considerably. Vladimir was once again living abroad at Beaulieu-sur-Mer, a small town on the Riviera between Monte Carlo and Nice, where he had gone for medical attention in 1905. His ailment, which Inessa still believed to be a cyst or abscess that could be cured by a minor operation,[1] was in fact tuberculosis. Unbeknownst to either of them, he had less than three months to live. Alexander was also abroad. After his arrest in late 1907, he had spent some time in jail and was then forbidden to live in certain major Russian cities for two years. Since Moscow and its environs, including Pushkino and Eldigino, were on the proscribed list, he chose at first to stay in the provincial town of Dmitrov, sixty kilometres northwest of Pushkino. When he found he could not manage family and business interests from there, Alexander requested permission to spend the rest of his term abroad. In August 1908, after permission had been granted, he took his two older sons to Switzerland for a holiday and then to Roubaix, near Lille, in northern France where they were to live until 1910.[2] He had chosen Roubaix – the so-called 'French Manchester' because of its heavy concentration of textile factories[3] – so that he could study modern methods of dyeing wool at the Higher School of Applied Art. It also would give his sons, Alexander and Fedor, a chance to fulfil their mother's wish that they perfect their language skills by attending a French school.[4]

Inessa's own situation was more precarious and uncertain. There is no indication that she made any attempt upon arrival in Moscow to contact the local party organization or had precise plans other than to see her younger children. She fortunately had limited freedom of move-

---

[1] Unpublished letter to Anna Asknazi ([April?] 1909), cited in Podliashuk, p. 77.
[2] See letters to A. E. Armand (16 February and 13 August 1908), 'Pis'ma Inessy Armand', pp. 211 and 212.
[3] John P. McKay, *Pioneers for Profit: Foreign Entrepreneurship and Russian Industrialization, 1885–1913* (Chicago, 1970), p. 48.
[4] See letter to A. E. Armand (13 August 1908), 'Pis'ma Inessy Armand', pp. 212–13.

ment, since she had managed to keep her passport from falling into police hands at the time of her earlier arrest,[5] and she may have counted on her absence from Mezen escaping immediate police attention.[6] Nevertheless, as a political fugitive, she was always vulnerable to arrest and to deportation to a place even more remote than Mezen. These considerations kept her from going to Pushkino – where three of her children were living with their grandmother – since her presence there would have been both predictable and obvious. Instead, she made arrangements for ten-year-old Inna and probably Varvara to visit her in Moscow where conspiracy was less of a problem.

Moscow also offered other things Mezen had lacked. Inessa went to a lecture on symbolism, to a new art exhibit at the Tretiakov Gallery, to concerts at the Bolshoi, and to several new plays. She even spent some time reading in the Rumiantsev Museum.[7] 'I listen with delight to the noise of carriages passing by,' she wrote to Vladimir,

to the commotion of the crowd, I look at the tall multi-storied buildings, at the trams ... Dear town, how I love you, how closely all the fibres of my being are tied to you. I am your child and I need your bustle, your noise, your commotion like a fish needs water ... I am very happy and excited.[8]

Inna Armand was probably right when she concluded that this month in Moscow was one of the happiest periods in her mother's life.[9] In her enthusiasm and optimism that she could avoid arrest, Inessa decided to take her children to Kiev and to remain in Russia until at least the summer of 1909. She hoped that by 'then it will be apparent what to do' next.[10]

Before leaving for Kiev, however, she wanted to attend the First All-Russian Women's Congress in St Petersburg with her sister-in-law, Anna Evgen'evna Konstantinovich. This congress, which the Women's Mutual Philanthropic Society first started talking about holding in 1902, represented the high-water mark of Russian feminism. It offered Armand a marvellous opportunity to re-visit an earlier period in her life and to learn about recent developments and problems in areas which once had been of great interest to her. Most of the ladies with whom she

---

[5] See letter to V. E. Armand of July 1907 asking him to retrieve her passport from her last place of residence (*ibid.*, p. 207).

[6] The police in Mezen did not in fact report her escape until three weeks after her departure. Sanov, 'Mezenskaia ballada', p. 86.

[7] See letters of 22 November and late November 1908 to V. E. Armand, 'Pis'ma Inessy Armand', pp. 214–16.

[8] Letter to V. E. Armand (10 November 1908), *ibid.*, p. 214.

[9] Inna Armand in Stasova (ed.), p. 79.

[10] Letter to V. E. Armand (10 November 1908), 'Pis'ma Inessy Armand', p. 214.

had been associated in the Moscow Society for Improving the Lot of Women had turned away from philanthropic work and concentrated their attention in recent years on the new legal opportunities and especially the State Duma promised by the October Manifesto. They hoped to get the support of the more liberal political parties within the Duma for extending to women the right to vote and to participate in the Russian parliament and ultimately to achieve through legislative action many of the goals they had failed to obtain through their philanthropic endeavours. The unresponsiveness of the male leaders in the First and Second Dumas to their demands, plus the general demoralization of Russian liberalism which accompanied the dissolution of these Dumas by the government, caused the women's movement to lose much of its momentum and its unity. It was this situation which the organizers of the 1908 Women's Congress hoped to correct. By revealing the common ground and the common interests of Russian women from differing backgrounds, they sought to broaden the base of their movement and ideally to create a new unified women's organization.

This possibility posed a dilemma for the Russian Social Democrats. No Marxist wanted to see a strong united women's movement under the control of so-called 'bourgeois feminists'. There were differing opinions, however, over the proper response to the congress itself. Almost all of the party leadership opposed meaningful participation in a gathering organized by the Mutual Philanthropic Society and devoted specifically to women's issues. Aleksandra Kollontai, a Menshevik who, in 1907, was one of the first Social Democrats to take an active interest in appealing to and organizing the female proletariat, argued to the contrary. She felt that the proposed congress offered a good opportunity for women workers to gain organizational experience, for Social Democrats to propose socialist solutions to women's problems, and for the party to weaken any future women's organization not under its control.[11] When these ideas were not received 'sympathetically' by the Bolshevik-controlled Petersburg Committee, she joined with the Mensheviks' Central Bureau of Trade Unions to organize the election of delegates and the drafting of reports for delivery at the congress. At the last moment, the Petersburg Committee sanctioned participation in the congress by the 45-member Workers' Group Kollontai had put together, but imposed leadership of its own in the persons of Vera Slutskaia and 'Comrade Sergei'.[12] Unlike Kollontai, who wanted to use

[11] Clements, *Bolshevik Feminist*, pp. 61–3.
[12] Z. V. Grishina, 'Pervyi vserossiiskii zhenskii s″ezd', *Vestnik Moskovskogo Universiteta*, series IX: *Istoriia*, 1976, no. 5, p. 58.

the debates of the congress to show how the positions of the workers differed from those of the feminists on basic women's issues, Slutskaia and 'Comrade Sergei' were primarily interested in organizing a demonstrative walk out by the entire workers' delegation.[13]

Inessa Armand was not part of this delegation, which had been chosen while she was still in Mezen. Because her illegal status required that she be as inconspicuous as possible, she was not even one of the 1053 official delegates who, for the most part, were professional women or represented 'the cream of Petersburg and provincial aristocracy and bourgeoisie, the wives of ministers, high officials, factory owners, merchants and well-known lady philanthropists'.[14] The congress, when it opened on 10 December 1908 in the St Petersburg City Hall, was divided into four sections – each of which was to meet half a dozen times to prepare resolutions for consideration at three plenary sessions. It is indicative of Armand's changed perspective that she attended the meetings which dealt with the economic situation of women and the family rather than those on philanthropic activity, the political situation of women, or education. At these meetings she heard reports on the economic problems of peasant women and women workers as well as on prostitution, divorce and maternity. 'Sometimes it is very boring', she wrote to Alexander, 'sometimes very interesting ... I am unable to say that all of these reports provided me with something new or striking' but they helped to clarify issues in her mind.[15] This was particularly true of the lengthy discussion concerning 'free love'. 'There is a contradiction in life', she informed Vladimir during the course of the debate.

On the one hand there are yearnings for freedom in love, and on the other women presently have so paltry an income that for the majority of them this freedom is unattainable or they must remain childless. The congress went around in this circle like a squirrel in a wheel. I would like to clarify this question for myself. Perhaps as a result of these thoughts, I shall write about it sometime.[16]

---

[13] Geoffrey Swain has suggested that Otzovist thought – that is, a dislike of party activity in all legal organizations – was behind the disruptive action of the Petersburg Committee, not simply a disinterest in work among women (G. R. Swain, *Russian Social Democracy and the Legal Labour Movement, 1906–14* [London, 1983], p. 48). Detailed accounts about the background and deliberations of the congress can be found in Edmondson, pp. 83–106; Goldberg, pp. 171–258; and Rose Glickman, *Russian Factory Women: Workplace and Society, 1880–1914* (Berkeley, 1984), pp. 253–64.

[14] This was the opinion of Anna Ivanova, a member of the Workers' Group, as cited in Goldberg, p. 181.

[15] Letter of 14 December 1908, 'Pis'ma Inessy Armand', p. 216.

[16] Letter of mid-December 1908, *ibid.*, p. 217.

Anna and Inessa did not stay until the congress ended on 16 December. When the resolution introduced by the Workers' Group at the economic section was not presented at the plenary session, they joined the Group in a poorly coordinated walkout. In Inessa's opinion, this action 'left a bad impression'. She felt 'it should have been done with fuss and commotion' to have been effective. 'In general the women Workers' Group at the congress demonstrated how inexperienced and untrained our female proletariat still is', she concluded. 'It would be good to organize ... the female proletariat in a better fashion but this is very difficult and up to now it has been unexplored territory.'[17]

It was 'unexplored territory' precisely because the party had shown no interest in organizing women workers or in recognizing the special needs of the female proletariat prior to the Women's Congress. Shortly before it disbanded, the Workers' Group sought to address this problem. It recommended the establishment of a 'Women's Commission' through the Central Bureau of Trade Unions and urged all workers' organizations to set up special committees to carry out agitational work among women. There even was some discussion of the need for a separate women's organization within the party such as existed in the German Socialist Party.[18] These recommendations did not fall in fertile ground in 1909 – neither the party leadership nor the tsarist police were willing to sanction a Marxist experiment in feminist separatism.

It would be interesting to know Inessa Armand's views on this issue at the time of the congress and whether she participated in these discussions. In late 1913 she led the fight to convince the male leaders of the Bolshevik Party that women workers constituted an important segment of the urban labour force, that they had to be appealed to by addressing issues of specific interest to them and that far more attention had to be given to organizing these workers. In 1918 she urged the establishment of special commissions for work among women within party organizations and, in 1919, she became director of the Women's Section of the Central Committee – thus fulfilling all of the organizational recommendations first made by the Workers' Group in December 1908. She also returned on several occasions in her writing to the questions of freedom of love, marriage and the family which had intrigued her at the congress.

Thus, while Armand did not play an active role in the 1908 Women's

17 *Ibid.*
18 See article on the congress by 'Chlen PK', *Sotsial-demokrat*, no. 4 (21 March/3 April 1909), p. 5.

67

Congress, the experience was important in that it revived her interest in women's issues, exposed her to the weaknesses of orthodox Marxist thinking on the woman question, and helped define the organizational role she would subsequently play within the Bolshevik and Communist parties. Moreover, many of the women she listened to at the congress – Kollontai, Slutskaia, P. F. Kudelli, Klavdiia Nikolaeva and Anna Ivanova – were to become her colleagues and sometime rivals within the socialist women's movement in the years to come.

*　　*　　*

Inessa stayed in St Petersburg for several weeks after the congress closed. During this time she came to the reluctant conclusion that it was easier to evade recapture there than in a smaller city such as Kiev, but that it was also difficult to find an apartment suitable for three children in the Russian capital. As a result, she was left alone in St Petersburg over the Christmas holidays – her three younger children were in Pushkino with Varvara Karlovna, her two eldest, whom she had not seen in a year and a half, were with Alexander in Roubaix, and Vladimir was sick on the French Riviera. Her euphoria and optimism of the previous month disappeared. She wrote Alexander on 26 or 27 December that she 'felt terribly lonely and completely despondent ... I did not know such loneliness in the North as I have experienced here because, even after Vladimir left, there was our circle which through living together became one big family.' She had to force herself to remember that 'many people are lonely their entire lives' and that she had at least 'established' herself in 'public life' through her involvement with the Social Democratic party. 'I greatly hope something good will develop in [my] private life', she added wistfully.[19]

This expectation was not to be realized in the near future. Shortly after writing to Alexander, Inessa hurriedly left St Petersburg, crossed the Finnish border illegally, and made her way to the Riviera. Her sudden departure was prompted by the unexpected news that Vladimir's health had deteriorated still further. By the time she arrived in Beaulieu in mid-January 1909, he 'was a dying man' and within two weeks succumbed to tuberculosis.[20] 'For me, his death was an irreparable loss', she wrote to her friend Anna Asknazi, 'since all of my personal

---

[19] 'Pis'ma Inessy Armand', p. 218.
[20] Inna Armand, introduction to 'Pis'ma Inessy Armand', p. 197. Both of Inessa's biographers, and most writers using them as their sources, claim that Vladimir died in Switzerland (Podliashuk, p. 77; Fréville, *Une grande figure*, pp. 64–5). Inessa's correspondence, however, was sent to Beaulieu and her daughter confirmed that Vladimir died in Nice ('Pis'ma Inessy Armand', pp. 197, 214–16).

happiness was tied to him and without personal happiness life is very difficult.'[21] Almost eight years later she tried to explain to her daughter what Vladimir's death meant to her.

I think, my dear Inochka, that everything ends with death ... This knowledge, it seems to me, becomes difficult only when you lose someone. It is hard to believe that everything is finished and that you will no longer meet with a favourite person. I remember when Uncle Volodia died; this knowledge was especially difficult for me, and I envied grandmother [i.e. Varvara Karlovna] who believes in an afterlife and for whom death is only a temporary parting.[22]

For the next seven months Inessa wandered about western Europe trying to regain her equilibrium and seeking to sort out her priorities and alternatives. She spent several months in the small Atlantic seaside town of les Sables d'Olonne where she was joined by her three younger children and her friend from Mezen, S. M. Zubrovich.[23] After Easter she moved to Paris where she met Lenin, probably for the first time, following a report which he gave at a café favoured by Russian émigrés on the Avenue d'Orléans. One of those at this meeting was her former Moscow roommate, Elena Vlasova, who later recalled how melancholy, thin and pale Inessa seemed.[24] From Paris she went to Brussels, probably visited Alexander and her sons in Roubaix,[25] and then returned briefly to the city of her birth.

This period of wandering in 1909 represented the second turning point in her life. Just as in 1903, she had to re-examine her personal and political commitments and decide what to do with her life. On the personal level, she had lost Vladimir, she was separated from her husband, and she had to accept a life apart from her children as long as she chose to remain in western Europe. Returning to Russia was not a realistic alternative even if she were willing to risk almost certain arrest for having fled Mezen. She could not re-enter the University of Moscow

[21] Cited in Vinogradskaia, p..212. Possony seems to have confused N. E. Vilonov, a young Moscow Bolshevik who died of tuberculosis in Switzerland, with Vladimir Armand (Possony, p. 121). While Inessa may have known Vilonov, there is no evidence whatsoever that she had an affair with him or that she went to see him before his death in Davos in 1910. On Vilonov, see Jutta Scherrer, 'Un "philosophe-ouvrier" russe; N. E. Vilonov', Mouvement social, no. 111 (1980), pp. 165–87.
[22] Letter to Inna Armand (late 1916), in Armand, Stat'i, p. 251.
[23] Bratskaia mogila, vol. II, p. 14.
[24] Vlasova in Krupskaia (ed.), Pamiati, p. 72.
[25] While there is no firm evidence that Inessa visited Alexander in Roubaix, owing in part to the fact that none of her correspondence to him after Vladimir's death has been published, it would stand to reason that she would want to see her older sons after a lapse of two years. For a photograph of Inessa with all five of her children taken in Brussels in 1909 or 1910, see Plate 8.

since Russian universities were once again closed to women. Nor was it feasible to think that she could resume her former life as an underground propagandist: police repression was so severe in 1909 and 1910 that the Social Democratic Party had virtually ceased to exist as an organized entity inside Imperial Russia.

Thus, like so many of the Russian intelligentsia of this period, she decided to stay abroad and to serve the party in some other capacity. Little did she know that she would not return to Russia for three and a half years. 'I want to try to occupy myself,' she wrote to Anna Asknazi from Paris, to gain 'some experience, some knowledge that would be useful for future work'.[26] For a while in the spring of 1909 she sought to take advantage of her fluency in French to familiarize herself with the policies and personalities of the French Socialist Party in the belief that this expertise and her new contacts would be useful to the Social Democratic leadership in Paris. She soon came to the conclusion, however, that 'I am completely unfit for [party] work just now. For it I need cheerfulness and energy, but especially now I have none.'[27] Since she lacked a profession, other than that of tutor, she could not seek conventional employment abroad. Another alternative, and the one which she finally chose, was to resume her university education at the Université Nouvelle de Bruxelles.

*   *   *

Inessa never explained why she picked the Université Nouvelle rather than the Sorbonne in Paris. Perhaps she wanted to get away from the memories associated with the large Russian émigré colony in the French capital; more likely she wished to be nearer those members of her family living in Roubaix only eighty kilometres from Brussels. The Université Nouvelle also had a tradition of being hospitable to political refugees from eastern Europe. It had been founded in 1894 as an offshoot of the Université Libre de Bruxelles by some followers of the French philosopher and early sociologist, Auguste Comte. Its faculty tended to be anti-clerical, liberal, even socialist, and included at one time or another such luminaries as the French Communard and geographer Elisée Réclus, the sociologist Maxim Kowalevsky, the criminologist Enrico Ferri and the economist/politician Emile Vandervelde. Initially housed in two old residential buildings in one of the poorer areas of Brussels, its bohemian and radical reputation attracted many foreign students interested in its innovative approaches to the social sciences. In 1897, over

---

26 Quoted in Vinogradskaia, p. 212.
27 Undated letter to Anna Asknazi, quoted in Podliashuk, p. 78.

8. Inessa Armand with her children in Brussels during 1909 or 1910
(*from lower left:* Andre, Inna, Fedor, Alexander and Varvara).

60 per cent of its 261 students came from Bulgaria, Romania or Russia.[28] It also welcomed women students, many of whom, like Angelica Balabanoff who studied there at the turn of the century, were involved in the revolutionary movement.[29]

Inessa Armand and her three younger children took up residence at 32 Avenue Jean Volders[30] not far from the Gare du Midi and the university's new quarters on rue de la Concorde. On 6 October 1909 she registered for the first year of the licence programme in the Faculty of Economic Sciences and paid the initial instalment of her 50 fr. registration fee. Under the heading of 'previous education' she listed the courses she had audited at the University of Moscow as being the equivalent of one year of full-time study.[31]

Her choice of economic science (or political economy as she put on her registration form) – rather than law, social science or philosophy – perhaps reflects her desire to improve her theoretical knowledge of Marxism and other economic systems. She was well aware that the RSDRP put great stress on a command of economic theory and political thought; its leaders always were persons adept at polemical disputation at party congresses and theoretical writing in the party press. Since these skills required an education and the confidence in one's abilities which an education can bring, the leadership of the party was monopolized by men with university degrees. Women, who rarely were admitted to Russian universities, lacked this preparation and self-confidence. As a result, they either were relegated to or sought out organizational and agitational work within the party, leaving the theory and leadership to their male colleagues.[32] Aleksandra Kollontai

---

28 Andrée Despy-Meyer, *Inventaire des archives de l'Université Nouvelle de Bruxelles (1894–1919)* (Brussels, 1973), p. 9. One possible explanation for the low native enrolment is that the Belgian authorities – for religious and political reasons – refused to recognize the degrees of the Université Nouvelle (*ibid.*, pp. 8, 13).

29 See Balabanoff's memories of her days at the university (*My Life as a Rebel* [London, 1938], pp. 25–33).

30 Krupskaia in Krupskaia (ed.), *Pamiati*, p. 11; Fréville, *Une grande figure*, p. 61. The Okhrana intercepted two letters to her in Brussels: one addressed to 32 Avenue Jean Volders (also used on her university registration form) and the other to 270 Chaussée de Waterloo. OA, file XIIIc(1), folder 1I, incoming dispatch 1577 (28 December 1909); file XIIIc(1), folder 1C, incoming dispatch 487 (March 1910).

31 Bulletin d'Inscription, no. 42, Université Nouvelle de Bruxelles. I am indebted to Dr Elizabeth Popoff-Böcker of Leuven University for providing me with a copy of Armand's registration form and examination record. While the licence was a teaching degree, she was not studying pedagogy as several Western writers maintain (see, for example, Robert D. Warth, 'Armand, Inessa Fedorovna', *The Modern Encyclopedia of Russian and Soviet History*, vol. II [1976], p. 94).

32 Clements, 'Baba and Bolshevik', pp. 168–70; Knight, pp. 247–8; R. H. McNeal, 'Women in the Russian Radical Movement', *Journal of Social History*, vol. V, no. 2

was one of the very few women who felt comfortable in congress debates or sought to make theoretical contributions of her own. Inessa, after six years' experience in the party, was keenly aware of the importance placed on theoretical abilities and of her own educational shortcomings. While she may not have aspired to be a theoretician such as Kollontai or Rosa Luxemburg, she nevertheless showed in her subsequent career that she wanted to be taken seriously by the male members of the party and to be appreciated for more than just her linguistic and organizational skills. To achieve this recognition, she needed theoretical training and felt she might as well take advantage of her forced exile to obtain it. She was moreover a woman in a hurry and well aware that she was already in her mid-thirties. Despite the fact the licence programme in Belgium usually took two years to complete, she decided to sit her examinations after only ten months of study, successfully passed them, and was duly awarded her diploma on 30 July 1910.[33]

While in Brussels Armand was involved on a casual basis in the work of the local Russian Social Democratic organization and she may have volunteered her services as a translator when the International Socialist Bureau met there in November 1909.[34] Since the Belgian capital was considered an innocuous postal address, she also served as a forwarding agent for party newspapers and other literature printed at the *émigré* headquarters in Paris and destined for Russia. Near the end of her stay she wrote to D. M. Kotliarenko, who was in charge of dispatching *Sotsial-demokrat* from Paris, asking that she be reimbursed for her postal expenses since she was short of money and wanted to attend the Eighth Congress of the Socialist International scheduled to meet in Copenhagen in late August 1910.[35]

The money must have been forthcoming for she spent at least ten days in the Danish capital attending the congress and probably the Second Conference of Socialist Women which preceded it. Little documentation exists about this excursion since none of her letters of this period have been published and her two communist biographers have chosen to pass over it in silence or with unhelpful platitudes.[36] One

---

(Winter 1971–72), p. 153. This problem is discussed at length in Beate Fieseler, 'The Making of Russian Female Social Democrats, 1890–1917', *International Review of Social History*, vol. XXXIV, no. 2 (1989), pp. 193–226.

[33] Copies of her university records in my possession confirm that she received her degree but not that it was awarded 'with distinction' as Podliashuk maintains (p. 78).

[34] Krupskaia in Krupskaia (ed.), *Pamiati*, p. 11; Singer, p. 186. Lenin was in Brussels attending this and other meetings, 5–8 November 1909.

[35] Podliashuk, p. 82.   [36] *Ibid.*, pp. 82–3; Fréville says nothing about the congress.

German writer asserts, without providing any evidence, that she was on her 'honeymoon' with Lenin[37] who, unexpectedly, showed up in Copenhagen without his wife Krupskaia.[38] It is equally plausible that Inessa spent the time with her sister-in-law, Anna Konstantinovich, whom she apparently visited in Leipzig during the month of August.[39] It would be natural that the two of them would end the summer by attending the Conference of Socialist Women in Copenhagen as observers just as they had gone together to the 1908 Women's Congress in St Petersburg twenty months earlier.

Inessa was familiar with the debates of the First Conference of Socialist Women, which was held in Stuttgart during 1907 in conjunction with the Seventh Congress, from her reading of the protocols of that congress in Mezen. About one hundred women delegates from Social Democratic parties, trade unions and socialist clubs in fifteen countries attended the Second Conference. Once again Clara Zetkin was the dominant force and once again the sharpest debate was over the degree to which socialist women should support the suffrage demands of feminist groups. It was clear from the reports of the various delegations that the socialist women's movement in Russia lagged behind those in most western European countries. Aleksandra Kollontai, the only official Russian delegate at the conference, reported that the first signs of a proletarian women's movement could be seen in the Workers' Group at the December 1908 Women's Congress, in the workers' clubs set up in St Petersburg, and in the textile union that sent her to the present conference.[40] Kollontai was named as the Russian representative to the International Women's Secretariat headed by Zetkin and as a contributor to the Secretariat's official paper *Die Gleichheit*.

One of the more interesting resolutions to come out of the conference was a proposal by Zetkin that

socialist women in each country shall organize, in agreement with the political workers' parties and trade unions, a special Women's Day, whose object it is

---

37 Singer, p. 186. See pages 180–1, below, for a further discussion of this suggestion.
38 In early August Lenin had written to M. V. Kobetskii asking him to secure 'a *cheap* room (or 2) for a week or longer' since he was planning to attend the congress with his wife and mother-in-law (Lenin, *PSS*, vol. XLVII, pp. 264–5 [emphasis in the original], where the letter is misdated 15–23 August). Krupskaia in the end chose to stay in Pornic where the Ul'ianovs had been spending their summer holidays.
39 Zubrovich noted that he visited Inessa and her 'sister' (he probably meant her sister-in-law Anna) in Leipzig for three weeks in 1910 (*Bratskaia mogila*, vol. II, p. 14).
40 Kollontai's report on the conference is in *Sotsial-demokrat*, no. 17 (25 September/8 October 1910), pp. 8–9. Inessa's own summary can be found in a brochure she wrote a decade later. See 'Rabotnitsy v Internatsionale', in Armand, *Stat'i*, pp. 154–5.

first and foremost to agitate for suffrage for women. This demand must be based on the general provisions of the socialist program.[41]

During the next two years International Women's Day was celebrated in half a dozen European countries. In Russia, however, police conditions and the reluctance of the male party leadership to sanction an idea that had feminist implications curtailed this and all other efforts to establish a viable Marxist women's movement.

Little did Inessa realize as she left the proceedings of the Second Socialist Women's Conference that she would be responsible for organizing what purported to be the Third Conference five years later or that she would be occupying the chair held by Clara Zetkin when the First International Conference of Communist Women opened in Moscow in the summer of 1920.

On Sunday, 28 August 1910, after the Women's Conference had closed, Inessa and perhaps Anna Konstantinovich attended the impressive opening ceremonies of the Eighth Congress of the Second International using two guest tickets obtained for Armand by Lenin.[42] Seated on the stage of the Copenhagen Concert Hall were the leaders of European socialism – Victor Adler, Karl Kautsky, Jean Jaurès, Ramsay MacDonald, Rosa Luxemburg, Emile Vandervelde, Camille Huysmans – many of whom Armand was seeing for the first time. The Russian delegation also included an impressive array of talent: Lenin, Kollontai, G. V. Plekhanov, G. E. Zinoviev, L. B. Kamenev, Iu. O. Martov, A. V. Lunacharskii and L. D. Trotskii were among the seventeen voting and non-voting Social Democratic delegates; Victor Chernov headed the seven-person Socialist Revolutionary group.[43] The week-long debate undoubtedly served as a continuation of her Brussels education and as a valuable introduction to the problems and personalities she would be dealing with in the next six years as Lenin's assistant and 'Girl Friday'.

The Copenhagen Congress marked the end of Armand's twenty-two months of wandering, indecision and political inactivity which had begun with her flight from Mezen. During this time she had survived a second personal crisis, added to her education, renewed her interest in

[41] Cited in Y. Bochkaryova and S. Lyubimova, *Women of a New World* (Moscow, 1969), p. 42. The first Women's Day was held in the United States in 1909. The resolution did not designate a specific day so as to permit flexibility by national organizations. See 'K istorii prazdnovaniia Mezhdunarodnogo zhenskogo dnia v Rossii', *Krasnyi arkhiv*, 1938, no. 2 (87), pp. 3–6.

[42] *Leninskii sbornik*, vol. XXI (1930), p. 184.

[43] *Sotsial-demokrat*, no. 17 (25 September/8 October 1910), p. 10. The Russians had twenty votes: ten allocated to the SDs, seven to the SRs, and three to trade-union representatives who apparently did not show up.

women's issues, and become familiar with many of the leading figures of Social Democracy in emigration. In September 1910 she moved to Paris and once again became fully involved in the work of the party organization.

CHAPTER 5

BUILDING A 'PARTY OF THE NEW TYPE'

When Inessa Armand returned to Paris in the fall of 1910 the melancholy and depression which had affected her on her earlier visit had disappeared. The black clothes she had worn after Vladimir's death gave way to refined, almost stylish, attire that enhanced her youthful appearance and set her apart from many of her revolutionary colleagues.[1] All those who met her during her second stay in the French capital were struck by her 'cheerfulness',[2] her 'happy dynamism',[3] and the fact that 'life in her seemed to spring from an inexhaustible source'.[4] Krupskaia later related how Inessa 'immediately won people over with her tact, her culture, her revolutionary dedication and strong-willed character that contrasted with the usual aimless Russian immigrant abroad'.[5]

Like many Russian *émigrés*, she chose to settle in the thirteenth or fourteenth arrondissement in the southern part of the city. At first, since she still had her three younger children in tow, she rented a pleasant set of rooms at 25 rue Reille[6] overlooking Parc de Montsouris. After they returned to Russia, probably in the company of Alexander when his term of exile was over, she moved a short distance to 91 rue Barrault where she rented a smaller furnished room from a Russian *émigré* couple named Mazanov. From both locations she could get reasonably easily to the Sorbonne, where she attended lectures on a casual basis in

---

[1] L. Stal', 'Pamiati Inessy Armand', in Krupskaia (ed.), *Pamiati*, p. 45.

[2] Krupskaia in Kon (ed.), p. 64. See also Krupskaia's comments in *Pravda*, 3 October 1920.

[3] Fréville, *Lénine à Paris*, p. 126.

[4] G. Kotov, 'Iz vospominanii o tov. Inesse', in Krupskaia (ed.), *Pamiati*, p. 74.

[5] Cited in Vinogradskaia, p. 213.

[6] Most secondary sources follow Fréville (*Une grande figure*, p. 63) in maintaining that Inessa and her children rented student-type accommodation nearer the Sorbonne at 241 rue St Jacques in October 1910 (see, for example, Podliashuk, p. 99). The more reliable police registry of names (OA, file XIIIg, folder 19), however, gives her address at this time as 25 rue Reille. Very possibly Inessa and her children lived on St Jacques during her earlier visit to Paris in the late spring of 1909. This seems to be confirmed by Stal' in Krupskaia (ed.), *Pamiati*, p. 39.

1910–11,[7] or to the Russian library on Avenue des Gobelins. She also was within walking distance of Avenue d'Orléans (now Avenue Général Leclerc), the centre of Russian *émigré* life in pre-war Paris. The party's central organ, *Sotsial-demokrat*, was published at number 110 and the Bolshevik Paris Section met regularly above a café at number 11. After buying wine or coffee from the proprietor, which served as rent for the spartan meeting room, the dozen or so *émigrés* would climb the narrow staircase to gossip and argue about party politics.[8]

In becoming a regular participant in these sessions, Inessa for the first time clearly identified herself with the Bolshevik faction. She was elected to the presidium of the Bolsheviks' Paris Section and much to Krupskaia's relief took over corresponding with Bolshevik groups elsewhere in western Europe.[9] The fact that her command of French was better than that of any of her colleagues meant that she was often called upon to assist new political *émigrés*, who at this time were flocking to Paris from other places in Europe,[10] in finding accommodation and employment in a large foreign city.[11] Even Lenin sought her assistance in rendering his Russian into acceptable French when he had to give a speech at the funeral of Paul and Laura Lafargue.[12] If she had known then how dependent he was to become on her linguistic skills in the future, she probably would have declined this first assignment in 1911. More to her liking was being named Bolshevik representative to the French Socialist Party[13] and being asked to bring greetings from the Russian workers to the congress of the French socialists in Lyon in February 1912. This rekindled her earlier interest in French socialism and raised the possibility of becoming in time her party's expert in all matters relating to France.

While in Paris Armand also returned to another earlier interest – organizing women workers – but with considerably less success. This activity had been begun by Liudmila Stal' and Krupskaia shortly after Lenin and his wife moved to Paris in December 1908. Because of their lack of fluency in French, they started out by establishing small propaganda circles for Russian women working in French factories. Through them they hoped to influence French women workers. Inessa's arrival

---

[7] Beliavskii and Sorokin, 'Neizvestnye stranitsy', p. 56. She did not, however, earn a degree at the Sorbonne, as suggested by Possony, p. 123.

[8] A. S. Shapovalov, *V izgnanii (sredi bel'giiskikh i frantsuzskikh rabochikh)* (Moscow, 1927), p. 153.

[9] Krupskaya, *Lenin*, p. 213; Krupskaia in Krupskaia (ed.), *Pamiati*, p. 11.

[10] Krupskaya, *Lenin*, p. 193.

[11] Fréville, *Lénine à Paris*, p. 126.   [12] Krupskaya, *Lenin*, p. 227.

[13] Shapovalov, p. 188.

in 1910 allowed them to extend their organizational activities directly to the French female proletariat. Not only could she lecture effectively in French, but she supposedly 'knew well the manners and morals of the French'.[14] Stal' was so impressed with her colleague's skill as a propagandist and by her 'ability to captivate her audience' by speaking to them in their native language that she and other Bolshevik women started to study French in earnest.[15]

The idea of Russian *émigrés* giving political instruction to the female descendants of the French Communards has appealed to Soviet writers with the result that these accounts have improved with repeated retelling.[16] Contemporary sources provide little evidence of the effectiveness or the longevity of these efforts. What is evident is the lack of cooperation the Bolshevik propagandists received either from the French Socialist Party, which was notoriously uninterested in the 'woman question' and in organizing its own female proletariat, or from the RSDRP itself. While Lenin gave his moral support to the scheme,[17] many Bolshevik men had reservations about having the consciousness of their wives raised or in having them absent from hearth and home because of study sessions in the evening.[18] Even some of the *émigré* milliners and dressmakers, when enticed to their first organizational session, asked 'What's the idea of a women's meeting, anyway?'[19] As a result of this lack of support and disinterest, these activities petered out during 1911 as the women who ran them became involved in helping Lenin create a 'party of the new type'.

In January 1910, when Inessa was still in Brussels, Lenin suffered a major political defeat at a plenum of his party's Central Committee. Called against his wishes in an attempt to impose unity on the centrifugal factions of Russian Social Democracy, the January Plenum forced him to close down the Bolshevik 'Centre' and his factional newspaper *Proletarii*, to hand over his factional treasury to the Central Committee

---

[14] L. Stal', 'Rabota Parizhskoi Sektsii Bol'shevikov sredi frantsuzskikh rabotnits v 1914–1916 gg.', *Bor'ba klassov*, 1934, no. 9, p. 17.

[15] *Ibid.*, pp. 17–18.

[16] Most Soviet sources stress the work among the French female proletariat rather than among Russian *émigré* women. See, for example, T. F. Liudvinskaia, 'V Teriokakh i v Parizhe', in *Vospominaniia o Vladimire Il'iche Lenine*, vol. II (Moscow, 1969), p. 286, and S. M. Levidova and S. A. Pavlotskaia, *Nadezhda Konstantinovna Krupskaia* (Leningrad, 1962), pp. 94–5.

[17] Krupskaya, *Lenin*, p. 226.

[18] Stites, *Women's Liberation Movement*, p. 256. According to Barbara Clements, Armand and Krupskaia planned to establish a school for Russian *émigré* women in Paris in 1911 but failed to receive sufficient party support to make it practical. Clements, *Bolshevik Feminist*, p. 77.

[19] Krupskaya, *Lenin*, p. 226.

and three impartial German 'trustees', and to accept parity with the Mensheviks in the leadership bodies it sought to revive.[20] For Lenin the three-week plenum had been 'torture' and an exercise in 'idiotic conciliationism'[21] in which he had been forced to make the 'utmost concessions' on organizational issues[22] in order to keep his faction in being.

As a result of the plenum, he came to the conclusion that he had to build what Soviet historians have called a 'party of the new type'. He decided to abandon the charade of working within a supposedly united Social Democratic Party and instead to turn what remained of the Bolshevik faction into a true Bolshevik Party. This party would be led by 'like-minded' individuals in emigration united behind his programme and accepting his unquestioned leadership. Through organizational subterfuge and artful propaganda he would try to equate this new entity with the old Social Democratic Party so as to gain the support of the rank-and-file in Russia who were often uncommitted to any faction and considered *émigré* squabbling a major deterrent to the revival of a strong party. He recognized that the disillusioned and isolated members of the underground wanted competent leadership and party policies consistent with changing conditions in Russia and that he could capitalize on the fact that they were not getting either from the superficially united but largely moribund central bodies then in existence. No party congress had been called since May 1907 despite statutory provisions for annual meetings; the Central Committee had met but twice since that congress; the Central Organ of the party had published only one issue between December 1906 and January 1909; the Russian Bureau of the Central Committee was hamstrung by police arrests and factional animosities – indeed, several of its Menshevik members refused to take part in its operations; and the Foreign Bureau of the Central Committee spent its time in polemical disputation rather than in uniting party groups abroad.

Lenin's immediate objective was to fill this organizational vacuum and to further his own long-term plans by creating a new all-Bolshevik Central Committee, a Bolshevik Central Organ, and Bolshevik-controlled Russian and Foreign Bureaux of the Central Committee. Once these were in place he could then turn his back on the howls of protest that would surely emanate from the other *émigré* leaders and concen-

---

[20] Institut marksizma-leninizma pri TsK KPSS, *Kommunisticheskaia partiia sovetskogo soiuza v rezoliutsiiakh i resheniiakh s"ezdov, konferentsii i plenumov. TsK*, vol. I (8th edn; Moscow, 1970), pp. 289–99 (hereafter *KPSS v rez.*).

[21] Letter to Maksim Gor'kii (11 April 1910) in Lenin, *PSS*, vol. XLVII, pp. 248–51; see also letter to I. F. Armand (before 26 January 1914), *ibid.*, vol. XLVIII, p. 253.

[22] Krupskaya, *Lenin*, p. 206.

trate instead on using his new leadership bodies to extend Bolshevik influence and authority inside Imperial Russia. This would ultimately involve setting up a new Bolshevik legal daily newspaper in St Petersburg, creating a new Bolshevik fraction inside the State Duma, and taking control of worker organizations such as trade unions and the proposed worker insurance councils. The essential step in creating this 'party of the new type' was the calling of an *émigré* conference which purported to be 'all-party' but was in fact 'all-Bolshevik'. This conference would be used to set up the leadership bodies Lenin had in mind and to approve new policies more appropriate to conditions in Imperial Russia. It took Lenin two years to lay the groundwork for this conference which finally met in Prague in January 1912.[23] Inessa Armand played an important role in the events leading up to Prague and in the building of the new Bolshevik Party. It is curious that this work, which culminated in her fifth arrest in St Petersburg in August 1912, has been largely ignored not only by Western scholars but also by Soviet writers.

*   *   *

As *Iskra*'s editors had shown in 1903, the success of any party gathering was determined in advance by those who called the meeting and selected its delegates. The editorial board had popularized its programme through the pages of *Iskra* itself and had used the paper's distributing agents in Russia to influence the selection of delegates who adhered to that programme. In the case of the Prague Conference, which was to turn the Bolshevik faction unexpectedly created at the Second Congress in 1903 into a Bolshevik Party, the essential preparatory work was done not by a party newspaper but by a party school. This school – which 'Inessa played an active role in organizing' at Longjumeau in the summer of 1911[24] – screened, trained and indoctrinated a group of undistinguished underground party workers who were to convene and in large measure comprise the Prague Conference.

Longjumeau was not the first party school in emigration. In 1909 A. A. Bogdanov and other of Lenin's rivals on the left-wing of the Bolshevik faction created the 'First Higher Social Democratic Propagandist-Agitator School for Workers' at Maksim Gor'kii's villa on Capri. Its purpose was two-fold: to train inexperienced workers from the underground in the practical arts of propaganda, agitation and illegal

---

[23] For more information on the background to the Prague Conference, see my introduction to *Vserossiiskaya konferentsiya Ros. Sots.-Dem. Rab. Partii, 1912 goda and Izveshchenie o konferentsii organizatsii RSDRP* (London, 1982).

[24] *Pravda*, 3 October 1920.

organization so that they could replace the intelligentsia which had left the revolutionary movement after the failure of 1905; and also to indoctrinate a select group of workers who, upon returning to Russia, could form the cadres and contacts Bogdanov needed to circumvent Lenin's control of the factional hierarchy.[25] Lenin's response was to condemn the school, to seek a split in its student body, to offer counter-lectures to Capri students in Paris, and to expel its organizers from his faction. Less than two years later, after the left Bolsheviks had held a second school in Bologna, Lenin decided that a similar school but one under his control was the key to the success of his proposed 'all-party conference'.[26]

Longjumeau offered none of the amenities of either Capri or Bologna. It was a dreary, one-street, rural town located in the valley of the Yvette River twenty kilometres south of Paris. Lenin had chosen it as the site for his school on one of his frequent bicycle trips in the area because it promised cheaper accommodation than the French capital, was less likely to be under observation by his factional opponents or police agents, and offered fewer distractions for his pupils.[27] The Paris Bolshevik Section divided up the responsibilities for preparing the school: Lenin and Zinoviev, in the name of the party's School Commission, convinced fourteen émigré intellectuals to lecture at the school; S. M. Semkov found thirteen would-be students in the Russian underground and five auditors in the émigré communities whom he felt would give the school body a 'strictly Leninist' character;[28] N. A. Semashko, as 'Minister of Finance', sought funds to pay the school's expenses from the German 'trustees' and other sources;[29] and Inessa Armand set up the school and, once it opened on 20 June 1911, supervised its daily operations.

During the month before the school opened, Armand helped Lenin and Krupskaia take care of some of the Russian students who had

25 A. V. Lunacharskii, *Velikii perevorot (Oktiabr'skaia revoliutsiia)* (Petrograd, 1919), p. 46.
26 For more detail on these schools, see S. I. Lifshits, *Partiinye universitety podpol'ia* (Moscow, 1929); R. C. Elwood, 'Lenin and the Social Democratic Schools for Underground Party Workers, 1909–11', *Political Science Quarterly*, vol. LXXXI, no. 3 (September 1966), pp. 370–91.
27 Lifshits, p. 116; Fréville, *Une grande figure*, p. 70.
28 OA, file XXIVj, folder 2, outgoing dispatch 976 (26 July 1911). For other police information on the school, see file XXIVj, folder 2, outgoing dispatch 837 (22 June 1911).
29 G. Urakadze, *Vospominaniia Gruzinskogo sotsial-demokrata* (Stanford, 1968), p. 225. See Lifshits, p. 132, for a discussion of the school's finances. The loss of the school's financial report makes it difficult to determine all the sources of its funding ('Otchet pervoi partiinoi shkoly v Lonzhiumo', *Istoricheskii arkhiv*, 1962, no. 5, p. 55).

arrived in Paris ahead of schedule. In early June, shortly after Alexander Armand had left seven-year-old Andre in her care for the summer, Inessa and the early arrivals moved to Longjumeau. With money provided by her estranged husband,[30] she rented a two-storey house at number 17 Grande Rue that became the centre of the school's activities. On the first floor was a large communal dining room and a kitchen presided over by Katya Mazanova, Inessa's Paris landlady, whom she hired as school cook for the summer. Inessa, her son and three of the older students had quarters on the second floor. She also rented a metalworker's shop adjoining number 17 that was to serve as the school's classroom. Before that could happen, however, she had to organize what one of the students referred to as the first Bolshevik *subbotnik*: everyone gave a day's free labour to clear out the rubbish and debris left behind by its previous occupant.[31] She then located twenty wicker chairs, a home-made table and a lecturer's desk to serve as the furnishings of what was officially known as 'La première université marxiste'.[32] She also dealt with local authorities on all matters relating to the school, purchased the daily provisions, and served as translator for the unilingual students in their dealings with the often confused townspeople. As one of the students later recalled, 'Inessa played a dominant role in the life of the school . . . without her no one could have managed.'[33] In some respects, living with the younger students must have seemed to the 37-year-old Armand like a return to her communal days in Mezen. Krupskaia, who lived at the opposite end of town with Vladimir Il'ich and was surprisingly uninvolved in the running of the school, acknowledged that 'the comradely atmosphere which was created was to a remarkable extent the work of Inessa'.[34]

The daily routine called for Lenin to begin with an hour and a half lecture at eight in the morning on dialectical materialism, political economy, agrarian reform or the party platform. Inessa then often led a class discussion of his lecture topic leaving Lenin free to cycle to Paris on party business. After lunch in the communal dining room, two of the other teachers gave two-hour lectures. Near the end of the summer, an occasional sparsely attended class was held after the evening meal in an

---

[30] As an Okhrana agent observed at the time, Alexander was 'a man of comfortable means' who was obviously able and willing to support Inessa's causes. OA, file XXIVj, folder 2, outgoing dispatch 976 (26 July 1911).

[31] B. A. Breslav, 'O V. I. Lenine (Beglye vospominaniia)', *Katorga i ssylka*, 1934, no. 1, p. 149.

[32] Urakadze, p. 221. The school's first name – 'Ecole supérieure du marxisme révolution-naire' – was abandoned so as not to frighten the local citizens.

[33] *Ibid.*, p. 236.   [34] Krupskaia in Kon (ed.), p. 64.

effort to cover the planned curriculum. The subject matter was mostly historical or theoretical, unlike at the two earlier party schools where more attention was given to practical matters. Zinoviev gave a 'clear and systematic history' of the RSDRP; D. B. Riazanov was 'dry, scholarly and hard to understand' when lecturing on trade unions in Russia and the West; and Inessa 'showed herself to be a very weak lecturer and nothing was gained' from her four talks on Belgian socialism.[35] Armand, who was the only woman to lecture at Longjumeau, was probably chosen because of her university education in Brussels and her experience as an underground propagandist. Perhaps the negative student reaction to her talks was more a comment on the topic, which had little relevance for workers from tsarist Russia, than it was an indictment of her skills as a lecturer. It is indicative of Lenin's priorities that she was not allowed to follow Kollontai's example at the Bologna school in discussing the problem of prostitution and the organization of women workers[36] – topics of more interest to her and of more importance to her audience.

On Sundays or holidays the students and some of their lecturers took cycling trips or walks through the hot French countryside, went swimming in the Seine, or made excursions to Paris where they saw the landmarks of the French Revolution and were given guided tours of the Louvre by A. V. Lunacharskii. Occasionally, 'the closest group – Il'ich [Lenin], Armand, Sergo [Ordzhonikidze], Lunacharskii – went to a theatre in the outskirts of Paris' to see *avant-garde* or proletarian plays.[37] The fact that Inessa rather than Krupskaia was included in this 'closest group', that she was the only woman to lecture at Longjumeau, and that she was the chief administrator of the school led some 'malicious tongues' to speculate that Krupskaia was 'jealous'.[38] A Menshevik student at Longjumeau, however, felt that this speculation was contradicted by Krupskaia's warm relationship with Inessa and that the 'romantic rumours which made the rounds both inside and outside the

[35] These course evaluations were provided to the Okhrana by one of their agents at Longjumeau. Tsiavlovskii (ed.), pp. 66–7.
[36] *Otchet vtoroi vysshei sotsialdemokraticheskoi propagandistsko-agitatorskoi shkoly dlia rabochikh* (Paris, 1911), p. 19; S. A. Lifshits, 'Partiinaia shkola v Bolon'e (1910–1911)', *Proletarskaia revoliutsiia*, 1926, no. 3 (56), p. 132.
[37] I. M. Dubinskii-Mukhadze, *Ordzhonikidze* (Moscow, 1963), p. 91.
[38] Urakadze, p. 236. It might be noted that Krupskaia's mother, who was aged and ill, was staying with the Ul'ianovs in Longjumeau and that Krupskaia still had to take care of much of the party's correspondence during the summer. According to her Soviet biographers, she did assist in some of the practical instruction at the school – how to publish leaflets, write letters to the party press, carry out conspiratorial correspondence, etc. Levidova and Pavlotskaia, p. 96.

school' were caused by a misunderstanding of Lenin's obvious confidence in Armand's abilities.[39]

On 30 August, after holding a farewell party in the local café, each of
the remaining students was given 200 fr., the address of a new underground organization, and instructions to work for the convening of the
Prague Conference and, if possible, for their own election to it. They
were assisted in their efforts by three of the auditors who had disappeared from Longjumeau in mid-July. After making the rounds of
selected party organizations in Russia promoting Lenin's version of
unity and his ideas about party revival, two of the auditors reappeared
in Tiflis where in early October 1911 they formed 'the Russian Organizing Commission for calling an all-party conference'. When the Prague
Conference met three months later, it was evident that Longjumeau and
its graduates had done their job well: eight of the eighteen delegates had
either taught or studied at the school[40] and all but two of the delegates
were Bolsheviks. This small group of 'like-minded men', over the objection of one of the non-Bolsheviks, declared themselves to be 'an all-party
conference of the RSDRP – the highest organ of the party'. After
occasionally spirited debate, they accepted Lenin's programme, stated
that a portion of the Mensheviks *'had placed themselves outside the
party'*,[41] and elected four new Bolshevik-controlled leadership bodies.
One of these – the Committee of Foreign Organizations – was headed by
Inessa Armand.

*   *   *

In September 1911 Inessa and Andre moved back to Paris where they
were joined once again by Varvara and Inna. Since her room at the
Mazanovs' could not accommodate a family of four, she rented a new
apartment – still close to the Parc de Montsouris and Avenue d'Orléans
– at 2 rue Marie Rose. Next door at number 4 lived the Ul'ianovs. It was
during the next nine months, Krupskaia remembered, that 'Inessa
became very close to us.'[42] So also did her children. The Ul'ianovs had
met Inessa's estranged husband when Alexander visited Paris before

[39] Urakadze, p. 236.
[40] A ninth had been in the Capri contingent to whom Lenin provided counter-lectures in Paris but this student, A. S. Romanov, was now employed by the Okhrana. Two other students – B. A. Breslav and I. I. Shvarts – were given mandates to the conference but were arrested before they could cross the border.
[41] *KPSS v rez.*, vol. I, pp. 327 and 341 (emphasis in the original). For a discussion of some of the tensions which surfaced at the conference, see G. R. Swain, 'The Bolsheviks' Prague Conference Revisited', *Revolutionary Russia*, vol. II, no. 1 (June 1989), pp. 134–41.
[42] Krupskaia in Krupskaia (ed.), *Pamiati*, p. 12.

Longjumeau opened, they often saw Andre at the school, and now the girls came calling regularly.[43] Vinogradskaia suggests that Inessa and her family introduced an element of personal happiness into Lenin's household, a sense of motherhood which the childless couple had not experienced before.[44] Krupskaia, in particular, developed a fondness for the girls that was to last long after their mother's death.

The principal activity during the fall of 1911 was soliciting support abroad for the 'all-party' conference to be held in Prague and laying the groundwork for a new organization uniting all Bolsheviks in western Europe. Prior to 1912, Paris was the exception in having separate Menshevik and Bolshevik sections; in most cities the two factions operated within a joint Social Democratic group and often did not have separate identities. The work of these groups was supposedly coordinated by the Foreign Bureau of the Central Committee. In May 1911, however, the Bolshevik representative to that body walked out after the Foreign Bureau refused to cooperate with Lenin's plans to call a party conference and thereafter Leninists refused to have anything to do with it. Unlike the Mensheviks, who in 1908 had set up a Bureau of Foreign Groups to keep their *émigré* supporters informed of factional activities in western Europe, the Bolsheviks had no body to coordinate their operations abroad. One Bolshevik in Bern complained that he did not even know what other Bolsheviks in Switzerland were doing, let alone elsewhere in Europe.[45]

While Lenin went on several extended speaking tours promoting the calling of an 'all-party' conference,[46] the Bolshevik Section in Paris dealt with the problem of factional coordination abroad. They put out a brochure in early November explaining why the Foreign Bureau of the Central Committee had outlived its usefulness and suggesting the need to call a conference of foreign Bolsheviks to discuss corrective measures. The actual organizing of this conference was left to a three-person Orgburo set up by the Paris section. The Orgburo, made up of Krupskaia, Inessa Armand and Elena Rozmirovich, drew up an agenda for the conference and tried to convince acceptable Social Democratic groups and individuals in twenty-four European cities to send representatives to it. While they had positive responses from 18 cities repre-

---

[43] Podliashuk, p. 127; V. Armand, 'Zhivaia nit' (Iz vospominanii i perepiski s N. K. Krupskoi)', *Novyi mir*, 1967, no. 4, p. 198.
[44] Vinogradskaia, p. 213.
[45] G. L. Shklovskii, 'Iz moikh vospominanii', *Zapiski Instituta Lenina*, vol. I (1927), p. 112.
[46] He supposedly spoke before seventeen party groups in the fall of 1911. A. P. Iakushina, *Lenin i Zagranichnaia organizatsiia RSDRP, 1905–1917* (Moscow, 1972), p. 146.

senting 188 Bolsheviks and 'Bolshevik sympathizers', only 7 groups had the financial resources and the inclination actually to send delegates.[47]

When the Conference of Foreign Organizations met on 27 December 1911 above the Bolshevik café on Avenue d'Orléans, there were twenty-two Social Democrats in attendance: eleven voting delegates from the seven groups in France, Switzerland and Belgium; six non-voting members of the Orgburo including Inessa Armand; the three non-voting editors of the Bolshevik newspaper *Rabochaia gazeta* – Lenin, Zinoviev and Kamanev; and two guests – Krupskaia and police agent A. A. Zhitomirskii.[48] Seven of the participants had spent the summer in Longjumeau. Inessa's report on 'Bolshevik Organizational Tasks' did not elicit much debate nor did the local reports wherein it was quite clear that Bolshevik groups throughout western Europe were in a 'chaotic condition', that they predominated in only three cities, and that they were badly in need of strong central leadership.[49] Lenin picked up on the last point in his report. He said that Bolsheviks abroad had to put their own house in order and that to do so they needed to organize themselves into a party rather than just a faction. He suggested that all Social Democrats abroad supporting the Bolsheviks' Russian Organizing Commission and the calling of the Prague Conference should form separate organizations and that these then be united by a new Committee of Foreign Organizations (KZO) that would replace the inactive Foreign Bureau of the Central Committee as the party's central institution abroad.[50]

This clear step toward the building of an all-Bolshevik 'party of the new type' was predictably opposed by some delegates who merely wanted to maintain Bolshevik sections within united Social Democratic groups abroad and by others who felt that the creation of a Committee of Foreign Organizations should be deferred until the meeting of the Prague Conference two weeks later. Armand strongly argued that an independent Bolshevik organization was needed abroad now in order to show support for the forthcoming conference. Before the meeting ended

---

[47] On the work of the Orgburo, see Shklovskii, 'Iz moikh vospominanii', p. 113; Iakushina, *Lenin i Zagranichnaia organizatsiia*, pp. 155–61; A. P. Iakushina, 'Parizhskoe soveshchanie bol'shevikov', *Voprosy istorii KPSS*, 1964, no. 12, pp. 40–3.

[48] OA, file XVIb, folder 2, outgoing dispatch 1709 (28 December 1911/10 January 1912), pp. 1–3. Police biographical information on sixteen of these delegates can be found in file XVIIa, folder 1B, incoming dispatch 608 (22 March 1912).

[49] OA, file XVIb, folder 2, outgoing dispatch 1709 (28 December 1911/10 January 1912), p. 5.

[50] *Ibid.* See also Lenin's conference notes in *Leninskii sbornik*, vol. XXV (1933), pp. 103, 108–9.

on 30 December, a compromise favouring Lenin was adopted. A five-person Committee of Foreign Organizations was set up in Paris[51] and at the same time a special commission was struck to draft a resolution for presentation to the Prague Conference wherein the delegates would be asked to approve actions already taken in Paris. Inessa Armand was put on both bodies. She was not, however, sent as the KZO's representative to the all-male, 'all-party' conference. That honour fell to Samashko. It is interesting, therefore, that when the Prague Conference duly approved the prior establishment of the KZO,[52] it named Armand as the Committee's secretary or chairperson rather than Semashko. This may have been in recognition of the experience she had gained corresponding with *émigré* Bolshevik groups since the fall of 1910 or of her active role in calling the December Conference of Foreign Organizations. It also may have been an acknowledgment of her energy and organizational abilities that had been noted by more than one *émigré* since she had arrived in Paris.[53]

She needed these talents for her work on the Committee of Foreign Organizations. In January 1912 the KZO issued a letter 'To all members of the RSDRP living abroad' informing them of the decisions of the December meeting, asking them to support the Prague Conference, and strongly suggesting that in each city a Bolshevik group be formed or old united sections be splintered with the resulting new bodies affiliating with the KZO. Draft statutes for foreign organizations were appended which stressed that the KZO would represent those groups in all dealings with other parties. Bolsheviks were urged to raise money through membership dues (90 per cent of which would go to the KZO), lotteries, concerts and other means to help the party press, striking workers and political prisoners.[54] The KZO put out three leaflets in January and

---

[51] There is some disagreement over the identity of the fifth and perhaps sixth members of the KZO. Cf. account by the police observer in OA, file XVIb, folder 2, outgoing dispatch 1709 (28 December 1911/10 January 1912), p. 5, and that of the chief Soviet scholar on the KZO, Iakushina, 'Parizhskoe soveshchenie bol'shevikov', p. 47. Armand, however, is on both lists.

[52] 'The [Prague] Conference recognizes the absolute necessity of the existence abroad of a single party organization rendering assistance to the party under the guidance of the Central Committee ... The Conference hereby states that groups abroad which do not submit to the Russian centre of Social Democratic activity, that is, to the Central Committee, and which cause disorganization by communicating with Russia independently of the Central Committee, are not able to use the name of the Russian Social Democratic Labour Party' (*KPSS v rez.*, vol. I, pp. 343–4). The sometimes acrimonious debate about party operations abroad is reproduced in 'Protokoly VI (Prazhskoi) vserossiiskoi konferentsii RSDRP', *Voprosy istorii KPSS*, 1988, no. 7, pp. 32–5.

[53] See, for example, Stal' in Krupskaia (ed.), *Pamiati*, p. 41.

[54] Iakushina, 'Parizhskoe soveshchenie bol'shevikov', p. 48. The KZO later claimed it raised 1111 francs in 1912. Iakushina, *Lenin i Zagranichnaia organizatsiia*, p. 198.

February and Inessa, as its secretary, carried out a 'huge correspondence'.[55] G. L. Shklovskii, who once complained about not knowing what other Bolsheviks in Switzerland were doing, was now getting two or three letters daily plus assorted telegrams from 'Lenin and other Parisians'.[56] In March Inessa sent him a detailed report on a meeting of Paris Social Democrats and encouraging news about support the Prague Conference was receiving in Russia.[57] In January she informed the Stuttgart group that the KZO 'had taken up the task' of drawing new 'lines of demarcation' in the party and two months later she urged the same group to follow the example of organizations in Russia where she claimed there was only one party and that one was united behind the new Bolshevik Central Committee.[58]

Armand was somewhat more candid about Bolshevik successes abroad in an internal report on the KZO's activities which she wrote in April 1912. She noted that contacts with Social Democrats had expanded from twenty-four cities to thirty-seven in the last three months and that twenty groups were now affiliated with the Committee. She had to admit, however, that only seven of these were formal Bolshevik organizations as stipulated by the December conference. The rest of the affiliations were with individual Bolsheviks or partially formed groups. Much more success had been achieved in bringing confirmed Leninists in western Europe under the umbrella of the KZO than in convincing 'conciliator' Bolsheviks or followers of Plekhanov to support the decisions of the Prague Conference and to affiliate with the KZO. She blamed these modest results on 'the foreign atmosphere' and on the fact that Lenin's opponents were organizing an 'all-party' conference of their own for August and were carrying out 'disorganizing activity against the Bolsheviks throughout Europe'.[59]

The life of the KZO and of its secretary in particular 'became further complicated'[60] on 17 June 1912 when Lenin decided to turn his back on the furor his 'raid on the party'[61] had created in émigré circles and to move his personal headquarters to Austrian Galicia. This meant that the KZO, in addition to its usual responsibilities, now had to take over

---

[55] Karavashkova, p. 16.   [56] Shklovskii, 'Iz moikh vospominanii', p. 114.
[57] Quoted in ibid., pp. 115–16.
[58] These two letters are reproduced in Iakushina, Lenin i Zagranichnaia organizatsiia, pp. 172, 185–6.
[59] This report is reproduced in 'Iz istorii zagranichnoi organizatsii RSDRP', Istoricheskii arkhiv, 1961, no. 2, pp. 112–14.
[60] A. P. Iakushina, 'Iz istorii deiatel'nosti Komiteta zagranichnoi organizatsii RSDRP (1911–1914 gg.)', Voprosy istorii KPSS, 1966, no. 4, p. 75.
[61] Pravda (Vienna), no. 24 (14 March 1912), p. 6.

dispatching party literature from Paris to Russian organizations, raising money for all Bolshevik ventures in western Europe, and carrying out the detailed instructions of its absentee leader. Inessa Armand must have become tired of her secretarial duties and have felt that it was someone else's turn to build a 'party of the new type' in western Europe. In mid-July she too left for Galicia on her way back to Russia armed with a hand-drawn map which Lenin had sent Kamenev for use by 'members of the Committee of Foreign Organizations and others coming to Cracow'.[62]

*　　*　　*

Lenin had gone to Galicia not only to get away from the 'bickering and abuse'[63] that had intensified in the Paris *émigré* colony but also, more importantly, to be in closer contact with changing conditions and increased worker unrest in Russia. In accordance with the Prague Conference resolutions that more energy, flexibility and ingenuity were needed in the area of 'legal' Social Democratic work,[64] he wanted to put greater emphasis on using the legal press, the State Duma and trade unions as 'front' organizations through which his party could increase the political consciousness of the workers and its own control over them. Immediately after the conference closed, Lenin and two other members of his new Central Committee went to Leipzig where they met with two Social Democratic Duma deputies to discuss the establishment of a legal daily workers' newspaper in St Petersburg under Bolshevik direction. The first problem they faced was to raise the 10,000–12,000 rubles the meeting felt was needed to start such a venture. The Central Committee agreed to give 1000 rubles, later supplemented by another 3000. The remainder was to be raised by the organizers in St Petersburg from Russian factory workers and wealthy individuals.[65] Several months later it was announced that workers had contributed 3858 rubles toward their new newspaper.[66] One of the wealthy sympathizers approached was Maksim Gor'kii who gave 2000 rubles. Another might have been Alexander Armand. On 10/23 February 1912 someone signing themselves 'S' wrote to Krupskaia about fund-raising efforts in St Petersburg and suggested that she 'read this letter to Inessa and ask

62 *Biog. khr.*, vol. III, p. 13.
63 Letter to A. I. Ul'ianova-Elizarova (24 March 1912), in Lenin, *PSS*, vol. LV, p. 323.
64 *KPSS v rez.*, vol. I, pp. 328 and 334.
65 Tsiavlovskii (ed.), pp. 102–3. Since two of the five participants in the Leipzig meeting were police agents, the Okhrana was well informed of its decisions.
66 *Zvezda*, no. 33 (22 April 1912), p. 4.

her to stir up her friends, give her my address'.[67] Several weeks later Inessa sent Alexander a letter from Lenin addressed to P. N. Maliantovich, a Menshevik lawyer in Moscow who had been used in the past to obtain money from wealthy industrialists such as Savva Morozov and N. A. Shmidt.[68] Before taking the letter to Maliantovich, Alexander was to read it and 'intercede with the two people mentioned in it . . . Say that the affair will go forward in the *very near* future, i.e., between March and May, thus it is necessary to act *as soon as possible.*'[69] One 'affair' which took place 'between March and May' was the publication of the first issue of *Pravda* on 22 April. On 2 April the Central Committee had been informed that 'the heir of a certain factory owner' had promised 3000 rubles to the paper.[70] While it is uncertain whether this 'heir' was Alexander Armand or perhaps V. A. Tikhomirnov, another wealthy merchant who gave money to *Pravda*[71], it is reasonable to conclude from this correspondence that Inessa's husband was actively involved in raising money for the paper.

When Inessa arrived in Cracow in mid-July 1912, Lenin was encountering a second problem with *Pravda*. In its first issue the editors had stated that '*Pravda* will call, first and foremost, for unity in the proletarian class struggle, for unity at all costs'. The editors defined this as meaning avoidance of pejorative terms such as 'Liquidator' and 'painful' factional questions which they felt would be of little interest to the average worker.[72] This policy even applied to Lenin himself. As Krupskaia remembered, 'Vladimir Il'ich was very upset when *Pravda* at first removed all polemics with the Liquidators from his articles. He wrote angry letters to *Pravda*.'[73] He was even more 'upset' when the editors turned down some of his articles:

Why did you kill my article on the Italian Congress? In general, it would do no harm to inform [authors] about rejected articles. This is by no means an excessive request. To write 'for the wastebasket', that is, articles to be thrown

---

[67] *Iz epokhi 'Zvezdy' i 'Pravdy'*, vol. III (Moscow, 1923), pp. 232–3. Because of her family connections and her own financial well-being, it was not unusual for Inessa to be approached with requests for help. The Okhrana Archives contain at least two other letters to her from people in Russia seeking funds (OA, file XIIIc [1], folder 1I, incoming dispatch 1577 [1909], and file XIIIc [1], folder 1C, incoming dispatch 497 [1910]).

[68] On Maliantovich, who had been Trotskii's defence attorney in 1905 and was to be the last Minister of Justice in the Provisional Government, see M. F. Andreeva, *Perepiska, vospominaniia, stat'i, dokumenty* (Moscow, 1968), pp. 134, 140, 168 and 611.

[69] Unpublished letter cited in Podliashuk, pp. 114–15 (emphasis in the original).

[70] *Iz epokhi 'Zvezdy' i 'Pravdy'*, vol. III, p. 236.

[71] *Deiateli SSSR*, vol. II, p. 63.   [72] *Iz epokhi 'Zvezdy' i 'Pravdy'*, vol. III, pp. 188–9.

[73] N. K. Krupskaia, *Vospominaniia o Lenine* (Moscow, 1957), p. 194.

out, is not very enjoyable. Unpublished articles should be returned. *Any* contributor, even to bourgeois newspapers, would demand this.[74]

It seemed to the Bolshevik leader that during the first three months of *Pravda*'s operations its editors were seeking to reverse the decisions taken at the Prague Conference. Rather than narrowing the definition of Social Democrat still further and contributing to the growth of Bolshevik influence, they apparently were seeking to re-unify the old party and to negate all of the steps he had taken to build a 'party of the new type'. When 'angry letters' did not bring improvement, he decided to send personal representatives to read the riot act to the editors. One of these was Inessa Armand.

Inessa stayed in Cracow for two days to get her instructions concerning *Pravda*. Lenin took advantage of her presence to have her translate into French a document which he wanted to send to a lawyer in Paris in an effort to recover money given to the German 'trustees'.[75] The two of them also discussed the need to restore the Petersburg Committee, which had been broken in a series of police raids around May Day, and to make better preparations in St Petersburg for the forthcoming elections to the Fourth State Duma. Lenin was particularly concerned that local Bolsheviks were joining forces with the Mensheviks to conduct joint Social Democratic election campaigns in violation of yet another Prague decision.[76] In addition, he wanted Inessa to set up a number of meetings in Galicia with individuals from St Petersburg.

She was to be accompanied on this mission by a 21-year-old Armenian, G. I. Safarov, and was to carry a passport bearing the name of a peasant woman, Frantsiska Kazimirovna Iankevich. Lenin had no illusions about her safety. As he wrote Kamenev on 11/24 July, 'the *two* of them are already on their way. If they are not arrested, this will be useful. But everything moves slowly with one arrest after another'.[77] Inessa apparently was willing to run the risk since the assignments she had been given were of obvious importance to the party and being in Russia might provide her with an opportunity to see members of her family.

Their first stop was Lublin where they met with N. V. Krylenko to discuss how future visitors to Cracow should cross the frontier.[78] From there Inessa went to Kharkov, perhaps to report on the results of the

[74] Letter to the editorial board of *Pravda* (28 or 29 July 1912), in Lenin, *PSS*, vol. XLVIII, p. 74 (emphasis in the original).
[75] *Biog. khr.*, vol. III, p. 16.   [76] Swain, p. 154.
[77] Lenin, *PSS*, vol. XLVIII, p. 72 (emphasis in the original).
[78] Krupskaya, *Lenin*, p. 241.

Prague Conference or to check up on the election campaign in the workers' curia there, and then she proceeded to St Petersburg where she stayed in the apartment of fellow Bolshevik Evgeniia Adamovich.[79] 'Being down to a half kopek', she gratefully acknowledged receipt of some money sent by Alexander.[80] She and Safarov found the situation in the Russian capital even worse than they had expected. The underground organization was in 'wretched shape' consisting since the May Day raids of isolated circles unconnected with one another. For several weeks they 'wandered about Petersburg in vain and at considerable risk'[81] dressed in old boots and clothes 'far from the Parisian style' she had adopted several years earlier.[82] The individual Social Democrats they encountered showed no enthusiasm for the work of the Prague Conference and a strong desire for continued party unity. As one old Bolshevik told Safarov: 'We believe in [Prague] as Protestants do [in the teachings of the Church]: we are quite prepared to pray on Sundays, but every other day of the week we sin.'[83]

A break came when they gave a report on the Bolshevik platform for the Duma elections to a group of Putilov workers. The report was well received and led to contacts with left-Bolshevik elements in the Narva district. A debate on Duma participation was arranged at the Putilov Works between Safarov and D. Z. Manuil'skii who argued the left-Bolshevik case. Much to their pleasure, the majority accepted the Prague position, Narva became a base of Bolshevik operations and, within a couple of weeks, an Inter-district Commission was established which later in the fall became a new Petersburg Committee. In an attempt to expand Bolshevik influence outside of St Petersburg, a five-person Northern Oblast Bureau was created with Armand and Safarov as two of its members.[84]

The two Bolsheviks experienced considerably less success in their principal task – bringing *Pravda* into line. The first indication of the

---

[79] E. Adamovich, 'Vosstanovlenie podpol'noi bol'shevistskoi organizatsii v Khar'kove v 1911–12 gg.', *Letopis' revoliutsii*, 1924, no. 1 (6), pp. 167–8.

[80] Undated and unpublished letter cited in Podliashuk, p. 119.

[81] G. Safarov, 'Nasha Piterskaia organizatsiia pered vyborami v IV Dumu', *Iz epokhi 'Zvezdy' i 'Pravdy'*, vol. III, p. 126.

[82] V. L. Malakhovskii, 'Pamiati nashego druga', in Krupskaia (ed.), *Pamiati*, p. 95. See also Krupskaia in Kon (ed.), p. 65.

[83] Quoted in Swain, pp. 154–5. See also I. Iurenev, *Bor'ba za edinstvo partii* (Petrograd, 1917), p. 6.

[84] This sequence of events is described by Malakhovskii in Krupskaia (ed.), *Pamiati*, pp. 55–6; and Safarov, 'Nasha Piterskaia organizatsiia', pp. 127–8. Robert C. McKean has recently questioned the veracity of these accounts and the longevity of Armand's organizational achievements. See his *St. Petersburg between the Revolutions: Workers and Revolutionaries, June 1907–February 1917* (New Haven, 1990), pp. 92–3, 133.

editors' uncooperative attitude came when they refused to print an appeal of the Inter-district Commission calling for separate Bolshevik candidates in several of the Duma curias.[85] Then N. D. Sokolov, a lawyer closely associated with *Pravda*, 'threatened to kick them down the stairs'[86] when they sought to discuss better relations with the paper. After this rebuff, Inessa contacted K. N. Samoilova, a Bolshevik working as a secretary to the editorial board. Finally, in late August, with Samoilova's help and pressure from the Northern Oblast Bureau, a meeting with the editors was arranged.[87] Soviet scholars claimed to see 'an improvement in *Pravda*'s position' after this intervention[88] but the paper nevertheless continued to reject many of Lenin's articles and to preach its own version of party unity for the next six months.[89]

Armand's third task in St Petersburg was to ensure the election of a Bolshevik from the workers' curia to the Fourth State Duma and to prevent alliances with other parties in the early stages of these elections. As one worker in St Petersburg noted, 'for the first time two comrades came officially from the Bolshevik [centre] to hold election meetings' in July and August 1912.[90] On sunny Sunday afternoons as many as one hundred workers would converge on a near-by field ostensibly to pick mushrooms but in reality to hear Armand and Safarov urge them to elect only Bolsheviks as 'authorized representatives' in the first stage.[91] Since almost half of the eighty-six representatives chosen turned out to be uncommitted 'Social Democrats',[92] pressure then had to be brought to bear to get them to vote for Bolshevik 'electors'. Perhaps as a result of Armand's and Safarov's insistence, a separate slate of six Bolshevik electors was put forward in St Petersburg – the only workers' curia in Russia where this objective of the Prague Conference was achieved. When only half of this slate was chosen to sit in the Guberniia Electoral Assembly, Armand summoned thirteen party members from various trade unions and workers' societies to a meeting at the Women's Mutual Aid Society on 14 September to discuss how they could ensure that one of the three Bolshevik electors would be picked as the Duma deputy. Before the meeting could even begin, the police surrounded the

---

[85] Safarov, 'Nasha Piterskaia organizatsiia', p. 127.

[86] V. T. Loginov, *Leninskaia 'Pravda', 1912–1914 gg.* (Moscow, 1972), p. 64.

[87] Safarov, 'Nasha Piterskaia organizatsiia', p. 127.

[88] Institut marksizma-leninizma pri TsK KPSS, *Istoriia kommunisticheskoi partii sovetskogo soiuza*, vol. II (Moscow, 1966), p. 393 (hereafter *Istoriia KPSS*).

[89] A more detailed account of Lenin's difficulties with *Pravda* can be found in my 'Lenin and *Pravda*, 1912–1914', *Slavic Review*, vol. XXXI, no. 2 (June 1972), pp. 355–80.

[90] I. P. Khoniavko, 'V podpol'e i v emigratsii (1911–1917 gg.)', *Proletarskaia revoliutsiia*, 1923, no. 4 (16), p. 162.

[91] Safarov, 'Nasha Piterskaia organizatsiia', p. 128.   [92] Swain, p. 156.

building and arrested all fourteen Social Democrats.[93] Two days later a Bolshevik elector, A. E. Badaev, was in fact selected to sit in the Fourth Duma. Whether this victory was more a result of anti-Semitic Octobrist support in the Electoral Assembly (the Menshevik candidate was a Jew) or of Armand's pre-election strategy[94] is a moot point.

It is also unclear to what extent Armand's arrest on 14 September was the work of R. V. Malinovskii[95], a member of Lenin's new Central Committee and an Okhrana informer, who was busy at the time with his own election campaign in Moscow. There is ample evidence that the police were aware of her presence in St Petersburg and simply saved their raid for a time when they could seize the largest number of people and do the greatest damage to the election campaign. The fact that they found several Social Democratic proclamations and part of a brochure on the Prague Conference in her apartment made them skeptical of her story that she was in Russia simply to arrange for the schooling of her children.[96] She spent the next six months in a solitary cell in the St Petersburg pre-trial prison charged under Article 102 and facing the likelihood of at least having to finish her interrupted term of exile in Mezen.[97] The police allowed her to enquire about her children and to request some books. They also permitted Alexander to visit her on occasion.[98] In the damp prison conditions, however, her health deteriorated and, like many prisoners, she started to show signs of tuberculosis. Finally, on 20 March 1913, Alexander was allowed to post 5400 rubles bail as a guarantee that she would appear at her trial in five months' time.[99]

Thanks to her husband's usual generosity, Inessa got to spend the spring with her family in Pushkino or Moscow and the summer with

---

[93] Khoniavko, 'V podpol'e', p. 162.
[94] For the latter case, see A. Sol'ts, 'Eshche odna smert'', *Pravda*, 12 October 1920, p. 1.
[95] As suggested by Singer, p. 189.
[96] Podliashuk (pp. 120–1) cites an informer's report about her activities submitted prior to her arrest. The police files also contain some very misleading information about her at this time. On 27 December 1912 an agent reported that a member of the Social Democratic Central Committee named Inessa Armand had been arrested in Moscow ten days earlier. This confused the Minister of Internal Affairs who thought she had been in custody in St Petersburg for several months (OA, file XIIIc [1], folder 1E, incoming dispatch 984 [24 July 1913]; file XIIIb [1], folder F, outgoing dispatch 1394 [31 August/13 September 1913]). There also are unconfirmed police reports that she was in Moscow on 28 August 1912 (Peregudova and Khmeleva, 'Dokumenty', p. 106) and that she had contacts with well-known SRs abroad in 1913 (Tsiavlovskii [ed.], p. 192). Quite possibly the police were confusing her on occasion with Lidiia Armand, a prominent SR who was married to Lev Emil'evich Armand.
[97] Elena Stasova in *Pravda*, 8 May 1964, p. 4.
[98] Inna Armand in Stasova (ed.), p. 80.
[99] Podliashuk, p. 124.

her children on a holiday trip along the Volga and in the Caucasus. She was delighted with their stay in Stavropol, glorying in watching early morning sunrises and getting to know her children better.[100] The prospects of returning to prison or to Mezen understandably had even less appeal after her holiday. Thus, on the eve of her scheduled court appearance on 27 August 1913, she crossed the Russian frontier into Sweden allegedly using a passport belonging to a member of the Finnish Diet.[101] Four weeks later her husband's rather substantial bail was forfeited. With good reason she remarked to him several years later that 'memories of the past are dear to me as is your very friendly attitude toward me ... I only now fully appreciate that such an attitude is very rare in contemporary society.'[102]

*   *   *

Armand's destination was once again Austrian Galicia – the place she had left thirteen months earlier at the beginning of her interrupted round trip to Imperial Russia. By the time she arrived in September 1913[103] Lenin had moved from Cracow to his summer residence in Bialy Dunajec, a small village of two thousand Polish peasants near Poronin in the foothills of the High Tatras. Lenin considered the area around Poronin to be 'pure Switzerland'. As he wrote to his sister Mariia, 'it is a marvellous place. The air is wonderful ... the villages are almost Russian in type ... We have started leading the rural life here – we get up early and go to bed almost with the roosters.'[104] To the somewhat less enthusiastic Krupskaia, 'this is the real summer cottage routine'[105] but at least 'it will be good to put Shkurka [i.e., Lenin] out to pasture'.[106]

---

[100] See letter to Inna Armand (summer 1915), in Armand, *Stat'i*, p. 231.

[101] Podliashuk, p. 125; Possony, p. 146.

[102] Unpublished letter of November 1915 cited in Podliashuk, pp. 35–6.

[103] The precise date of her arrival is uncertain. As noted above, she fled Russia sometime before her scheduled trial on 27 August/9 September. The editors of the *Leninskii sbornik* (vol. XXXVII, p. 21) say she arrived in Galicia during August 1913. The police note that she attended a meeting of the Central Committee that began in Poronin on 23 September/6 October (OA, file XVIb [2], folder 1, incoming dispatch 119 [25 January 1914]; Tsiavlovskii [ed.], p. 141) whereas Krupskaia (*Lenin*, p. 266) maintains she arrived half-way through that meeting. It is possible that Krupskaia, whose memory for dates during this period was rather vague, was confusing this Central Committee meeting with a less formal one held in Poronin during August ('Novyi pod"em rabochego dvizheniia, 1910–1914', *Krasnyi arkhiv*, 1934, no. 62, pp. 242–3).

[104] Letter of 12 or 13 May 1913, in Lenin, *PSS*, vol. LV, p. 339.

[105] Letter to Lenin's mother (25 May 1913), in *ibid.*, p. 341.

[106] Letter to M. I. Ul'ianova (10 April 1913), in *ibid.*, p. 446.

The Ul'ianovs had rented a large peasant cottage for the summer which they shared with Zinoviev and his family and short-term visitors such as Inessa and Kamenev. In nearby Poronin an expanded version of the Bolshevik Central Committee met for eight days in early October 1913. To Inessa, who found herself representing the party organization in St Petersburg,[107] it was obvious from the reports given at the meeting that the Bolsheviks had achieved a great deal since she had last spoken to Lenin in July 1912. The Mensheviks' answer to the Prague Conference – their August or Vienna Conference – turned out to be a 'babel of voices and jangle of creeds'[108] that was unable to exploit the discontent caused by Lenin's schismatic activities. Their new Organizational Committee was virtually inoperative in contrast to the Bolshevik Central Committee which was in the midst of its second expanded meeting as well as having held several smaller sessions since Prague. It was evident from these reports that worker unrest was still on the rise in Russia; that the Bolsheviks' echoing of this militancy was gaining them new adherents in trade unions, insurance councils and other legal workers organizations; and that *Pravda*, now firmly under Lenin's control, was having considerably more success than the Mensheviks' *Luch* in reaching this new generation of discontented Russian workers.

As a result of these gains, the meeting took two further steps toward the final building of Lenin's 'party of the new type'. The six Bolshevik deputies in the Fourth Duma were instructed to demand parity with their seven Menshevik colleagues. When this ultimatum was predictably rejected in November 1913 the Bolshevik deputies declared themselves to be an independent 'Fraction of the Russian Social Democratic Workers'. The second step was to lay plans for the calling in 1914 of an all-Bolshevik party congress that would confirm the organizational changes and programmatic revisions Lenin had instituted at the Prague Conference. Building on the experience of Longjumeau, the potential delegates to this congress would receive prior indoctrination at a new party school to be held in Poronin.[109]

After the Central Committee meeting ended on 14 October, Inessa

---

[107] OA, file XVIb (2), folder 1, incoming dispatch 119 (25 January 1914), p. 2. Alojzy Siwecki's oil painting *Narada poronińska* portrays Armand and some of the other delegates at this meeting (see Plate 9).

[108] Bertram D. Wolfe, *Three Who Made a Revolution: A Biographical History* (Boston, 1948), p. 533.

[109] Extensive police reports of this meeting are to be found in OA, file XXIV 1, outgoing dispatch 1909 (30 November/13 December 1913); file XVIb (2), folder 1, incoming dispatch 119 (25 January 1914). The resolutions can be found in *KPSS v rez.*, vol. I, pp. 380–90.

9. 'Meeting in Poronin' by the Polish artist Alojzy Siwecki (oil, 1962), portraying a group of

decided to remain in Galicia and to take over responsibility for turning Krupskaia's notes into a publishable protocol.[110] Before getting down to work, however, she and the Ul'ianovs and perhaps a few other delegates spent six days pursuing Lenin's favourite pastime. As Krupskaia remembered, 'we took long walks, went once to Czarny Staw, a mountain lake of remarkable beauty, and other places in the mountains'.[111] Ever since her first visit to Switzerland in 1899, Inessa had marvelled at the 'majestic tranquillity' of mountains which she found 'soothing and satisfying'.[112] Lenin's appreciation of mountains, whether they be in Switzerland or the Carpathians, was more physical than aesthetic: he 'liked scrambling up'[113] them and had no hesitation in taking his hiking companions on exhausting dawn to dusk expeditions. These excursions continued after the Russian Social Democrats returned to Cracow on 20 October. 'After all', wrote Krupskaia to Lenin's mother, 'what else is there to do in Cracow but to go walking?'[114] 'Ilyich and I went for long walks with Inessa ... outside the town, to the meadows – called *blon* in Polish. Inessa in fact took the pseudonym of Blonina.'[115] The three of them came to be known as the 'excursionist party' or 'anti-cinemist (anti-Semitic) party' in contrast to Zinoviev and Kamenev, Lenin's two Jewish colleagues, who preferred the 'absurd local cinema' to walking.[116]

When muddy trails discouraged even Lenin from hiking in the winter, Armand persuaded the Ul'ianovs to buy tickets to a series of five Beethoven concerts given by the Brussels Quartet in Cracow. Krupskaia later confessed to Lenin's mother that the music 'made us terribly bored' even though 'an acquaintance of ours, an excellent musician [i.e., Inessa] was ecstatic over it'.[117] Lenin went to only a few of these concerts and left early on at least one occasion.[118] One wonders if he really did 'love music' and Beethoven in particular as his wife,[119] his siblings and most of his biographers assert. While he may indeed have asked Inessa to play the 'Sonate pathétique' and the 'Appassionata'

---

[110] A. M. Volodarskaia, *Lenin i partiia v godu nazrevaniia revoliutsionnogo krizisa, 1913–1914* (Moscow, 1960), p. 185.

[111] Krupskaya, *Lenin*, p. 268.

[112] Letter to A. E. Armand (early May 1899), in 'Pis'ma Inessy Armand', p. 198.

[113] See Krupskaia's letter to Lenin's mother (16 March 1914), in Lenin, *PSS*, vol. LV, p. 352.

[114] Letter of 26 December 1913, *ibid.*, p. 346.   [115] Krupskaya, *Lenin*, pp. 268–9.

[116] Krupskaia to Lenin's mother (26 December 1913), in Lenin, *PSS*, vol. LV, pp. 346–7.

[117] *Ibid.*

[118] Walentyna Najdus, *Lenin wśród przyjaciół i znajomych w Polsce, 1912–1914* (Warsaw, 1977), p. 253.

[119] Krupskaya, *Lenin*, p. 269.

many times in Cracow and Paris, the topic never enters into his voluminous correspondence with her, he rarely went to concerts, and he gives the general impression of being unmusical. Other forms of culture, especially Polish culture, had even less appeal: the Ul'ianovs were unenthusiastic about the local Polish theatre; Lenin did not visit the library of the Jagellonian University during his first year and a half in Cracow; 'You couldn't get him to go and see the Polish painters for love or money';[120] and he showed no interest in increasing his vocabulary beyond the 'five words of Polish' he knew when he first arrived in Poronin.[121] His 'thirst for good literature' in Cracow was restricted to Russian literature with the result that he was reduced to pouring over 'with envy the advertisements of second-hand book dealers', 'burying himself in ... an old catalogue of the Tretiakov Gallery', and reading *Anna Karenina* – 'the only odd volume we have – about a hundred times'.[122]

To Krupskaia, who found life in 'the local swamp' (as she referred to Cracow) 'very monotonous' and lonely,[123] Inessa's company was a welcome relief: she was Russian, female, interesting and the two women got along well. This is evident in a lengthy passage in her *Reminiscences of Lenin*:

That autumn all of us – our entire Cracow group – were drawn very close to Inessa. She was just brimming with vitality and exuberant good spirits. We had known her in Paris, but the colony there had been a large one, whereas in Cracow we lived together in a small close and friendly circle. Inessa rented a room in the same house where Kamenev lived. My mother was greatly attached to her. Inessa often came to have a chat with her, or sit and smoke. Things seemed cozier and more cheerful when Inessa was there ... Our home life was more like that of students, and we were very glad to have Inessa. During this visit of hers, she told me a great deal about her life and her children, and showed me their letters. There was a delightful warmth about her stories ... It was originally planned that Inessa was to remain in Cracow and bring her children over from Russia. I had even gone with her to look for rooms.[124]

Then, rather abruptly and without having finished the protocols of the Central Committee meeting, Armand left Cracow bound for Paris on 18 December 1913. Krupskaia may be partially correct in her expla-

120 See Krupskaia's letter to Lenin's mother (26 December 1913), in Lenin, *PSS*, vol. LV, p. 347.
121 See Lenin's letter to M. I. Ul'ianova (12 or 13 May 1913), in *ibid.*, p. 339.
122 See Krupskaia's letter to Lenin's mother (26 December 1913), in *ibid.*, p. 347.
123 See *ibid.* and Krupskaia's letter to Lenin's sister Anna and mother (4 January 1913), in *ibid.*, pp. 443–4.
124 Krupskaya, *Lenin*, pp. 268–9.

nation for her friend's departure: 'Life in Cracow . . . was very secluded, and reminded one a bit of Siberian exile. Inessa's energies, with which she was bubbling over at that time, found no outlet there.'[125] It is certainly true that she always preferred the hustle and bustle of big cities such as Moscow and Paris to small ingrown communities like Push-kino, Mezen or even Cracow. Krupskaia is less accurate when she adds that Inessa left in order to revive the Committee of Foreign Organi-zations.[126] That body, which had indeed fallen on hard times, met for a second time in August 1913 and elected a new Committee which did not include Armand.[127] She showed little enthusiasm for becoming involved in its operations after her return to Paris. There are, however, other possible explanations for her sudden departure which Krupskaia chose to overlook.

As Armand had shown from the time she entered the Université Nouvelle in Brussels, she wanted to carve out a niche for herself in the Bolshevik Party and to be taken seriously by its male leadership. She had taken steps in that direction by supervising operations and lectur-ing at the Longjumeau school, by chairing the Committee of Foreign Organizations, and by serving as an emissary of the Central Committee in St Petersburg. But the traditional way of influencing and making policy within the Social Democratic Party was through writing – not letters to émigré organizations or protocols of Central Committee meet-ings, as she had been asked to do in the past, but newspaper articles and political brochures. This was not an area where Russian Social Demo-cratic women, with the notable exception of Aleksandra Kollontai, had been very productive in the past. Even Krupskaia had reconciled herself to the fact that she was not a 'competent writer'.[128] Armand's first attempt at making her mark as an author may have been an unsigned article written in Mezen.[129] In 1912 she apparently started collecting material from the writings of Joseph Chamberlain and Cecil Rhodes for an article or brochure on England's role in increasing tensions among the great powers.[130] She returned to writing once again while in Galicia, perhaps on one of those rainy days that kept even Lenin indoors and at his desk. The topic she chose was again English: opportunism in the British labour movement and worker unrest in Ireland. She prob-ably decided to concentrate on England because she was one of the few

[125] *Ibid.*, p. 269.
[126] *Ibid.* Podliashuk likes this explanation. To him, 'the revolution called' in the form of the KZO (p. 130).
[127] 'Novyi pod"em', p. 243; Iakushina, *Lenin i Zagranichnaia organizatsiia*, p. 223.
[128] Letter to A. I. Ul'ianova-Elizarova (11 February 1914), in Lenin, *PSS*, vol. LV, p. 448.
[129] See page 58, above.   [130] Podliashuk, p. 81.

Russian School Democrats with a knowledge of the language. Moreover, Liudmila Stal' was now reporting for *Pravda* on the situation in France[131] which she once considered to be her own speciality. The result of her labours in 1913 was a three-page manuscript which she gave to Lenin for comment. She must have been surprised and a bit angered at his response. He told her she should pay more attention to the opportunism of Philip Snowden and to the importance of James Larkin as well as to the dangers of syndicalism. He finished up by informing her that for her 'Note' to become an article she must provide it 'with a beginning and an end, it must give *an account of something* for Russian workers, [it must] have hands and feet and a conclusion'.[132] Armand's reaction to this rather deflating criticism is unknown except that the article went unpublished.

While in Galicia Inessa also tried to convince the male Bolshevik leadership that the 'party of the new type' had to take into account the growing importance of women workers in Russia. She argued that this group, which now made up almost a third of the urban labour force, had to be propagandized, organized and brought into the Bolshevik Party. If it were not, then other parties would channel growing female militancy in the wrong direction. Here too her initiative met with a marked lack of encouragement and support. Out of frustration and in protest, she left Galicia to pursue this project as well as her own writing in a more conducive atmosphere elsewhere in Europe.

131 See, for example, *Za pravdu*, no. 38 (17 November 1913), pp. 1–2.
132 *Leninskii sbornik*, vol. XXXVII, p. 21 (emphasis in the original).

CHAPTER 6

IN DEFENCE OF WOMEN WORKERS

Inessa Armand's interest in issues of concern to women in general had been formed fifteen years earlier when she joined the Moscow Society for Improving the Lot of Women. Her concern for the condition of the female proletariat, however, developed somewhat later. At the 1908 Women's Congress in St Petersburg and at the 1910 Conference of Socialist Women in Copenhagen she learned in more detail about the double burden of working in a factory and running a household which she herself had never had to bear. She also became aware that women workers were poorly organized and that the Social Democratic Party had little interest in their problems.

These observations were reinforced when Armand was in St Petersburg in the summer of 1912. In the course of trying to make *Pravda* more responsive to Lenin's instructions, she had long conversations with Konkordiia Samoilova, secretary of the paper's editorial board. One of Samoilova's duties was to collect correspondence from women workers and to arrange for its publication. These letters drove home to her the growing frustrations of the female proletariat and led her to develop some ideas which she discussed with Armand about how these concerns might be addressed.[1]

One fact which no visitor to the industrial districts of St Petersburg or Moscow could ignore was the tremendous growth in the number of women working in Russian factories. Between 1901 and 1914 the Russian industrial labour force grew by 37 per cent. The majority of these new workers – 64.1 per cent – were women.[2] Women, who made up 24 per cent of the factory workers in 1887, now comprised 31 per cent[3] and in some industries such as textiles they made up well over half. One of the reasons for this growth in the female proletariat was the

---

[1] Clements, *Bolshevik Feminist*, pp. 76–7.
[2] Robert E. Drumm, 'The Bolshevik Party and the Organization and Emancipation of Working Women, 1914–1921: or, A History of the Petrograd Experiment' (unpublished Ph.D. dissertation, Columbia University, 1977), p. 12. See also Hayden, p. 76.
[3] Knight, pp. 102–3.

introduction of labour-saving devices which eliminated physical strength as a prerequisite in hiring. Employers considered women raised in the patriarchal tradition of Russian villages more submissive to authority and less likely to strike.[4] Moreover, according to one factory inspector, women were often hired in preference to men because of 'their greater industry, attentiveness and abstinence (they do not smoke or drink), their compliance and greater reasonableness in respect to pay'.[5] As child labour was phased out in many industries, employers hired women, often illiterate, to fill the unskilled jobs formerly held by children. Women were considered 'reasonable' because they were willing to accept child wages and to work for one-half to two-thirds what an employer would have to pay a man.[6] In St Petersburg, for example, the average daily wage of a man in heavy industry on the eve of the war was 1 ruble 41 kopeks; for a woman it was 72 kopeks.[7] Women workers also had limited maternity benefits, little opportunity to care for infants while working, and were subject to sexual harassment by male supervisors.[8]

Not only were female workers exploited by their employers, they also received little support from their fellow workers. Male proletarians showed no inclination before the war to fight for the right of women to be paid an equal wage for equal work.[9] Nor were women particularly welcome in Russian trade unions where they made up only 6 per cent of the total union membership in 1912.[10] *Pravda* explained this low figure by citing the commonly held belief that women were politically backward and were opposed by male members on the grounds that they

4 Barbara Alpern Engel, 'Women in Russia and the Soviet Union', *Signs*, vol. XII, no. 4 (summer 1987), pp. 183–4.

5 Cited in S. A. Smith, *Red Petrograd: Revolution in the Factories, 1917–18* (Cambridge, 1983), pp. 23–4. See also a similar report in Victoria E. Bonnell, *Roots of Rebellion: Workers' Politics and Organizations in St. Petersburg and Moscow, 1900–1914* (Berkeley, 1983), p. 320.

6 Rose L. Glickman, 'The Russian Factory Women, 1880–1914', in D. Atkinson, Alexander Dallin and G. W. Lapidus (eds.), *Women in Russia* (Stanford, 1977), p. 69.

7 Dale Ross, 'The Role of the Women of Petrograd in War, Revolution and Counter-Revolution, 1914–1921' (unpublished Ph.D. dissertation, Rutgers University, 1973), p. 92. Comparable figures can be found in Marcelline J. Hutton, 'Russian and Soviet Women, 1897–1939: Dreams, Struggles, and Nightmares' (unpublished Ph.D. dissertation, University of Iowa, 1986), p. 374.

8 Hutton, p. 375.

9 'Zhenskoe sotsialisticheskoe dvizhenie', *Sotsial-demokrat*, nos. 21/22 (19 March/1 April 1911), p. 10.

10 'Zhenshchiny i rabochiia organizatsii', *Pravda*, no. 170 (16 November 1912), p. 4. See also 'Ot zhenshchin-metallistok', *Severnaia pravda*, no. 18 (23 August 1913), p. 1, wherein two women note both the relative absence of their sex in the Metalworkers' Union and the opposition of male members to the election of women to union offices.

undercut men by accepting lower wages. In some instances, husbands were reluctant to pay two sets of union dues out of modest family earnings.[11] It has also been suggested that the lower literacy rate among women workers made them 'ill-equipped to appreciate the virtues of collective organization'[12] and that because of 'daily life bonding patterns ... women were expected to inhibit any other on-going commitment in their lives which might contend with the family for their time and energy'.[13]

These factors did not prevent women workers from writing to *Pravda* in increasing numbers to complain about working conditions and a lack of support from their colleagues. Samoilova was impressed by the tone and the volume of this correspondence but powerless to get much of it published. One solution, which she suggested without success to the editorial board, was to publish a separate journal directed specifically at women workers which would serve as a forum for these complaints.[14] She also discussed this solution with Inessa Armand. The two women were in agreement that such a journal would not only satisfy immediate needs in St Petersburg, it also could be used to raise the class consciousness of women workers, to overcome resistance to joining trade unions, and to win their allegiance to the Bolshevik Party. While the initial idea to publish a women's journal may have come from Samoilova, it became Inessa's job to sell it to the Bolshevik leadership abroad or to find other means of bringing it to fruition.

When she arrived in Poronin in September 1913 she immediately sought the backing of Krupskaia and Zinoviev's wife, Zinaida Lilina, for the scheme. As Krupskaia later recalled, 'we had long talks together about women's work. Inessa strongly urged that propaganda work be widely developed among the women workers and a special women's magazine be published in St Petersburg.'[15] Two new arguments strengthened her case. The first of these was the unexpected success of International Women's Day, initially held in tsarist Russia on 17 February 1913. After ignoring the day for two years as a suffragette ruse, the party was forced to make preparations when the Duma, in response to feminist pressures, designated it a holiday in 1913. Planning was delegated by the Petersburg Committee to a special commission headed by Samoilova and P. F. Kudelli. Under their direction, *Pravda* devoted

---

[11] *Pravda*, no. 170 (16 November 1912), p. 4.   [12] Bonnell, p. 365.

[13] Bobroff, p. 750. For an excellent discussion of the negative attitude of Russian trade unionists toward both the problems of women workers and female participation in unions on the eve of the war, see Glickman, *Russian Factory Women*, pp. 196–218.

[14] *Borets za raskreposhchenie rabotnitsy: K. N. Samoilova* (Moscow, 1925), pp. 36–7.

[15] Krupskaya, *Lenin*, pp. 269–70.

the first three pages of its 17 February issue to articles on women workers and a 'scientific meeting' was arranged for that day to discuss the right to vote and other issues of interest to women.[16] While some party members had reservations about paying too much attention to 'feminist views', the spontaneous response of women workers exceeded expectations. Lenin's sister, Anna Elizarova, considered it 'the first major action by working women [which] played an immense, decisive role in the women workers movement',[17] if only in making the Bolshevik leadership aware of the latent militancy of the female proletariat.

The second new development had been the government's introduction of a workers' insurance scheme. According to the law promulgated on 23 June 1912, precise insurance rules and the organizational structure of the sickness funds and insurance councils were to be worked out on the factory level by elected representatives of the workers in consultation with management. The party was well aware of the agitational value inherent in the ensuing 'insurance campaign' and of the organizational advantage to be gained by electing Bolshevik supporters to these insurance bodies. To be successful in this venture, however, a way had to be found to appeal to women workers who had equal voting rights with men in the elections. In particular, it was necessary to neutralize the support the Mensheviks would receive for their persistent advocacy of greater maternity benefits for women workers.[18] It seemed to Armand that one logical way of countering the feminist arguments concerning women's suffrage and Menshevik arguments on maternity benefits was to publish a women's newspaper that would give the Bolshevik view on these issues.

Perhaps at Armand's urging, Krupskaia buttonholed the Bolshevik Duma deputies at the Poronin meeting of the Central Committee in October 1913. She urged them to pay more attention to revolutionary work among the 'families of workers', to setting up propaganda circles for women workers, and to 'organizing the women's movement rather than leaving this to the Mensheviks'.[19] According to Armand, the question of doing revolutionary work among the female proletariat through the publication of a special women's newspaper was also discussed at Poronin and at a subsequent meeting of the Central

16 S. N. Serditova, *Bol'sheviki v bor'be za zhenskie proletarskie massy* (Moscow, 1959), pp. 84–9.
17 Cited in Bochkaryova and Lyubimova, p. 51.
18 Clements, *Bolshevik Feminist*, p. 76.
19 G. I. Petrovskii, 'Zhizn', polnaia blagorodstva i predannosti idee kommunizma', in A. M. Arsenev *et al.* (eds.), *Vospominaniia o Nadezhde Konstantinovne Krupskoi* (Moscow, 1966), pp. 83–4.

Committee in January 1914.[20] It may have been discussed but no resolution supporting the scheme was passed at either meeting and no mention of a women's newspaper was made in two lengthy resolutions on the party press.[21]

In the two months following the Poronin meeting, Armand continued to advocate the publication of a women's journal. According to Liudmila Stal', the sentiment of many male party members was that scarce party resources should not be spent on such a venture when more pressing tasks remained under-funded.[22] The Central Committee offered no financial support and Lenin's sister advised Krupskaia that 'nothing could be diverted from the daily paper', i.e., *Pravda*, for the scheme.[23] Anna Elizarova suggested instead that *Pravda* publish a weekly supplement aimed specifically at women workers. Krupskaia doubted if this alternative would save much money and noted that it would not have the 'organizational significance' of a separate paper.[24] She was undoubtedly correct in this assumption and, perhaps to a greater degree than Armand, she realized there were theoretical, historical and organizational as well as financial reasons behind the leadership's reluctance to endorse Inessa's project.

*   *   *

The theoretical reasons for the Bolsheviks' reluctance to sanction a separate women's newspaper in a curious way go back to Karl Marx's avoidance of the 'woman question'. To Marx, women workers were oppressed in the same fashion as male workers by the capitalistic system and needed therefore to join their class brethren in a common fight against economic oppression. He did not recognize that there were specific women's problems that should be addressed and settled separate from general class and economic problems. As Alfred Meyer has concluded, the woman question was 'an unwanted side issue of distinctly marginal importance that took attention away from the key struggle. In

---

[20] Elena Blonina [I. F. Armand], 'Rabotnitsy i Internatsionale', in Armand, *Stat'i*, pp. 156–7. See also Loginov, p. 271.

[21] *KPSS v rez.*, vol. I, pp. 384, 393–4. Neither the well-informed police (OA, file XXIV 1, folder 1, outgoing dispatch 1909 [30 November/13 December 1913]; file XVIb [2], folder 1, incoming dispatch 119 [25 January 1914]) nor the most detailed and perceptive Soviet account of the Poronin meeting (Volodarskaia, pp. 183–263) makes any mention of discussion of a women's newspaper.

[22] L. Stal', 'Istoriia zhurnala "Rabotnitsa"', in A. V. Artiukhina *et al.* (eds.), *Zhenshchiny v revoliutsii* (Moscow, 1959), p. 109.

[23] 'K istorii izdaniia zhurnala "Rabotnitsa"', *Istoricheskii arkhiv*, 1955, no. 4, pp. 26–7.

[24] N. K. Krupskaia to A. I. Elizarova (29 January/11 February 1914), in *ibid.*, p. 36.

short, relative neglect of the "woman question" was built into Marxist theory'.[25]

It was left to Friedrich Engels and to the German socialists – August Bebel and Clara Zetkin in particular – to develop a socialist theory of women. Bebel argued in *Die Frau und der Sozialismus* (1879) that the enslavement of women resulted from the development of private property and the capitalistic system. Women could free themselves from male domination by joining the industrial labour force. Their true liberation would come with the victory of socialism which would abolish private property and emancipate the entire working class. Bebel, however, was 'unsystematic, ambiguous', vague and unhelpful in discussing 'the appropriate strategy and tactics of a [socialist] women's movement' seeking to achieve this agreed-upon end.[26]

Clara Zetkin added specificity and an organizational approach to the generalities of Marx, Engels and Bebel. She agreed that women workers should fight side by side with male workers and not beside women of other classes since they were being oppressed as workers and not specifically as women. She therefore was adamantly opposed to any cooperation with the feminist movement which she felt emphasized 'a battle of the sexes' rather than a 'class war'. Zetkin, however, recognized that women workers were more politically backward than their male counterparts and that they had particular problems as women that needed to be addressed. Therefore, to educate them politically, to draw them into the general political struggle, and to counteract the appeal of feminist groups, she argued for the publication of a special women's journal (*Die Gleichheit*) and for the establishment of women's sections within the German Socialist Party (SPD). Ironically, even though these innovations contributed to the enrolling of 190,000 women in German trade unions and 140,000 in the German Socialist Party,[27] Zetkin encountered 'indifference and even hostility on the part of male socialists who thought [that her] efforts smacked of bourgeois feminism'.[28] After 1908 the separate women's organizations which she had established were gradually abolished as the interests of women

---

[25] Alfred G. Meyer, 'Marxism and the Women's Movement', in Atkinson *et al.* (eds.), p. 99.

[26] Stites, *Women's Liberation Movement*, p. 234. One recent writer has concluded that while Bebel tried to portray himself as a 'veritable feminist', he was in fact infected with 'virulent male chauvinism'. Raya Dunayevskaya, *Rosa Luxemburg, Women's Liberation and Marx's Philosophy of Revolution* (Atlantic Highlands, N.J., 1982), p. 27.

[27] Knight, p. 139.

[28] Richard Stites, 'Women and the Russian Intelligentsia: Three Perspectives', in Atkinson *et al.* (eds.), p. 61.

workers were subordinated to those of the party as determined by the party's male leadership. As one scholar has noted, 'a serious discrepancy existed between the theory and practice of many socialist men' within the SPD.[29]

Marxist theory and German practice were not irrelevant to the way the Russian Social Democratic Labour Party dealt with the woman question before 1913. Even more than their German counterparts, most early Russian Marxists considered women workers to be backward, passive and a brake on the revolutionary movement. These deficiencies might be ameliorated by contact with more advanced male workers but it was generally felt that it was not worth the party's time, energy or money to develop special programmes for them. In *The Development of Capitalism in Russia* (1898) Lenin merely noted that factory work was progressive in that it liberated women from the patriarchal home, supposedly made them economically independent, and conceivably could lead to the development of their class consciousness by revealing to them the evils of the capitalistic system. In 1901 Krupskaia published a brochure on the *Woman Worker* which discussed the condition but not the theory of female labour and repeated the standard formula that the liberation of the entire proletariat would bring with it the liberation of women. The 1903 party programme paid little attention to female emancipation other than advocating universal suffrage and the introduction of labour legislation that would provide maternity leave, day nurseries, time off for nursing mothers and prohibition of female employment in industries harmful to their health.[30] As Rose Glickman has concluded, 'in the decade before the 1905 revolution ... the Social Democrats said little and did nothing about women workers'.[31]

The first Russian Social Democrat to suggest that special approaches should be made toward working women was Aleksandra Kollontai. She was concerned that 'the exploration of problems which affected women workers as women, and the defence of their interests as mothers and housewives, was left without any struggle in the hands of feminists of the bourgeois camp'.[32] This concern was heightened in 1905 when new feminist political groups started to appeal to factory women on these issues as well as to women students and the female intelligentsia.

[29] Karen Honeycutt, 'Clara Zetkin: A Left-wing Socialist and Feminist in Wilhelmian Germany' (unpublished Ph.D. dissertation, Columbia University, 1975), p. 338. On Zetkin, see also Stites, *Women's Liberation Movement*, pp. 236–9; Elena Blonina [I. F. Armand], 'Rabotnitsy i Internatsionale', in Armand, *Stat'i*, pp. 148–9.

[30] *KPSS v rez.*, vol. I, p. 64.   [31] Glickman, *Russian Factory Women*, p. 250.

[32] Alexandra Kollontai, *Women Workers Struggle for their Rights* (London, 1971 [1918]), p. 14.

Kollontai agreed with the feminists that the woman question was a question of gender but one based on securing economic rights for proletarian women rather than political rights for bourgeois women. Like Zetkin, she was opposed to any cooperation between Social Democrats and feminists.

Kollontai argued that the party should proceed along two lines. First, it should appeal to women workers *per se* and in doing so recognize that they had concerns relating to maternity, child care and sexual abuse that differed from those of men and ought to be addressed as such. The object of these approaches would be to raise the consciousness of working women, to counteract the influence of feminist propaganda, and to 'increase the numbers, strength and significance of the workers' party'.[33] Secondly, she suggested that much of this work should be done through separate organizations made up primarily of women workers under Social Democratic control such as the Women's Political Club established in St Petersburg in 1906 and the Women's Mutual Aid Society set up a year later. Both of these groups sought to recruit and to politicize working women through offering lectures and educational programmes specifically of interest to them. At the same time Kollontai was also attracted to Zetkin's concept of a separate women's section inside the Social Democratic Party that could coordinate propaganda work among women. After visiting a congress of the German Socialist Party in 1906, she advocated the establishment in Russia of an autonomous women's bureau on the German model that could get more women involved in party operations.[34]

The response of the Russian party hierarchy to these overtures was even harsher than that of the male leadership in Germany. The RSDRP saw no need to promote in practice the granting of benefits to women which it had approved in theory in its 1903 programme since women workers would ultimately gain equality with men and a better way of life after the triumph of socialism. Attempts to appeal to women workers now by discussing issues of specific interest to them were branded as feminism and as divisive of the working class. Efforts to set up women's organizations were seen as separatism and as a weakening of the unitary Social Democratic Party. When Kollontai sought the assistance of the party's most prominent female member, Vera Zasulich, in arranging special work among women, she was told such activity was

---

[33] *Ibid.*, p. 27.
[34] For an excellent summary of Kollontai's thought and activities during this period, see Clements, *Bolshevik Feminist*, pp. 44–8.

'unnecessary, if not harmful'.[35] When she scheduled a meeting in St Petersburg to discuss the formation of a women's bureau in 1906, she found a sign on the door announcing that 'the meeting *for women only* has been called off. Tomorrow a meeting *for men only*'.[36] The Women's Mutual Aid Society was denied financial support by the party and, as already noted, the Petersburg Committee sought to scuttle her efforts to organize a Workers' Group at the 1908 Women's Congress. In her autobiography Kollontai related that 'I realized for the first time [in 1905] how little our Party concerned itself with the fate of women of the working class and how meagre was its interest in women's liberation'.[37] The situation had not changed three years later when she wrote her major theoretical work – *Sotsial'nye osnovy zhenskogo voprosa* (The Social Bases of the Woman Question) – in which she provided not only a vitriolic Marxist condemnation of bourgeois feminism but also more indirectly a feminist condemnation of her own party's lack of interest in working women.

Social Democratic agitation and propaganda among working-class women decreased still further after Kollontai's emigration to western Europe in December 1908. Leaflets addressed specifically at women were virtually non-existent; the woman question was omitted from the Longjumeau curriculum; only six articles on topics of interest to women appeared in thirty-one issues of the party's central organ, *Sotsial-demokrat*; despite Soviet claims to the contrary, there were surprisingly few articles on women's issues in *Pravda* during 1912 and 1913; and Kollontai was initially told her idea of celebrating International Women's Day in Russia 'smacked of feminism'.[38] It is no wonder then that the party attracted few women to its ranks and had little influence among the broad masses of working women before 1914.[39] It is also not surprising that the Russian feminist movement, as Kollontai feared, found a proletarian audience when it started to address questions Social Democracy avoided.[40]

One explanation for this history of official Russian Social Democratic disinterest in the woman question is that party policy was argued out in journals edited by men and approved at congresses and conferences

[35] Quoted in Goldberg, p. 100.
[36] Kollontai, as cited in Clements, *Bolshevik Feminist*, p. 46 (emphasis Kollontai's).
[37] Quoted in Lapidus, p. 46.   [38] Clements, *Bolshevik Feminist*, p. 66.
[39] P. Kudelli, *K. N. Samoilova-Gromova ('Natasha'), 1876–1921 gg. (biografiia)* (Leningrad, 1925), p. 51.
[40] See, for example, an article on a meeting sponsored by the League for Women's Equality to discuss a factory inspector's report on working conditions for women. *Za pravdu*, no. 50 (3 December 1913), p. 4.

dominated by men – men who had no interest in questioning Marxist orthodoxy on this issue. With the exception of Vera Zasulich, who had an honorary position on *Iskra*'s editorial board, no woman was involved in the editing of the party's four pre-revolutionary central organs or major *émigré* factional newspapers. Of the 394 voting delegates at the first five party congresses and the Prague and Vienna conferences in 1912, only thirteen (3 per cent) were women. Of the 69 Central Committee members between 1898 and 1912, only five (7 per cent) were women.[41] Those few women who did attend these meetings were reluctant to speak out on theoretical issues, on women's issues, or even on their own subordinate position in the party. Zasulich almost never spoke at party congresses and accepted the 'benevolent domination' and condescension of Plekhanov, Aksel'rod and Deich.[42] Elena Stasova, a candidate member of the Bolshevik Central Committee in 1912, 'did not like to speak at meetings … since I did not consider myself sufficiently competent in political questions'.[43] Others, such as Samoilova and Krupskaia, simply did not think of themselves as theoreticians or policy makers and much preferred to remain in the background carrying out policies determined by their male colleagues.[44] This attitude was a product of a variety of factors: a submissiveness inculcated during childhood, a lack of higher education, an absence of personal ambition, an illusion that women were indeed equal within the revolutionary movement, a desire to maintain party harmony in the common fight against tsarism, a faith that the ultimate revolution would bring equality in all areas, and a fear of being accused of 'feminism'.[45] One of the consequences of this attitude and of low representation at national party gatherings was that no aspect of the woman question or of Social Democratic work among proletarian women was discussed at party congresses or conferences during the decade before the war.

[41] Knight, pp. 209–10. It should be noted that 9 of the 96 delegates holding consultative votes at the party congresses were women. Estimates on the relative number of women in the party at this time range from 11.5 per cent (Knight, p. 195) to 15 per cent (Fieseler, 'The Making of Russian Female Social Democrats', p. 195). Another measure of the unimportance of women in the upper echelons of the Bolshevik Party is that only 8 of the 248 (3 per cent) revolutionaries prominent enough to be included in *Deiateli SSSR i Oktiabr'skoi Revoliutsii* were women. McNeal, 'Women in the Russian Radical Movement', p. 159.
[42] Jay Bergman, *Vera Zasulich: A Biography* (Stanford, 1983), p. 172.
[43] Quoted in Knight, p. 218.
[44] *Ibid.*, p. 229.
[45] For a more detailed discussion of these factors, see *ibid.*, pp. 215–48; Clements, 'Baba and Bolshevik', p. 170.

For Lenin and others who shared his orthodox views of the woman question there were some disquieting signs that female 'separatism', while never brought up at party conferences, was not entirely dead within the RSDRP. Perhaps at Kollontai's suggestion, the Workers' Group at the 1908 Women's Congress called for the formation of a Women's Commission within the Central Bureau of Trade Unions and discussed the merits of a separate women's bureau 'along German lines' within the party.[46] In 1911 *Sotsial-demokrat* carried an unsigned article praising the work of the German bureaux and suggesting that Russian Social Democrats 'learn from our German colleagues and carry out propaganda work among women workers'.[47] In 1913, Kollontai repeated her call, this time in *Pravda*, for the establishment of special party committees and women's bureaux that would attract women workers to the party.[48] And later that same year Liudmila Stal' lauded Zetkin's organizational work and suggested that 'women's groups, organized through workers organizations [i.e., the party] and trade unions, could bring women up to the consciousness of men' in Russia. She bridled at the idea that such groups might be considered as the same type of 'separatism' as that represented by the national organizations within the old RSDRP.[49]

*   *   *

It is against this theoretical and historical background that Lenin's unenthusiastic response to Inessa Armand's suggestion that the party sanction a paper addressed to women and written by women must be viewed. In Armand's favour was her lack of interest in establishing a women's bureau or in organizational autonomy for its own sake which often led Kollontai to be branded as a separatist. Nor did she evoke the feminist arguments that women were best appealed to by other women or that the oppressors of women were essentially men. Moreover, she showed no sign in 1913 of wanting to pursue some of the broader aspects of the woman question such as female sexuality, prostitution and maternity benefits which intrigued Kollontai. Like many of her colleagues, she was unconcerned about the theoretical aspects of the question but unlike some she did not want simply to execute someone

---

[46] *Sotsial-demokrat*, no. 4 (21 March/3 April 1909), p. 5.
[47] 'Zhenskoe sotsialisticheskoe dvizhenie', *Sotsial-demokrat*, nos. 21/22 (19 March/1 April 1911), p. 10. Ironically, these bureaux were finally abolished by the German party at about the time this article appeared.
[48] 'Zhenskii den'', *Pravda*, no. 40 (17 February 1913), pp. 1–2.
[49] 'Organizatsiia zhenshchin-rabotnits', *Za Pravdu*, no. 2 (3 October 1913), p. 2.

else's orders. She was above all a pragmatist. She recognized that women workers, who represented a growing section of the Russian proletariat, were being ignored by the Social Democratic Party; that the grievances of these women were real even if in many cases they were the same as those of male workers; and that unless the Bolsheviks propagandized and organized these workers, other opposition groups would do so. She would have welcomed a general party undertaking that sought to remedy these deficiencies but, since none was forthcoming, in late 1913 she was prepared to take the initiative herself or in concert with other Social Democratic women.

Lenin remained at best ambivalent toward the scheme. Unlike many of his male colleagues, he shared many of Armand's assumptions and saw a women's paper as less of an evil than a women's bureau. It also would have been in keeping with his rather devious and opportunistic nature to seek a loyal woman supporter to implement his own ideas with respect to the woman question just as he sought a Caucasian such as S. G. Shaumian or J. V. Stalin to advance his views on the nationality question. And yet, while Lenin may not have been a male chauvinist, he certainly retained his male arrogance. He firmly believed in the backwardness and passivity of Russian women workers and he doubted if this state of mind could be changed. He also lacked confidence in the ability of the inexperienced Bolshevik women around him to organize, finance, edit and publish a party journal by themselves. If Armand wanted to try, then he had no overt objections but neither would he extend material support or hold out much hope that the venture would be successful. This patronizing attitude, plus a desire to prove that the project was feasible and that she was capable of pulling it off, undoubtedly contributed to Armand's sudden decision to leave Cracow in mid-December 1913.

Armand's destination was Paris but on the way she stopped in a number of European cities where she lectured to Russian *émigré* groups on the woman question,[50] on the necessity of publishing a newspaper aimed at women workers and, above all, on the need to collect money for this venture. The refusal of the Central Committee and *Pravda* to extend financial assistance made fund-raising her top priority. In early January 1914 she sent an appeal to *Put' pravdy* calling on women workers and their husbands to send in their contributions. *Pravda*'s editors apparently were still unenthusiastic about such a paper or pessimistic about its chances for success since they delayed publishing

---

[50] Wolfe, 'Lenin and Inessa Armand', p. 103.

114

the appeal for nearly a month.[51] While some money was realized through this means,[52] Anna Elizarova acknowledged that many husbands were reluctant to spend scarce family funds on a women's paper.[53] Armand also used trade-union contacts she had developed in 1912 to urge the metal workers and textile workers to organize collections for the paper.[54] And, once again, she tapped the private resources of the Armand family. In early January she reported to Krupskaia:

As regards money, things are in a shambles. I shall write Anna [Konstantinovich] and ask her to visit a mutual friend of ours; perhaps she [i.e., Anna] will give something (but of course not the entire amount) ... I would like to go with Liudmila [Stal'] tomorrow to visit a rich individual here – perhaps something will come of it.[55]

Since Alexander Armand had already supported the Longjumeau school and *Pravda*, it stands to reason that he was the 'mutual friend' Inessa would turn to through her sister-in-law when trying to finance her own newspaper. In the absence of a detailed financial report and because of the reluctance of Soviet authorities to admit that wealthy industrialists such as the Armands helped to pay for their own demise, it is impossible to determine how much money Inessa raised from these and other sources. It at least was enough to get the paper started. After that Krupskaia was optimistic that the mere appearance of a women's newspaper would generate sufficient revenue to keep it going.[56]

After arriving in Paris, Inessa rented an apartment from her old landlords, the Mazanovs, at 91 rue Barrault[57] and even acquired a piano which she found 'so calming and reconciling' to play 'especially at sad moments'.[58] She spent most of her time in Paris, however, happily sitting in small cafés along Avenue d'Orléans with Liudmila Stal' working out a precise organizational structure and operating rules

[51] *Put' pravdy*, no. 13 (5 February 1914), and no. 20 (23 February 1914); Armand, *Stat'i*, p. 23.
[52] Stal' in Artiukhina *et al.* (eds.), p. 109.
[53] A. Elizarova, 'Zhurnal "Rabotnitsa" 1914 g.', *Iz epokhi 'Zvezdy' i 'Pravdy'*, vol. III, p. 66.
[54] Pavel Podliashuk, 'Pravda i zhizn' – za nas!' in V. Vavilina (ed.), *Vsegda s vami: Sbornik posviashchennyi 50-letiiu zhurnala 'Rabotnitsa'* (Moscow, 1964), p. 57.
[55] 'K istorii ... "Rabotnitsa"', p. 30. 'Anna' is conveniently but mistakenly identified as Anna Elizarova by the editors of this correspondence.
[56] Letter to A. I. Elizarova (29 January/11 February 1914), in *ibid.*, p. 36. The four reports on donations published in *Rabotnitsa* indicate that the paper received about 300 rubles from its readers. One of these small donations came from Inessa's former friends in Mezen. *Rabotnitsa*, no. 3 (1 April 1914), p. 14.
[57] OA, file XIIIc (1), incoming dispatch 377 (8 March 1914); file XIIIb (1), folder 1E, outgoing dispatch 687 (3/16 April 1914).
[58] Letter to Inna Armand (1914), in Armand, *Stat'i*, p. 218.

for the proposed paper.[59] Inessa and Krupskaia had already decided that their 'little journal' should be called *Rabotnitsa* and that its foreign editorial board should consist of themselves plus Stal' and Zinaida Lilina. On 12 December they had written Samoilova to suggest that she approach Kudelli about forming the Russian portion of the board[60] together with Lenin's sister, Anna Elizarova.[61] This suggestion caused problems. Samoilova felt Kudelli was too conciliatory toward the Mensheviks and was bothered when she wanted to invite Kollontai, a Menshevik, to be a contributor and suggested cooperating with the Mensheviks during the forthcoming Women's Day. Moreover, there was a general feeling that Elizarova was a difficult person with whom to work.[62] By 20 January, however, these differences had been resolved and a Russian board made up of Samoilova, Kudelli, Elizarova and Rozmirovich held its first meeting in Samoilova's apartment.

One of the items they discussed was the draft set of rules governing relations between the two sets of editors which had been compiled in Paris and forwarded to St Petersburg by Krupskaia in Cracow. Armand and Stal' proposed that each group have equal voting rights; that all important issues such as acceptance of unsigned articles or theoretical pronouncements had to be decided by vote; and that, in case of a tie, the editor of *Sotsial-demokrat* in Paris would have the deciding vote.[63] The Russian editors, who apparently were more aware than Armand of the inherent problems of a tripartite editorial board, ultimately accepted these rules 'with minor amendments'. They insisted that articles sent abroad had to be approved by a certain date or a satisfactory substitute provided. They also wanted the deciding vote to rest with the Central Committee in Galicia, i.e., with Lenin, rather than with someone informed of the situation by Armand in Paris.[64]

Inessa also drew up an outline of the contents of the first issue. Her scheme called for a concentration on theoretical articles written largely by herself and Stal' which would reveal to Russian women workers why their lives were so hard, their working hours so long, their pay so

[59] Stal' in Krupskaia (ed.), *Pamiati*, p. 42.   [60] OA, file XVIIa, folder 1a.
[61] Elizarova, 'Zhurnal "Rabotnitsa"', pp. 63–4.
[62] Rozmirovich to Krupskaia (19 January/1 February 1914), and Samoilova to Krupskaia (25 January/7 February 1914), in 'K istorii ... "Rabotnitsa"', pp. 32–3 and 35.
[63] Armand to Krupskaia (first half of January 1914), in *ibid.*, pp. 31–2.
[64] Rozmirovich to Krupskaia (21 January/3 February 1914), in *ibid.*, p. 34. There was a general feeling on the part of the St Petersburg editors that they preferred working with their colleagues in Galicia rather than with Armand and Stal' in Paris. See, for example, letter from Rozmirovich to Krupskaia (19 January/1 February 1914), in *ibid.*, p. 33.

low. The weak and unorganized women were to be told how they could fight back against the oppressive capitalistic system.[65] The Russian editors were to take care of local correspondence and provide a chronicle of events of interest to women workers. At Krupskaia's suggestion, some articles would be included on general themes so as 'not to give the paper an exclusively "women's" character'.[66]

To the surprise of some, the authorities in St Petersburg granted permission for the publication of *Rabotnitsa*. After considerable difficulty, Elizarova finally found a press willing to print two issues a month of the paper, and D. F. Petrovskaia, the wife of a Bolshevik Duma deputy, agreed rather reluctantly to serve as its official publisher.[67] At Inessa's suggestion, an official endorsement for the paper was to be sought from another of the Duma deputies, perhaps Badaev or Malinovskii.[68] These preparatory arrangements and especially acquiring financial backing took more time than the editors anticipated. Armand originally hoped the first issue would come out before the end of January; then the target date was mid-February; finally it was agreed that its appearance should coincide with International Women's Day on 23 February.[69]

The only item lacking was an article from Lenin. Samoilova wrote to Krupskaia suggesting that such an article would be welcome and would prove that *Rabotnitsa* was not a feminist organ.[70] Lenin did not in fact contribute to the first issue or indeed to the six that followed it. Had he done so Soviet scholars would have found it easier to justify their often stated claim that the journal was published on his initiative and subsequently functioned under his guidance.[71] This claim, which was contradicted by the Central Committee's total lack of support for the paper, is based on three letters Lenin allegedly wrote in December 1913. The first, sent on 12 December, six days before Armand left Cracow and

---

[65] See appeal in *Put' pravdy*, no. 13 (5/18 February 1914); letter from Armand to Krupskaia (early January 1914), in 'K istorii ... "Rabotnitsa"', pp. 29–30.
[66] Unpublished letter from Krupskaia to Rozmirovich, cited in 'K istorii ... "Rabotnitsa"', p. 27.
[67] Elizarova, 'Zhurnal "Rabotnitsa"', pp. 66–7.
[68] Armand to Krupskaia (early January 1914), in 'K istorii ... "Rabotnitsa"', p. 30. The portion of the letter referring to police agent Malinovskii is omitted from the version published in Armand's *Stat'i* (p. 214). The endorsement, if it were indeed forthcoming from a male Duma member, did not appear in *Rabotnitsa*.
[69] See Armand's draft appeal and Samoilova's letter to Krupskaia (25 January/7 February 1914), in 'K istorii ... "Rabotnitsa"', pp. 31 and 35.
[70] *Ibid.*, p. 36.
[71] See, for example, Volodarskaia, p. 299; Yemelyanova, p. 12; Levidova and Pavlotskaia, p. 102.

first published in *Krasnyi arkhiv* in 1938, was addressed to Samoilova and attributed to Krupskaia alone. In it she wrote:

Lately *we* have been talking a lot here [i.e., in Cracow] about the need to start publishing a small periodical especially for women ... *We* have outlined the following rough plan for our little journal which it would be good to call *Rabotnitsa*: 1) an editorial on a general political subject; 2) the labour movement and the participation of the woman worker in its various aspects (political struggle, trade union movement, insurance campaign, cooperatives); 3) conditions of women's work in the factory, workshop, as saleswomen, in home industries, conditions of domestic servants; 4) protection of female labour; 5) foreign section; 6) general review of current events; 7) chronicle; 8) working woman and the family.[72]

By inference, 'we' referred to Krupskaia and her husband and according to one Soviet author the 'rough plan' was personally worked out by Lenin.[73] In a copy preserved in the Okhrana Archives at the Hoover Institution two signatures do indeed appear on the letter: one is Krupskaia's but the other is Armand's rather than Lenin's. The ellipses in the *Krasnyi arkhiv* version are replaced by a list of proposed women editors and a favourable comment about the venture by Zinoviev.[74] Lenin was in no way connected with the letter.

The second letter was sent by him to Armand in Paris sometime after 27 December 1913. In it he commands her rather cryptically to '*get going* super-energetically on the women's journal'.[75] Nowhere else in the thirty-one published letters he sent her before the war does he refer to *Rabotnitsa*. He does, however, mention the journal, perhaps disparagingly, in two archival letters of the period which for unexplained reasons Soviet authorities chose not to publish.[76]

The third letter used to 'prove' Lenin's key role in establishing *Rabotnitsa* has also not been published. According to Anna Elizarova writing in 1923, she received a letter from Lenin in December 1913 in which he discussed plans to publish a journal for women and the possible composition of its editorial board.[77] There is, however, no record of this letter in his 'Complete Collected Works', in the register of his writings in the Central Party Archives of the Institute of Marxism-Leninism,[78] or in the police files of intercepted correspondence at the Hoover Institution.

---

72 'K istorii ... zhenskogo dnia', p. 8 (emphasis added).   73 Serditova, p. 91.
74 OA, file XVIIa, folder 1a.
75 Lenin, *PSS*, vol. XLVIII, p. 243 (emphasis in the original).
76 *Biog. khr.*, vol. III, pp. 192 and 208.
77 Elizarova, 'Zhurnal "Rabotnitsa"', p. 63.
78 The editors of *Biog. khr.*, vol. III, p. 168, state that Lenin wrote the letter but cite Elizarova's 1923 article as their source. They do not provide a *fond* number as is usually done when an unpublished letter is held in the Central Party Archives.

Perhaps Elizarova's memory was vague about dates and correspondents of a decade earlier. On 31 January 1914 Krupskaia rather than Lenin wrote to her that plans for the publication of *Rabotnitsa* 'seem to be developing sporadically. Some people appear to have taken the matter seriously. I don't know how it will turn out but Volodia [i.e. Lenin] will write to you about it.'[79] Twelve days later 'Volodia' finally got around to writing to his sister but the only reference to *Rabotnitsa* here or elsewhere in his published correspondence to her was an afterthought at the very end of his letter: 'N.K. [i.e., Krupskaia] will write about the women's magazine.'[80] Krupskaia's accompanying letter discussed the background to the paper and many of the problems the would-be editors (including Elizarova) had encountered. It also raises questions not only about Lenin's role in establishing the paper but about her own as well. Written five months after Armand had initially discussed with her the possibility of publishing a women's journal and three weeks before the first issue of *Rabotnitsa* appeared in St Petersburg, Krupskaia's enthusiasm for the project was limited to 'I am beginning to get an appetite for it.'[81] It would hardly seem that she was the guiding spirit behind *Rabotnitsa*'s creation, as has been argued.[82] Armand's letters to Krupskaia from Paris give the clear impression that it was Inessa who was doing the work of raising money, drawing up operating rules and assigning articles. Krupskaia, because she had up-to-date addresses in St Petersburg and clandestine means of getting correspondence to Russia, simply served as a secretariat for Inessa just as she did for Lenin. Sixteen years later Krupskaia herself acknowledged that *Rabotnitsa* was created 'on Inessa's initiative'.[83]

*   *   *

Rabotnitsa was almost still-born. To prevent the type of demonstrations that had erupted on International Women's Day in 1913, the Okhrana staged a series of preventive raids on radical women's groups of various political persuasions on 18 and 19 February 1914. Among the more than thirty women arrested were Kudelli, Rozmirovich and Samoilova who had gathered in Kudelli's apartment on the 18th to discuss last-minute details concerning the paper's publication scheduled for the 23rd. As a result of these raids, the Okhrana reported that Women's Day was 'generally quiet in the capital' with only one public meeting of

---

[79] Lenin, *PSS*, vol. LV, p. 447.   [80] *Ibid.*, p. 350.   [81] *Ibid.*, p. 449.
[82] 'K istorii ... "Rabotnitsa"', p. 27; Kudelli, p. 52.
[83] N. Krupskaia, 'Inessa Armand', *Pravda*, 24 September 1930, p. 5.

any consequence being held.[84] *Rabotnitsa*, however, came out more or less as planned thanks to the fact that Anna Elizarova was late in arriving at Kudelli's and thus able to avoid the police roundup. Fortuitously, most of the manuscripts were already at the press and thus escaped seizure as well. With the help of the party's insurance journal, Elizarova was able to print twelve thousand copies of the first issue.[85] While this amounted to less than a tenth of the press run of Zetkin's *Die Gleichheit*[86] and was insufficient for circulation outside the capital, it nevertheless represented the first Russian Social Democratic attempt at appealing specifically to working women.

Rabotnitsa's existence remained precarious for the next four months. Elizarova could count on several of the other Russian editors, who had been exiled to Liuban, eighty kilometres from St Petersburg, for occasional advice and some articles but not for administrative assistance.[87] She quite rightly considered the division of editorial responsibilities with the foreign editors 'too unwieldy'[88] and found the ensuing correspondence with Galicia and Paris to be slow, unreliable and often a source of unwanted controversy. Money remained scarce and on three occasions the censor interfered with publication. It is no wonder that Lenin was pessimistic about the paper's ability to survive.[89] His sister nevertheless managed to put out seven issues, all but the last at the projected two-week intervals. Each issue was sixteen pages in length and was given away in the factories or sold for four or five kopeks a copy.

The content of the paper, which Armand had been so instrumental in bringing to fruition, was not what she had anticipated nor was it particularly to her liking. At Krupskaia's suggestion, the largest portion of the first issue was to have been written in Paris by Armand and Stal'.[90] This allocation of work agreed with Armand's earlier outline for that issue in which she assigned herself four articles and Stal' three.[91] Most of these were to be serious pieces on historical, political or theoretical issues in keeping with the propagandistic character of most Social Democratic publications in emigration. The paper, when it appeared on 23 February/8 March, contained only one article by Stal' and none by

84 Report 5147 (23 February 1914), in 'K istorii ... zhenskogo dnia', p. 10.
85 Elizarova, 'Zhurnal "Rabotnitsa"', p. 65.
86 Honeycutt, p. 296.   87 Kudelli, p. 52.
88 Elizarova, 'Zhurnal "Rabotnitsa"', p. 70.
89 See notation of unpublished letter of 8 March 1914 to Inessa Armand in *Biog. khr.*, vol. III, p. 192.
90 Krupskaia to Samoilova (13/26 February 1914), in 'K istorii ... "Rabotnitsa"', p. 39.
91 Armand to Krupskaia (early January 1914), in *ibid.*, pp. 29–30.

the other foreign editors. At least one by Armand, as well as Krupskaia's lead editorial which Inessa had edited in Paris, were omitted.[92] These omissions might have been explained by the belated publication of the issue and by the need to print topical articles relating to International Women's Day but this excuse could not be used to justify their exclusion from the next issue as well. In number two, which appeared on 16/29 March 1914, all but one article by Stal' on the socialist women's movement in western Europe were popular or agitational in character and written by the Russian editors. Armand vented her displeasure in a letter to Krupskaia:

> We have here the second issue and I must say it is very, very poor. In essence, it is utterly frivolous, almost empty. There should be various short agitational articles in the issue but there must also be discussion – even if in a very popular and agitational form – of the different questions in our minimum and maximum programmes. Otherwise *Rabotnitsa* in no way fulfils its mission of [providing] a socialist education for women workers.[93]

She was also concerned that the editors in St Petersburg had chosen to print a Menshevik account of Women's Day in Russia rather than following the *Pravda* version of events on 23 February. It seemed to her that there were 'conciliators or even worse' on *Rabotnitsa*'s editorial board and she suggested that Krupskaia try to reassert the foreign editors' ideological control over the board.[94]

In 1923 Elizarova admitted that her vision of the journal was different than that of the foreign editors whom she felt were isolated from events in Russia and unaware of the desire on the part of women workers for a popular mass organ.[95] Rather than filling up *Rabotnitsa* with propaganda pieces written by foreign authors as Armand had projected, she devoted only about 35 per cent of the journal's columns to this type of material. An equal amount of space was given over to correspondence from women workers and accounts of current events of interest to the female proletariat. The remaining 30 per cent, much to Armand's disgust, was taken up by proletarian poetry and popular

---

[92] Compare Krupskaia's letter to Samoilova of 13/26 February 1914 ('K istorii ... "Rabotnitsa"', p. 39) and her draft editorial (*ibid.*, pp. 37–9), with *Rabotnitsa*, no. 1 (23 February 1914) and especially 'Ot redaktsii' (pp. 1–2). Several Western writers have mistakenly assumed that the draft was in fact the editorial published (see, for example, Lapidus, p. 48; Anne Bobroff, 'The Bolsheviks and Working Women, 1905–1920', *Soviet Studies*, vol. XXVI, no. 4 [October 1974], p. 546).
[93] Written between 16/29 March and 1/14 April 1914, in 'K istorii ... "Rabotnitsa"', p. 41.
[94] *Ibid.*   [95] Elizarova, 'Zhurnal "Rabotnitsa"', pp. 68–72.

fiction designed to divert and amuse rather than to edify the paper's readership.[96]

Elizarova's assessment was probably correct. Tired, over-worked and poorly educated factory women were more interested in picking up a readable and relevant publication along the lines of *Pravda* than they were in having their consciousnesses raised by theoretical and sometimes condescending articles more appropriate for the *émigré* intellectual audience of *Sotsial-demokrat*. One suspects they also would have been interested in editorial comment, which was not forthcoming in either *Rabotnitsa* or *Pravda*, about the complaints constantly raised in their letters concerning male hostility or indifference encountered at work or in the trade-union movement.

Because of these philosophical differences, communication problems, and perhaps the delay in publishing her initial contributions, Armand was the least active of the foreign editors. Stal' and Lilina each submitted seven articles and Krupskaia three.[97] Inessa wrote only two: 'Electoral Rights of Women' in issue number three and 'Women Workers and the Eight-hour Working Day' in number four.[98] In the first she made a sensible argument, long ignored by orthodox Social Democrats, that the political struggle takes place in parliaments just as it does on picket lines; that this is a common struggle of male and female workers and to deprive women of the right to vote is therefore to weaken the overall class struggle. She argued that women needed the right to vote, not to promote and defend specifically women's issues such as maternity benefits which they supposedly knew best, but rather to fight for general worker demands such as the eight-hour day, the right to form trade unions and to hold meetings, etc. 'Women workers do not have special demands separate from general proletarian demands', she asserted, and even if they did, male workers were just as interested in obtaining these demands as were their female colleagues.[99] One wonders what Lenin would have said had he had a chance to review this manuscript as he had her earlier one on British trade unionism. He probably would have been less concerned by its contra-

96 For a discussion of *Rabotnitsa*'s contents, see Janet Hyer, 'Pre-Revolutionary *Rabotnitsa*: A Study of Bolshevik Policy towards Working Women' (unpublished MA thesis, Carleton University, 1985), especially pp. 70–5.
97 While the identification of the initials and pseudonyms of the Russian editors is not always certain, it would appear that Samoilova wrote three signed articles and Elizarova and Kudelli two each.
98 Podliashuk (p. 144) and Krupskaia (*Pamiati*, p. 14) suggest that several of the unsigned articles in *Rabotnitsa* were probably by Armand. Judging from the topics of the very few unsigned articles, this seems unlikely.
99 'Izbiratel'nyia prava zhenshchin', *Rabotnitsa*, no. 3 (1 April 1914), pp. 1–2.

dictory statements than by the assertion that parliaments and dumas could produce meaningful reform as well as serving as forums for socialist agitation.

Armand's second article foreshadowed some unconvincing arguments she was to make five years later as the first director of Zhenotdel. After quoting English statistics concerning the detrimental effects of overtime work on women's health, she argued that one of the chief benefits of an eight-hour working day was that it allowed women to go to study circles and union meetings in the evening and thus further the class struggle. She noted in passing that women, unlike men, also had to fulfil their roles as mothers and housewives after work and before going to meetings.[100] In 1919 she was to carry this one step further by suggesting some rather more interesting ways of relieving the second part of the double burden women workers had to carry (see Chapter 12, below).

When Krupskaia proved unable or unwilling to bring *Rabotnitsa* back under the control of its foreign editors, Inessa appeared to lose interest in the women's paper she had been instrumental in establishing. Even Lenin's rare words of encouragement about the paper in late April[101] failed to change her attitude. She wrote nothing for the last three issues[102] and made virtually no reference to the journal in her published correspondence. Increasingly, her time in Paris was taken up with running various errands for Lenin and in planning a summer holiday with four of her children on the Adriatic. In mid-May she departed for Lovran near Trieste leaving it to Krupskaia to explain the lack of foreign contributions to Elizarova. 'Our articles are going badly,' Lenin's wife wrote on 18 June, 'because Lilina is sick in hospital, Stal' was sick, and Blonina's [i.e., Armand's] child [Andre] was sick. I was busy. Almost all of us live in different places and we rely on one another.'[103]

Despite the numerous internal and external problems *Rabotnitsa* encountered, and Armand's declining interest in it, the venture was

---

[100] 'Rabotnitsa i 8-mi chasovoi rabochii den'', *Rabotnitsa*, no. 4 (19 April 1914), pp. 5–6. Both of these articles were written under the pseudonym 'Elena Blonina' which the editor failed to recognize as being of Polish origin and rendered as 'Bloshina'. Perhaps this was a simple problem of transcription or a typographical error. It is also possible that Elizarova, who had her fill of Armand's complaints, took perverse pleasure in seeing her referred to as Elena 'the flea'.

[101] Unpublished letter noted in 'K istorii ... "Rabotnistsa"', p. 26.

[102] Her interest was so slight that in 1919 she thought that it ceased publication after its fifth issue on 4 May 1914. See Elena Blonina [I. F. Armand], 'Bor'ba rabotnits za poslednie gody', in Armand, *Stat'i*, p. 76.

[103] OA, file XVIIa, folder 4, incoming dispatch 713 (10/23 June 1914).

valuable both as a learning experience for its editors and as a precedent for future party activities. It is impossible to determine how much seven issues of an unevenly written, occasionally condescending and often uninteresting paper increased the class consciousness of St Petersburg's female proletariat. It did, however, make them realize that some people within the Bolshevik Party were interested in their problems and were prepared to offer encouragement and organizational assistance. The loyalties won and contacts made among women factory workers in St Petersburg in 1914 were to stand the Bolsheviks in good stead in Petrograd in 1917. Perhaps the readers of *Rabotnitsa*, through their correspondence to the paper, also broke down some of the stereotypes concerning the backwardness of Russian factory women and male attitudes toward them. There is evidence that some trade unions lowered their dues in 1914 to get women workers to join rather than trying to remain exclusive male preserves.[104] Inside the party, despite a continued lack of male enthusiasm for *Rabotnitsa*, no longer was a female workers' paper viewed as a feminist or separatist threat. The precedent that women socialists could address women workers on issues of interest to women through an organization run by women had been established and would be recalled when the party returned to organizing women workers in 1917.

For Inessa Armand, *Rabotnitsa* represented a renewed involvement in working with women. Just like her earlier experience with the Moscow Society, so also the six months she spent on *Rabotnitsa* were not entirely successful. She had proven, however, that she was capable of organizing a substantial enterprise without male assistance and she was instrumental finally in putting the woman question on her party's agenda. One reflection of her increased stature in the Bolshevik ranks was her nomination by the Central Committee in late May or early June 1914 as the Bolshevik representative to the International Women's Secretariat.[105] Since the RSDRP was entitled to just one seat on that body and that position had been held by Aleksandra Kollontai since 1910, a confrontation between Russian Social Democracy's two foremost feminists seemed inevitable at the Third Conference of Socialist Women scheduled to meet in Vienna during August 1914. The outbreak of the First World War, however forced the cancellation of the conference and delayed this encounter until after the Revolution.

[104] Serditova, p. 102.
[105] Lenin, *PSS*, vol. XLVIII, p. 338; OA, file XVIIa, folder 4, incoming dispatch 713 (10/23 June 1914).

CHAPTER 7

LENIN'S 'GIRL FRIDAY'

When Inessa Armand left Cracow bound for Paris, she may have intended to devote her energies to getting *Rabotnitsa* off the ground but Lenin had other ideas on how she should use her time. Shortly after her departure on 18 December 1913 he wrote her a letter – the first of forty-one she was to receive during the seven months before the war. Despite the incomplete and one-sided nature of this correspondence, it reveals a great deal about Lenin, about Armand, and about their changing relationship. In it he uses the *ty* form of address – a familiarity he employed with no other party member of this period and a sign of both his friendship and his trust in her. The correspondence also reflects the new role he wanted her to play in the party. She was to be his 'Girl Friday': a loyal and trusted subordinate who could utilize her knowledge of western European languages and her presence in Paris to carry out a variety of personal and political tasks. Even more than Trotskii during the *Iskra* period, she became Lenin's 'cudgel' – someone to beat wavering Bolsheviks back into line, to deliver uncompromising messages to his political opponents, to carry out uncomfortable missions which Lenin himself preferred to avoid. Much of the time this work involved trivial, almost menial tasks such as fetching books Lenin wished to read or translating his pronouncements into French or German. On other occasions, these assignments brought her into contact and conflict with the leaders of European socialism and perhaps justified the Okhrana's conclusion of 1914 that she was 'an extremely prominent, popular and active figure in international socialist ranks and [was] considered in Russian revolutionary circles to be the right hand of Lenin'.[1] That Armand did not particularly like being Lenin's 'Girl Friday', a role she was to play for over two years, is also evident in much of their correspondence. This unhappiness ultimately led to a marked change in their relationship in 1916.

*   *   *

[1] Cited in Podliashuk, p. 157.

125

A sign of what was in store for her was evident in that first letter which she received after arriving in Paris.

What is the story with the C[entral] O[rgan]? It is a disgrace and a scandal!! It has not appeared yet, not even proofs. Enquire and get an explanation, please. The issue of *Vorwärts*, where Kautsky used the foul phrase 'there is no party [in Russia] . . . ', is no. 333, 18 December 1913. You must get hold of it (49 rue de Bretagne, or some other place) and organize a protest campaign.[2]

A couple of weeks later he was still annoyed with the editing of *Sotsial-demokrat*:

I received the C[entral] O[rgan]. Page 8 is disgraceful. Why the devil were we not informed? We could have found more material!! And it should not have been dated 28 December, but earlier, since there is not a word about the International [Socialist] Bureau . . . Who wrote the article on the Bailis affair in the C[entral] O[rgan]? Why were we not sent the proofs? . . .[3]

In April he ordered her to gather together all of the books he and Kamenev had left in various places in Paris and to concentrate them in the hands of N. I. Sapozhkov. 'Make him *swear an oath not to let them be pilfered.*' The same letter asked her to 'send us *all* the copies' she could find in Paris of *Sotsial-demokrat*, no. 11, published four years earlier.[4] Since the mail was his major form of contact with western Europe, he was distressed when items were delayed or went astray. 'I still have not received the collection (*Nachalo*)', he wrote on 11 April. 'Is it the post again?'

If you still have the wrapper, there should be postmarks on it. I would advise that you lodge a protest with the ministry, enclosing the wrapper. It is terribly exasperating to lose the letter about Rakhmetov [A. A. Bogdanov], and I consider complaints, protests, etc., to be absolutely essential. I have a strong suspicion that letters to Russian *émigrés* are stolen in Paris (and taken to the police to be read before being delivered to the addressees). It is necessary to note down the dates on which letters are received.[5]

Lenin was particularly distressed with the conduct of the Committee of Foreign Organizations (KZO) and the Paris Bolshevik Section since he and Inessa had left the French capital a year and a half earlier. Despite his personal intervention at the KZO's second conference in Bern during early August 1913, he felt that the body had fallen behind in collecting

---

[2] Lenin to Armand (after 18 December 1913), in Lenin, *PSS*, vol. XLVIII, p. 238.
[3] Lenin to Armand (after 28 December 1913), in *ibid.*, pp. 248–9.
[4] Lenin to Armand (14 April 1914), in *ibid.*, p. 282 (emphasis in the original).
[5] *Ibid.*, p. 281.

money abroad and in publishing *émigré* literature. In early January 1914 he instructed Inessa to 'make sure that the KZO does not give a *single* kopek to *anybody* but us ... Bring up the question in the KZO of lambasting Kautsky and put it to a vote: if the majority turns it down, I'll come and give that majority a lathering they will never forget.'[6]

Lenin did in fact go to Paris to help Inessa read the riot act to the KZO. In mid-January 1914 he and R. V. Malinovskii – the new head of the Bolshevik Duma fraction as well as an agent of the tsarist secret police – left Cracow for a 23-day trip through western Europe. After consulting with some Latvian Social Democrats in Berlin, they continued on to Paris arriving on the 17th or 18th and remaining for a week.[7] According to the police and a fellow Bolshevik lodger, they too stayed at the Mazanovs'.[8] During his free moments, Lenin sat quietly in a corner of the main room listening to Inessa, accompanied by the Bolshevik violinist Andre Grechnev-Chernov, play pieces from Chopin, Beethoven, Mozart and Wieniawski on her rented piano.[9] Lenin enjoyed the social aspects of his visit to Paris. As he wrote to his mother after his return to Cracow, 'there is no better or more lively a city to stay in for a short time, to visit, to roam around in. It was a good change for me.'[10]

Politically, the stay was less successful. Malinovskii was heckled by a large and hostile audience when he tried to justify the split he and Lenin had engineered in the Social Democratic Duma fraction. The talk ended with Malinovskii in tears and the crowd chanting 'Lenin, Lenin, Lenin'.[11] While the Bolshevik leader refused to speak on that occasion, he gave three lectures of his own: the first two on the anniversary of

---

6 Lenin to Armand (between 9 and 15 January 1914), in *ibid.*, pp. 253–4 (emphasis in the original).
7 Much confusion surrounds the details and timing of this trip. Podliashuk, perhaps because of Malinovskii's presence, ignores it altogether; Wolfe, certainly because of Inessa's presence, claims Lenin stayed in Paris for one and a half months ('Lenin and Inessa Armand', p. 103); several Paris *émigrés* (Khoniavko, 'V podpol'e', p. 166, Shapovalov, p. 157, V. Degot, *Pod znamenem Bol'shevizma: zapiski podpol'shchika* [Moscow, 1927], p. 86) and at least one Soviet historian (Iakushina, 'Iz istorii ... KZO', p. 77) assert that Lenin visited Paris twice between the fall of 1913 and the spring of 1914. From Lenin's letters, Krupskaia's memoirs and *Biog. khr.*, it is evident that his only stay was between 17/18 and 25 January 1914.
8 OA, file XIIIb(1), folder 1E, outgoing dispatch 687 (3/16 April 1914); Degot, p. 86.
9 A. S. Grechnev-Chernov, 'Vospominaniia o V. I. Lenine', in *O Vladimire Il'iche Lenine* (Moscow, 1963), p. 98. Other writers, basing themselves on Grechnev-Chernov, have assumed that this informal recital took place during Inessa's first stay at the Mazanovs' (see, for example, Fréville, *Lénine à Paris*, p. 126, and Najdus, pp. 252–3). She, however, is quite explicit about renting a piano in 1914 (see letter to Inna Armand [before summer 1914], in Armand, *Stat'i*, p. 218).
10 Lenin to M. A. Ul'ianova (21 February 1914), in Lenin, *PSS*, vol. LV, p. 351.
11 Khoniavko, 'V podpol'e', pp. 166–7; Degot, p, 86.

Bloody Sunday (9/22 January) in an effort to help Inessa raise money for the Paris Section, and a third sponsored by the KZO on the nationality question. He was disturbed when he arrived at the large hall of the Société de Géographie to find only a small number of people were willing to pay up to five francs to hear him speak. He was even more distressed that most of the audience were Poles or members of the Jewish Bund known to be unsympathetic to his point of view on the nationality question. After lecturing for two hours, he left without waiting for the usual questions and rejoinders from his critical listeners.[12] When asked by Inessa whether he was 'angry because of the unsuccessful lecture', he replied 'You bet I am angry' and blamed 'that idiot' A. V. Popov, a member of the KZO who had organized the talk, for apparently not having packed the audience with a larger number of his faithful supporters.[13] Lenin may have given the KZO a 'lathering' while in Paris but he was unsuccessful in bringing the recalcitrant committee back into line. Three days after leaving France, he wrote to Armand:

there is an important job to be done in Paris – the reorganization of the KZO. It is now more important than ever before ... It is of *utmost* importance to the party that the publication in Paris [of the Central Committee's new *Bulletin*] be *straightened out*. I beg you to *do* this 'both as a duty and as a friend' ... Make sure that [my instructions to the KZO] are followed *precisely*. Convince the people there that we shall get rid of the KZO and replace it with our own committee (named by the Central Committee) – really, I am not joking – unless the publication and distribution of the *Bulletin* is done with great care ... I demand *literally* the strict execution of my instructions concerning the *Bulletin*. That is one thing. Secondly, the KZO must establish a business *commission* so that Antonov [A. V. Popov] ... has *nothing* to do with the practical side of affairs ... Put this through the KZO and *get the commission going*. I repeat, this is a matter of utmost importance.[14]

How Armand – who was no longer a member of the Committee, had little interest in its operations, and obviously lacked Lenin's political clout – was to carry out these instructions was left unstated. Perhaps at her prodding, one issue of the *Bulletin* did appear during January. She in addition lent a hand in her speciality – raising money: she helped the KZO solicit funds for the party in the United States and through the 'political' Red Cross in Switzerland.[15] By the time she left Paris in May, the Bolshevik Section, which had been 'leaderless' since Kamenev's

---

12 Degot, p. 86.
13 Lenin to Armand (26 January 1914), in Lenin, *PSS*, vol. XLVIII, p. 255.
14 Lenin to Armand (28 January 1914), in *ibid.*, pp. 256–7 (emphasis in the original).
15 Iakushina, 'Iz istorii ... KZO', p. 76; Iakushina, *Lenin i Zagranichnaia organizatsiia*, p. 200.

departure the previous summer,[16] had been revitalized and could claim over ninety members.[17]

Lenin also asked his 'Girl Friday' to intercede on his behalf with some Ukrainian Social Democrats in Paris and Zurich. His intentions were devious and divisive. 'It would be good', he wrote in the middle of March, 'for us to have a Ukrainian Social Democratic group of our own, however small. Write whether you can make the contacts and do something in this direction.'[18] A month later, he reiterated: 'I beg you, if you go to Zurich, to do everything you can to see the Ukrainian SDs, find out their attitude on the question of a separate national Ukrainian SD organization, and try to organize even a small group of anti-separatists.'[19] While she was unsuccessful in these schismatic activities, she was able to assist Lenin in carrying out a related subterfuge. On 1 April he sent her a draft appeal in which he attacked the Ukrainian Social Democrat, Lev Iurkevich.

I ask you to be very tactful in getting it accepted (not in my name, of course, and not in yours) by [O.N.] Lola and a couple of other Ukrainians ... You will understand why it is awkward for me to send a draft such as this in my own name [to a party newspaper] ... Re-write my draft (I agree to all changes ...), have Lola alone or with someone else pass it and translate it into Ukrainian, and then send it through me to Put' pravdy in his name or better yet in the name of a group (even two or three people) of Ukrainian Marxists (better still, Ukrainian workers). This should be done tactfully, quickly, against Iurkevich and without his knowledge since this rogue will cause trouble.[20]

After Inessa got Lola to agree to the content of the appeal but not to sign it, it was sent to Trudovaia pravda where it duly appeared over Lola's name and with a Central Committee endorsement which also had been written by Lenin.[21]

During the course of these rather questionable dealings, Armand became intrigued with Ukrainian Social Democracy and carried out some investigations of her own. She reported at length to Lenin on speeches she heard Lola and Iurkevich give and she sent him V.K. Vinnichenko's popular new novel Zavety ottsov. The latter caught her attention not only because it was written by a leading Ukrainian socialist but also since it dealt with prostitution, a problem of great

[16] Degot, p. 86.   [17] Iakushina, 'Iz istorii ... KZO', p. 77.
[18] Lenin to Armand (after 15 March 1914), in Lenin, PSS, vol. XLVIII, p. 272 (emphasis in the original).
[19] Lenin to Armand (24 April 1914), in ibid., pp. 281–2.
[20] Ibid., pp. 277–8 (emphasis in the original).
[21] Ibid., pp. 410–11, n. 311 and 316.

interest to her over a decade earlier, and was frank in its discussion of sexuality. She must have found Lenin's response to these initiatives discouraging. 'Frankly speaking, I was angry with you', he wrote on 1 April, 'you did not understand the *main point* of Iurkevich's speech.'[22] His reaction to Vinnichenko's novel was equally unenthusiastic.

This is balderdash and stupidity! To combine together every conceivable kind of 'horror', to collect in one story 'depravity' and 'syphilis' and romantic crime and blackmail . . . All this with hysterical outbursts, eccentricities, claims to having a 'personal' theory for organizing prostitutes . . . This pretentious, complete idiot Vinnichenko . . . has made this into a collection of horrors – a kind of 'two-penny dreadful'. Brrr, what filth, what nonsense; too bad I spent so much time reading it.[23]

There was of course not a word of thanks to Inessa for having sent him the book or for having taken an interest in Ukrainian affairs. On the basis of Lenin's own outburst she should not have been surprised seven months later, when she herself started to address problems of human sexuality, that her correspondent turned out to be priggish and uninterested.

*   *   *

It was with understandable relief that Armand temporarily abandoned her 'Girl Friday' role in mid-May 1914 and moved to the Adriatic coast for what she hoped would be a 'glorious and inexpensive' vacation with four of her children.[24] She had not seen them since the previous summer and was well aware she was missing out on their formative years. Alexander, now twenty years old, was no longer taking family vacations; Fedor was eighteen, the two girls in their teens, and Andre ten. The mood of the family, as she later recalled, was 'frivolous': 'we wanted to enjoy everything together – the sun, the sea'[25] (Plate 10). All of this came to an end in early July when, after a lapse of a month, she received another letter from Lenin.

Dear Friend,
    Information was received today that the Executive Committee of the I[nternational] S[ocialist] B[ureau] has scheduled a so-called 'Unity' Conference for Brussels on 16, 17 and 18 July.
    A delegation must be formed. It is uncertain whether we shall go. Perhaps Gregorii [Zinoviev will go] but most likely he will not.

---

22 *Ibid.*, p. 278 (emphasis in the original).
23 Lenin to Armand (before 5 June 1914), in *ibid.*, pp. 294–5.
24 See letter to Inna Armand (spring 1914), in Armand, *Stat'i*, p. 217.
25 Letter to Inna Armand (1915), in *ibid.*, p. 234.

10. Inessa Armand with her children Andre and Varvara vacationing on the
Adriatic coast during the summer of 1914.

On behalf of the C[entral] C[ommittee], I would like to ask you to agree to be a
member of the delegation. We shall pay the expenses of the trip. The tactics will
be worked out in minutest detail.

If you have the slightest possibility of making arrangements for your children
for 6–7 days (or even less since the conference is only 3 days), then *I* would ask
you to agree. You are familiar with [party] affairs, you speak perfect French,
you read *Pravda*. We also have in mind [I. F.] Popov, Kamskii [M. F. Vladimir-
skii], Iurii [A. A. Bakzadian]. All have been written.

So, answer immediately, without an hour's delay. Agree!

Very truly,

V.I.

... Agree, really. It will do you good to rouse yourself and you will help the
cause!! ...[26]

---

[26] Lenin to Armand (before 4 July 1914), in Lenin, *PSS*, vol. XLVIII, pp. 297–8 (emphasis
in the original). Greeting and salutation written in English in the original.

The idea of a 'unity' conference to determine the conditions necessary for the re-establishment of a unified RSDRP had first been raised by Rosa Luxemburg at a meeting of the International Socialist Bureau (ISB) in December 1913. After brief debate, the ISB decided instead to accept Karl Kautsky's suggestion that the Executive Committee simply offer its services as a mediator and facilitate an 'exchange of opinions' among the various factions of Russian Social Democracy.[27]

Lenin at first had no objection to an 'exchange of opinions' with his factional opponents.[28] He, after all, was dealing from a position of strength in late 1913. The Bolsheviks had scored gains in the elections to the Fourth Duma; *Pravda* had a vastly greater circulation than the Mensheviks' *Novaia rabochaia gazeta*; his party was steadily taking over one after another the directorates of formerly Menshevik trade unions and it was registering similar victories in the new workers' insurance councils. Abroad, Lenin's Central Committee was more active and unified than the Mensheviks' Organizational Committee in trying to provide guidance and coordination for these activities in Russia. Plans were well underway for the calling of a Sixth Party Congress in August 1914 that would complete the work of the 1912 Prague Conference in building an all-Bolshevik 'party of the new type'. Thus Lenin could write with confidence to Inessa in January that what 'we are witnessing is a new wave of idiotic conciliationism which the ISB is trying to exploit to stage a comedy in the spirit of the January 1910 Plenum. Well, we are now standing on our own two feet and will expose this riff-raff.'[29]

Lenin's attitude started to change during the spring of 1914 as the ISB procrastinated in fulfilling its December mandate. As Krupskaia had foreseen,[30] new groups such as those around Trotskii's *Bor'ba* and Plekhanov's *Edinstvo*, started springing up in Russia demanding consideration in whatever plans the Bureau might ultimately devise. Lenin also was having problems with the Second International's influential leaders. In March, he threatened to break off all personal relations with the Bureau's secretary, Camille Huysmans, over what he considered to be an intemperate letter.[31] Several months later, Emile Vandervelde, the

---

[27] *Proletarskaia pravda*, no. 2 (8/21 December 1913), pp. 1–2. The following account incorporates portions of my article on 'Lenin and the Brussels "Unity" Conference of July 1914', *Russian Review*, vol. XXXIX, no. 1 (January 1980), pp. 32–49. I am indebted to the editor of the *Russian Review* for permission to reproduce that material.

[28] Lenin, *PSS*, vol. XLVIII, pp. 238 and 249.

[29] Lenin to Armand (between 5–15 January 1914), in *ibid.*, p. 253.

[30] See letter to V. M. Kasparov (13 January 1914), 'Perepiska TsK RSDRP s mestnymi partiinymi organizatsiiami v gody novogo revoliutsionnogo pod"ema', *Istoricheskii arkhiv*, 1957, no. 1, p. 16.

[31] Lenin to Huysmans (7 March 1914), in Lenin, *PSS*, vol. XLVIII, pp. 268–9.

chairperson of the ISB, showed up unannounced in St Petersburg. Lenin was concerned when he heard that Vandervelde had broached the question of whether the various Russian groups would accept the International's arbitration rather than just its mediation and implied that his own sympathies were definitely on the side of the Mensheviks.[32] Moreover, Malinovskii's sudden resignation from the State Duma in early May, amid rumours that he was an agent of the tsarist police, put the Bolshevik leader in a much more vulnerable position than had been the case five months earlier.

When the Bureau finally issued invitations on 29 June to ten Russian Social Democratic groups to attend a 'unity conference' in Brussels two and a half weeks later, Lenin was 'furious'.[33] Not only was a formal conference involving *émigré* party leaders something more than a simple 'exchange of opinions', but also its delayed convocation meant that it would come on the eve of the Bolsheviks' own long-awaited Sixth Congress. With his limited resources, he could not plan for both at the same time with the result that the party congress was tacitly postponed. For a while Lenin debated boycotting the conference altogether. This, he felt, would have been the 'wiser' policy in the long run but one 'which the Russian workers would not have understood'.[34] Under no circumstances would he go himself, however. He justified this on unexplained grounds of 'principle' and by claiming that 'the Germans are out to annoy us'. 'I would probably have *blown up* at them', he wrote Armand, '*and that is what they want.*'[35] In reality, his schismatic activities within the RSDRP, the Malinovskii affair, his quarrel with Huysmans and legal troubles with the German 'trustees', all put the Bolshevik leader in a vulnerable and embarrassing position which his enemies, as he realized, would surely have capitalized on had he gone to Brussels. They 'only want to scold me before the International', he supposedly remarked, 'and I'm not going to give them the pleasure'.[36] None of his leading male subordinates was willing to take the scolding either. Zinoviev, a long-time member of the Bolsheviks' Central Committee,

---

[32] For differing accounts of this trip, see A. Shliapnikov, *Kanun semnadtsatogo goda*, vol. I (Moscow, 1923), pp. 8–9; *Pis'ma P. B. Aksel'roda i I. O. Martova* (Berlin, 1924), pp. 290–1.

[33] I. S. Ganetskii, 'Lenin nakanune imperialisticheskoi voiny', in *Vosp. o V. I. Lenine*, vol. II, p. 330; Krupskaya, *Lenin*, p. 274. For the invitation dated 16/29 June 1914, see 'Bol'sheviki na briussel'skom soveshchanii 1914 g.: dokumenty Instituta marksizma-leninizma pri TsK KPSS', *Istoricheskii arkhiv*, 1959, no. 4, p. 20.

[34] Lenin to Armand (19 July 1914), in Lenin, *PSS*, vol. XLVIII, p. 323.

[35] Lenin to Armand (before 4 July and 19 July 1914), in *ibid.*, pp. 298 and 323 (emphasis in the original).

[36] Ganetskii in *Vosp. o V. I. Lenine*, vol. II, p. 331.

begged off on the grounds that his wife was ill. Besides, added Lenin, 'his nerves are shot' and 'he speaks only German (and bad German at that)'.[37] Kamenev was otherwise engaged in editing *Proletarskaia pravda* in St Petersburg while Maksim Litvinov, who had represented the Bolsheviks at the December meeting of the ISB, claimed that he could not take time off from his job with the London Tourist Bureau.[38] Lenin's choice thus fell to Inessa Armand.

I am terribly afraid that you will refuse to go to Brussels and thus put us in an *absolutely impossible position*. Therefore, I have come up with another 'compromise' which you will be unable to refuse.

Nadia [i.e., Krupskaia] thinks that your older children have already arrived and that you could easily leave them for 3 days (or take Andre with you.)

If the older children have not arrived and it is *absolutely* impossible for you to leave the [other] children for 3 days, I suggest that you go *for one day* (the 16th, *even for half a day*, to read the report), either leaving the children for the day or even as a last resort sending for K—vich [Inessa's sister-in-law, Anna Konstantinovich] for that day. (We shall pay the expenses) . . .

Of course, in addition to excellent French, *an understanding of the principal points* and tact are necessary. There is *no one* but you. Therefore, I beg you, with all my strength I beg you – agree to go, if only for one day . . .[39]

Judging from the imploring tone of this and the four other letters Lenin sent her[40] before she eventually gave in on 9 July, Inessa was reluctant to accept the assignment. Since none of her letters of this period has been published, one can only speculate on the reasons for her reluctance. Surely she did not wish to leave her children, especially at a time when Andre was sick.[41] It is equally understandable that she had no desire to be the Bolshevik sacrificial lamb in Brussels and to take the 'scolding' for Lenin's schismatic policies. It is also possible that she had doubts about her ability to do battle with such experienced protagonists as Plekhanov, Trotskii, Martov and Aksel'rod. Lenin, in his initial letter, sought to bolster her confidence by noting that 'you are more sure of yourself now, you have been giving lectures and can carry it off splendidly'.[42] He continued in the same patronizing vein a week or so later:

---

[37] Lenin to Armand (before 6 July 1914), in Lenin, *PSS*, vol. XLVIII, p. 301.
[38] Litvinov to Lenin (5 May 1914), in 'Neopublikovannye pis'ma M. M. Litvinova V. I. Leninu (1913–1915 gg.)', *Novaia i noveishaia istoriia*, 1966, no. 4, pp. 125–6.
[39] Lenin to Armand (before 6 July 1914), in *PSS*, vol. XLVIII, pp. 300–1 (emphasis in the original).
[40] *Ibid.*, pp. 297–304, 313–14; *Biog. khr.*, vol. III, p. 244.
[41] See letter to Krupskaia (1914), in Armand, *Stat'i*, pp. 219–20.
[42] Lenin to Armand (before 4 July 1914), in Lenin, *PSS*, vol. XLVIII, p. 298.

I am convinced that you are one of those people who develop, grow stronger, become more forceful, more confident when they are by themselves in a responsible position – and therefore I absolutely refuse to believe pessimists who say that you . . . can hardly . . . Stuff and nonsense! I do not believe it! You will do marvellously![43]

The other two members of the Bolshevik delegation were even less experienced. I. F. Popov, who Inessa had known in Mezen, was chosen primarily because he lived in Brussels and could take care of local arrangements. He and M. F. Vladimirskii, who Lenin admitted was 'dead wood',[44] had as their 'chief duty (since Inessa will do the speaking in French) to write down everything as accurately as possible, especially the speeches of the Germans, and *especially those of Kautsky*, and to send a report to the Central Committee'.[45]

If Lenin was unwilling to expose himself personally to the assaults of his rivals, this did not mean that he was not going to fight back. He devoted much of the two weeks before the conference opened to collecting documentation in support of the Bolshevik position. Popov was deluged with protocols of past party gatherings, proofs of Lenin's as yet unpublished book *Marxism and Liquidationism*, long runs of *Pravda*, *Novaia rabochaia gazeta* and even some SR and bourgeois newspapers.[46] Lenin also spent eight days drafting a lengthy formal report, which was made legible by his wife or mother-in-law before being sent, section by section, by registered mail to Armand in the Balkans. She was to translate it 'immediately' into idiomatic French, '*tone down*' passages which were 'too sharply worded' or involved 'name calling', and then dispatch it to Popov in Brussels for reproduction.[47]

Lenin readily acknowledged that she was 'going to have [her] work cut out' since 'everybody will be very mad at my not being there and will probably take it out on you'. He therefore took the liberty of offering her 'heaps of advice' as to how she should react. 'Please don't take [this] occasional advice in a "bad sense". It is only meant to make your difficult task easier.'[48] 'I advise you to ask for the floor first to make your report on the grounds, if necessary, that your children are sick and that

[43] Lenin to Armand (between 10–16 July 1914), in *ibid.*, p. 307 (ellipses in the original).
[44] Lenin to Armand (28 January 1914), in *ibid.*, p. 257.
[45] Lenin to I. F. Popov (before 10 July 1914), in *ibid.*, p. 307 (emphasis in the original).
[46] See, for example, Lenin's instructions of 11 July 1914 to the Priboi publishing house, in *ibid.*, pp. 312–13.
[47] Lenin to Armand (before 10 July 1914), in *ibid.*, p. 305 (emphasis in the original). It is not surprising, given the manner in which the report was written and translated, that the final version was poorly organized and admittedly incomplete (*ibid.*, vol. XXV, pp. 363–405, 526 n. 142; for variants, see *Leninskii sbornik*, vol. XXXVII, pp. 24–9).
[48] Lenin to Armand (July 1914), in Lenin, *PSS*, vol. XLVIII, pp. 304, 314, 317.

you may have to leave for home in a hurry.' 'Try to make it sound as if you are giving a speech while merely referring to your notes. Take the Russian text with you but *do not give it* to the Liquidators; say that you didn't bring it' if they ask for a copy.[49] She was to 'deliver her speech in *excellent* French ... otherwise nine-tenths will be *lost* in translation'.[50] Moreover, 'the Germans will hardly understand you, if they understand at all – sit close to the Executive Committee and speak *to them*. After every German speech, [however,] ask Huysmans for a French translation as you have *every* right to do.' She was warned that 'Plekhanov likes to "disconcert" female comrades with "sudden" gallantries in French' and that he also 'liked to "interrogate" and mock' his opponents. She should respond with 'quick repartees ("you old spark, you") ... that would politely *rebuff* him'. If this did not work, then she was to 'take the offensive' against him.[51] Additional counsel was given on how she should handle Luxemburg, Vandervelde, Kautsky and others who Lenin preferred not to tackle himself, as well as detailed answers to a dozen or so questions she might be asked. 'The most important thing', he emphasized, 'is to prove that only we are the party ... Unless they accept our conditions, there will be no rapprochement let alone unity!!'[52] Armed with little more than this 'occasional advice' and a haphazard two-hour report, Inessa reluctantly set off for the Belgian capital.

The Brussels 'Unity' Conference opened at 10 am on Thursday, 16 July 1914, in the Maison du Peuple. Vandervelde sat in the chair flanked by five members of the International Socialist Bureau. In front of them were twenty-two delegates representing eleven different Russian organizations.[53] As they arranged their chairs, Huysmans asked 'Et Lénine, est-il venu ou viendra? Pourquoi donc il n'est pas venu? Franchement, pourquoi?' Popov replied that the Bolshevik delegation had been named by the Central Committee and that he 'frankly' did not know why Lenin had not been designated.[54] To several this answer was

---

[49] Lenin to Armand (before 10 July 1914), in *ibid.*, pp. 305–6 (emphasis in the original).
[50] Lenin to Armand (before 6 July 1914), in *ibid.*, p. 300 (emphasis in the original).
[51] Lenin to Armand (after 7 July 1914), in *ibid.*, pp. 314–15 (emphasis in the original).
[52] Lenin to Armand (between 10–16 July 1914), in *ibid.*, p. 308.
[53] In addition to the Bolshevik Central Committee, the Menshevik Organizational Committee, the Menshevik Duma fraction, Plekhanov's *Edinstvo*, the Vperëdists, the Bund, the Latvian Social Democrats and the Lithuanian Social Democrats, there were three different Polish groups represented.
[54] Popov to Lenin (16 July 1914), in 'Bol'sheviki na briussel'skom soveshchanii', p. 25. Unless otherwise indicated, all citations concerning the debates of the conference come from this letter (pp. 24–5), Popov's previously unpublished report to *Pravda* (pp. 26–7), or his second letter to Lenin of 21 July 1914 (pp. 30–5).

evasive and the rumour soon made the rounds that the Bolshevik leader was in fact hiding somewhere in Brussels directing the work of his delegation.[55]

Vandervelde opened the session by saying that the ISB felt unity was entirely possible and that the matter should not be reduced to figures and arguments purporting to prove the supremacy of one faction over another. 'The question', he said, "begins not with statistics but with conditions for unification.' Aksel'rod, Plekhanov and Kautsky expressed their wholehearted agreement. Kautsky then introduced a three-point agenda. The conference, he suggested, should first discuss programmatic differences preventing unity, then turn to tactical differences, and finally look at organizational differences. This beginning did not augur well for the Bolshevik delegation. Not only was Vandervelde going beyond the December resolution by suggesting a solution rather than just facilitating an 'exchange of opinions', but also much of Lenin's case was built precisely on statistics derived from newspaper circulations, trade-union resolutions and Duma elections. Moreover, Inessa had been given a long and detailed report unrelated to the suggested agenda. 'Statistics', she informed the gathering, 'are closely related to the question of unity. We have produced figures [which she promptly circulated]; the other delegations ought to do likewise.' The first order of business, she insisted, should be the hearing of prepared reports by all delegations.[56] However, since only the Latvian Social Democrats agreed with her, Kautsky's agenda was adopted.

After lunch the conference began to debate programmatic differences. G. A. Aleksinskii and S. I. Semkovskii, representing the Vperëdists and the Menshevik Organizational Committee, respectively, stated that there simply were no major differences concerning the interpretation of the party's 1903 programme. The Latvian delegate disagreed. He noted that his party rejected national-cultural autonomy as contrary to the official programme and called on the conference to affirm this position. As expected, the Bund and several Mensheviks defended the concept which had received wide support at Trotskii's August 1912 Conference. The Executive Committee sought to paper over this apparent contradiction by introducing a resolution whereby 'all Social Democratic organizations in Russia acknowledge that they accept one and the same

55 *Ibid.*, p. 30; and V. M. Kasparov to Lenin (27 July 1914), in *ibid.*, p. 35.
56 S. S. Shaumian, 'V. I. Lenin i briussel'skoe "ob"edinitel'noe" soveshchanie', *Istoriia SSSR*, 1966, no. 2, p. 35; and A. V. Ovcharova and K. V. Shakhnazarova, 'Briussel'skoe "ob"edinitel'noe" soveshchanie (iiul' 1914 g.)', *Voprosy istorii KPSS*, 1959, no. 5, p. 156 (both citing from archival sources).

programme; that 'this programme is presently subject to interpretation exclusively on the basis of the decisions of pre-split congresses'; and that 'only the restoration of unity makes new interpretations possible'.[57] At this point Armand, who, lacking a script, had been inactive in the afternoon debate, intervened to say that her delegation did not have instructions on this question and would therefore abstain. She reiterated that the conference should be listening to reports rather than taking votes. After 'warm debate' on proper procedure, one of the members of the ISB sought to preserve the semblance of unity by suggesting that the vote be postponed, the agenda discarded, and the reports heard as Inessa insisted.

That evening Popov wrote to Lenin saying that the Bolshevik dele-gation had indeed 'blundered' in the morning session 'and had not adopted a bold and independent approach'. 'But don't judge us too harshly', he implored. He urged Lenin to remember the unusual and high-powered surroundings in which they were operating and noted that 'the presidium conducted itself dictatorially toward us while showing favouritism to Plekhanov and Rosa [Luxemburg]. Many times we were not permitted to speak in the debate' and thus could not use much of the material Lenin had sent. He felt that the 'plan of the Executive Committee is clear: [to secure passage of] a plump resolution. The plan of the Liquidators is to jabber and to ignore principles.' He was certain that 'tomorrow things will go more satisfactorily' now that the meeting had given in to Bolshevik obstinacy.

The next morning the three Bolsheviks caucused at 7 am and then met with their Polish and Latvian allies to plot common strategy. Inessa was obviously nervous when she began to deliver Lenin's report. According to Popov, she 'read it in such a quiet voice' that Kautsky and Vandervelde were forced to cup their hands behind their ears and thus much of the 'value of the report was lost'. Vandervelde also started to look at his watch. After Inessa finished the first section, in which Lenin sketched the substance and history of his differences with the Menshe-viks, the chairperson interrupted to say that her allotted time was running out. As a result she was forced to omit or to summarize the second and third sections in which Lenin had provided detailed statistics to 'prove' Bolshevik superiority and traced the breakup of the Menshe-vik August Bloc to demonstrate the inability of his rivals to unite even amongst themselves. The concluding section, which Lenin considered the most important, contained his 'fourteen conditions' for unity with

---

[57] 'Bol'sheviki na briussel'skom soveshchanii', p. 26.

his opponents: 'if our *dear* comrades want unity, then here are our conditions ... take them or leave them!!'[58] These included condemnation of Liquidationism and national-cultural autonomy, closure of Menshevik newspapers where they were in competition with Bolshevik ones, subordination of the Menshevik Duma fraction to the Bolshevik Central Committee and communication only through the latter by groups abroad, acceptance by the national organizations of a unified RSDRP, etc.[59]

Lenin had foreseen that 'people will go out of their way to attack us for our "monstrous" proposals'.[60] He was not wrong. According to the police, 'the majority of the delegates were greatly disgusted with Petrova's [i.e., Armand's] report. No one expected that the impudence of the "Leninists" would reach such dimensions.'[61] Semkovskii acted 'as if his virtue had been insulted'. Plekhanov called Lenin's conditions 'the articles of a new criminal code' and felt that his uncompromising attitude was a consequence of not wanting to give up his claim to party funds now in his or the 'trustees' hands.[62] Kautsky charged that the conditions were a 'slap in the face' and a 'demand for self-destruction which no one could accept'. Vandervelde concluded that 'if they are accepted, they will create an atmosphere in which it will be impossible to breathe' and implied that the International would not sanction unity on these grounds.[63]

Debate on Lenin's report went on for the rest of the day despite the fact that the speakers were limited to one statement each of no more than fifteen minutes in duration. Hesitant support came only from Inessa's rather inarticulate Latvian and Polish allies. Some delegates, such as Trotskii, remained silent throughout the entire debate despite suggestions from the chair that statements of their positions would be welcome. Others appeared quite content to allow the Bolsheviks to dig their own grave. The Executive Committee concluded that the length and the tone of the day's debate made it inadvisable to return to the original agenda. To bring matters to an amiable conclusion, Huysmans the next morning introduced in the name of the Committee a mild resolution drafted by Kautsky. The delegates were asked to confirm 'that at the present moment there are no tactical disagreements between them

---

58 Lenin to Armand (before 4 July 1914), in Lenin, *PSS*, vol. XLVIII, p. 298 (emphasis in the original).
59 *Ibid.*, vol. XXV, pp. 384–96.   60 *Ibid.*, p. 404.
61 Report 261 in Tsiavlovskii (ed.), p. 147.
62 *Ibid.*; Lenin, *PSS*, vol. XXV, p. 528 n. 142.
63 Shaumian, 'Lenin i briussel'skom ... soveshchanie', p. 37 (citing from archival sources).

which are sufficiently important to justify the split'. Unification, it was suggested, could be achieved on the basis of the acceptance of the present programme, subordination of the minority to the decisions of the majority, recognition that the party must be illegal and that blocs with bourgeois parties were unacceptable. All groups had to agree to participate as soon as possible in a 'general congress that would resolve all questions now under dispute'.[64]

Armand was in a quandary. She could not vote for the resolution, despite its innocuous nature, since Lenin had given her explicit instructions 'not to consent to any steps in the direction of a general congress, a federation or a rapprochement, even in the slightest degree, so long as the Liquidators do not agree to our conditions'.[65] Not only had they not done so but she realized that a 'general congress' would seriously compromise Bolshevik plans for a Sixth Party Congress in August. At the other extreme, she did not have the courage to follow Lenin's other piece of advice: 'agree to *nothing*, walk out'.[66] Popov argued that it would be better simply to vote against the resolution. Inessa hesitated. She protested to the chair that the resolution was beyond the competency of the meeting and that only the Central Committee could make a decision on the matter. Vandervelde ignored these objections and in anticipation of Armand's only other alternative, threatened 'that those who do not take part in the voting will be held responsible before the International for wrecking attempts at unity and that this would be reported to the Vienna Congress' of the Socialist International scheduled to meet in August.[67] Armand, backed by Vladimirskii and the Latvians, chose Vandervelde's wrath over Lenin's or decisive action of her own by once again abstaining. The nine other delegations voted in favour of the Executive Committee's resolution. The meeting then, to the relief of its organizers and most of its participants, adjourned after passing without debate a very general resolution endorsing the unification of the various Polish factions.

Lenin anxiously awaited word on the outcome of the proceedings in Poronin. Throughout the conference he criticized his hard-pressed delegation for failing to keep him informed. He bombarded them with last-minute instructions, new information concerning Vandervelde's trip to Russia, and protests about rumours that he was in Brussels.[68]

---

[64] The resolution was first published in *Informatsionnyi listok zagranichnoi organizatsii Bunda*, no. 7 (January 1915), p. 15.

[65] Lenin, *PSS*, vol. XXV, p. 400.   [66] *Ibid.*, p. 403 (emphasis in the original).

[67] Cited in V. I. Lenin, *Sochineniia*, 2nd edn, vol. XVII (Moscow, 1935), p. 745 n. 177.

[68] Lenin, *PSS*, vol. XLVIII, pp. 318 and 323; *Biog. khr.*, vol. III, pp. 254, 258–9; Shaumian, 'Lenin i briussel'skoe . . . soveshchanie', pp. 41–2.

When information about the results of the Brussels Conference finally reached Poronin, an impromptu meeting of the Central Committee thanked the delegation for its 'skilful and vigorous defence of the party line'[69] and Lenin started to make plans to counteract the harm done.

The consequences of his heavy-handed attempt to 'prove that only we are the party' at Brussels could have been disastrous. The day after the conference ended all but the Latvian and Bolshevik delegates met privately to plot common strategy. They agreed to forget past differences, to open their respective journals to one another, and to meet again on the eve of the Tenth Congress of the Socialist International where they would be represented by a joint delegation. They undoubtedly would have been supported by the leaders of the ISB who made it quite clear that Bolshevik conduct at Brussels would be called to the attention of the congress. Those 'idiots and intrigants [*sic*] with the aid of Kautsky will get a resolution *against* us at the Vienna Congress', wrote Lenin in English to Armand. 'Soit!!'[70] Very likely the result of this resolution would have been the expulsion of his party from the European socialist movement. Lenin's response to this threat was to turn his back on Vienna and to reschedule his own Sixth Congress for the same time in Poronin.[71]

On 19 July he asked Armand to come to Galicia beforehand, since 'there is tons of work to be done', and to report on the Brussels Conference to the Bolshevik congress. In the same letter he once again thanked his 'dear and dearest friend':

> You have rendered a very great service to our party! I am especially thankful because you have replaced me ... Write – are you very tired, very upset? Are you angry at me for having persuaded you to go?[72]

Not surprisingly, she was upset both with having been pressured into going and with the criticism she had to endure from Popov, from leaders of the ISB and, at times, from Lenin himself. As a result, she found the

---

[69] 'Podgotovka s"ezda bol'shevistskoi partii v 1914 g.', *Istoricheskii arkhiv*, 1958, no. 6, p. 27.

[70] Lenin to Armand (before 24 July 1914), in V. I. Lenin, *Collected Works*, 45 vols. (Moscow, 1960–70), vol. XLIII, p. 426 (emphasis in the original). Huysmans, in his correspondence with various European socialist leaders, made it quite clear that 'we shall impose *unity* at Vienna'. See, for example, his letter of 18 July 1914 to Friedrich Adler, quoted in *Aspects of International Socialism, 1871–1914: Essays by Georges Haupt* (Cambridge, 1987), p. 130 (emphasis in the original).

[71] The Sixth Party Congress was rescheduled for 20–25 August. Since the congress of the Second International was to open on the 23rd, it is possible the Bolsheviks might have adjourned in time to show up in Vienna en masse.

[72] Lenin, *PSS*, vol. XLVIII, pp. 323–4. The salutation and first two sentences quoted are in English in the original.

prospect of making a report on the conference at the party congress 'extremely unpleasant'[73] and she made plans to return to Russia with her children rather than going to Poronin as Lenin had requested. These signs of independence and disobedience caused Lenin to write her two more letters in July 1914 which Soviet authorities chose not to publish.[74] While he would write another ninety-eight letters to her during the course of the next six years, never again would he use the familiar *ty* form of address.

*   *   *

These internal problems kept Lenin from paying much attention to the rising tensions in the Balkans. The day before the ISB issued its invitations to attend the 'Unity' Conference, Archduke Franz Ferdinand was assassinated at Sarajevo not far from where Inessa was vacationing. Ten days after the conference closed Austria declared war on Serbia. The outbreak of the Great War wiped the slate clean: the new anti-Bolshevik coalition dissolved, the Vienna Congress was cancelled, Lenin found himself under arrest in Galicia rather than presiding over a party congress of his own, and Inessa's trip to Russia was called off. She instead sent her children back by way of Italy, England and Archangel while she made her own way from Lovran to Switzerland.[75]

Armand arrived without a passport after a difficult trip in mid-August 1914.[76] For the next month and a half she lived in the small resort town of Les Avants high above Montreux – an area which she knew from earlier visits to Switzerland. Poor health may have been the reason she chose Les Avants, which was well known for its sanatoria. Lenin had been concerned about her health immediately after the Brussels Conference and again in late September enquired in broken English 'Do you make walks? Do you feed better now?'[77] It is also plausible that she picked the Montreux area because of Nicholas Rubakin's renowned Russian library in Baugy-sur-Clarens, a suburb of the city. Rubakin's library and the musical soirées that were held there on many evenings served as a magnet for Russian *émigrés* in Switzerland.[78] Among the Bolsheviks who made Baugy their headquarters

---

[73] Cited in Lenin to Armand (before 24 July 1914), in *ibid.*, p. 325.

[74] *Biog. khr.*, vol. III, pp. 258–9, 261.

[75] Podliashuk, p. 158. Fréville ('Portrait d'Inessa Armand', p. 96) claims that she sent her children back on the last boat from Trieste to Odessa.

[76] Stal' in Krupskaia (ed.), *Pamiati*, p. 42; Podliashuk, p. 176.

[77] Lenin, *Collected Works*, vol. XLIII, p. 433. See also Lenin, *PSS*, vol. XLVIII, p. 326.

[78] Alfred Erich Senn, *Nicholas Rubakin: A Life for Books* (Newtonville, Mass., 1977), pp. 24–6.

during the first year of the war were Elena Rozmirovich, A. A. Troianovskii, N. V. Krylenko, G. L. Piatakov and E. B. Bosh. N. I. Bukharin,
who lived in nearby Lausanne, frequently came over for political discussions and to use the library. Armand formed reasonably close ties
with the 'Baugy Group': she was invited to contribute to their proposed
journal Zvezda[79] and she later joined them in questioning and at times
opposing some of Lenin's policies both during the war and again
immediately after the October Revolution.

One of Inessa's first chores after arriving in Switzerland was to raise
money to enable Lenin and Krupskaia to make the trip from Galicia. On
25 August she wrote to Olga Ravich in Geneva telling her that a letter
had been received from Zinoviev by other comrades in Bern informing
them that 'V. I. had been arrested – that is for certain.' Zinoviev was
reasonably confident Lenin would soon be released but added that 'he
had been picked up without any money and asked that some be
obtained'.[80] Three days later Inessa reported that the money had been
raised through unspecified sources and had been sent to Lenin. With the
help of this money and of Victor Adler's intercession with the Austrian
authorities, Lenin and his wife made it to Bern on 5 September. Lenin
liked the Swiss capital. It 'is a small, dull but quite civilized town', he
wrote to his sister Mariia, and 'the libraries here are good'.[81] At his
urging,[82] Inessa joined them in early October.

Getting permission to live in Bern proved to be a problem. She
reported to the police, as required, on 7 October. Two months later,
when it became evident that her stay in Switzerland was going to be
prolonged, she applied for an *aufenthaltsbewilligung* or foreigner's residence permit that would allow her to remain in the canton for a year. In
her application Armand stated that she wished to continue her studies
at the University of Bern and, in lieu of a valid Russian external
passport, she submitted her licence certificate from the Université
Nouvelle of Brussels. To the legalistic Swiss this did not constitute proper
documentation and she therefore was informed on 22 January that she
would have to post a bond of 1160 Swiss francs in order to get a
provisional residence permit. When she pointed out that she was cut off
from her usual source of support, since her husband was in Moscow, the
authorities relented by agreeing to accept 100 francs if she promised to

---

[79] V. Karpinskii, 'Vladimir Il'ich za granitsei v 1914–1917 gg.', *Zapiski Instituta Lenina*,
   vol. II (1927), p. 74.
[80] Cited in Iakushina, *Lenin i Zagranichnaia organizatsiia*, pp. 258–9.
[81] Lenin to M. I. Ul'ianova (22 December 1914 and 9 February 1915), in Lenin, *PSS*,
   vol. LV, pp. 357 and 358.
[82] *Ibid.*, vol. XLIX, p. 7.

pay an additional 75 francs each quarter. A month later, when the 100 francs was not forthcoming, the director of the Bern police rescinded her temporary permission to stay in Switzerland and ordered that deportation proceedings be commenced in eight days time. At this point, the harassed and apparently impoverished Armand sought political and financial assistance. Perhaps with Lenin's help, she contacted Karl Moor, a socialist member of the Bern Council. Moor intervened with the police but was told he would have to guarantee in writing to cover 'the costs of any damages Mme Armand might cause the state' before a provisional *aufenthaltsbewilligung* would be granted. He did so and on 16 June 1915 Armand received her long-awaited permit.[83]

While these technicalities were being worked out, Inessa rented an apartment at 23 Drosselweg several blocks from the Ul'ianovs and close to the Bremgartenwald. As Krupskaia remembered:

we used to roam for hours along the woodland paths, which were bestrewn with yellow leaves. Mostly the three of us went on these walks together – Vladimir Ilyich, Inessa and myself ... Sometimes we would sit for hours on a sunny wooded hillside, Ilyich jotting down notes for his articles and speeches, and polishing his formulations, I studying Italian with the aid of a Toussaint textbook, and Inessa sewing a skirt and basking in the autumn sunshine – she had not quite recovered yet from the effects of her imprisonment [in 1912–13]. In the evening we would all gather at Grigory's (Zinoviev's) tiny room ...[84]

While Ilyich was 'polishing his formulations', Armand was engaged in more productive pastimes than just sewing and sunbathing. In December she published a long unsigned article on 'The Women Workers Movement and the War' in *Sotsial-demokrat* in which she argued that the war put greater responsibility on female workers since male workers were now in the army. Women could not by themselves cause a revolution but they could do the preparatory work and they could contribute to the restoration of a true international socialist movement.[85] The need for a new body to replace the Second International, many of whose leaders had supported their governments' war

---

[83] The record of these legal and financial formalities is preserved in the Bern Staatsarchiv, BB4. 1. 946. Akten der Polizei-Direktion. 1914, file 4352/14. I am indebted to John Keep for his generous assistance in obtaining this information. A year later, when Lenin and Krupskaia found that their Bern residence permit was invalid in Zurich, two other Swiss socialists – Otto Lang and Fritz Platten – came to the rescue by guaranteeing their bond of 3000 francs (*Biog. khr.*, vol. III, p. 503). See also Alfred Erich Senn, 'Russian Émigré Funds in Switzerland, 1916: An Okhrana Report', *International Review of Social History*, vol. XIII (1968), pp. 77–8.

[84] Krupskaya, *Lenin*, p. 292.

[85] 'Zhenskoe rabochee dvizhenie i voina', *Sotsial-demokrat*, no. 34 (5 December 1914), p. 2.

efforts, was emerging as a major theme in Lenin's own writing at the time, though he did not attribute much of a role to women either in its creation or in preparing the way for revolution in Russia. At his suggestion, Armand went to Geneva in late 1914 to give a lecture in French on 'Different Tendencies among Russian Socialists concerning the War'.[86] All things considered, 'life here [in Bern] is relatively quiet', she wrote to her daughter Inna. 'I keep myself busy in the usual way – I go to the library, read and write articles.'[87]

In the same letter she mentioned a new and rather controversial project she was working on.

I want to write a pamphlet on the family. I already have some interesting material. If it comes out, I'll dedicate it to you and Varia [Varvara]. Your questions – remember last fall [in Lovran]? – about love, the family, etc., were largely responsible for spurring me on to write this pamphlet.[88]

Other factors in her own past – her unconventional married life, her work with prostitutes, her interest in the free love debate at the 1908 Women's Congress, perhaps her recent reading of Vinnichenko's novel – also contributed to her decision to write a pamphlet on love, marriage and the family. It was a time when the theories of Sigmund Freud and the writings of the Bloomsbury Group were making discussions of sexuality commonplace in European intellectual circles. There is little evidence, however, that much of this discussion permeated the male bastions of the Russian Social Democratic Party. These topics were not discussed at party schools, in party newspapers or even in *Rabotnitsa*. The only Russian Marxist to have approached them from a socialist and feminist perspective was Aleksandra Kollantai and her writings were still relatively unknown and even less appreciated.

In January 1915 Armand left Bern for a few weeks to work on her pamphlet in the solitude of the Swiss mountains. The first result of these endeavours was an outline on the 'family question' which she sent to Lenin for comment. What she got back on 17 January was typical Lenin – it should not have surprised her but it also certainly could not have pleased her.

Dear Friend!
I very strongly advise you to write the prospectus for the pamphlet in greater detail. Otherwise, too much is unclear.
One opinion I must express right at the outset: I would advise you to throw

---

[86] See letter from Lenin to V. A. Karpinskii and S. N. Ravich (21 November 1914), in Lenin, *PSS*, vol. XLIX, p. 33.
[87] Letter to Inna Armand (1915), in Armand, *Stat'i*, p. 239.   [88] *Ibid.*

out completely point 3 – 'the demand (on the part of the women) for freedom of love'. This is not really a proletarian but rather a bourgeois demand.

After all, what do you mean by this phrase? What *can* be meant by it?

1 Freedom *from* material (i.e., financial) considerations in love affairs?
2 [Freedom] *from* material worries?
3 From religious prejudices?
4 From parental prohibitions, etc.?
5 From societal prejudices?
6 From the narrow circumstances of one's environment (peasant or petty-bourgeois or bourgeois-intellectual)?
7 From the restraints of the law, the courts and the police?
8 From seriousness in love?
9 From childbirth?
10 Freedom of adultery, etc.?

I have listed many (but of course not all) of the nuances. You mean, of course, not nos. 8–10 but either nos. 1–7 or something *like* nos. 1–7. But you must choose a different designation for nos. 1–7 since 'freedom of love' does not express this idea precisely.

The public, the readers of the pamphlet, will *inevitably* understand 'freedom of love' to mean something like nos. 8–10 despite *your intentions to the contrary.*

Just because in contemporary society the most vocal, noisy and 'elite' classes understand freedom of love to mean nos. 8–10, for this very reason it is not a proletarian but a bourgeois demand.

For the proletariat nos. 1–2 are the most important, and then nos. 1–7, and these, properly speaking, are not 'freedom of love'.

It does not matter what you *subjectively* 'mean' by this term. What does matter is the *objective logic* of class relations in affairs of love.

Friendly shake hands!

W.I.[89]

Lenin quite obviously ignored all aspects of her prospectus except point 3 – the right of women to freedom of love – and he then tried to impose his own 'objective logic of class relations' on 'affairs of love'. Armand's response, which like the prospectus itself has never been published, must have been spirited for it elicited a much longer, even more pedantic, didactic and disdainful reply from Lenin on 24 January. She rejected his contention that free love was simply a bourgeois demand; to her, freedom in love and in sexual relations was a woman's demand which transcended class. 'If you refute [my contention]', responded Lenin,

---

[89] Lenin to Armand (17 January 1915), in Lenin, *PSS*, vol. XLIX, pp. 51–2 (salutation and farewell in English in the original, emphasis in the original).

then you must show that this interpretation is 1) wrong (and replace it with another ...) or 2) incomplete (and add what is missing) or 3) cannot be divided into proletarian and bourgeois [views of the question].

You did not do either one, or the other, or the third.[90]

Armand also 'did not understand how it is *possible to identify* "freedom of love"' with 'freedom of adultery' which she certainly had not done in her prospectus. This reasonable observation caused Lenin to snap back:

So it appears that *I* 'identify' the one with the other and you mean to shatter and destroy *me* for it. How are you going to do this? *Bourgeois women* understand freedom of love to mean points 8–10 – that is my thesis ... You are completely forgetting the objective and class point of view, you are going over on the 'offensive' against *me* as if I am 'identifying' freedom of love with points 8–10. This is marvellous, simply marvellous ....

In defending her earlier position, Inessa had suggested that a 'short-lived passion and/or love affair' could be 'more poetic and pure' than 'the love-less kisses ... of a married couple'. To Lenin this was 'not a contrast of class *types* but something like an "incident"' better 'worked out as a theme of a novel' than used as an example in a serious party pamphlet.

As Inessa and others were to find out, arguing with Lenin was a frustrating experience. He showed a marked lack of comprehension of her viewpoint, he persisted in translating her arguments into his own terms and then turning them against her, and he tried to overwhelm her with 'logic' and class 'analysis' that could not be questioned. He justified his none-too-subtle attack on her initiative by saying he was afraid the enemies of the party would take 'appropriate passages' like free love out of context 'and turn your pamphlet into grist for their mill and distort your ideas in the eyes of the workers ... The only reason I am sending you this letter is so that you might examine the prospectus in greater detail.' In condescending fashion, he suggested that she translate his ten points and her rejoinder and then read them to a female French socialist friend: 'watch her [reactions], listen to her as attentively as possible' and then presumably she would drop the demand for freedom of love as he suggested.

What is clear from this one-sided correspondence is that to Lenin and Armand 'free love' meant two very different things: Lenin stressed the negative side and Inessa the positive. While he may have framed his arguments in a class analysis, free love meant to Lenin promiscuity and

90 This, and all succeeding quotes, are from Lenin's letter to Amand of 24 January 1915, in *ibid.*, pp. 54–7 (emphasis, where used, is Lenin's).

147

multiple marriage partners. In capitalist society it was a reflection of bourgeois decadence; in socialist society it was a narcotic, a stimulus that undermined the concentration, self-control and self-discipline of communist youth. He accepted the 'glass of water' analogy with free love and he specifically rejected its implication – that when one is thirsty, one should drink. This theory, he told Clara Zetkin in 1920, 'is completely un-Marxist, and moreover, anti-social ... Of course, thirst must be satisfied. But will the normal man in normal circumstances lie down in the gutter and drink out of a puddle, or out of a glass with a rim greasy from many lips?'[91]

Since Lenin's Victorian, prudish outlook on sex was shared by his Stalinist successors, it is not surprising that these two letters were the first of his voluminous correspondence with Inessa Armand to appear in print. 'The publication of these letters', noted the Marx-Engels-Lenin Institute in 1939, 'has great significance for the strengthening and development of the socialist family, for the communist education of workers, and for the fight against remnants of capitalism in marriage.'[92] Inessa Armand and her version of freedom of love were ignored as writers concentrated on attacking 'the enemies of socialism – Trotskyites, Zinovievites, Bukharinites – who preach a wrecker's bourgeois-anarchist theory about the disappearance in a socialist society of the family and of "free love".'[93]

Some Western writers have accepted Lenin's definition of free love and have without justification accused Armand of both preaching and practising this theory.[94] Nowhere in any of her published writings or letters does she advocate sexual adventurism or promiscuity or the 'glass of water' theory. There is no evidence in her private life after the death of Vladimir in 1909 of casual romantic attachments. Apart from Lenin himself, only one man. G. I. Safarov, appears with any regularity in her life and he was seventeen years her junior.[95] There is perhaps

91 Clara Zetkin, *Lenin on the Woman Question* (New York, 1934), pp. 11–12.
92 'Pis'ma V. I. Lenina Inesse Armand', *Bol'shevik*, 1939, no. 13, p. 58.
93 O. Voitinskaia, 'Leninskie pis'ma k Inesse Armand', *Pod znamenem marksizma*, 1939, no. 11, p. 72.
94 McNeal, 'Women in the Russian Radical Movement', p. 155; Hayden, p. 76; Cathy Porter, introduction to Alexandra Kollontai, *A Great Love* (New York, 1981), p. 13. Solzhenitsyn (p. 75) has Lenin worrying in Zurich that Inessa was practising what he thought she was preaching with regard to 'free love'.
95 Safarov was a member of the KZO in 1912, travelled to St Petersburg with Armand during that summer, was in Paris and Switzerland at similar times from 1914 to 1917, and returned with his wife on the same 'sealed train' to Russia. There is, however, no evidence to support Stefan Possony's assertion (pp. 147 and 208) that they were romantically involved.

more circumstantial evidence of a continuing intimate relationship with her former husband Alexander, whom she saw and wrote to on numerous occasions after 1909, than there is of casual affairs with *émigré* Bolsheviks such as Safarov.

In contrast to Lenin's conventional, negative, male and bourgeois interpretation of free love, Inessa equated freedom of love with a freedom to choose one's marriage partner, with marriage based on personal commitments between two equal people rather than on a contract, with a monogamous relationship free of religious and societal hypocrisy, and perhaps with the freedom of no love. She followed these precepts in her relations with Alexander and Vladimir Armand. She argued against the economic and legal constraints placed on women by bourgeois marriage in 1908.[96] There is no doubt that her 1915 pamphlet, had it appeared, would have advocated sexual emancipation and sexual equality. To her, these were women's demands, not class demands, and were based on her own feminist instincts and background rather than on economic analysis. Since she and Lenin came at the problem from different directions, it is not surprising that they reached different conclusions.

That she did indeed believe in 'seriousness' in love and saw love as involving feeling and commitment and not just as an exercise in erotic pleasure is evident in a long letter which she sent to her sixteen-year-old daughter Inna at the same time as she was working on her prospectus for Lenin.[97] In the letter she contrasted the views of love and women held by Tolstoy and the classical Greeks. She began by quoting Tolstoy's statement in the *Kreutzer Sonata* which apparently had bothered Inna: 'Chastity is not a rule or an order, but an ideal.' Tolstoy, she said,

considered love the greatest sin and disgrace which people should avoid in every possible way. This worldview is rooted in the Middle Ages, and the founding of women's and men's monasteries is nominally based on this view. In the monasteries they sought complete chastity, i.e., the same ideal which Tolstoy invites us to pursue ... Ascetics of the Middle Ages ... considered women to be a tool of the devil, sent to earth especially to lead people astray. And their attitude toward love? Asceticism can arise only because of the most crude and primitive attitudes toward love. And what about Tolstoy? Tolstoy, of course, does not look at woman as the tool of the devil – he was born too late for this – but his view on love is as crude and primitive as that of the ascetics of the Middle Ages, and he protests against the poeticization of love because he does not understand its poetry.

[96] See letter to V. E. Armand (mid-December 1908), in Armand, *Stat'i*, p. 208.
[97] This letter in Armand's *Stat'i* (pp. 246–50) is dated by the editor as 'fall in 1916' but from internal evidence it is obvious it was written in December 1914.

Inessa then juxtaposed these views with those of the Greeks whom she felt had 'a completely different outlook on life and love'.

The Greeks worshiped beauty – they looked freely at love and considered it is wonderful to love, that it is necessary to love, but there was little that was spiritual in their attitude toward beauty and love. They loved the beauty of the body and they did not need the 'soul' at all. In contemporary society the most vivid representatives of Hellenism are perhaps the French. Read, for example, the stories of Maupassant (by the way, I ask you not to delve deeply into Maupassant – there is a lot in him which would be unpleasant for you) ... [The Greeks] didn't seek either a friend or a comrade in woman – they sought beauty, a bit of wit, the ability to sing, to play or dance; in a word, delight and diversion. As a wife, she is a slave, locked up in her own house, as in a dungeon, and abandoned by her husband. She does not exist for herself, as befits a human being, but only to bear children and keep house. Not only respect but also love are usually out of the question – she is simply the head slave of her husband.

Inessa concluded that

the attitudes of both asceticism and Hellenism with respect to women and love are coarse and primitive. Hellenism is more beautiful, more natural, and it doesn't have that specific aftertaste of sin which makes asceticism especially repulsive ... As life becomes more complex (like the relationships among people), that which we call culture has grown; not only thought but also feeling has been enriched; that, which earlier among animals and primitive peoples was only instinct (as, for example, with respect to maternity), has turned from instinct into feeling with a thousand tints and nuances; new attitudes and new feelings have arisen among people, which animals and savages do not know at all or know only in embryonic form. Love is also a product of culture and civilization – animals and savages do not know love, do not know that complex 'poeticization', full of the most complex psychological interaction (and such love does exist). But read the *Kreutzer Sonata* and you will see that there is not a particle of love – only instinct reigns. It seems that in today's society – alongside the highest, most complex and precise manifestations of love – there are people who in love feel completely like savages. I would add that the *majority* still feels this way in love. *Everyone* marries or indulges in lust but *very few* love or have loved. But more about this ... in the next letter [Armand's emphasis].

Unfortunately, the 'next letter', if it were ever written, has not been published and thus her more detailed views on sexuality *per se* are unknown.

After receiving Lenin's unhelpful and discouraging critique of her prospectus, Inessa still continued to collect material on the question of marriage and the family.[98] In March and April 1915, however, she was

98 Podliashuk, p. 165.

once again called upon to serve as Lenin's 'Girl Friday' at three socialist conferences held in Bern. That summer, she told her daughter in confidence, whenever rain kept her from hiking in the mountains, she had resumed work on the pamphlet.[99] Regrettably, for anyone interested in the evolution of Armand's feminist thought, the brochure was never finished or at least never published. According to her Soviet biographer, this was because 'Lenin's critique destroyed her arguments; to write it all the same, without considering Lenin's opinion, she organically could not do.'[100] One suspects that this is only part of the answer. Perhaps the project was too much for her. She was never a prolific writer and unlike Kollontai never felt comfortable writing about theoretical matters. Perhaps, like Kollontai in this regard, she came to the conclusion that in wartime she should devote her attention to more pressing political problems. It is also possible that she decided that the pamphlet simply was not worth having to endure Lenin's continued criticism and brow beating.

*   *   *

In 1915 four socialist conferences were held in or near Bern – the Conference of Foreign Sections of the RSDRP (27 February–4 March), the International Socialist Women's Conference (26–28 March), the International Socialist Youth Conference (4–6 April), and the Zimmerwald Conference (5–8 September). Inessa Armand was the only Bolshevik to attend all four meetings; she was the leading organizer of the Women's Conference; and she served as Lenin's spokesperson at the Women's and Youth Conferences just as she had in Brussels less than a year earlier. As a result of these conferences, she gained increased familiarity with the workings of the international socialist movement and perhaps more confidence in her own abilities. She also on occasion differed with her party leader in public and questioned his right to be her ventriloquist in private.

The Conference of Foreign Sections of the RSDRP was called in an attempt to repair the damage done by the war to the organizational structure of the Bolshevik Party and to endorse Lenin's theses concerning the war. The party's Central Committee, formerly located in Galicia, had disintegrated with the outbreak of the war and the concurrent arrest or isolation of most of its members in Russia. By 1915 it existed only in the persons of Lenin and Zinoviev in Bern. The Committee

---

[99] See letter to Inna Armand (summer 1915), in Armand, *Stat'i*, p. 230.
[100] Podliashuk, p. 192.

of Foreign Organizations was in even worse shape. Three of its remaining four elected members in Paris volunteered for service in the French army and the fourth suggested that the body should be disbanded. Liudmila Stal' and her husband G. N. Kotov, who had been co-opted to the committee just before the war, tried to pick up the pieces. When their own efforts failed, they wrote Armand asking that she rejoin the KZO or at least that she use her influence to get the Paris Bolshevik Section to back their work.[101] There is no evidence that her intervention, even if it were forthcoming, had a positive result.

Since the war made the calling of a true party congress or conference with elected representatives from Russia impossible, Lenin had to settle for a conference of representatives from Bolshevik sections abroad. It was in fact almost entirely a conference of Bolshevik sections in Switzerland. Of the nineteen delegates, nine lived in Bern and six in Baugy-sur-Clarens. Only A. G. Shliapnikov, representing Paris, came from outside the country.[102] Inessa Armand represented an otherwise non-existent 'Women's Group'. This homogeneous group of Bolsheviks gathered in the Schweizerbund Café which offered a cramped, extremely dirty but cheap meeting room on Lenggasstrasse, within walking distance of Lenin's apartment.[103]

The creation of a new KZO was accomplished with relative ease. The only point of contention was whether its members should be drawn from several cities, as Armand proposed, or concentrated in one place as before. It was ultimately decided that it should be made up of five Bolsheviks living in Bern – Inessa, Krupskaia, Zinaida Lilina, G. L. Shklovskii, and V. M. Kasparov.[104] Much to Inessa's relief, Krupskaia took over as secretary of the body and thus had the prime duty of corresponding with the various sections and trying to unify Bolshevism in western Europe. The new KZO also took on an additional function of assisting Russian prisoners of war in German and Austrian camps. Under Shklovskii's leadership, a Commission for Intellectual Help to Prisoners was established with Inessa Armand as one of its members. The commission sent letters and literature to POW camps and helped to

---

101 Iakushina, *Lenin i Zagranichnaia organizatsiia*, pp. 249–54.
102 M. Syromiatnikova, 'Bernskaia konferentsiia zagranichnykh organizatsii RSDRP v 1915 g.', *Proletarskaia revoliutsiia*, 1925, no. 5 (40), p. 158. Krupskaia held by proxy the vote of the London Section, Piatakov and Bosh, who had just arrived in Baugy by way of New York, Japan and Siberia, were said to represent organizations in Russia.
103 G. L. Shklovskii, 'Vospominaniia uchastnikov Bernskoi konferentsii', *Proletarskaia revoliutsiia*, 1925, no. 5 (40), p. 182.
104 Syromiatnikova, 'Bernskaia konferentsiia', pp. 164 and 175.

set up libraries and camp newspapers. By 1917 ties had been established with more than 300 POWs in 75 different camps.[105]

From Lenin's point of view, the most important question discussed at the Bern Conference was the party's stand on the war. He had originally spelled out his theses to a small group of Bolsheviks on 6 September 1914, the day after his arrival in Bern. While these had subsequently been approved by a group of Bolsheviks in Petrograd and issued in the form of a party manifesto,[106] Lenin wanted a wider endorsement abroad and particularly from the 'Baugy Group' which had expressed reservations about some of his key slogans.[107] The ensuing debate, which was the 'most complicated and confused' of the conference,[108] began before the Baugy contingent arrived. To Lenin's relief, his basic slogans – 'transformation of the present imperialist war into a civil war', the defeat of tsarist Russia as the 'lesser evil', and the establishment of a new International – were accepted.[109] A subsidiary slogan, however, caused long and acrimonious debate in which Inessa Armand was a major participant. According to the original manifesto, 'the immediate political slogan of European Social Democrats should be the formation of a republican United States of Europe'. Inessa 'vehemently opposed' this slogan[110] on the grounds that democracy of the type found in the United States was impossible in Europe because of imperialistic pressures and conflicts of interest among nations of the area. Even if a United States of Europe did emerge, it would be used only to attack the more progressive United States of America. In the debate Armand and her two supporters were branded 'the anarchists' and they in turn charged Lenin with 'opportunism'.[111] While Inessa's amendment aimed at watering down the slogan was overwhelmingly defeated,[112] she was put on a revision commission with Lenin and Zinoviev to draft the final wording for Lenin's resolution which the conference had

[105] Shklovskii, 'Vospominaniia . . . Bernskoi konferentsii', pp. 191–2; Iakushina, *Lenin i Zagranichnaia organizatsiia*, pp. 360–73.
[106] *Sotsial-demokrat*, no. 33 (19 October 1914), p. 1.
[107] Alfred Erich Senn, 'The Bolshevik Conference in Bern, 1915', *Slavic Review*, vol. XXV, no. 4 (December 1966), p. 676.
[108] Syromiatnikova, 'Bernskaia konferentsiia', p. 159.
[109] The resolutions of the conference will be found in Olga H. Gankin and H. H. Fisher, *The Bolsheviks and the World War: The Origins of the Third International* (Stanford, 1940), pp. 182–6.
[110] Krupskaya, *Lenin*, p. 297. See also M. Kharitonov, 'Iz vospominanii', *Zapiski Instituta Lenina*, vol. II (1927), p. 120; and Shklovskii, 'Vospominaniia . . . Bernskoi konferentsii', p. 186.
[111] O. Ravich, 'Iz vospominanii o Vladimire Il'iche', *Proletarskaia revoliutsiia*, 1929, nos. 8/9, p. 99.
[112] Syromiatnikova, 'Bernskaia konferentsiia', p. 175.

accepted in principle. Before the commission could complete its work, however, Lenin had a talk with Karl Radek who was not a delegate to the conference. Radek also expressed reservations about the slogan and said these were shared by Rosa Luxemburg. When the Bolshevik leader returned to the Schweizerbund Café the next day, he reversed his original position and suggested that the slogan be removed from the resolution and referred to *Sotsial-demokrat* for further discussion of its economic implications.[113] The only article to appear was ironically an unsigned one by Lenin himself attacking the idea of a United States of Europe. This was followed by a statement of the editors that the slogan was incorrect and thus had been withdrawn.[114]

Armand was also involved, though more indirectly, in Lenin's efforts to patch up relations with the Baugy Group. He had been concerned when she told him earlier of the group's plans to publish *Zvezda*. Lenin felt that at a time when the party was hard pressed to pay for the publication of *Sotsial-demokrat*, private groups should not be putting out their own papers even if they had the resources to do so. After extensive correspondence and at least one 'extremely long' telephone call in January, Bukharin and his friends backed down.[115] Before their arrival in Bern, the conference duly approved the more frequent publication of *Sotsial-demokrat*. Once the group appeared, Lenin hastened to effect a reconciliation. He had long conversations with Bukharin on points already agreed upon in the resolution on the war and reached a consensus on almost all issues. For tactical reasons, he found it advantageous to drop Inessa from the revision commission and replace her with Bukharin.[116] Armand's reaction to this slight is unknown. Also unknown was her reaction to some of the reservations raised at the conference by Bukharin and other members of the Baugy Group concerning Lenin's theories on 'defence of the fatherland' and the 'right of nations to self-determination'.[117] As these debates sharpened over the

---

113 Shklovskii, 'Vospominaniia . . . Bernskoi konferentsii', pp. 187–8.
114 *Sotsial-demokrat*, no. 40 (29 March 1915), p. 2; [V. I. Lenin], 'O lozunge Soedinennykh Shtatov Evropy', *Sotsial-demokrat*, no. 44 (23 August 1915), p. 2.
115 Karpinskii, 'Vladimir Il'ich', p. 74. Much of this correspondence has recently been published in 'Iz perepiski N. I. Bukharina', *Izvestiia TsK KPSS*, 1989, no. 11, pp. 199–202, 211 n. 27. In the spring of 1915 a new theoretical journal *Kommunist* did appear but with Lenin and Zinoviev on its editorial board along with Bukharin, Bosh and Piatakov.
116 Syromiatnikova, 'Bernskaia konferentsiia', pp. 159, 165, 174; Shklovskii, 'Vospominaniia . . . Bernskoi konferentsii', p. 184.
117 Stephen F. Cohen denies these were issues of contention as early as the Bern meeting (*Bukharin and the Bolshevik Revolution: A Political Biography, 1888–1938* [New York, 1974], pp. 23–4). For evidence to the contrary, see Ravich, 'Iz vospominanii', p. 99, and Gankin and Fisher, p. 174.

course of the next two years, Inessa increasingly found herself disagreeing with her mentor on these issues as well.

Once he had his own party in line, Lenin sought support for his theses from radical elements in other European socialist parties. His first chance to get this support came when the Conference of Socialist Women opened in Bern three weeks after the Conference of Foreign Sections of the RSDRP disbanded. The women's conference had been in the planning stage for over four months. 'A good deal of preliminary work was involved', recalled Krupskaia, 'the brunt of which was borne by Inessa.'[118] Had this work been successful and had the conference been called solely by female Bolsheviks in Bern, as originally intended, Lenin might have received the endorsement he sought albeit from a very small group of women. Instead, his assistants, and Armand in particular, were outmanoeuvred by Clara Zetkin with the result that the Bolsheviks were badly outvoted at the ensuing conference.

In November 1914 Armand, in the name of foreign editors of *Rabotnitsa*, wrote to Zetkin suggesting that an informal or unofficial conference of left-wing socialist women be called to discuss common attitudes toward the war and the Second International. By implication, the conference would be limited to women who were likely to support the transformation of the present war into a civil war, the condemnation of the leaders of the Second International who had voted for war credits, and the creation of a new Third International. A month later an appeal based on this letter was drafted by Armand and sent to left-wing socialists throughout Europe calling on them to join in the 'struggle against every kind of civil peace and in favour of a war against war, a war closely connected with civil war and social revolution', by attending the proposed informal conference.[119] Favourable responses were supposedly received from women in seven countries.[120] The key, however, was Zetkin's response of 2 January 1915. The long-time head of the International Women's Secretariat and one of the leading left-wing German socialists wrote Armand that the conference would be useful but that certain obstacles might prevent its convocation in the manner the Bolsheviks suggested. She was concerned with the problem

---

[118] Krupskaya, *Lenin*, p. 300.
[119] Armand, *Stat'i*, pp. 27–8; Gankin and Fisher, p. 286. See also 'O mezhdunarodnoi zhenskoi sotsialisticheskoi konferentsii v 1915 g.', *Istoricheskii arkhiv*, 1960, no. 3, p. 109.
[120] 'Iz istorii bor'by Bol'shevikov za proletarskii internatsionalizm v mezhdunarodnom zhenskom sotsialisticheskom dvizhenii (1915 g.)', *Novaia i noveishaia istoriia*, 1959, no. 4, p. 108.

of identifying a 'left-wing socialist' and with getting funding for delegates' travel to an unofficial conference. She noted that some women
would not wish to oppose openly the moderate policies of their own
party leaders or risk losing popular support at home by attending an
exclusively radical conference abroad. Zetkin also lectured Armand on
her poor conspiratorial technique. It was 'extremely careless to write
openly about the question. Your letter was opened and read by the
military authorities.' Henceforth, she would write only in German, talk
about the conference as a concert or family affair, and leave the
envelope unsealed.[121]

Inessa took this criticism to heart and optimistically chose to read
Zetkin's letter as qualified support. 'We are very happy that you approve
of Lucy's marriage', i.e., the proposed left-wing women's conference,
she responded in late January.

Although we were worried that the family would be against the marriage, it
has, quite to the contrary, gained general sympathy and all our relatives are
offering their best wishes to the bride and groom-to-be and promise to come to
the wedding ... It seems to me that the wedding should not be put off too long.

After raising the crucial point of where Zetkin proposed to draw the line
of demarcation between left and right socialists, Inessa concluded that
'there are other questions I want to ask you, but unfortunately, I must
do my housework'.[122] While Armand was busy with 'housework', in
this instance writing another set of letters to the Bolsheviks' initial
supporters claiming that she now had Zetkin's backing,[123] Zetkin was
consulting with Rosa Luxemburg, Angelica Balabanoff and other
leading socialist women. As a result of these consultations, Zetkin
decided to take over the calling of the conference herself in the name of
the International Women's Secretariat, to make it an official conference
with elected representatives, and to invite centrists or pacifists who the
Bolsheviks had specifically wished to exclude. The emphasis of the
conference would be more on how women could bring about peace
than on how the war could be turned into a civil war.[124] According to
one participant, Lenin considered holding a parallel conference of his
own[125] but ended up by instructing Armand to send out another round

121 Zetkin to Armand (2 January 1915), in *ibid.*, p. 111.
122 Armand to Zetkin (end of January 1915), in Armand, *Stat'i*, pp. 222–4.
123 See various letters of January and February 1915 in *ibid.*, pp. 28–30 and 220–1; and
   in 'Iz istorii bor'by Bol'shevikov ...', pp. 109–12.
124 Gankin and Fisher, p. 287.
125 O. Ravich, 'Mezhdunarodnaia zhenskaia sotsialisticheskaia konferentsiia 1915
   goda', *Proletarskaia revoliutsiia*, 1925, no. 10 (45), p. 168.

of letters urging the election of delegates sympathetic to the Bolshevik position.[126]

These letters did little good. When the twenty-seven delegates from eight countries assembled in Bern on 26 March 1915, it was evident that the pacifists outnumbered the left-wing socialists.[127] The opening speeches of the various delegates 'put a definite stamp on the work of the conference', according to one of the five Bolshevik delegates. 'The struggle for peace was the fundamental task' to most of the women; no one spoke of civil war or the break up of the Second International.[128] These sentiments were reflected in a conciliatory resolution introduced by the chair, Clara Zetkin, in the name of the International Women's Secretariat. The Bolsheviks then submitted a counter-resolution written by Lenin and incorporating the defeatist slogans approved by his own conference three weeks earlier. As Krupskaia recalled, 'the carrying out of our line rested chiefly on Inessa',[129] perhaps because she was the only one of the five with previous international experience and with an adequate spoken command of French and German. Unlike in Brussels, in Bern she reportedly talked 'with amazing precision and clarity'[130] and her 'splendid report', which was delivered in French, 'made a great impression'.[131] Nevertheless, most of the delegates wanted to talk about means of achieving peace. It seemed to them premature to discuss civil war, inappropriate to criticize their own party leaders who had voted for war credits, and inadvisable to precipitate a split in either the Second International or their own socialist parties. Few could accept Lenin's logic that 'peace can be achieved only through revolution'.[132] When the two resolutions were put to a vote, Lenin's was defeated 21 to 6 and Zetkin's accepted by the same margin.[133]

These results were greeted with dismay by both leaders. Lenin spent most of the conference sitting in the café of the Volkshaus waiting for

---

[126] See, for example, letters from Lenin and Armand to David Wynkoop (12 and 13 March 1915), in Lenin, *PSS*, vol. XLIX, pp. 68–9; and Armand, *Stat'i*, p. 226.

[127] For conspiratorial reasons, no official list of delegates was kept. In the memory of participants, the number varies from twenty-five to thirty; twenty-seven, however, voted on the key resolutions. The number of Bolshevik delegates is sometimes given as four. In fact, the delegation was made up of Armand, Krupskaia, Lilina, Rozmirovich and Ravich.

[128] Ravich, 'Mezhdunarodnaia . . . konferentsiia', p. 170.

[129] Krupskaia in Krupskaia (ed.), *Pamiati*, p. 17.

[130] Ravich, 'Mezhdunarodnaia . . . konferentsiia', p. 171.

[131] Ravich, 'Iz vospominanii', p. 99.

[132] Ravich, 'Mezhdunarodnaia . . . konferentsiia', p. 173. For the Bolshevik resolution and some of Armand's remarks in support of it, see 'O mezhdunarodnoi zhenskoi sotsialisticheskoi konferentsii', pp. 108, 119–20.

[133] *Ibid.* One of the Polish delegates joined the Bolsheviks in each vote.

reports from his female subordinates. 'It was very difficult for him to put up with the role of a sort of shadow-leader', reported Krupskaia. She recalled one occasion during a break in the conference when 'Inessa and I were visiting Abram Skovno in hospital (he had undergone an operation) . . . Ilyich came along and urged Inessa to go and see Zetkin, and persuade her of the correctness of our position.' Inessa, who had already been chastised by Zetkin in correspondence and had listened at length to her arguments during the conference, was reluctant to do Lenin's dirty work for him in Bern as she had eight months earlier in Brussels. 'Ilyich cited argument after argument that was to be used to convince Zetkin', continued Krupskaia. 'Inessa was not keen on going. She did not believe that anything would come of it. Ilyich insisted and pleaded warmly. Nothing came of Inessa's talk with Zetkin.'[134] Balabanoff, who attended the conference on behalf of the Mensheviks, tells a slightly different story. According to her, 'again and again Clara Zetkin appealed [to the Bolshevik delegation] to withdraw their resolution' so that the conference could present a united front against the war. When they refused, she went with the delegation to see their 'shadow leader' so as to plead her case in person.[135] As a result of this conversation, a compromise was arranged whereby the Bolsheviks would go along with the majority resolution on the condition that theirs would be printed in the official record of the conference.

Despite having preserved a united front, the conference was not a 'moral victory' for Zetkin as Balabanoff suggests. The ailing German socialist was fired as editor of *Die Gleichheit* by the defensist leaders of her party shortly after her return from Bern and she was arrested by the German police in August 1915. The Bolsheviks in turn were irritated that their resolution did not appear in *Beilage zur Berner Tagwacht*, no. 77 (3 April 1915), as Zetkin had promised,[136] and Inessa later saw the conference as a lost opportunity to have taken the first step toward the creation of a Third International.[137] On the positive side, the women's conference was the first organized expression of international socialist opposition to the war and it allowed Lenin to stake out his claim to represent the only radical alternative should the moderate policies of the other socialists fail to produce peace in the foreseeable future.

---

[134] Krupskaya, *Lenin*, p. 303.   [135] Balabanoff, *My Life*, p. 151.
[136] See letter from Armand to Wynkoop (April 1915), in Armand, *Stat'i*, p. 228. The resolution and their side of the story did, however, appear in *Sotsial-demokrat*, no. 42 (1 June 1915), *prilozhenie*, pp. 1–2.
[137] Elena Blonina [I. F. Armand], 'Rabotnitsy v Internatsionale', in Armand, *Stat'i*, p. 164.

One week after the women's conference closed, the International Socialist Youth Conference opened in Bern's Volkshaus on Easter Sunday 1915. The initiative this time came not from the Bolsheviks but from Willi Münzenberg, a German who served as secretary of the Swiss Youth League. On 10 November 1914 he had written to Robert Danneberg, the Austrian Secretary of the Bureau of the International Socialist Youth League, suggesting that a conference be called to revive the dormant international organization and to discuss the solidarity of youth against the war. When Danneberg refused to take action, Münzenberg summoned a conference without the authorization of the Bureau or the support of socialist organizations in most of the major belligerent countries. He attracted fewer delegates than the women's conference – fourteen from ten countries[138] – but they tended to be more radical in their attitudes toward the war. The RSDRP, which did not have a youth auxiliary, was short of appropriate delegates. The day before the conference opened, Lenin personally mandated Inessa Armand – who was youthful in appearance but one month short of her forty-first birthday – and Safarov to represent his Central Committee.[139]

The conference began peacefully enough with greetings from the Swiss and Italian socialist parties being delivered by Robert Grimm and Angelica Balabanoff followed by reports on the strength and activities of youth organizations in the countries represented. Armand's report on the situation in Russia was full of revolutionary optimism but short on facts and precision.[140] Sometime during these reports Balabanoff wandered down to the café where she found Lenin sitting at the same table he had occupied during the women's conference. 'Vladimir Ilyich', she enquired, 'did you come here for tea or for the resolution? He answered me with an annoyed glance'[141] and soon thereafter left for his apartment where he could follow further developments more peacefully by telephone.

Peace in the conference hall itself was disrupted early on the second day when Münzenberg suggested that each country should have one vote on all resolutions. The Russian delegation protested, perhaps favouring the formula used at the women's conference where each delegate had a vote. When their objections were voted down by the other delegates, the two Bolsheviks walked out in protest and went to

---

[138] For a discussion of the preliminaries to this conference, see V. Miuntsenberg, *S Libknekhtom i Leninym: piatnadtsat' let v proletarskom iunosheskom dvizhenii* (Moscow, 1930), pp. 93–6.   [139] Lenin, *PSS*, vol. XLIX, p. 457.
[140] Her report is summarized in Miuntsenberg, p. 98.
[141] Balabanoff, *My Life*, p. 152.

Lenin's apartment for instructions.[142] They returned only after a compromise was arranged whereby each country would have two votes
and Poland (whose delegate usually supported the Bolsheviks) would be
considered a separate country.[143] While they were out of the hall the
other delegates had proceeded to the next and most important item on
the agenda: discussion of a draft resolution introduced by Grimm and
Balabanoff on 'The War and the Tasks of Socialist Youth Organizations'.
Freed momentarily from Bolshevik intransigence, the conference unanimously adopted a statement 'regretting' the failure of most socialist
leaders to adhere to the pre-war decisions of the Second International in
August 1914, noting that the war was caused by the 'imperialist
policies of the ruling classes of all the capitalist countries', renouncing
the concept of 'civil peace' between the classes even in time of war, and
calling for an 'immediate end to the war'.[144]

When the out-manoeuvred Bolshevik delegates returned on the third
and last day, Inessa introduced a counter-resolution which was much
more critical of the role of the Second International on the eve of the war
and of its national leaders during the war. It also stressed the imperialist
nature of the war and the need for youth organizations to continue
conducting revolutionary activity.[145] After this resolution was voted
down 14 to 4, the Bolsheviks introduced an amendment to the resolution passed on the preceding day. When this was defeated by the same
margin,[146] they adjourned to the corridor to consult Lenin by phone.
He suggested a compromise similar to that used to settle the dispute at
the women's conference: the Bolsheviks would accept the majority
resolution if their own resolution was printed in the official record.[147]
After this arrangement was duly approved, the conference concluded
on a more harmonious note by expressing itself in favour of complete
disarmament (with the Russian delegation dissenting) and by setting up
a new International Socialist Youth League headed by Willi Münzenberg in Switzerland. This first organizational move toward a new

---

[142] *Biog. khr.*, vol. III, p. 332.   [143] Miuntsenberg, pp. 99–100.
[144] The resolution is reproduced in Gankin and Fisher, pp. 307–8.
[145] According to Gankin and Fisher (p. 302), no copy of the Bolshevik resolution is
extant. See a summary of it in Miuntsenberg, p. 100, and a draft of Armand's
statement in her *Stat'i*, pp. 30–1.
[146] Münzenberg said the vote was 13 to 3 (p. 100) but the larger figure, which comes
from the report in *Berner Tagwacht*, is more consistent with the new voting arrangements. Poland and Russia voted against; Norway and Denmark voted with the
majority but were treated as one country since they were represented by the same
delegate (see note in Gankin and Fisher, p. 306).
[147] Cf. Balabanoff, *Impressions of Lenin*, pp. 42–3; Miuntsenberg, p. 100. Balabanoff
claims the Bolsheviks walked out a second time over this vote.

International and the explicit break with the previous secretariat in Vienna pleased Lenin. The conduct of his delegates, however, displeased almost everyone else. It 'created an even more discouraging impression upon those of us who had witnessed it' at the women's conference, recalled Balabanoff,[148] and probably led to the exclusion of all Bolsheviks from the newly elected five-person International Youth Bureau. The ventriloquist and his two puppets must share the responsibility, although perhaps not equally, for the understandable criticism Bolshevik tactics evoked.

In early June 1915 Lenin and Krupskaia departed from Bern on their annual summer retreat to the countryside. Krupskaia had been ill since the death of her mother in March and both were tired from the round of spring conferences. This time they chose to stay at the Hotel Marienthal in the small mountain village of Sörenberg, eighty kilometres east of Bern. Krupskaia described it as a 'non-fashionable locality' which her husband had found while perusing advertisements for cheap summer accommodations. They liked their choice: 'the mail was delivered with Swiss punctuality', books could be obtained 'free of charge' with 'no questions asked' from libraries in Bern and Zurich in two days, and 'all around there were woods and mountains'.[149]

Soon after they arrived Lenin sent Inessa detailed instructions on how she too could reach Sörenberg. First, however, she had to take messages from him to Zinoviev, Kasparov and Radek as well as picking up lemon crystals, French novels, and thirty large envelopes ('the cheapest but strong') 'for sending thick manuscripts'.[150] He acknowledged that 'you will get quite crushed under the load of things and requests . . . It is a bad idea – going out into the country *after* everyone else.'[151] His last request was a portent of things to come. After pouring over his Baedeker, Lenin had become intrigued by the prospect of visiting some of the nearby high mountain cabins run by the Swiss Alpine Club. He asked Inessa to enquire at the headquarters of the SAC in Bern about the cost for non-members to stay in these huts and whether there were any group expeditions that climbed peaks between 3000 and 3500 metres 'just in case we should have an opportunity to go on a *long* excursion'.[152]

Apparently, the 'opportunity' did not arise or there were no group excursions and Lenin was cautious enough not to risk changing the

---

148 Balabanoff, My Life, p. 151.   149 Krupskaya, Lenin, pp. 306–7.
148 Balabanoff, *My Life*, p. 151.   149 Krupskaya, *Lenin*, pp. 306–7.
150 Lenin to Armand (after 4 June 1915), in Lenin, *PSS*, vol. XLIX, p. 79.
151 *Ibid.*, pp. 78–9 (emphasis in the original).
152 *Ibid.*, p. 80 (emphasis in the original).

course of Russian history by attempting a major climb on his own. He, Krupskaia and Inessa did, however, take numerous short hikes during the summer of 1915. Krupskaia recalled that they would get up early so that she and Vladimir Il'ich could spend the morning working

in different nooks of the garden. Inessa often played the piano during these hours, and it was very pleasant to work to the sounds of music drifting down into the garden. In the afternoon we used to go for walks in the mountains sometimes for the rest of the day ... coming home with armfuls of alpine roses and berries.

'We were all passionate mushroomers', she added, 'there were edible mushrooms galore ... and we used to argue fiercely over the different kinds and names as if it were a resolution on some vital issue.'[153] On several occasions they climbed the Rothorn,[154] the mountain immediately in front of the hotel, whose summit was over 2300 metres and snow covered during much of the summer. Inessa wrote to her daughter that 'from these tall peaks a magnificent view opens up of almost all of Switzerland. You can see not only the Bernese Oberland, not only Lake Luzern, but also on a clear day (so they say) Mont Blanc. Unfortunately, there are not many clear days.'[155]

During the frequent periods of rainy weather, Armand stayed in the hotel reading, surreptitiously working on her pamphlet concerning the family, and writing to her children. In the spring she had developed the habit of sending a postcard to a different one of her children each day. Now she turned to writing long letters, particularly to her seventeen-year-old daughter Inna. These letters show another side to the reserved, aloof and uncompromising woman encountered at party conferences or in correspondence with Bolshevik associates. Her letters to Inna are warm, often humorous and self-deprecating, and always deeply concerned about her daughter's feelings, aspirations and development. She tried to bolster Inna's flagging confidence in herself, telling her she was stronger than she imagined, not to worry about the superficial impressions she thought she was making on others, and reminding her that 'in femininity and gentleness there is a charm which is also a strength'. She urged her daughter to develop a strength of will and ability to assert herself while young[156] not mentioning that she herself was still fighting this battle in her forties. In other letters they discussed programmes of

---

153 Krupskaya, *Lenin*, pp. 307–8.
154 See letter from Krupskaia to M. A. Ul'ianova (24 September 1915), in Lenin, *PSS*, vol. LV, p. 452.
155 Letter to Inna Armand (summer 1915), in Armand, *Stat'i*, p. 230.
156 Letter to Inna Armand (1915), in *ibid.*, p. 236.

study Inna might follow in university, careers she might consider,[157] and books they had read. During the summer vacation,

rather than political economy, busy yourself with good belles lettres while you rest. After all, one ought to treat belles lettres seriously as well, it can give a lot in the sense of understanding life and help therefore in the solution of difficult problems ... It seems to me that you ought to consider keeping a diary or writing down your thoughts ... This helps to develop coherent thinking and pursuing a thought to the end because the act of writing helps to focus your thoughts.[158]

Inessa was greatly distressed by her physical separation from her children. 'I simply cannot reconcile myself with the thought that you cannot come and visit me this summer', she wrote in late June or early July. 'I still hope to arrange it'[159] – if not in Switzerland, then perhaps for a month in Sweden.[160] 'It is terribly difficult for me to be on my own here because I am isolated from everything which is dear and close [to me].' Nevertheless, she ruled out Inna's spending a year in Switzerland:

it would be a real crime on my part to agree to this. First, because it is necessary that your studies proceed normally to their end; secondly, you should not be torn away from Russian soil – you should develop there, put down roots there, because it is precisely there that you are faced with living and working, with applying the knowledge that you have accumulated.[161]

'In a foreign country', she wrote later in a similar vein, 'there are no roots and you live as if in a vacuum, and that is why it becomes so suffocating.'[162] By the end of the summer Inessa had come to the conclusion that the military situation in Europe was still too unsettled to arrange a meeting with her children. Moreover, Lenin had more errands he wanted her to run and another conference for her to attend.

On the second or third of September, Lenin and probably Inessa Armand left Sörenberg bound for Bern where the Bolshevik leader wanted to make final preparations for the Zimmerwald Conference. Like the women's and youth conferences which preceded it, Zimmerwald brought together European socialists opposed to the war, only in this

---

157 Letter to Inna Armand (late 1916), in *ibid.*, pp. 250–1.
158 Letter to Inna Armand (late June–early July 1915), in *ibid.*, p. 231.
159 *Ibid.*, p. 229.
160 Letter to Inna Armand (summer 1915), in *ibid.*, p. 233. It is interesting to note that Lenin also was considering 'risking' a trip to Scandinavia in 1915 (see letter to Armand [15 March 1917], in Lenin, *PSS*, vol. XLIX, p. 399).
161 Letter to Inna Armand (late June–early July 1915), in Armand, *Stat'i*, p. 229.
162 Letter to Inna Armand (summer 1915), in *ibid.*, p. 233.

instance it was party or opposition leaders rather than their subordinates who were in attendance. The initiative for the conference came from the Italian and Swiss socialist parties. In April 1915 the Italian socialist deputy Oddino Morgari asked Emile Vandervelde to call, on behalf of the International Socialist Bureau, a conference of socialists from neutral countries. When Vandervelde refused, the Swiss Social Democrat Robert Grimm summoned a meeting in Bern on 11 July to discuss procedures for calling an unauthorized conference but one which would include representatives of socialists in belligerent as well as neutral countries who were opposed to civil peace and militarism.[163]

From the Bolshevik point of view, the Bern organizers were once again not selective enough in who they intended to invite to the conference. As Zinoviev, who represented the Central Committee at the preparatory meeting, reported: 'it is clear that the so-called conference of the Lefts will in reality be a conference of "conciliators" of the "Center" with social chauvinists.'[164] During the rest of July and August, Lenin spent his mornings in Sörenberg writing letters to political allies in other countries and preparing resolutions for the conference.[165] The half dozen would-be supporters he lined up were asked to come to Bern before the conference opened. As they arrived at the train station, they were met by his 'Girl Friday' and taken to the Volkshaus for a private preliminary meeting of what came to be known as the Zimmerwald Left.

On the morning of 5 September all the delegates met at the Volkshaus for transportation to the actual site of the conference which, for conspiratorial reasons, Grimm had not revealed in advance. As Trotskii later recalled, 'half a century after the founding of the first International, it was still possible to seat all of the internationalists in four coaches'.[166] The motor coaches travelled twelve kilometres south through rolling foothills to the small agrarian community of Zimmerwald which offered not only privacy but also a marvellous view of the Bernese Oberland in the distance. For the next four days thirty-eight official delegates from eleven countries, who Grimm had said belonged to an 'ornithological society' when he booked rooms in the Hotel-Pension Beau Séjour,[167]

---

[163] The background to Zimmerwald is discussed in more detail in Gankin and Fisher, pp. 309–14, and R. Craig Nation, *War on War: Lenin, the Zimmerwald Left, and the Origins of Communist Internationalism* (Durham, 1989), pp. 73–85.

[164] Quoted in Gankin and Fisher, p. 315.

[165] Lenin, *PSS*, vol. XLIX, pp. 95–137; vol. XXVI, pp. 282–5.

[166] Leon Trotsky, *My Life: An Attempt at an Autobiography* (New York, 1970), p. 249.

[167] Nation, p. 85.

met for what Soviet historians have referred to as the 'First International Socialist Conference'. Lenin had initially suggested that Inessa Armand, as a member of the KZO, should represent Russian women's and youth groups at Zimmerwald.[168] This is precisely what Grimm and the other organizers wanted to avoid: the domination of the conference by the many factions and organizations of Russian and Polish Social Democracy. To prevent this the Russian socialists were allocated only eight votes: two each from the Bolshevik Central Committee (Lenin and Zinoviev), the Menshevik Organizational Committee (Aksel'rod and Martov), the Socialist Revolutionaries (M. A. Natanson and Victor Chernov); and one each to Trotskii (representing *Nashe Slovo*) and J. Berzen from the Latvian Social Democrats.[169] Inessa, as a result, attended the conference in an informal capacity and her participation was limited to providing Lenin and Zinoviev with linguistic assistance during the course of the debate.[170]

'The days of the conference', wrote Trotskii, 'were stormy ones.'[171] This political climate was caused largely by Lenin's tactics of incessantly protesting the resolutions of the majority, introducing counter-resolutions of his own, insisting that votes be recorded, etc., but never walking out as his surrogates had done in Bern or permitting himself to be isolated from the other delegates at Zimmerwald. He felt that these tactics were successful 'in introducing a number of the fundamental ideas of revolutionary Marxism'[172] into the final manifesto which Trotskii and Grimm drafted and the conference unanimously accepted. The manifesto condemned the actions of the leaders of the Second International, it noted that the demands of the proletariat as an international class superseded national demands based on patriotism, and it called on the workers of all countries to take immediate action to secure a peace based on no annexations, no reparations and the right of all nations to self-determination. 'The manifesto adopted by the conference does not give us complete satisfaction', stressed six delegates of the Zimmerwald Left. It did not call for the turning of the imperialist war into a civil war nor did it demand a decisive break with patriotic socialists and the establishment of a Third International. Nevertheless, 'we vote for the manifesto because we regard it as a call to struggle, and

---

168 Walentyna Najdus, *SDKPiL a SDPRR, 1908–1918* (Warsaw, 1980), p. 345.
169 *Leninskii sbornik*, vol. XIV (1930), pp. 186–7.
170 Nevskii (ed.), *Deiateli*, p. 129; Krupskaia, 'Plamennye bortsy za sotsializm', pp. 18–19. Balabanoff, who represented Italy at Zimmerwald, served as the official interpreter.
171 Trotsky, p. 250.   172 Lenin, *PSS*, vol. XXVII, p. 38.

in this struggle we are anxious to march side by side with the other sections of the International'.[173]

While the delegates may not have abolished the Second International, they did approve the establishment in Bern of an International Socialist Commission (ISC) to take over the work of the International Socialist Bureau on a temporary basis. Shortly after the conference adjourned, the ISC proposed the creation of an 'Enlarged Committee' to maintain contacts between the various organizations associated with the Zimmerwald movement. Lenin was quick to 'express our complete sympathy with the plan to establish a permanent international "Enlarged Committee"' and to name Zinoviev as the Central Committee's representative to that body with himself and Inessa Armand ('Comrade Petrova') as alternates.[174]

Even though his motions never received more than twelve votes, Lenin gained in respectability and in exposure at Zimmerwald. He was no longer simply the head of a small band of Russian extremists, but the recognized leader of the Zimmerwald Left – the new left-wing of the international socialist movement. His policies and slogans, which received wider publicity as a result of the conference, offered a clear alternative not only to social patriotism but also to the pacifism of the Zimmerwald majority. His next task would be to find supporters for the Zimmerwald Left in countries unrepresented at the conference or whose delegates voted with the majority. Here, once again, Inessa Armand could play an active organizational role.

*   *   *

After Zimmerwald Inessa joined the Zinovievs at Hertenstein for a short vacation on the shores of the Vierwaldstätter See before returning to Bern for the fall. Her immediate plans were more cerebral than organizational. At Lenin's request, she translated into French a brochure entitled *Socialism and War* in which he and Zinoviev had set down their views on the nature of imperialist wars for the Russian and German delegates at Zimmerwald.[175] She also contemplated writing some fictional short stories[176] and made preparations for resuming her academic studies at the University of Bern now that her residence permit had finally been granted. She was not enthusiastic, therefore,

---

[173] This minority statement is reproduced in Gankin and Fisher, pp. 333–4. The manifesto itself is found on pp. 329–33.
[174] Lenin, *PSS*, vol. XXVII, p. 31.
[175] See letter from Lenin to Zinoviev (11–15 September 1915), in *ibid.*, vol. XLIX, p. 140.
[176] Rusakov and Solov'ev, 'Stanovlius' bol'shevichkoi', p. 80.

when Lenin suggested that she go to Paris to spread the message of the Zimmerwald Left and seek supporters for his movement from among the French socialists. She was well aware that the two French delegates to the September conference – Alphonse Merrheim and Albert Bourderon – were unreceptive to Lenin's ideas but she lacked a passport and had made other plans for the winter. Besides, crossing international borders with forged documents and preaching defeatism in wartime to a party favouring defensism was at best a risky venture even for someone who had long-standing ties with the French Socialist Party and who felt at home in the French capital.

As she had when Lenin had asked her to go to Brussels against her will, Inessa eventually gave in. She found a reliable woman in Geneva to take over her translating duties for Lenin.[177] She also acquired from an unknown source a new Russian passport made out to Sophie Popoff which chopped seven years off her age and noted that she was travelling to Paris in order to do research at the Bibliothèque Nationale.[178] Armand arrived early in the New Year and went immediately to the area of the city which she knew best – the fourteenth arrondissement – where she stayed in the Hotel de Belfort on rue Sophie Germain,[179] not far from her earlier apartment on rue Marie Rose and close to the 'Bolshevik café' on Avenue d'Orléans.

According to the Okhrana, Armand came to Paris to agitate for a split in the Confédération Générale du Travail (CGT) and the French Socialist Party.[180] Such a mission was difficult if not impossible. The leadership of both groups was overwhelmingly in favour of the French war effort and actively supported the French coalition government. She had no chance even to present the defeatist views of the Zimmerwald Left in these circles. A much more modest and realistic objective was to seek converts from within the pacifist Comité d'action internationale and its successor Comité pour la reprise des relations internationales (CRRI) set up by Merrheim and Bourderon after their return from Zimmerwald. From the two meetings of the CRRI which she attended in January, however, she

---

177 See letter from Lenin to S. N. Ravich (before 16 December 1915), in Lenin, *PSS*, vol. XLIX, p. 169.

178 Podliashuk, pp. 176–7.

179 According to the Okhrana, she stayed at 16 rue Sophie Germain from 9 January to 9 March 1916 and then moved two doors down the street to what was probably another small residential hotel at number 12 where she stayed until 11 April. OA, file XVIIa, folder 4z (report of 19 April 1916); file XVIIa, folder 5 (report of 31 May 1916).

180 OA, file XVIIa, folder 5m (undated report [after April 1916]); file XVIIa, folder 5 (report of 19 April 1916, p. 11).

realized that Lenin's extreme views had few if any supporters in that body.

She had more success stimulating renewed party activity among her fellow Russian socialists in Paris. She was able to organize a group of Russian workers from the old Paris Bolshevik Section to spread anti-war propaganda among their French friends at work; she arranged for the reproduction of articles taken from an anti-war Swiss newspaper and from *Sotsial-demokrat*; she circulated 1000 copies of the Zimmerwald Left manifesto; and she made arrangements for the printing and distribution of Lenin's and Zinoviev's *Socialism and War*.[181] An inordinate amount of time was also spent getting a reader's ticket at the Bibliothèque Nationale and learning how to use its formidable catalogues so that she could maintain her 'cover' as a library researcher.[182]

Since she had been busy and had nothing significant to report, Inessa was slow in communicating with Lenin. The Bolshevik leader was impatient with her silence and perhaps worried about her safety. 'Not a scrap of news from you. We do not know if you have arrived or how you are getting on', he wrote on 13 January.[183] 'I'm rather surprised that there is no news from you', he complained on the 15th. 'Let me confess, while I am at it, that the thought occurred to me for a moment that you might have "taken offence" at my not having seen you off the day you left [Bern]. I repent, I repent and reject such an unworthy thought; I have driven it from my mind.'[184] Four days later he sent her another letter in care of *poste restante* in Paris stressing 'the great anxiety you are causing me' by not writing but after thinking it over he was reassured that 'if you were offended with me, you would probably have written to other friends' which apparently she had not done.[185] Finally, on the 21st Krupskaia got a friendly letter in which Inessa talked about the sombre mood evident in the streets of wartime Paris which were filled with women in mourning. She reported on her modest accomplishments to date and on her 'initial impression' that it was going to be very difficult to accomplish anything in the short term in the pacifist CRRI.[186] Even this letter did not satisfy Lenin since

[181] See letter from Armand to Krupskaia and Lenin (January 1916), in Krupskaia (ed.), *Pamiati*, pp. 18–19; Degot, p. 91; T. F. Liudvinskaia, 'V gody emigratsii (1914–1917)', *Istoricheskii arkhiv*, 1962, no. 4, pp. 155–7.
[182] See postcard from Armand to Lenin (25 January 1916), in Krupskaia (ed.), *Pamiati*, pp. 20–1.
[183] Lenin, *PSS*, vol. XLIX, p. 173.   [184] *Ibid.*, p. 174.   [185] *Ibid.*, p. 175.
[186] Krupskaia (ed.), *Pamiati*, pp. 18–19.

Inessa had written not to *him* but to Krupskaia; *his* first letter was not sent until the 25th.[187]

During the course of the next several weeks Armand's initial appraisal about the slim chance for success within Merrheim's Committee was borne out. She attended two more meetings of the CRRI where she passed out translations of relevant Central Committee documents and several of Lenin's articles relating to the Zimmerwald Conference and French socialism.[188] She also intervened in debates and sought the adoption of resolutions favourable to the position of the Zimmerwald Left. On one occasion, when Merrheim's draft resolution stated that 'the International should be based on the class struggle, on the struggle against imperialism, on the struggle for peace', Inessa introduced an amendment stressing that 'we shall *reorganize* the International on the basis of the class struggle, etc.' Merrheim and Bourderon 'pounced' on her for hinting at the creation of a Third International and insisted that 'the socialists in France do not wish to hear about a split in the Second International'.[189] Needless to say, the amendment was defeated. One reason for her lack of success may have been the influence of Leon Trotskii who had been in contact with the anti-militarist, semi-pacifist French socialists since the beginning of the war. He travelled to Zimmerwald with Merrheim and Bourderon and he now sat on the CRRI's executive.[190] Even though he may have been on 'excellent terms' with Armand as the police claimed,[191] as the author of the manifesto of the Zimmerwald majority he was not yet ready to encourage his French friends to support the Zimmerwald Left.

During late January and February, Inessa established more promising contacts with a socialist youth group and a couple of trade unions in Paris. Here too she passed out translations of Bolshevik literature and discussed the position of the Zimmerwald Left. According to a report received by the Okhrana, she was 'able to win the confidence of the young syndicalists because of her knowledge of the Russian and French revolutionary movements and by virtue of her command of the language and her enticing manner'.[192] Another factor in her favour was,

---

[187] See Lenin to Armand (21 January 1916), in Lenin, *PSS*, vol. XLIX, pp. 176–7, in which the personal pronoun is also emphasized.

[188] OA, file XVIIa, folder 4z (report of 19 April 1916); file XVIIa, folder 5m (undated report [after April 1916]).

[189] Armand to Lenin (late January 1916), in Krupskaia (ed.), *Pamiati*, p. 21 (emphasis added).

[190] Robert Wohl, *French Communism in the Making, 1914–1924* (Stanford, 1966), p. 76; Trotsky, p. 249. Trotskii makes no mention of Inessa Armand when discussing the work of the CRRI.

[191] OA, file XVIIa, folder 4z (report of 19 April 1916). [192] *Ibid.*

of course, the absence of formidable rivals such as Trotskii and Merrheim in these lower-echelon bodies. She was delighted when these
groups passed resolutions calling for revolutionary mass action and for
the creation of a new International.[193] Before she left France, a section
within the young socialists of the Seine region and another within the
Mechanics Union in Paris had affiliated with the Zimmerwald Left and a
group of Paris workers had named her as their delegate to the Second
International Socialist Conference scheduled to meet in Switzerland
during April 1916.[194] She wrote to Lenin that while she had been
unable to win any converts 'from above', i.e., in the Comité pour la
reprise des relations internationales, she had won some allies for the
Zimmerwald Left 'from below'.[195]

The content of Lenin's next letter therefore came as a shock. He
apparently ridiculed her gains among French youth groups and syndicalists and insisted that she try harder to cause a split, if not in the
French Socialist Party or the CGT, then at least in the CRRI. 'Don't be
afraid of a split', he lectured her. He wanted a group of respected
socialist leaders to be affiliated with the Zimmerwald Left in France just
as there was an organized group of International Socialists supporting
him in Germany. It did not matter whether this group was called the
'International Socialists of France' or the 'Revolutionary Internationalists of France', he wrote, but it had to include more than just a few
young socialists and unknown syndicalists.[196]

Armand was understandably upset by this response. She had after all
gone to Paris against her wishes; she had taken on a very difficult task;
she had spread the word of the Zimmerwald Left[197] and she had at least
won some new supporters for it. And then, rather than thanks for her
efforts, she received criticism. Not surprisingly, she responded to Lenin's
letter with what he characterized as an 'angry postcard'. 'Nothing is
accomplished', he wrote on 19 March, 'even in a fit of temper by using

---

[193] Armand to Krupskaia and Lenin (January 1916), in *Blizhe vsekh*, pp. 152–5; *Biog.
khr.*, vol. III, p. 440.
[194] Iakushina, *Lenin i Zagranichnaia organizatsiia*, p. 323; S. Pogodin, 'Komandirovka',
Sovetskie profsoiuzy, 1986, no. 17, p. 16.
[195] Quoted in Krupskaia (ed.), *Pamiati*, p. 18.
[196] *Leninskii sbornik*, vol. XXXVII, p. 35. This letter, which was not published until 1970,
is obviously incomplete and includes several sets of ellipses. See also a cold and rather
obtuse letter written on 26 February which in similar fashion argues in favour of a
split in the CRRI (Lenin, *PSS*, vol. XLIX, p. 186).
[197] In 1957, after ignoring Inessa Armand for a quarter of a century, a Soviet journal
published an article by Maurice Thorez in which he praised her wartime work in
creating a following for the Zimmerwald Left in France. Moris Torez, 'Oktiabr' ukazal
nam put'', *Voprosy istorii KPSS*, 1957, no. 3, p. 87.

rude words . . . this is not an encouragement to further correspondence.' He then rubbed salt into her wounds by adding that he had read their exchange to four of their friends in Zurich where he was now living and they all agreed he was right.[198] This was the last straw as far as she was concerned. She virtually stopped corresponding with Lenin and spent more time during her last month in Paris working on things of interest to her in the Bibliothèque Nationale.[199] She attended two more meetings of the CRRI – participating in a bitter debate on 3 April and suggesting that the Committee foment unrest in the French army on 10 April.[200] The latter action was quickly noted by the French police[201] but on 11 April, before they could arrest her, she left the country.

Armand returned to Bern but not to Lenin. On 24 April she was present at the Volkshaus for the opening session of the Second International Socialist Conference. Since the conference's organizers felt that the Swiss capital was 'overrun with dubious elements',[202] she and the other forty-two delegates were told to be at the train station at 7:15 the next morning for the sixty-five kilometre trip to the purer mountain surroundings of Kienthal. There, in the dining room of the Hotel Bären, she participated in the Kienthal Conference not as a representative of French syndicalists but as an official delegate of the Russian Central Committee. Once again she offered linguistic advice and provided background information for the other two Bolshevik delegates – Lenin and Zinoviev – who took care of almost all of the debating.[203] During the next five

---

[198] *Leninskii sbornik*, vol. XXXVII, p. 38.

[199] See Lenin to Armand (7 April 1916), *Leninskii sbornik*, vol. XL (1985), pp. 49–50. Other than a card which Lenin received on 31 March (*PSS*, vol. XLIX, p. 209), there is no evidence of further correspondence after the 'angry postcard'.

[200] Annie Kriegel, *Aux Origines du Communisme Français, 1914–1920*, 2 vols. (Paris, 1964), vol. I, p. 139; Annie Kriegel, 'Sur les rapports de Lénine avec le mouvement Zimmerwaldien Français', *Cahiers du Monde Russe et Soviétique*, vol. III, no. 2 (April–May 1962), p. 303. The split which Lenin wanted Armand to engineer in the CRRI did not take place until April 1917 and then only under much more favourable conditions.

[201] Report of Prefect de Police for 14 April 1916 in OA, file XVIIa, folder 5 (report of 19 April 1916, p. 10).

[202] Quoted in Alfred Erich Senn, *The Russian Revolution in Switzerland, 1914–1917* (Madison, 1971), p. 157.

[203] *Biog. khr.*, vol. III, p. 491. A series of notes and questions which Lenin passed to Armand at the conference is published in *Leninskii sbornik*, XIV (1930), pp. 183–4, but is erroneously identified as being to Zinoviev at Zimmerwald. According to the incomplete minutes of the conference, Armand intervened once to read two resolutions. See Horst Lademacher (ed.), *Die Zimmerwalden Bewegung*, vol. I: *Protokolle* (Hague, 1967), p. 130.

days she witnessed the growth of the Zimmerwald Left from eight delegates at the first conference to twelve at the second and saw this minority push the resolutions of the majority slightly further to the left.[204]

After the conference closed at 4 am on 30 April, she left Kienthal and also Lenin's immediate entourage. Contact henceforth was limited to correspondence and occasional telephone calls. She continued to take on party assignments which she thought were reasonable but she reserved the right to criticize the Bolshevik leader and she refused any longer to be his 'Girl Friday'.

[204] See Gankin and Fisher, pp. 371–478, for the background and resolutions of this conference. A perceptive interpretive account will be found in Nation, pp. 136–43. For Armand's own report on the work of the conference, which was sent to Russian socialists in Paris, see 'Pis'mo o Kintal'skoi konferentsii', *Krasnaia letopis'*, 1926, no. 2 (17), pp. 161–6.

CHAPTER 8

THE END OF AN AFFAIR?

In April 1916 Inessa Armand came close to breaking off all personal relations with V. I. Lenin. It is ironic that during that same month the Russian police were for the first time identifying her as the 'mistress' of the Bolshevik leader.[1] A half-century later four new Western biographies of Lenin appeared, three of which accepted without question that the two revolutionaries had been lovers intermittently or continuously from 1910 to 1916 or even to her death in 1920.[2] In the last decade novels and semi-novels of Lenin,[3] television programmes in Europe and even stage plays in Moscow[4] have perpetuated this image of their relationship to the point where it is now the conventional wisdom. Just as the love affairs of Catherine II absorbed her biographers and titillated their audiences, with far less evidence Lenin's relations with Inessa Armand have been blown out of proportion. Whether or not they were lovers is, of course, irrelevant to the course of Russian history or even to that of the Russian revolutionary movement. Lenin's relations with Armand, just like Catherine's with her lovers, never affected his judgments or his actions as a political leader. The 'affair', if such occurred, is at most a vignette in his life but one which makes this remote, seemingly repressed, sometimes too perfect individual seem more human.

The nature of their relationship is of somewhat more importance to an understanding of Inessa Armand's life. In most accounts, her relations with Lenin have overshadowed and obscured her achievements as a revolutionary and a feminist. In a few instances, Lenin's patronage is used as an explanation for contributions which she made in her own right.[5] The period of their friendship was a time when she was attempt-

---

[1] OA, file XVIIa, folder 5 (report of 19 April 1916).
[2] See the works by Stefan Possony, Robert Payne and Louis Fischer already cited. The one exception to this trend was Adam Ulam's *The Bolsheviks*.
[3] Solzhenitsyn, *Lenin in Zurich*; Alan Brien, *Lenin: The Novel* (New York, 1987).
[4] See comment on Mikhail Shatrov's play 'Brestski mir' (The Brest Peace) in the Toronto *Globe and Mail*, 4 January 1988.
[5] See, for example, Body, 'Alexandra Kollontai', p. 17, and Balabanoff, *Impressions of Lenin*, p. 14.

ing to carve out a niche for herself in the revolutionary movement, seeking to gain practical experience and theoretical knowledge, and ultimately trying to free herself from Lenin's domination and to establish her intellectual independence. The nature of her relationship with Lenin would therefore be important to her and it has a bearing on a biographer's understanding of her evolution as a revolutionary and as a person.

It is impossible to prove that two persons who saw each other frequently over a six-year period and also were obviously very close friends were not at the same time emotionally involved or that they did not have an isolated affair. It is almost as difficult to prove that they did not have an extended romantic involvement with one another. It is possible, however, to examine the evidence that has been used to support the hypothesis that they were lovers and to suggest, if the veracity of this evidence is in question, other possible interpretations of their relationship.

The only contemporary evidence of a love affair that has come to light so far are five reports issued by the Prefect of Police in Paris or the Foreign Agency of the Okhrana between April 1916 and January 1917. On 14 April 1916 the Prefect of Police reported that 'la maitresse de Lénine, nommée Popoff, Sophie, dite "Inessa"', had been in Paris.[6] On 19 April the Okhrana noted that 'la demoiselle Popoff est la maitresse de Lénine';[7] an undated report filed after April 1916 again referred to Inessa as 'la maitresse de Lénine' who was sent to Paris 'par son amant Lénine';[8] a hand-written report of 31 May identified her as 'la maitresse de Lénine';[9] and a final note of 18 January 1817 mentioned 'Popoff, Sophie, dite Inessa, maitresse de Oulianoff, dit Lénine'.[10]

All of these reports were written in French, none indicates when or where they supposedly were lovers, or what evidence was used in reaching this conclusion. Much of the accompanying biographical information is obviously wrong. The second and fourth reports repeat the same errors concerning the date and place of Inessa's birth which is given as 6 or 16 June 1881 in Baku. The second report also states incorrectly that Lenin was living in Geneva and the fourth claims that Inessa sometimes went by the pseudonym of 'Smirnoff'. The last two of these reports were submitted by Jean Henry Bint and, given the simi-

---

[6] OA, file XVIIa, folder 5 (in report of 19 April 1916, p. 10).
[7] OA, file XVIIa, folder 4z.
[8] OA, file XVIIa, folder 5m.   [9] OA, file XVIIa, folder 5.
[10] OA, file VIk, folder 5.

larity of the data and the terminology, it is reasonable to assume that he supplied the information for the other three as well. Bint was a 64-year-old Alsatian private detective who had been employed on an occasional basis since 1880 by the Foreign Agency in Paris. In 1886 he helped to blow up a printing plant of Narodnaia Volia in Geneva on the orders of the Russian police. He was later arrested by the authorities in Switzer-land for attempting to bribe Swiss mailmen to supply information on Russian *émigrés*. In 1908 he apparently had a falling out with the Okhrana and started to sell information to Vladimir Burtsev, the Russian Socialist Revolutionary who specialized in spying on the police. By the time of the war he was back working for the Okhrana, and in 1917 he offered his services to the Provisional Government in its investigations of his former employer, the Foreign Agency in Paris.[11] Bint's political allegiances, therefore, were doubtful; his methods were dubious; and, according to Burtsev, his intelligence was questionable. At best, he collected and sold gossip; at worst, he invented it. Gossip, it might be added, is never scarce when an attractive single woman is the subject of an investigation. It is instructive that all five of these reports appear to be raw sources of information and that none was apparently digested, signed by a Paris Okhrana official, and dispatched to Petro-grad. Nowhere in the seventeen other and more official Okhrana reports about Armand's revolutionary activity before 1916 is she identified as Lenin's 'mistress'. Indeed, after intercepting in June 1915 a letter from Natalia Kempler in Paris to Krupskaia which mentioned both 'Vladimir Il'ich' and 'Inessa', the police managed to misidentify Lenin and acknowledged that they did not know the identity of Inessa.[12]

According to one former Bolshevik writing in emigration in 1953, the affair was 'never a secret for [Lenin's] old comrades such as Zino-viev, Kamenev and Rykov'[13] and presumably for Mensheviks and other Russian *émigrés* of the post-revolutionary period. What is striking is that these *émigrés*, many of whom were arch-enemies of the Bolshevik regime, chose not to publicize their knowledge of the affair for over three decades after the revolution. Several commentators attributed this silence to a puritanical streak in these former revolutionaries and to a

[11] For information on Bint, see Senn, *Revolution in Switzerland*, pp. 5, 220, 232; Norman Cohn, *Warrant for Genocide* (Chico, Calif., 1981), pp. 78–9; Richard J. Johnson, 'Zagranichnaia Agentura: The Tsarist Political Police in Europe', *Journal of Contempo-rary History*, vol. VII, no. 1 (January 1972), pp. 221–41; Bianca D. Pelchat, 'Vladimir Burtsev: Wilful Warrior in Dubious Battle' (unpublished MA research essay, Carleton University, 1988), pp. 63, 76 and 132 n. 77.
[12] OA, file XVIIa, folder 1b, outgoing dispatch 928 (20 July/2 August 1915).
[13] Valentinov, p. 97.

code of conduct that would not allow them to discuss personal matters of this nature.[14] One ex-Bolshevik, Grigory Aleksinskii, who had few scruples in this regard and no liking of Lenin,[15] co-authored a book in 1937 entitled *Les Amours secrètes de Lénine*.[16] This rather unreliable exposé of Lenin's love life, which concentrated on his relations with a mysterious 'Lise de K...', does not mention Inessa Armand among the 'amours secrètes'. Indeed, in his unpublished memoirs, Aleksinskii specifically denied that Lenin had an affair with Armand.[17]

Émigré reticence seemingly diminished after Marcel Body published his brief reminiscence of Aleksandra Kollontai in 1952. According to Body, Kollontai told him during the 1920s in Oslo that Lenin had been 'very much attached' to Inessa, that Krupskaia knew of the affair and offered to leave her husband in the summer of 1911, that Lenin had been 'unrecognizable' at Inessa's funeral, and that her death hastened a deterioration in his own health.[18] It should be noted that Body's verbatim recollection of this conversation was written shortly after Kollontai's death and in anger at the Soviet refusal to honour her long career by publishing an obituary of their own. Either his or Kollontai's memory was faulty in such matters of detail as the year and cause of Inessa's death and her family background. Kollontai implied that she got her information from Inessa at some unspecified date. Before the revolution, when Kollontai was still a Menshevik, the two women attended several of the same conferences but never corresponded and saw each other informally only once, briefly in Paris in 1911. After 1917 they were in frequent contact but, as one contemporary noted, 'they did not get along very well together'.[19] They were of very different temperament: Inessa was 'deep, serious, complex' while Kollontai was 'expansive, impetuous, and easily carried away'.[20] It seems inconceiva-

[14] *Ibid.*; Wolfe, 'Lenin and Inessa Armand', pp. 111–12.
[15] According to Lydia Dan, Aleksinskii not only had long-standing political differences with Lenin but he also believed that the Bolshevik leader had had an affair with his wife. See interview in Haimson, pp. 124–5.
[16] Andre Beucler and G. Alexinsky, *Les Amours secrètes de Lénine* (Paris, 1937).
[17] R. H. McNeal, 'Lenin and "Lise de K...": A Fabrication', *Slavic Review*, vol. XXVIII, no. 3 (September 1969), p. 473.
[18] Body, 'Alexandra Kollontai', p. 17.
[19] Vinogradskaia as cited in Stites, 'Kollontai, Inessa, and Krupskaia', pp. 87–8. There is no evidence to support Moira Donald's contention that Armand was 'Kollontai's old friend and collaborator' before 1917 ('Bolshevik Activity Amongst the Working Women of Petrograd in 1917', *International Review of Social History*, vol. XXVII, no. 2 [1982], p. 140) or that she was 'an intimate of Inessa' as claimed by Lenin's most recent biographer (Ronald W. Clark, *Lenin: The Man Behind the Mask* [London, 1988], p. 138).
[20] Vinogradskaia as cited in Stites, 'Kollontai, Inessa, and Krupskaia', p. 88.

ble that a person as reserved as Armand would share this type of intimate information with any political associate, let alone with Aleksandra Kollontai. As Barbara Clements notes, Kollontai had a 'tendency to gossip' and this gossip cannot be considered 'wholly reliable' especially when reported second-hand a quarter-century later.[21]

Kollontai further complicated the picture by writing a novella in 1923 entitled *Bol'shaia liubov* (A Great Love). This book, which was virtually unknown in the West until the 1960s, is about a Russian revolutionary (Senya) who wears a cloth cap and has a sick wife (Aniuta) and his affair with a beautiful wealthy fellow revolutionary (Natasha) who just happens to be a good linguist. Several Western writers were quick to conclude that these characters were modelled after Lenin, Krupskaia and Inessa and that the story was a thinly fictionalized account of their love triangle.[22] It was conveniently forgotten that Kollontai also was attractive, from a privileged background, and a good linguist. In some unpublished notes she acknowledged that the novella was in fact autobiographical and that Senya was patterned after the Menshevik P. P. Maslov with whom she had had an affair.[23]

Once the Body/Kollontai revelations were in print, several other *émigrés* unburdened their memories. Angelica Balabanoff, in particular, now 'felt that she too might break the puritanical silence she had hitherto observed concerning Inessa'. In an interview with Bertram Wolfe, she observed that 'Lenin loved Inessa. There was nothing immoral in it, since Lenin told Krupskaia everything. He deeply loved music, and this Krupskaia could not give him. Inessa played beautifully – his beloved Beethoven and other pieces.'[24] Balabanoff, who was close to eighty when this interview took place, was not the most accurate of witnesses. She told Wolfe that Lenin 'had a child by Inessa. She married the German Communist, Eberlein.'[25] This would have been Inna Armand, Inessa's eldest daughter, who was born in 1898 while Lenin was in Siberia and Inessa in Eldigino and eleven years before the two met. Balabanoff also acknowledged that she 'did not feel close to [Inessa]

---

[21] Clements, *Bolshevik Feminist*, p. 298 n. 71.
[22] Kendall Bailes, 'Alexandra Kollontai et la nouvelle morale', *Cahiers du Monde Russe et Soviétique*, vol. VI, no. 4 (October–December 1965), pp. 471–96; McNeal, *Bride of the Revolution*, pp. 141–2. This is also the argument of Cathy Porter's introduction to her translation of *Bol'shaia liubov*: Alexandra Kollontai, *A Great Love* (New York, 1981), pp. 7–29.
[23] Stites ('Kollontai, Inessa, and Krupskaia' p. 89), citing Carsten Halvorsen's Swedish biography of Kollontai; Clements (*Bolshevik Feminist*, p. 280, n. 71), citing Kaare Hauge's unpublished Ph.D. dissertation on Kollontai.
[24] Wolfe, 'Lenin and Inessa Armand', pp. 111–12.   [25] *Ibid.*, p. 112.

nor really know her well'.[26] As a result of their crossing swords at four wartime conferences in Switzerland, she had come to the conclusion that Armand was

the perfect – almost passive – executrix of [Lenin's] orders ... she was so saturated with the master's authority and infallibility that the possibility of any divergence was inconceivable to her. She was the prototype of the perfect Bolshevik of rigid, unconditional obedience.[27]

This may have been the impression that Armand gave at public meetings before the war but it was increasingly untrue of their private relations. As Balabanoff should have known, Inessa was anything but an unquestioning Bolshevik after the revolution.

Another ex-Bolshevik who found this 'very intimate subject' an 'awkward one' before 1952 was Nikolay Valentinov (N. V. Vol'skii). Valentinov knew Lenin well in 1904, then broke with him and had no contact with either of the principals during the period of their friendship.[28] He wrote in 1953 that 'Lenin was greatly attracted by – indeed, he was in love with – Inessa Armand ... Of course, he was in love in his own way – no doubt stealing a few kisses between discussions of the perfidy of the Mensheviks and drafting a resolution stigmatizing imperialism and the capitalist sharks.'[29] He produced no new or personal evidence to back up his flippancy other than to quote 'so unobservant a person as the French pro-Bolshevik socialist Charles Rappoport. "Lenin" [Rappoport wrote with reference to the 1911–12 period], "avec ses petits yeux mongolés il épait toujours cette petite Française"'.[30]

---

26 Ibid., Lydia Dan, who like Balabanoff was in her ninth decade when interviewed in the early 1960s, related that 'Kuskova told me in great deal about [Lenin's] romance with Inessa Armand; it was a very stormy affair' (Haimson, p. 125). She does not explain why she had to get her information from E. D. Kuskova when the Dans themselves were living in Paris during 1911 and 1912 – allegedly the 'stormiest' period of the 'affair'. Leopold Haimson, while not discounting this gossip, notes that Lydia Dan's memory of events of this period 'lacks sharpness and depth of detail' (p. 20).
27 Balabanoff, Impressions of Lenin, p. 14. Though it is clear that she is referring to Armand, Balabanoff does not mention her by name either in this book or in her autobiography. In one of her interviews with Bertram Wolfe, she repeated: 'I did not warm to Inessa. She was pedantic, a one hundred per cent Bolshevik in the way she dressed ... in the way she thought, and spoke. She spoke a number of languages fluently, and in all of them repeated Lenin verbatim' (Wolfe, 'Lenin and Inessa Armand', p. 101).
28 His knowledge of Armand's background is questionable at best. He managed to make several mistakes in one sentence when he asserted that 'her husband's elder brother, Boris Evgen'evich, set her on the path of revolutionary activity' and that she had three children (Valentinov, p. 97).
29 Ibid.   30 Ibid., p. 98.

Even for puritanical revolutionaries, looking at an attractive woman should not have been a sin or proof of an illicit relationship.

Not all former Social Democrats still living and writing in emigration after the Second World War jumped on the Body/Kollontai bandwagon. G. Urakadze, a Menshevik who attended Longjumeau at the time Krupskaia was allegedly offering to leave Lenin, rejected all of the 'romantic rumours' which he heard.[31] David Shub, another former Menshevik, made no mention whatsoever of Inessa Armand in his 1948 biography of Lenin. When he revised this work in 1966, he repeated Rappoport's and Kollontai's observations as well as some mistaken biographical information picked up elsewhere but made no judgment on the veracity of the 'affair' other than noting that Lenin was 'deeply involved' with Armand.[32]

It was left to Bertram Wolfe to knit together these flimsy pieces of evidence and to popularize what Richard Stites had aptly dubbed the 'romantic school'.[33] Mr Wolfe called attention to the physical proximity of Lenin and Armand: in Paris and Longjumeau in 1911–12, in Cracow and Poronin in 1913, in Paris again in early 1914, in Bern and Sörenberg in 1914–15. Unfortunately, he sometimes puts them too close together for historical comfort. He quotes Krupskaia's statement that 'in Krakow ... Inessa rented a room in the same family with which Kamenev lived' and then adds a subtle footnote of his own that 'the Kamenevs lived on an upper floor in the same building as the Ulianovs'.[34] One can only assume that he was misled by Krupskaia's earlier comment that in *Poronin* 'Kamenev moved into the rooms above ours'.[35] In Cracow, on the other hand, Inessa and the Kamenevs rented rooms from the Polish socialist Alexander Bagocki at 3 Rakowicka – not far from the Ul'ianovs at 51 Lubomirskiego but certainly not under the same roof. Wolfe also found grist for his particular mill in Krupskaia's vague and misleading comment that Inessa lived 'across the road' in Bern whereas her house at 23 Drosselweg was several blocks from the Ul'ianovs flat at no. 11 Distelweg.[36] He produces no evidence to support his claim that Lenin spent a month and a half alone with Armand in Paris during January and February 1914.[37] His stay in Paris was in fact

---

[31] Urakadze, p. 236.
[32] David Shub, *Lenin: A Biography*, rev. edn (London, 1966), p. 138.
[33] Stites, 'Kollontai, Inessa, and Krupskaia', p. 90.
[34] Wolfe, 'Lenin and Inessa Armand', p. 103.
[35] Krupskaya, *Lenin*, p. 266.
[36] Cf. Wolfe, 'Lenin and Inessa Armand', p. 104; Krupskaya, *Lenin*, p. 292; Bern Staatsarchiv, BB4. 1. 946. Akten der Polizei-Direktion. 1914, file 4352/14.
[37] Wolfe, 'Lenin and Inessa Armand', p. 103.

limited to a week, he shared Inessa's company with Malinovskii, and he was back in Cracow by 6 February as his correspondence, his wife and his editors all confirm.[38]

Since the publication of Mr Wolfe's article in 1963, Western writers with even less justification have found other women in Lenin's life but have added little to the existing evidence of an affair with Armand. Some, however, have found additional locales where they maintain assignations took place. Robert McNeal, in his study of Krupskaia, concluded 'it is highly probable that Inessa was Lenin's mistress for about a year in 1911–1912 and quite possible that they renewed their love affair for a bit more than a year in 1914–1915'.[39] He suggested that a temporary moratorium was agreed to during May 1912 when the lovers met alone in the small seaside town of Arcachon near Bordeaux. There is evidence that some friends of the Ul'ianovs were indeed in Arcachon in early March[40] and that Inessa was on vacation in late April.[41] The only proof that these two facts are related is a police report dated 30 April 1912, which McNeal saw at the Hoover Institution, stating that Armand was in Arcachon.[42] The 'proof' that Lenin was in Arcachon at the same time is a statement by the editors of his *Polnoe sobranie sochinenii* that 'prior to 23 May Lenin was away from Paris for several days'.[43] The editors of his *Biograficheskaia khronika* correctly add that he spent these days in Germany not Arcachon.[44]

Two other rendezvous have been noted in recent literature. Ladislaus Singer claimed that Inessa and Lenin had their 'honeymoon' at the time of the Copenhagen Congress of the Second International in August 1910[45] and both Singer and Possony assert that the two Bolsheviks travelled together in Switzerland in September 1911 while Krupskaia minded the shop in Paris.[46] Unlike McNeal, neither of these authors provided evidence to support their assertions. There is no doubt that Lenin and Armand were both in Copenhagen (a large city) at the time of

---

[38] *Biog. khr.*, vol. III, p. 184; Lenin, *PSS*, vol. XLVIII, p. 260; Krupskaya, *Lenin*, p. 271.
[39] McNeal, *Bride of the Revolution*, p. 135.
[40] See letter from Lenin to his mother (8 or 9 March 1912), in Lenin, *PSS*, vol. LV, p. 322.
[41] See letter from Krupskaia to Shklovskii (30 April 1912), in 'Pis'ma N. K. Krupskoi k G. L. Shklovskomu', *Proletarskaia revoliutsiia*, 1925, no. 8, p. 122.
[42] McNeal, *Bride of the Revolution*, p. 142. This report, unfortunately, could not be located by the Hoover archivists in June 1986.
[43] Lenin, *PSS*, vol. XXI, p. 658.
[44] *Biog. khr.*, vol. III, p. 4. I would not spend so much time discussing what I consider to be a minor error by a highly respected historian except that the 'Arcachon meeting' now is appearing in other secondary literature. See, for example, Porter's introduction to Kollontai, *A Great Love*, p. 19; Clark, p. 144.
[45] Singer, p. 186.   [46] *Ibid.*, p. 188; Possony, p. 125.

this congress. One Russian resident of the Danish capital, whose husband arranged for Lenin's accommodation and who personally prepared Lenin's meals throughout his stay, attests to the fact that he was extremely busy but makes no mention whatsoever of Inessa Armand.[47] As suggested earlier, Inessa very likely was accompanied by her sister-in-law, Anna Konstantinovich, rather than by Lenin during the days of the 1910 congress. Lenin did attend a meeting of the International Socialist Bureau in Zurich on 22 and 23 September 1911, he climbed the Pilatus near Luzern on the 27th or 28th, and after that spent some time in Bern and Geneva on party business.[48] The only evidence that Inessa was even in Switzerland at the time is a statement by a member of the Lausanne Bolshevik group that she first met Armand in 1911 and that at some unspecified time then or later arranged a meeting in Lausanne at which Armand reported on revolutionary work in Russia.[49] It would be grasping at straws to use this vague statement as a springboard for a long intuitive leap from lecture hall to love nest on the shores of Lac Léman.

If Lenin had an affair with Inessa Armand sporadically or continuously from 1910 to 1916, then evidence of this relationship would surely have been found in their voluminous correspondence which started in December 1913 and continued until shortly before her death in September 1920. The fact that the editors of the various editions of Lenin's collected works were reluctant to publish his share of the correspondence in its entirety has only served to reinforce the *émigré* gossip and the Western speculation so dear to the 'romantic school'.

Lenin is known to have written 139 letters and postcards to Armand. None of these appeared in the second or third editions of his *Sochineniia*. Following the initial publication of the two letters concerning free love in *Bol'shevik* in 1939, twenty-three letters appeared in the fourth edition of his *Sochineniia* in 1950. In 1964, more complete versions of some of these letters, along with seventy-seven new communications, were published in volumes XLVIII and XLIX of Lenin's supposedly 'complete' *Polnoe sobranie sochinenii*. As a matter of fact, eighteen additional letters, most of them dealing with the post-revolutionary period, are to be found

---

[47] Aleksandra Kobetskij, 'Der Hvor Lenin Boede', *Fakta om Sovjetunionen* (Copenhagen), 1964, no. 8, pp. 19–21. See also Erli Ol'sen (Erlie Olsen), 'Lenin v Kopengagene v 1910 gody', *Voprosy istorii KPSS*, 1960, no. 5, pp. 125–30.

[48] *Biog. khr.*, vol. II, pp. 124–7.

[49] E. Rivlina, 'Pamiati pervoi rukovoditel'nitsy tsentral'nogo otdela', in Krupskaia (ed.), *Pamiati*, p. 52. It might be noted that Rivlina was active in the Lausanne organization during the war when Armand without a doubt gave a talk in that city.

in the *Leninskii sbornik* or in *Izvestiia TsK KPSS*[50] while seventeen more letters remain unpublished in the Central Party Archives.[51] Four communications of one sort or another are acknowledged to have been lost. Of the 118 letters that have been published, eight are missing one or more pages, six are without salutation or farewell (and thus may be incomplete), and at least eight others include unexplained ellipses which may or may not have been a stylistic device employed by Lenin himself. On the face of it then it would seem that this belated and incomplete publication of Lenin's letters is proof that the Institute of Marxism-Leninism had something it wanted to hide.[52] But was it trying to keep Soviet readers from seeing evidence of Lenin in love or are there other plausible explanations for their subjective editing?

In many of the 118 published letters Lenin discusses personal matters as well as party business and political gossip. He is at times solicitous about Armand's health and her feelings; he is interested in what she is doing; he recalls incidents in their past; and he allows his impersonal mask to drop on occasion to reveal his own frustrations and irritations. Nowhere in these letters, however, are there comments of a clearly romantic nature – endearments, arrangements for assignations, personal asides between lovers. It is of course possible that portions of some letters were excised and other letters suppressed entirely to conceal comments of this nature. If this be the case then Lenin was highly sporadic in the expression of his affections since the unpublished material is spread throughout his entire correspondence and is interspersed with many innocuous letters.

One indication of the type of material Soviet editors wanted to conceal can be seen in those portions left out of letters published in the fourth edition but restored in the *Polnoe sobranie sochinenii*. Three

---

50 *Leninskii sbornik*, vols. XXXV, pp. 108–9; XXXVII, pp. 35–8, 52–8, 233; XL, pp. 49–50; *Izvestiia TsK KPSS*, 1989, no. 1, pp. 215–16.

51 Brief descriptions of the content of these letters will be found in *Biog. khr.*, vol. III, pp. 189, 192, 208, 244, 251, 258–9, 261, 511, 528, 549, 555, 566, 572, 608; vol. IX, p. 146; and in Lenin, *PSS*, vol. XXIV, p. 556. All but the last are to be found, according to the editors of *Biog. khr.*, in the Central Party Archives of the Institute of Marxism-Leninism, *fond* 2, *opis'* 1, *dela* 3214, 3221, 3238, 3297, 3317, 3335, 3341, 4091, 4147, 4222, 4239, 4279, 4281, 4303, 4737, 14867.

52 Armand was not unique in the volume and intensity of the correspondence she received from Lenin or in the subsequent suppression of that correspondence. During 1912 and the first half of 1913, L. B. Kamenev received thirty-five letters, only two of which appeared in the fourth edition of Lenin's *Sochineniia* and both of these were abriged. Two-thirds of the thirty letters to Kamenev published in volume XLVIII of the fifth edition are acknowledged to be 'damaged' to the extent that words or phrases or more have been omitted. The same pattern holds true for Lenin's extended correspondence with Zinoviev during 1915 and 1916.

omissions are of particular interest. In the first the editors of the fourth edition chose to drop the following from a letter written on 20 November 1916:

Of course I want to correspond. Let's continue to write. I really laughed over your postcard, I had to hold my sides, as they say. 'In France [Inessa had written] there is no such measure as the ha, only an acre, and you [i.e. Lenin] don't know how large an acre is ...'
   This really is hilarious!
   It was *France – imaginez-vous* – that introduced the metric system. According to the metric system, which has been adopted by most countries of the world, a ha = hectare = 100 ares. An acre is *not* a French measure but an English one, and is about 4/10th of a hectare.
   You mustn't be offended at my laughing. I didn't mean any harm. After all, it isn't surprising that you don't often come across words like hectare, ha, etc. They are dull, technical words.[53]

Inessa's sin was that she had queried Lenin's use of the abbreviation ha for hectare in a manuscript she was translating at his request into French. While he may have been right on the question of measurements, his condescending tone was apparent even to his Stalinist editors.
   In 1950 the editors of the fourth edition also decided to eliminate a curious comment which Lenin had made in a letter written on 1 April 1914:

Again, I am sorry I called you the Holy Virgin. Please don't be angry – it is because I am fond of you, because we are friends – but I cannot help but be upset when I see 'something that reminds me of the Holy Virgin'.
   Reply as quickly as possible whether you can carry out this assignment properly and quickly.
   On Monday I sent you [*Nachalo*] and a note attached to Nadia's [i.e., Krupskaia's] letter. Have you received them?[54]

It would be intriguing to know why Lenin called Inessa 'the Holy Virgin' (*bogoroditsa*) but unfortunately the original reference was apparently made in a letter of 26 March of which only the last page has been found.[55] The final exclusion of early June 1914 is seemingly more innocuous:

---

[53] Cf. Lenin, *Sochineniia* (4th edn), vol. XXXV, pp. 196–9; *PSS*, vol. XLIX, pp. 323–5 (emphasis in the original).
[54] Cf. Lenin, *Sochineniia* (4th edn), vol. XXXV, pp. 100–1; *PSS*, vol. XLVIII, pp. 277–8.
[55] Lenin, *PSS*, vol. XXIV, p. 403, and vol. XLVIII, p. 280.

P.S.: How are things going with your arrangements for the summer?
Yours, V. I.
Franchement, continuez vous à fâcher ou non?[56]

What probably bothered the editors is that once again Lenin was concerned that Inessa might be 'angry' (fâcher) or upset just as in the two previous letters he had apologized and had sought to continue their correspondence. These sentiments, while admirable, do not necessarily reflect the desired master–pupil image. Moreover, by dropping the concluding paragraph of the last two letters cited, the editors were also able to eliminate Lenin's troublesome and overly familiar farewell 'Tvoi' just as they simply dropped the same farewell in yet another letter.[57]

These concerns about Lenin's image may explain why fourteen letters are still incomplete in the Polnoe sobranie sochinenii and seventeen others remain unpublished in Russian archives. Much of this suppressed material was written at controversial times in Lenin's dealings with Armand and may concern problems which the editors of the earlier fourth edition tried to ignore altogether.[58]

One such problem was Lenin's trip to western Europe in January 1914. Seven of the incomplete letters were written just before, during or immediately after that trip. The missing portions may of course refer to Lenin's seeing Inessa Armand in the absence of Krupskaia or to his arrangements for staying at the Mazanovs. It is equally possible that they refer to Lenin's travelling companion – police agent Roman Malinovskii. All letters to Malinovskii and favourable mention of him have been removed elsewhere from the Polnoe sobranie sochinenii. One example of this subjective editing can be seen in a letter written to G. L. Shklovskii in May 1914 in which Lenin referred to the 'action of Mal[inovskii]' in resigning from the Duma as being that of a 'nervous adventurer. Rumours about [his] provocation are baseness and nonsense on the part of the Liquidators.' When the editors of the Leninskii sbornik finally got around to publishing this letter in 1975 the quoted material about Malinovskii was replaced with ellipses.[59] It is also possible that the missing portions of the Paris letters as well as two unpublished letters of 8 March and mid-April 1914 dealt with Rabotnitsa and specifically with Inessa's efforts to raise money for the paper

[56] Cf. Lenin, Sochineniia (4th edn), vol. XXXV, p. 107; PSS, vol. XLVIII, pp. 294–5.
[57] Cf. Lenin, Sochineniia (4th edn), vol. XXXV, p. 101; PSS, vol. XLVIII, p. 282.
[58] A more detailed discussion of this problem will be found in my article, 'Lenin's Correspondence with Inessa Armand', Slavonic and East European Review, vol. LXV, no. 2 (April 1987), pp. 218–35.
[59] Cf. Leonhard Haas, V. I. Lenin: Unbekannte Briefe, 1912–14 (Zurich, 1967), p. 60; Leninskii sbornik, vol. XXXVIII (1975), p. 146.

from the Armand family. Soviet scholars and editors have always sought to ignore the fact that wealthy industrialists such as the Armands contributed substantial sums of money to the party and have sought to forget that Lenin was unenthusiastic about the newspaper for women workers that he allegedly inspired.

A second controversial problem for Lenin's editors was the Brussels 'Unity' Conference of July 1914. Lenin wrote seventeen letters or notes in an effort to get Inessa to go to the conference, to tell her what to do in Brussels, and to patch up differences after the conference. In contrast to the fourth edition, which published only one of these letters, the fifth includes thirteen. Perhaps four letters still remain unpublished because they show Lenin as too much of a supplicant before she agreed to go to Brussels and too petulant when she refused to return to Poronin after the conference. The preferred image of a benevolent, considerate but unquestioned leader was also tarnished by Lenin himself in his letters to Armand when she was in Paris during 1916. The editors of the fourth edition avoided this problem by publishing none of the nine letters he wrote between 13 January and 7 April. The fifth edition includes six in which he complains that she has not written and worries that she was 'offended' because he did not see her off at the Bern train station. The remaining three letters, one of them incomplete, have subsequently appeared in the *Leninskii sbornik*. Soviet readers, just like Armand herself, might be upset by the patronizing and childish tone of these letters. The missing portion of the one letter, rather than containing 'sweet nothings', probably shows the once supposedly omnipotent leader in an even more unflattering light.

Until *glasnost'* results in the opening of the Central Party Archives to researchers or allows for the publication of some of its contents, one can only speculate on the reasons a portion of Lenin's correspondence to Inessa Armand has been suppressed.[60] It is, of course, possible that he sent her an occasional unpublishable *billet-doux* but it seems more likely from a study of his published correspondence that there are other and often more mundane aspects of his image that Soviet editors tried

---

[60] Roy Medvedev recently implied that Lenin's still unpublished correspondence with Armand is sufficient to fill an entire volume of his *Polnoe sobranie sochinenii* but that it 'has been held back due to the "sanctimoniousness" of Mikhail Suslov, the chief Soviet ideologist of the Brezhnev years' (Paul Quinn-Judge, 'Soviets Touch the Big Taboo: Lenin's Reputation', *Christian Science Monitor* [weekly edition], 7–13 November 1988). Seventeen letters would hardly fill an entire volume. A close reading of Lenin's 103 letters written between December 1913 and April 1917 does not reveal internal evidence of extensive additional unpublished correspondence. It is, of course, possible, though unlikely, that Medvedev is referring to letters written before Lenin's departure to Galicia in July 1912 or after his return to the Finland Station.

202 OF 324 ?

to protect through their restrictive policies. Whatever the reason, one would think that the current and long overdue trend to de-mythologize Lenin will soon lead to the publication of these letters in their entirety. It is unfortunate that a similar investigation of Inessa's correspondence cannot be made since only a couple of her letters to Lenin have been published.[61] According to Singer, as long as the others remain unpublished, 'one must assume that they are love letters'.[62] Singer, of course, starts from the premise that they were lovers in arriving at this assumption. He may find some support from Jean Fréville, a French communist and the only writer who apparently has had access to these letters in the Soviet Union. Without citing from them, he comes to the conclusion that Inessa felt for Lenin 'a love without limit'.

As for Lenin, how could he help not being brought under the spell of this exceptional being who combined beauty with intelligence, femininity with energy, practicality with revolutionary zeal, joy of life with dedication, ideological steadfastness and softness of manner?[63]

This speculation, however, begs the question and proves nothing. It is also contradicted by a Polish scholar, Walentyna Najdus, who had access to Lenin's Galician archives which presumably contained Armand's pre-war letters before these archives were returned to the Soviet Union in the early 1950s. Dr Najdus, while very candid about embarrassing material relating to Malinovskii found in Lenin's unpublished papers, was adamant that nothing she saw would support Fréville's or Singer's interpretation.[64]

Reading Lenin's correspondence to Inessa Armand leaves no doubt that she occupied a special place in his life. He wrote more letters to her than to any other person except his mother, often communicating several times a week. The tone of these letters is far more personal than that used in addressing his other frequent correspondents of this period – Zinoviev, Kamenev, Gor'kii, Shklovskii, Karpinskii, Shliapnikov and Kollontai. While he often treated Armand as a subordinate and could be condescending and even rude, he at other times was considerate of her well-being and very much concerned about her opinion of him. Twenty-four of the letters written in the seven months before the war are also distinguished by the fact that Lenin used the familiar *ty* form of address. As Bertram Wolfe has pointed out, 'it is hard to convey how unusual, and how intimate, it is for an educated Russian to address a woman as

---

[61] See page 8, note 30, above.
[62] Singer, p. 179.
[63] Fréville, *Lénine à Paris*, p. 108.
[64] Interview with Walentyna Najdus in Warsaw, 19 June 1982.

ty' rather than the more polite second-person plural pronoun *vy*.[65] Wolfe notes that Lenin used the term with only two other persons outside his own family – Martov and G. M. Krzhizhanovskii – both close friends from the 1890s and both relegated to the *vy* form after they disagreed politically with him just as Inessa was after she refused to go to Galicia in July 1914. Wolfe cites five women – Stal', Kollontai, Balabanoff, Elena Stasova and Zinaida Lilina – who did not qualify.

Armand was addressed as *ty*, at least from January to July 1914, but perhaps not for the reason Wolfe implies. For two years in Paris and for three months in Galicia she lived in the same neighbourhood as the Ul'ianovs, she was a frequent visitor to their house, a good friend of Krupskaia, and a special protégée of Lenin's. More than anyone else of the inter-revolutionary period and certainly more than any of the women mentioned by Wolfe, she could be termed a close family friend.[66] In Paris the Ul'ianovs had met Inessa's estranged husband and they had come to know her younger children. She delighted in showing them the children's letters and in discussing family matters. Krupskaia relates how Inessa frequently came over to chat and smoke with Krupskaia's aged mother[67] who lived with them in Paris, Galicia and Bern until her death in 1915. After the revolution, Krupskaia told Polina Vinogradskaia that Inessa 'was our closest friend'.[68] Given this warm family friendship, it is not surprising that Lenin addressed her as *ty*; what may be surprising is that he did not use this same form of address in the fourteen letters he sent her between September 1914 and the near break in their relations in April 1916.[69]

Lenin was always a fastidious individual: neat and formal in dress, reserved and correct in manner, Victorian and sedate in behaviour. He detested the bohemian lifestyle that some revolutionaries affected and he avoided many of the usual excesses of human existence. His diversions were always healthful – skating, hiking, cycling – and seem almost intentionally chosen to keep him fit for his intellectual and revolutionary endeavours. 'Confronted with so much virtue', Adam Ulam

[65] Wolfe, 'Lenin and Inessa Armand', p. 97.
[66] Zinoviev's wife Lilina also lived in close proximity to the Ul'ianovs during these years but she was not nearly as active as Inessa in party affairs, was the recipient of only one letter from Lenin during this period, and apparently was not particularly liked by Lenin and Krupskaia (see Krupskaia to M. A. Ul'ianova [16 March 1914], in Lenin, *PSS*, vol. LV, p. 352).
[67] See page 100, above.   [68] Vinogradskaia, pp. 221 and 232.
[69] Wolfe suggests that the change to *vy* was for conspiratorial reasons since 'wartime censors [were] opening letters on every frontier' ('Lenin and Inessa Armand', p. 98). This may be valid for the letters sent to Paris but it does not explain the use of *vy* in letters sent within neutral Switzerland.

has written, 'the modern writer gropes for some evidence of the weaknesses of the flesh.' 'The non-Soviet biographer', he continues, 'has an almost irresistible temptation to catch Lenin in love.'[70] Ulam, unlike most other recent biographers, has resisted this temptation to see Inessa as more than just a very close friend of the Ul'ianov family. Perhaps there was a fleeting romance. But not only is there no convincing evidence of a long-term affair, it also was alien to Lenin's moral code. He disagreed with Armand about freedom of love because for him the term could only mean adultery and promiscuity. His 'glass of water' analogy accurately reflected his repressed view of sexuality. As Marie Mullaney has pointed out, 'Lenin was particularly harsh on those women [such as Aleksandra Kollontai after 1917] who overstepped the bounds of "proper" respectability.'[71] It is very difficult to conceive of a man who had what Trotskii called an 'inborn revulsion from vulgarity'[72] having a long drawn-out love affair in front of his revolutionary colleagues in Copenhagen and Bern and his mother-in-law in Paris and Galicia, all the while continuing to live with his wife of several decades who just happened to be one of the 'other woman's' closest friends.

If Lenin's character has to be distorted in order to 'catch him in love', then it is necessary to make Krupskaia into a female version of Chernyshevskii's Lopukhov to explain her willingness to live with an unfaithful husband and to honour his lover. This may happen in novels (at least in Russian novels) but it is rare in everyday life. Krupskaia corresponded regularly and warmly with Inessa during the same period as the latter's more famous correspondence with Lenin.[73] Here too the 'thou' form of address was frequently used. Krupskaia took a great interest in the growing up of Inessa's children and after Inessa's death she served as a surrogate mother for Inna and Varvara Armand. She kept a picture of her friend on her dresser in the Kremlin.[74] When Inessa died, Krupskaia noted that 'it is difficult to write an obituary about a dear person'.[75] She subsequently wrote several other necrologies and short biographical sketches of Armand[76] as well as editing a memorial volume in her honour.[77] Perhaps the picture which Krupskaia paints of Inessa in

---

[70] Ulam, pp. 208 and 284.
[71] Marie Marmo Mullaney, *Revolutionary Women* (New York, 1983), p. 76.
[72] Leon Trotsky, *The Young Lenin*, trans. by Max Eastman (Garden City, N.Y., 1972), p. 202.
[73] There are four letters to Krupskaia in Armand's *Stat'i* (pp. 211–20) as well as several more in Krupskaia (ed.), *Pamiati*, pp. 18–22.
[74] Vinogradskaia, p. 213.   [75] *Pravda*, 3 October 1920.
[76] *Kommunistka*, 1920, no. 5, pp. 17–20; *Pravda*, 24 September 1930, p. 5; Kon (ed.), pp. 63–6; *Sputnik kommunista v derevne*, 1938, no. 4, pp. 16–19.
[77] Krupskaia (ed.), *Pamiati*. See especially her own long entry, pp. 5–33.

Reminiscences of Lenin should be accepted at face value. In it she emerges as a close friend of the family, an intelligent and cultured woman, a mother isolated from her family who brings youthfulness and vitality into an otherwise staid Ul'ianov household. If Kollontai was right and Krupskaia knew that her husband had an affair with one of her best friends, then the woman who wrote those warm reminiscences was hypocritical or masochistic in the extreme. To believe such is unfair to Krupskaia and contrary both to logic and to most of the available evidence.

It also does a disservice to Armand to believe that she would be willing to be part of this unusual triangle. As much as it is tempting to make an attractive single woman, who had had an unconventional married life and wrote about free love, into the mistress of a famous revolutionary, such an interpretation is inconsistent with other aspects of Armand's character. She always retained traces of her aristocratic upbringing: she was aloof, reserved, almost ascetic, cultured and well-mannered.[78] Like Lenin, she eschewed a bohemian lifestyle. Unlike Kollontai, she was not flamboyant and, with the exception of her short life with Vladimir Armand, she did not flout society's usual conventions. Her letters to her daughters and even to her estranged husband indicate a sensitivity and a morality inconsistent with secret rendezvous, stolen kisses and the deception of a close friend. Inessa wanted to achieve something in her own right and to be recognized for what she was – an intelligent, committed revolutionary. Biographers should give her the benefit of trying to achieve this goal without resorting to self-seeking and unsubstantiated romances with influential men.

[78] These qualities are mentioned repeatedly by Armand's contemporaries. See, for example, comments by Kamenev and Vinogradskaia, in *ibid.*, pp. 36, 60, 62–3.

CHAPTER 9

ON THE EVE OF REVOLUTION

The year 1916 marked the third turning point in Inessa Armand's life and, just like the other two, the decisive events took place in or near the Alps. In 1903, while awaiting the birth of her fifth child in Switzerland, she decided to abandon charitable work in the Moscow Society and the comfortable life with Alexander Armand in favour of propaganda work in the RSDRP and a student's life with Vladimir Armand. In 1909, after fleeing exile in Mezen and watching over Vladimir's death on the French Riviera, she decided to resume her education and to assist in the building of 'a party of the new type'. In 1916, after returning from a difficult if not impossible party assignment in Paris, she decided to forego her role as Lenin's 'Girl Friday' and to seek more personal and political freedom in the Russian *émigré* community in Switzerland. Independence meant living free of Lenin's daily dictation and of the sense of his intellectual superiority which had pervaded their relations since 1910. Like Rosa Luxemburg in breaking with Leo Jogiches, 'she needed to be free, to be independent, to be whole'.[1] Obtaining this objective was not going to be easy.

Just as in 1909, she was faced with the twin problems of where to live and what to do with herself. It would have been simplest to join Lenin and Krupskaia at their new residence in Zurich or on their annual summer retreat in Flums. This she refused to do. Her other options were limited since she had few close friends in Switzerland and most of her family were cut off in Russia by the war.[2] For a while after the Kienthal Conference she stayed on in Bern, before joining the Zinovievs at their summer home in Hertenstein on the Vierwaldstätter See. In September she returned to 'non-fashionable' Sörenberg and stayed there alone until late November when her hotel probably closed for the season. She

---

1 Dunayevskaya, p. 92.
2 Judging from Lenin's correspondence, Anna Konstantinovich was in Switzerland in March 1917 and was married to a good friend of Inessa's, Abram Skovno (Lenin, *PSS*, vol. XLIX, pp. 405, 427 and 641). A month later, both Anna and Skovno returned to Russia with Armand on the 'sealed train'. One would have expected, had Anna been in Switzerland in 1916, that Inessa would have sought out the company of her sister-in-law after Kienthal.

then retreated to the milder climate in Baugy-sur-Clarens near Montreux where she rented a cold-water flat in Maison Vincent across from Rubakin's Russian library.

This peripatetic and lonely existence caused periods of depression. Lenin sensed this and did his best on occasion to cheer her up. 'Do you go skiing?' he asked on 17 December 1916. 'I strongly recommend it – it is extremely healthy.'[3] The very next day he returned to the subject. 'Do you ski? You really should! Learn how, get some skis and go to the mountains – you must. It is good in the mountains in the wintertime! It's lovely and smells of Russia.'[4] 'I know how terribly bad you feel', he wrote in January, 'and I am very anxious to help you in any way I can. What about trying to live someplace where there are friends and where you can regularly talk about party affairs and take a regular part in them?'[5] In case she did not get the message, he repeated it the next day: 'have a change of scenery, visit new and old friends. I would terribly like to say a few friendly words to you to make things easier for you until you get adjusted to work that will completely absorb you.'[6]

While she continued to resist Lenin's entreaties to 'visit old friends' in Zurich, finding 'absorbing' work proved difficult. Just as in 1909, she still did not have an occupation to pursue. Her choice of isolated residences made it impossible for her to resume her education at the University of Bern as she had in Brussels after the death of Vladimir. She decided instead to spend her time reading, writing and giving occasional public lectures.[7] For these purposes, living in Baugy with its Russian community and its easy access to Rubakin's library made good sense and she stayed there until April 1917 when revolutionary events in Petrograd offered a belated chance to return to Russia.

Physical separation from Lenin did not mean a lack of contact with the Bolshevik leader. During the eleven months that followed the Kienthal Conference he bombarded her with seventy letters and they conversed on occasion by telephone. The correspondence of this period, while more frequent than before, is different in tone from that of 1914. With the exception of the few letters cited above, Lenin was less personal, less apologetic and less open. From Inessa's point of view, it was a pleasant change for him to discuss party affairs with her as a

---

[3] Lenin, *PSS*, vol. XLIX, p. 339.   [4] *Ibid.*, p. 341.
[5] Letter of 14 January 1917, in *ibid.*, p. 364.
[6] Letter of 15 January 1917, in *ibid.*, p. 366.
[7] On 21 January 1917 she gave a lecture attacking pacifism in Montreux or Lausanne. Lenin urged her to repeat this talk in Geneva and La Chaux-de-Fonds as well as lecturing on various trends in the Swiss Socialist Party. See his letters written between 14 January and 14 February 1917, in *ibid.*, pp. 364–86.

colleague, if not as an equal, and even to deign to explain theoretical matters to her. From Lenin's perspective, it was aggravating that her new-found sense of independence led her to argue back and to question some of his theoretical assumptions.

Armand continued to do party work for Lenin but now she exercised her option to turn down assignments she did not like or which seemed to fall into the 'Girl Friday' category. Such was the case when Lenin wanted her to return to Imperial Russia as an agent of the Central Committee. He must have sensed she would be unenthusiastic about taking on this obviously dangerous mission since in late March 1916 he informed Zinoviev 'Inessa would be good, but she will refuse to go.'[8] Judging from later letters, she did refuse, especially in light of her recent experiences on a similar trip to Paris. Three months later Lenin employed subterfuge to get her to change her mind. He wrote that he had heard from Krupskaia that Inessa's children were in Sweden and suggested that she go there or to Norway for a few months to see them, to replace Shliapnikov as the Central Committee's representative in Scandinavia, and perhaps once there to continue on to Russia on behalf of the party.[9] This time Armand wavered: she wanted to see her children and had already explored the possibility of going to Scandinavia for that purpose the previous summer. Lenin took the initiative in making the necessary arrangements. On 27 June he wrote Olga Ravich 'that Inessa badly needs a passport' and instructed her to see if one could be obtained in Geneva.[10] When nothing materialized, he suggested to Krupskaia that she give up hers for the purpose.[11] Inessa was bombarded with advice on approaching the German embassy, on alternate routes by way of England, and even with an offer to loan her money for the trip.[12] By mid-July, Lenin had to accept the fact that her lack of enthusiasm and logistical problems could not be overcome by a barrage of letters. What had worked in getting her to go to Brussels in 1914 no longer had the same effect in 1916.

In January 1917 Vladimir Il'ich came up with two less dangerous make-work projects for her consideration. 'If Switzerland is drawn into the war', he wrote on the 16th,

the French will immediately occupy Geneva. To be in Geneva then is to be in France and from there, to be in touch with Russia. I am therefore thinking about

---

[8] *Leninskii sbornik*, vol. XXXVII, p. 39.
[9] Letter written after 27 June 1916 in Lenin, *PSS*, vol. XLIX, pp. 245–6.
[10] *Ibid.*, p. 255.
[11] See letters to Armand of 4 and 7 July 1916, in *ibid.*, pp. 260 and 261.
[12] Letter of 2 July 1916 in *Leninskii sbornik*, vol. XXXVII, p. 53.

transferring the *party* treasury to you – to be kept *on your person*, in a special little bag, since the bank will not allow withdrawals during wartime.[13]

Armand apparently had no objections to becoming the Bolsheviks' walking treasury but she was concerned about the prospect of Switzerland being drawn into the war. Lenin reassured her that mobilization would be delayed until the spring and promptly forgot about the project.[14] His other scheme would have made her the Bolsheviks' official publisher in French Switzerland. 'I have hit on a plan for establishing a small publishing house and issuing leaflets, handbills and *small* brochures', he wrote her on 6 January.

Would you care to take on this business? It would work approximately in the following tentative manner: You would be the publisher of the French brochures. I would take on myself the editorial work (writing and editing). You would be the translator. You would go to La Chaux-de-Fonds for a short time (for a few days; I do not think you would have to live there) and clear up all the financial and printing details. You would also find out whether you could raise (or borrow) the money for this publishing house.[15]

Two weeks later he was pestering her to 'hurry up with your trip to La Chaux-de-Fonds' but by 19 February he had almost accepted the inevitable: 'Well, what about your visit to La Chaux-de-Fonds? Have you completely given up on the idea ... ?'[16]

One of the problems with the scheme from Inessa's point of view was that Lenin would do the writing and she as usual would be relegated to doing the translating. Lenin had used her as his interpreter on occasion before the war and at several of the wartime conferences. His first letter to her in Switzerland had raised the possibility of her translating some 'interesting documents' into French for publication in a local newspaper[17] and she had taken on the large project of translating his and Zinoviev's 48-page brochure *Socialism and War* into French in 1915. The situation got out of hand in late 1916-early 1917 and served to exacerbate her already strained relations with the Bolshevik leader.

Lenin was not a particularly considerate employer of unpaid translators. His instructions tended to be abrupt: 'I am sending you a leaflet', he wrote in February 1917, 'Please translate it into French and English ... [using] vigorous language and short sentences. Please do it in

[13] Lenin, *PSS*, vol. XLIX, p. 367 (emphasis in the original).
[14] Letter of 20 January 1917, in *ibid.*, p. 372.
[15] *Ibid.*, pp. 352–3 (emphasis in the original).   [16] *Ibid.*, pp. 372 and 391.
[17] See letter written before 28 September 1914, in *ibid.*, p. 6.

duplicate and as clearly as possible so as to avoid misprints.'[18] He also insisted on speed: '... still no article!! And I asked you to return it noting that I needed it and you *long ago* promised to send it "tomorrow". What is the meaning of this? I demand that you send it immediately!'[19] It must have been particularly galling for Armand to be reminded several times that the translation of a speech was essential and then to be told after it was done that he did not need it after all.[20] On occasion she would suggest a point be added to something she was translating or she would question a particular phrase or term. Sometimes Lenin accepted these suggestions[21] but more often he ridiculed her idea as he had done when she queried his use of hectare (see page 183, above) or when she questioned his use of the term 'imperialist economism' (which she understood as 'economic imperialism').[22] Much to Lenin's angry 'surprise', rather than engaging in further exchanges of this nature, she once simply refused to translate several passages which she considered erroneous and which 'made her blood boil'.[23] Matters came to a head when he sent her the draft of a May Day leaflet shortly after 19 February 1917 to be translated into French and English. He asked her on the 25th to 'hurry up' with the work and noted that 'there still is no sign of the French text!' on the 27th. After receiving it shortly thereafter, he wrote her an ungrateful (and unpublished) postcard on 2 March noting gaps and mistakes in the translation. Six days later he reminded her about the missing English translation. Her response must have been another 'angry postcard' and more 'rude words'. On the 13th Lenin innocently asked:

> You did not 'take offence' at my writing you about your not having gone over the French text, did you? Incredible! ... Is it conceivable that anyone can *take offence* at such a thing? Inconceivable!! On the other hand, your complete silence on the matter of the English translation is strange...[24]

Lenin's manner was only part of the problem. Inessa much preferred to spend her time writing articles of her own rather than translating someone else's. She had made a start toward proving herself as a writer

[18] *Ibid.*, p. 389.   [19] Letter of 9 October 1916 in *ibid.*, p. 306 (emphasis in original).
[20] *Ibid.*, pp. 315, 316, 318.
[21] See, for example, letter to Armand of 20 November 1916, in *ibid.*, p. 324.
[22] See letter to Armand of 25 December 1916, in *ibid.*, p. 346.
[23] Cited in letter to Armand of 22 January 1917, in *ibid.*, pp. 374–5. Their disagreement was over the 'defence of the fatherland' controversy discussed in more detail on pages 196–8, below.
[24] This exchange can be followed in *ibid.*, pp. 389–98 (emphasis in the original). It might be noted that at least five of Lenin's communications relating to translation problems in 1916 and 1917 remain unpublished in Russian archives (*Biog. khr.*, vol. III,

with the two articles she had published in *Rabotnitsa* and the one on the women workers' movement in *Sotsial-demokrat* in late 1914. In May 1916, while working on a draft table of contents for the second issue of *Sbornik Sotsial-demokrata*, Lenin scheduled another article on women workers.[25] Much to Inessa's displeasure, this article was later assigned to Zinaida Lilina who had recently given a report on the topic in Bern[26] and just happened to be the wife of Lenin's co-editor. Inessa, who was staying with the Zinovievs at the time, must have protested this perceived slight and offered to write an article of her own. Lenin 'had to humour her unfortunate passion for writing theoretical articles', mused Alexander Solzhenitsyn.

Frank criticism was impossible, and he had to choose his words carefully, or sometimes lie. 'What could I possibly have against publishing your article [in the *Sbornik?*', Lenin replied on 20 July 1916]. 'Of course I'm all for it.' Then, afterward, he would pretend that unforeseen circumstances prevented it.[27]

In this instance, Solzhenitsyn got it right: Armand completed sometime in the next few months a four-page manuscript entitled 'Who Will Pay for the War?' which she presumably submitted to Lenin for comment.[28] Her article was never published; Lilina's appeared as scheduled in December 1916.[29]

If Inessa was not encouraged to write articles then at least she could take the initiative in revitalizing the international women's movement – an area where Lenin had welcomed her efforts in the spring of 1915. In November 1916, while living in Sörenberg, she sent him the draft of a letter from the editors of *Rabotnitsa* to 'A German Woman Social Democrat'. This letter, which presumably was intended for Clara Zetkin, suggested an exchange of views on the women's movement and the calling of another unofficial conference of left-wing women socialists. 'It seems to us', Inessa had written in her draft, 'that during the war the [women's] movement can play a very important role for socialism. When most of the proletariat – the men – are at the front, the other part of the proletariat – the women – should take our socialist cause into their own hands.' Lenin's reaction was categorical and uncomfortably familiar: 'I do not advise you to send *such* a letter', he wrote in late

pp. 549, 555, 566 and 608). Reasons for their suppression were suggested in the previous chapter.

[25] *Leninskii sbornik*, vol. II (1924), p. 268.

[26] Iakushina, *Lenin i Zagranichnaia organizatsiia*, p. 341.

[27] Solzhenitsyn, p. 82. Lenin's letter is in *PSS*, vol. XLIX, p. 263.

[28] See manuscript version of 'Kto budet platit' za voinu?', in Armand, *Stat'i*, pp. 38–40.

[29] Z. Lilina, 'Ocherednoi vopros', *Sbornik Sotsial-demokrata*, no. 2 (December 1916), pp. 62–7.

November. '"We should take into our own hands" – if this gets into the press, you will be a laughingstock!!' In his opinion, the letter 'should be redrafted with the greatest of care' if she intended it for wide circulation or otherwise sent through safe channels '*only* to the closest of friends'. Once again Inessa 'took offence' at Lenin's 'remarks'. He suggested rather sarcastically on the 26th that perhaps she had 'misinterpreted them just a wee bit' and claimed he had 'expressed *not the slightest* "displeasure" with your letter, *none whatsoever*. You asked for my opinion; I gave it to you and *merely* suggested *only* slight alterations.'[30] In the wake of this 'slight' criticism, the letter, just like the proposed pamphlet on the family, ended up unfinished in her desk drawer.

Lenin might be able to discourage her from writing but he could not stop her from using her time in Sörenberg and Baugy-sur-Clarens to read and to improve her theoretical knowledge. In the past Marxist theory had largely been a male preserve, at least within the Bolshevik Party. She had ventured to question Lenin on his slogan 'the United States of Europe' in 1915 and she occasionally queried formulations in articles he asked her to translate. In late 1916 she challenged his use of the slogan 'defence of the fatherland' and by the time the dust had cleared in March 1917 she had driven him to distraction and had put further strain on their relations.

The confrontation started innocently enough when Inessa noted that Marx had said in the *Communist Manifesto* that 'the worker has no fatherland'. If this be so, she wondered, was it not redundant for Lenin constantly to argue against the slogan 'defence of the fatherland' with respect to the World War? Lenin responded on 20 November that there were some situations, such as the struggle of colonies for emancipation, when war and thus defence of the colony's right to have an independent fatherland was justified. The master then informed his student, 'I shall send you my article against Kievskii [G. L. Piatakov] on this issue.'[31] Much to his surprise, she read the article and then proceeded to cite some of his own earlier work against it. 'You apparently want to establish a contradiction between my present writing and that of an earlier date (when? 1913? where precisely? what precisely?)', he wrote on the 25th. 'I do not think that there are any contradictions. Find the exact texts, then we shall look at it again . . . If you need books, write.'[32] She answered by return mail that his article 'Marxism and Revisionism' written eight years before and published in *To the Memory of Marx*

---

[30] For excerpts from Armand's draft and Lenin's two letters in response, see Lenin, *PSS*, vol. XLIX, pp. 326–7, 545 n. 400 (emphasis in the original).
[31] *Ibid.*, p. 324.   [32] *Ibid.*, p. 325.

seemed at variance with his present stand on 'defence of the fatherland'. Lenin, who must have realized by now that she was not going to drop the issue, responded reasonably patiently on 30 November.

You find a contradiction between my [earlier] article ... and my present statements *without quoting* either precisely. It is impossible for me to respond to this. I haven't got *To the Memory of Marx*. Of course, I cannot remember word for word what I wrote in it. Without *precise* quotations, past and present, I am unable to reply to *such* an argument on your part.

Generally speaking, it seems to me that you are arguing in a slightly one-sided and formalistic manner. You have taken *one* quotation from the *Communist Manifesto* ... and you want to apply it without reservation, *up to and including the repudiation of national wars.*[33]

He then proceeded to explain his understanding of Marx and Engels on this issue at considerable length and without the usual condescension.

By now Inessa had access to Rubakin's library and with this new ammunition she continued their discussion. Lenin's patience was wearing thin after a month of defending himself. 'I would find it extremely unpleasant if we should go different ways', he wrote on 23 December.

Let's try once again to come to terms. Here is some 'material for reflection':
– War is the continuation of politics;
– Everything depends on the *system* of political relations before a war and during a war ... Think about this;
– Caesarism in France + tsarism in Russia against *non-imperialist* Germany in 1891 – that was the historical situation in 1891. Think about this![34]

Even though Inessa did not appreciate the pedantic tone of this letter, she did 'think about' the situation in 1891 and she fought back. She suggested that they were 'talking past one another', that Lenin was inconsistent in saying that Germany's defence of the fatherland against the threat of Russia and France was justified in 1891 but unjustified in 1914, and that even Engels could be wrong on Germany in 1891 as he was in his views on a strike by Belgian workers. For good measure, she added that 'Englels was the father of passive radicalism.' Lenin simply ducked the defence of the fatherland issue by accusing her of being 'extremely unhistorical' when she tried 'to identify, even to compare the international situation in 1891 and 1914'.[35] It was another matter to attack Engels. 'Engels was right', Lenin wrote on Christmas Day.

[33] *Ibid.*, pp. 328–9 (emphasis in the original).
[34] *Ibid.*, pp. 344–5 (emphasis in the original).
[35] *Ibid.*, p. 370.

In my time I have seen an awful lot of rash charges that Engels was an opportunist, and my attitude to these is extremely distrustful. Try, I say, to prove first that Engels was wrong!! You won't prove it! . . .

His statement about the Belgian strike? When? where? What? I do not know it.

No. No. Engels was *not* infallible. Marx was *not* infallible. But if you want to point out their 'fallibility' you must go about it differently; I'm serious, much differently.[36]

But then, when Inessa produced the statement by Engels on the Belgian strike that Lenin did not know about, he backed down. 'It is quite possible', he wrote on 19 January 1917, 'that in this question of fact, on a particular question, Engels was mistaken.' But in general, he concluded,

your attacks on Engels, I am convinced, are totally groundless. Excuse my frankness. One must prepare much more seriously before writing something such as this! Otherwise, it is easy to disgrace yourself – I warn you *entre nous*, as a friend, confidentially, just in case you begin talking *in this way* someday in the press or at a meeting.[37]

Armand still would not give up and in her next letter cited an obscure text by Marx to back up her position. Lenin had had enough. On 2 February he responded; 'I am aware of Marx's English works; they are special things which I shall have to read in due course . . . but *I do not have the time now.*'[38]

While Lenin did not acknowledge it, Armand's position in the defence of the fatherland debate was more internationalist than his own.[39] She would not accept his argument that there were just wars and times when the proletariat was justified in supporting national war efforts. Indirectly, she was supporting earlier accusations made against Lenin on this same issue by members of the Baugy Group – most notably Bukharin, Piatakov and Bosh. During the course of the debate, differences between Armand and Lenin over the question of national self-

[36] *Ibid.*, p. 348 (emphasis in the original).
[37] *Ibid.*, pp. 368–9 (emphasis in the original).
[38] *Ibid.*, p. 379 (emphasis in the original).
[39] None of the numerous letters Armand wrote to Lenin on this issue has been published nor did she or their contemporaries subsequently comment on the debate in print. Her position must therefore be inferred from Lenin's arguments against her and the few passages he quotes out of context from her letters. Several writers have concluded, mistakenly I believe, that she stood to the right of Lenin on the defence of the fatherland issue. Rather than taking an internationalist position criticizing Lenin's justification of national defence in certain circumstances, they see her as adopting a pacifist (Tamara Deutscher [ed.], *Not by Politics Alone . . .: The Other Lenin* [London, 1973], p. 39) or even a defensist (Fischer, p. 80) position.

determination also became apparent. Here too she took an internationalist position close to that of Piatakov and Bosh. Once again she accused Lenin of contradicting himself in his article on 'The Socialist Revolution and the Right of Nations to Self-Determination' and she suggested that acknowledging the right of self-determination would weaken the future socialist state. To Lenin her arguments were 'unclear, unthought out [and] confused' even though he admitted that 'in a certain sense for a certain period, *all* democratic aims (not only self-determination! Note this! You have forgotten this!) are capable of slowing down the socialist revolution.'[40] Armand was not alone in wondering at what stage in the revolutionary process Lenin's opportunistic policies did or did not apply. Lenin, however, would not be drawn into another protracted theoretical debate. 'You must be in an excessively nervous state', he wrote in late March 1917. 'This is my explanation for the number of theoretical "oddities" in your letters.'[41] These 'theoretical oddities' would in fact crop up again a year later when Inessa and the Baugy Group became the core of the Left Communist opposition. In the meantime, it was Lenin who was 'in an excessively nervous state' since a week and a half earlier revolution had broken out in Petrograd and he needed help in getting back to Russia.

*   *   *

'We in Zurich are in a state of agitation', Lenin had written Armand on 15 March 1917. 'There is a telegram in the *Zürcher Post* and the *Neue Zürcher Zeitung* of 15 March that in Russia the revolution *was victorious* on 14 March after three days of struggle ... If the Germans are not lying, then it is true.'[42] The Germans were not lying. On the same day that Lenin sent this letter, Nicholas II abdicated and on 3/16 March a new Provisional Government tried to pick up the reigns of power.

Lenin's thoughts immediately turned to the problem of getting back to Russia. He first considered returning by way of Russia's allies – through France to England and then by boat to Holland and Scandinavia. This route ran the risk not only of torpedoing but also of arrest or detention in England where the authorities had already enquired about Lenin's contacts with German socialists. He came to the conclusion that 'I cannot personally make any move unless very "special" measures have been arranged.'[43] For this he needed a 'Girl Friday'. On 18 March,

---

[40] Letter to Armand of 25 December 1916, in Lenin, *PSS*, vol. XLIX, p. 346 (emphasis in the original).
[41] *Ibid.*, p. 414.   [42] *Ibid.*, p. 399 (emphasis in the original).
[43] Letter to Armand of 19 March 1917, in *ibid.*, p. 405.

while returning to Zurich by train from giving a lecture in La Chaux-de-Fonds, he sent Inessa Armand a postcard. 'I would very much like you to find out discreetly for me in England if I would be granted passage', he wrote.[44] The next day he talked to her by telephone and was 'keenly disappointed' to learn that she was 'undecided and wanted to think over' his proposal. 'I was certain that you would rush off to England', he wrote the same day, 'since only there is it possible to find out how to get through and how great is the risk.' He came to the conclusion that 'you probably have special reasons, maybe your health is bad, etc.' for not wanting to test the torpedo-infested waters on his behalf.[45]

Lenin also asked Inessa to take care of three less dangerous chores in connection with his return to Russia. First, she was to find out if there were any Russians or Swiss in Baugy-sur-Clarens who were willing to give up their passports 'without saying it is for me'. Secondly, she was to get her sister-in-law, Anna Konstantinovich, to enquire of the Russian embassy in Bern about procedures for Russians to get visas for re-entry into their own country. And thirdly, she was to get a

wealthy or not-so-wealthy Russian social patriot in Clarens (e.g., Troianovskii, Rubakin) to ask the Germans to allow for the passage of a railway coach to Copenhagen for various revolutionaries ... You will say, perhaps, that the Germans *will not* give a coach. I bet they *will*! Of course, if they learn this idea came *from me* or from *you*, then the scheme will be ruined.[46]

Lenin won his bet though not with the help of the 'social patriots' in Clarens. After despairing in late March that 'we will probably *not* manage to get to Russia!! Britain *will not let us through*. It cannot be done through Germany'[47] – word was received that the German authorities were willing to provide railway passage through their country to Scandinavia. In early April Lenin sent Inessa 100 francs to take care of travel expenses for herself and Anna Konstantinovich.[48] On the night of 6 April Armand joined Lenin, Zinoviev and seven other Social Democrats at the Volkshaus in Bern to draw up a protocol listing

---

[44] *Ibid.*, p. 403.
[45] *Ibid.*, p. 405. On 23 March Lenin wrote telling Armand that Safarov's wife had learned from the British embassy in Bern that passage via England was indeed impossible (*ibid.*, p. 409).
[46] *Ibid.*, pp. 405–6 (emphasis in the original). Lenin also endorsed Olga Ravich's scheme of marrying 'a convenient old man' with a Swiss passport which would entitle both to enter Germany and Russia. He even recommended she try P. B. Aksel'rod (who had taken out Swiss citizenship) and offered 100 francs to cover expenses (*ibid.*, pp. 416, 554 n. 470).
[47] Letter to Armand (25–31 March 1917), in *ibid.*, p. 414 (emphasis in the original).
[48] *Ibid.*, p. 424.

the conditions under which they were returning to Russia. After midnight they had to transfer their discussions to Karl Radek's apartment where Inessa translated the agreement into French and German. This document was duly signed on Easter Sunday, 8 April 1917.[49] The next day they met for lunch at the Zahringerhof in Zurich where more documents were signed before proceeding to the train station.

Thirty-two Russians – ten of them women and two children – were on board the Swiss train bound for Singen when it pulled out of the Zurich Bahnhof at 3.10 pm on 9 April. The majority were Bolsheviks but there were a few Mensheviks and Bundists as well. At the German border town of Gottmadingen they disembarked and boarded the special 'sealed train' provided by the German government. Their new coach had eight compartments – three second class with upholstered seats for married couples and some of the women and five third class – in addition to a baggage wagon. Lenin and Krupskaia had a second-class compartment to themselves; Inessa shared hers with Radek, Olga Ravich, and Safarov and his wife; the Zinovievs, G. A. Usievich and his wife Helen Kon were given the third. One of the third-class compartments was reserved for two German officers who accompanied the Russians on the three-day trip from Gottmadingen to Sassnitz by way of Singen, Stuttgart, Karlsruhe, Frankfurt and Berlin. Lenin insisted that a chalk line be drawn separating the officers from the *émigrés* and that only the Swiss socialist Fritz Platten could cross over or communicate with them. Of the ten outer doors, only the one next to the Germans was left unlocked and no contact was allowed along the way with any German citizens. The officers also were given exclusive use of one of the two toilets; the other, at Lenin's insistence, had to do double duty as a smoking room. The Bolshevik leader also insisted on a reasonable degree of quiet and personally moved Olga Ravich to a more distant third-class compartment after her high-pitched laugh got on his nerves.[50] Conditions in the coach were spartan: since the train lacked both sleeping accommodation and a dining car, everyone had to doze in their seats and make do with whatever food the German officers could obtain along the way.

When the small party finally reached Sassnitz on 12 April, they boarded the ferry *Queen Victoria* for a rough crossing of the Baltic to Trelleborg in southern Sweden. There they were met by anxious

49 N. Krutikova, *Na krutom povorote* (Moscow, 1965), pp. 53–61.
50 Ravich herself blamed Radek for the noise (Ravich, 'Iz vospominanii', p. 103). Information on this portion of the trip, which is surprisingly sparse, can be found in Michael Pearson, *The Sealed Train* (London, 1975), pp. 82–7.

11. A group of Bolsheviks in Stockholm on 13 April 1917 on their way back to Petrograd from Switzerland. This is the only known photograph of Armand and Lenin together. *From right to left*: Ture Nerman (Norwegian socialist), Lenin (with umbrella), unknown man, Carl Lindhagen (mayor of Stockholm), unknown man, Krupskaia (wearing big hat), Karl Radek.

Swedish and Polish colleagues, one of whom, Jakob Hanecki, had been waiting three days for their arrival. The Russians were taken by train to Malmö, fed their first good meal since Zurich, and then given the comfort of a sleeping-car for the overnight train trip to Stockholm. Much to their surprise, after an inconspicuous trip across Germany, they were met at the central station by correspondents, photographers and the socialist mayor of Stockholm, Carl Lindhagen. He and a Scandinavian member of the Zimmerwald Left, Ture Nerman, escorted the party on foot to the luxurious Hotel Regina on the Drottninggatan where a banquet had been arranged in their honour by several Swedish socialists.[51] After lunch, thanks to the generosity of the Vera Figner Society for Assistance to Émigrés and Returning Exiles, some of the group were able to go shopping for clothing and footware.[52] Others went to the Russian embassy to obtain further travel documents.

By 6.30 pm they were back at the central station for the three-day trip around the Gulf of Bothnia through Finland to Petrograd. According to a Swedish correspondent, they were in an 'exceptional mood' at the station buoyed by one hundred well wishers and the singing in a 'non-professional' manner of the 'Marseillaise'.[53] Inessa, who from all accounts had been very subdued during the trip through Germany,[54] spent the next portion writing an account of their odyssey for a Swiss newspaper[55] and sending letters to her children informing them that 'soon I shall be with you'.[56] One wonders if she told them that her

---

51 Ravich, 'Iz vospominanii', p. 103; R. A. Skovno, 'Samoe dorogoe v zhizni', in *Nash Il'ich: Sbornik vospominanii starykh Bol'shevikov zamoskvorech'ia o vstrechakh s V. I. Leninym* (Moscow, 1960), p. 18. A famous photograph of the walk shows Lenin with Lindhagen, Nerman and Krupskaia close at hand (Plate 11). Another cropped picture, which appeared in *Dagens Nyheter* on 23 November 1954, has part of Inessa Armand's coat next to Lenin. A search of newspaper morgues and Stockholm film archives failed to turn up the original or any of the many other pictures that were taken on that day. Outside the Modern Art Museum in Stockholm is a cross-section of a cobblestone street and tram line marked with an X. It is entitled 'Lenin in Stockholm'.

52 D. Suliashvili, 'Vstrechi s Leninym v emigratsii', *Neva*, 1957, no. 2, p. 143.

53 Cited in *Izvestiia*, 22 April 1962, p. 4.

54 Pearson, p. 87, who notes that the memoirs of three of her travelling companions (Radek, Safarov and Ravich) make virtually no mention of her activities during the trip. She is, however, the central figure in Tom Hyman's novel, *Seven Days to Petrograd* (New York, 1988). By disarming and then seducing a would-be American assassin on the train, she supposedly saved the life of Lenin and the fate of the revolution. One wonders if this was also the theme of the Italian movie 'Lenin ... Train', starring Dominique Sanda as Inessa Armand, which 'for some reason disappeared from the programme' of the 1989 Moscow Film Festival. *Moscow News*, 23 July 1989, p. 11.

55 Unsigned 'Pis'mo iz Stokgol'ma', in *La Sentinelle* (La Chaux-de-Fonds), no. 93 (23 April 1917), reproduced in Krutikova, pp. 82–3.

56 Cited in Podliashuk, p. 202.

sleeping companions on the first night out of Stockholm were Lenin, Krupskaia and an obscure Georgian Bolshevik named David Suliashvili. According to Suliashvili, who, like Lenin, had an upper bunk, the future head of the Soviet state spent his time reading newspapers, talking to himself, and ignoring Krupskaia's entreaties to put on his pyjamas so as not to catch cold.[57]

On the evening of 14 April they reached the small Swedish fishing village of Haparanda where they disembarked and boarded eight horse-drawn sleds for the short trip across the frontier to Tornio in Russian Finland. After a careful search of their luggage and an eighteen-hour delay, all but one of the party were allowed to proceed. The exception was Fritz Platten, the Swiss socialist who had made most of the logistical arrangements for the trip, who was denied entry because he lacked a Russian visa. Lenin spent the long train trip through Finland worrying about the reception that awaited them in Petrograd. As a precaution, he had already left his manuscripts in Stockholm. Because of his fear that the Provisional Government would misconstrue the assistance received from the Germans, he had insisted that the party pay regular prices for their train tickets, that contacts with all Germans be minimized, and that the refusal of the British to grant passage be publicized. Both in Zurich and in Stockholm he got neutral socialists to endorse the trip across Germany. In Malmö telegrams had been sent to the Bolshevik Central Committee and the Petrograd Soviet requesting formal permission to return to Russia.[58] Even so, long discussions were held during the last leg of the journey about what should be done if they were arrested in Petrograd and, at Lenin's insistence, only five persons were authorized to speak publicly about the political aspects of their trip.[59] Lenin need not have worried. After spending the last night sleeping in their clothes, the week-long trip ended for the weary travellers at 11 pm on 3/16 April with a friendly and boisterous welcome at the Finland Station in Petrograd.

[57] Suliashvili, 'Vstrechi s Leninym', p. 143.
[58] [I. F. Armand], 'Pis'mo iz Stokgol'ma', in Krutikova, p. 83.
[59] Krutikova, pp. 84–5.

CHAPTER 10

RETURN TO MOSCOW

Nineteen seventeen was the fulcrum of Russian history. In the space of less than a year, the Romanov dynasty was overthrown, a liberal Provisional Government collapsed, and a revolutionary Soviet regime came to power. Management of industry passed into the hands of the workers, peasants seized the land, and Russia's vast armies withdrew from the war. The year also witnessed an exponential growth in the membership, organization and responsibilities of the Bolshevik Party. Quite obviously the party needed experienced and trusted leaders for the seizure of power, for the exercise of that power, and for the guidance of its vastly expanded cadres.

It is curious in this situation that Inessa Armand played such an inconspicuous and insignificant role in the great events of the revolutionary year. Unlike in 1905, when she also was relatively inactive, she now had experience as an underground propagandist, as the editor of a party newspaper, and as the organizer of numerous *émigré* party operations. This practical experience, plus her theoretical training and her international contacts, should have made her a valuable commodity for a party not overly blessed with talented leaders. There are a number of explanations why her contributions in 1917 were so modest. It could be argued, for instance, that revolutionary events require *men* of action like Trotskii who could lead street demonstrations, influence army garrisons and speak forcibly before large political gatherings. And yet other women, such as Aleksandra Kollontai, played important roles in these difficult and often dangerous circumstances. It is also true that the party in 1917 needed different skills and types of expertise than those possessed by Armand. A knowledge of international socialism, contacts within the French Socialist Party, and an ability to translate into three languages would be important once the Bolsheviks started to exercise power but were marginal to the process of seizing power. If the Bolshevik Party had paid more attention to organizing and influencing women workers in 1917, it might have consolidated its power in a smoother fashion and it would have had a natural role for Armand to play. But, as shall be seen, the male leaders of the party felt that women workers were of secondary or tertiary importance in comparison to the problems of bread, peace, land and the transfer of power to the soviets. Many Bolshevik women, Armand among them, shared this view during 1917 and the first half of 1918.

Another possible explanation for her temporary eclipse was that because she had 'taken offence' so often during 1916 and refused repeatedly to be his 'Girl Friday' during the last year in Switzerland, Lenin no longer viewed her as a reliable protégée to be entrusted with important party assignments. Moreover, he was in Petrograd while she spent most of the revolutionary year in Moscow isolated from the party leadership and from the decisive events of 1917. One other factor, which had a bearing on her political inactivity both in 1905 and in 1917, was her commitment to family and the precedence personal loyalties sometimes took over political responsibilities. Just as in 1905, when the poor health of Vladimir Armand kept her in western Europe for the second half of the year, so also in 1917 she chose to spend the fall with her ailing son in Pushkino rather than being involved in the seizure of power in Moscow. Inessa Armand in 1917 very much resembled another, more famous Russian revolutionary who produced on N. N. Sukhanov 'the impression of a grey blur, looming up now and then dimly and not leaving any trace'.[1] The fact that she did not leave much of a 'trace' and, unlike Stalin, did not spawn a host of sycophantic biographers makes it difficult now to chart her course during this, the most important year in Russian history.

*   *   *

After their train arrived at the Finland Station on 3/16 April, Armand stayed in Petrograd long enough to hear Lenin elaborate his 'April Theses' the next day at the Tauride Palace. Kollontai, who was one of the few Bolsheviks to defend Lenin, remembered that 'in the first row sat Nadezhda Konstantinovna [Krupskaia] and next to her Inessa Armand. They both were smiling at me, as if encouraging my speech.'[2] Inessa also encountered Lev Kamenev at the palace and chastized him for arguing against the quick transition to socialism advocated by Lenin.[3]

A day or so later she returned to Moscow and immediately went out

---

[1] N. N. Sukhanov, *The Russian Revolution: 1917*, 2 vols., trans. by Joel Carmichael (New York, 1962), vol. I, p. 230.
[2] Quoted in Clements, *Bolshevik Feminist*, p. 109. Kollontai became a Bolshevik in 1915 as a result of sharing Lenin's view of the war.
[3] Kamenev in Krupskaia (ed.), *Pamiati*, p. 37.

to Pushkino which she had not visited since the summer of 1913. At the family estate she saw her younger children – thirteen-year-old Andre, sixteen-year-old Varvara and perhaps Inna who was now in university. Her sons Fedor and Alexander, however, were both away on active duty in the Russian army. While in Pushkino she also met with N. P. Bulanov, whom she had known during her early years as an underground propagandist, and supposedly encouraged him to organize a local Soviet of Workers' Deputies.[4]

On 19 April she attended the opening of a three-day Moscow Oblast Conference which brought together representatives from twenty-two Social Democratic organizations in the Moscow region. Once again she defended the April Theses 'at a time when not everyone understood the worldwide-historical significance of Lenin's prognosis and conclusions'.[5] She also spoke in favour of the election of officers in the army and the fraternization of opposing forces in the trenches so as to encourage soldiers to turn their guns against their own governments and thus bring about a 'proletarian peace'. In another speech she condemned the opportunism of the leaders of the Second International and insisted that the conference's resolution should give more emphasis to urging the European proletariat to rebel against their imperialist governments.[6] Just as in Switzerland, she stood on the left wing of her party in arguing for the acceleration of revolution at home and its spread abroad. At least one person at the conference felt she made an 'irresistible impression' by the combination of her forceful speeches and her 'attractive appearance'. Polina Vinogradskaia described Armand, who at the time was a couple of weeks shy of her forty-third birthday, as slender, above average in height, with a thin face, 'aquiline nose', 'large greenish expressive eyes', and 'long luxuriant hair' collected behind her head (Plate 12).[7] Recent editors of *Pravda* have concluded that she was indeed 'one of the most beautiful women of the Revolution'.[8] She must have made an 'irresistible impression' in more important ways as well since she was chosen as one of Moscow's representatives to the Seventh Party Conference scheduled to meet in three days' time in Petrograd.

The Seventh or April Conference was the first 'all-party' gathering Inessa attended. The 151 delegates in attendance reflected both the four-fold increase in the party's membership since the February Revolution

4 Podliashuk, p. 209.   5 Vinogradskaia, p. 219.
6 'Protokoly pervoi (Moskovskoi) oblastnoi konferentsii tsentral'no-promyshlennogo raiona RSDRP(b) proiskhodivshei v g. Moskve (2–4 mai) 19–21 aprel'ia 1917 g.', *Proletarskaia revoliutsiia*, 1929, no. 10, pp. 163–4.
7 Vinogradskaia, p. 219.   8 *Pravda*, 28 January 1988, p. 6.

12. Inessa Armand in 1918.

and also Lenin's success in regaining control of the party. In contrast to the ignominious defeat of his April Theses three weeks earlier, his key slogans – down with the war, no support for the Provisional Government, and all power to the soviets – now were accepted by near-unanimous votes. Armand's active participation in the Moscow Oblast Conference did not carry over to Petrograd. The incomplete protocols of the Seventh Conference do not indicate that she spoke at any of the plenary sessions.[9] She did, however, give an 'interesting talk' on the various tendencies within the French Socialist Party to a sub-section of the conference which met in Kshesinskaia's mansion to discuss the international socialist movement.[10] Kollontai was less impressed with her non-committal attitude toward the establishment of women's sections within party organizations – an idea which was discussed and rejected by a private meeting of Bolshevik women attending the conference.[11]

When Inessa returned to Moscow in early May 1917 she once again took up residence in the Arbat district, at 14 Denezhnyi Lane, in an apartment owned by her husband Alexander Armand.[12] For the next three months she carried out a wide variety of assignments for the Moscow Committee. On the instructions of the committee, she attended as an 'observer' a preparatory meeting in May for an All-Russian Women's Congress which the bourgeois League for Women's Equality planned to call in early June to solicit female support in the forthcoming elections to the Constituent Assembly. After giving a speech in which she claimed that proletarian women had nothing in common with bourgeois women and should have nothing to do with the proposed congress, Armand led a walkout of six other worker representatives just as Kollontai had led a walkout from the First All-Russian Women's Congress over eight years earlier.[13] In June, when women could vote for

---

[9] Institut marksizma-leninizma pri TsK KPSS, *Sed'maia (Aprel'skaia) Vserossiiskaia konferentsiia RSDRP (bol'shevikov), Petrogradskaia obshchegorodskaia konferentsiia RSDRP (bol'shevikov). Aprel' 1917 goda: Protokoly* (Moscow, 1958), p. 326.

[10] F. Raskol'nikov, *Kronshtadt i Piter v 1917 g.* (Moscow, 1925), p. 87.

[11] See also below, p. 212.

[12] Lenin sent three short letters to this address in April and May 1917 as well as several packages of personal effects forwarded from Switzerland or perhaps Stockholm (*Leninskii sbornik*, vol. XXXVII, pp. 56–8).

[13] See Blonina [I. F. Armand], 'Rabotnitsa i Vserossiiskii zhenskii s"ezd', *Zhizn' rabotnitsy*, no. 1 (20 June 1917), pp. 5–6, as reproduced in Armand, *Stat'i*, pp. 36–8. Also M. Petrova, 'Moskovskii Komitet v 1917 goda', *Put' k Oktiabriu*, vol. I (1923), p. 159. Most other sources claim Armand disrupted the congress itself but disagree on when it took place. Stites (*Women's Liberation Movement*, p. 303) and Podliashuk (p. 212) say it was in April, Karavashkova says 'early summer' (p. 74), Drumm (p. 471) maintains

the first time in Moscow City Duma elections, she ran as a Bolshevik candidate and was one of twenty-three of her party to be elected. According to her Soviet biographer, she 'excelled' in defending the Bolshevik position[14] within the same body that her husband had sat in during the first Russian Revolution of 1905. Throughout May and June she also was active as a party propagandist giving lectures in Moscow and surrounding areas on such diverse topics as 'Women Workers and the Class Struggle' and the 'History of the Second International'. Here too there must have been a sense of *déjà vu* but, unlike her propaganda work in the same region in 1906 and 1907, now her talks could be announced in the newspaper and there was no fear of arrest. Just as in Longjumeau, she participated in a party school set up by the Moscow Committee in early June that offered two-month crash courses for would-be agitators and propagandists.[15]

As a result of this varied activity and her past experience, Armand was elected to the seven-person Executive Commission of the party's Moscow Committee on 21 June 1917. This body was responsible for all of the organizational work of the Moscow Committee and for implementing the decisions of the larger committee. Two weeks after her election, the Moscow Committee had to deal with the crisis caused by the July Days in Petrograd. Inessa, in the name of the Executive Commission, recommended on 5 July that mass demonstrations supporting 'all power to the soviets' be held in Moscow as evidence of solidarity with Bolsheviks in Petrograd and that pressure be brought to bear for the quick re-election of deputies to the Moscow Soviet.[16] Following the suppression of the premature uprising in Petrograd, many of the leaders of the Moscow party organization were also arrested.

Perhaps by virtue of not having been arrested, Armand was sent as a non-voting delegate of the Moscow organization to the Sixth Party Congress which convened conspiratorially in Petrograd on 26 July 1917. Once again, she did not prove to be an active participant in rough and tumble party debate. The congress protocols indicate that she made

there were *two* congresses – one on 7/8 April (which was too early for Armand to attend) and the other in May.

[14] Podliashuk, p. 210.

[15] For her work as a propagandist, see E. Levi, 'Moskovskaia bol'shevistskaia organiza-tsiia ot fevralia do iiul'skikh dnei', and E. Popova, 'Moskovskaia okruzhnaia organiza-tsiia v 1917 godu', in *Ocherki po istorii Oktiabr'skoi revoliutsii v Moskve* (Moscow, 1927), pp. 77 and 365; 'Protokoly zasedanii Moskovskogo oblastnogo biuro (mai-iiun' 1917 g.)', *Proletarskaia revoliutsiia*, 1927, no. 4, p. 249; Podliashuk, p. 208.

[16] E. Levi, 'Moskovskaia organizatsiia bol'shevikov v iiule 1917 goda', *Proletarskaia revoliutsiia*, 1929, nos. 2/3, pp. 134–5.

only one intervention and that was a procedural motion which was defeated.[17] She may have lacked confidence in her ability to perform effectively in this milieu. For whatever the reason, she did not attend the next three party congresses before her death. Not surprisingly, the delegates at the Sixth Congress chose *in absentia* Aleksandra Kollontai – who was a much more forceful orator than Armand – as the first woman to sit as a full member on the Bolshevik Central Committee.

Armand was particularly interested in A. S. Bubnov's report to the Sixth Congress. Bubnov, a member of the Moscow Oblast Bureau and of the new Bolshevik Central Committee, reported that the Moscow organization was attempting to conduct work among factory women and cited the publication of *Zhizn' rabotnitsy* as evidence of this commitment.[18] *Zhizn' rabotnitsy* had been started in June 1917 by Armand and Varvara Iakovleva as Moscow's version of Petrograd's revived *Rabotnitsa*. It was at best a pale imitation. Scheduled to come out bi-weekly, the editors managed to publish only two issues – one of eight pages on 20 June and another of sixteen pages on 15 July – in comparison to *Rabotnitsa's* thirteen larger issues. Its circulation never got over 15,000, a third of that of its big sister in Petrograd. Newsprint was hard to obtain in Moscow and printing methods were primitive in comparison to either the pre-revolutionary or the 1917 *Rabotnitsa*. Articles started immediately under the masthead and often employed large type. An attempt was made to include a couple of simple popular articles in each issue in addition to ones reprinted from *Pravda*, interviews, and a chronicle of events. Unlike in the case of the pre-revolutionary *Rabotnitsa*, men such as M. S. Ol'minskii and N. L. Meshcheriakov (but not Lenin) occasionally contributed to *Zhizn' rabotnitsy*.[19]

Inessa Armand published four articles in her new paper. It is indicative of her current interests that two dealt with general political issues – the Kerenskii offensive and accusations after the July Days that Lenin was a German agent – and the other two with issues of special interest to the female proletariat: the bourgeois women's congress and the continuation of the class struggle in Russian factories after the February Revolution.[20] These reinforced the general line of the paper that female workers did not have interests which were different from those of male workers. Inessa did, however, urge women to join the party in greater

---

[17] Institut marksizma-leninizma pri TsK KPSS, *Shestoi s"ezd RSDRP (bol'shevikov), avgust 1917 goda: Protokoly* (Moscow, 1958), p. 106.
[18] *Ibid.*, p. 80.   [19] Karavashkova, pp. 75–6.
[20] Copies of *Zhizn' rabotnitsy* do not appear to be available outside Russia. Armand's articles are reproduced in her *Stat'i*, pp. 33–8, 41–6.

numbers so as to improve the general conditions of their life. If Armand's articles lacked in feminist sentiment, they certainly were not short of political militancy. The answer to Russia's internal problems, she argued, lay in all power being transferred to the Soviets of Workers and Soldiers Deputies and the subsequent institution of worker control in the factories. On questions of cooperation with the Provisional Government or with other socialist parties, she was uncompromising, orthodox and a hard-line Leninist.

Zhizn' rabotnitsy ran into difficulty at about the time of the Sixth Party Congress. Paper was scarce, there were more pressing claims on the party's limited funds, and anti-Bolshevik sentiment after the July Days made party publications vulnerable. Iakovleva felt that too much effort had already been expended on the paper for its marginal return and that henceforth all energies should be concentrated on Petrograd's *Rabotnitsa*. Armand, who did not always get along well with her co-editor, wanted to continue the paper[21] but she found she did not have the resources to do so alone.

One of the reasons Iakovleva may have lost interest in *Zhizn' rabotnitsy* was the establishment by the Moscow Oblast Bureau in August 1917 of a 'Commission for Agitation and Propaganda among Working Women' subordinate to the Oblast Bureau and the Moscow Committee. Other commissions were to be set up by all lower party committees to coordinate activity among working women in the Moscow area. In many respects, these commissions resembled the women's sections Kollontai had proposed in April but which had been turned down by the other Bolshevik women in Petrograd. At the time, Kollontai was upset that 'Inessa wasn't against, but she wasn't for our project.'[22] Now in August, according to Liudmila Stal' and several secondary Soviet sources,[23] Armand suggested that similar women's commissions be created in Moscow. Sofia Smidovich, one of the five members of the new Moscow commission, however, claimed that the initiative came not from Armand but from Iakovleva, the secretary of the Oblast Bureau, who subsequently became the leader of the only women's commission established in Moscow before the October Revolution.[24]

While Inessa may have been at the Oblast Bureau meeting which

---

21 Podliashuk, p. 214.   22 Quoted in Clements, *Bolshevik Feminist*, p. 112.
23 Stal' in Krupskaia (ed.), *Pamiati*, p. 44; Inna Armand in Stasova (ed.), pp. 85–6; A. T. Barulina, 'Iz istorii bor'by partiinykh organizatsii Petrograda i Moskvy za zhenskie proletarskie massy v 1917 godu (iiul'-oktiabr')', *Vestnik Moskovskogo Universiteta*, series IX: *Istoriia*, 1962, no. 5, p. 60.
24 S. Smidovich, 'Rabota sredi zhenshchin v Moskve i Moskovskoi gubernii', *Kommunistka*, 1923, no. 11, p. 19.

adopted the idea, she certainly did not participate in the work of the commission. Sometime in August she returned to the family estate in Pushkino and remained there throughout the three crucial months of the October Revolution. This departure from Moscow may have been a result of frustration in trying to keep *Zhizn' rabotnitsy* alive or of a general feeling that party work would be unproductive, if not dangerous, in the aftermath of the July Days. The major factor in her decision, however, was the illness of her son Andre whom she feared had contracted tuberculosis.[25] She must have felt that the country air of Pushkino was more suitable than the pollution of the Arbat and that he would need more care than the aged Varvara Karlovna alone could provide. In her unpublished 'autobiography' she merely noted that 'in the fall of 1917 I worked in the [party's] Moscow District [*Okruzhnyi*] Committee and in the Moscow Guberniia Soviet'.[26] The only sign of this activity was a lecture which she gave for the District Committee on 'Soviet Power and the Constituent Assembly'.[27] There is no evidence whatsoever to support the contention that she 'participated in the planning of the armed uprising in Moscow'[28] or that she organized assistance for the Moscow insurgents from the surrounding areas.[29]

At least one member of the Armand family was active in the seizure of power in Moscow but on the wrong side. I. V. Got'e, a childhood friend of Inessa's but far more moderate in his political beliefs, wrote in his diary on 30 October 1917/ 12 November: 'There was an inspection of the attics of our building. Among the officer-volunteers were Fedia [Fedor] and Andriushka Armand; Fedia is making amends for his bolshevik mama. We treated them to lunch.'[30] That Fedor Armand was defending the remnants of the Provisional Government and preparing for street fighting against the Bolsheviks is not entirely surprising. He had entered the Imperial Army in December 1914, graduated from the Alekseev Military School in 1915, and served as a company commander in an infantry regiment until being sent to flying schools first at Gatchina and later in England. In 1917 he was attached to the English

[25] Podliashuk, p. 215; Fel'dman, 'Inessa Armand', p. 77.
[26] Cited in Podliashuk, p. 215.
[27] *Put' k Oktiabriu*, vol. II, p. 284.
[28] *Velikaia Oktiabr'skaia sotsialisticheskaia revoliutsiia* (Moscow, 1968), p. 38.
[29] As suggested by A. Abramov, *U kremlevskoi steny*, 5th edn (Moscow, 1983), p. 124.
[30] Got'e, p. 72. It seems unlikely that Got'e was referring to Inessa's 13-year-old son Andre when he used the diminutive 'Andriushka'. Perhaps the second officer was a cousin of her children, i.e., a son of Boris or a grandson of Emil or Adolf Armand.

Mission as a translator and was stationed at the Central Depot for Aviation Equipment in Moscow.[31]

* * *

Immediately after power had been consolidated in Moscow Inessa Armand was named to the Presidium of the new Moscow Guberniia Soviet[32] and delegated by that body to attend the Guberniia Congress of Peasant Deputies called earlier by the SR leaders of the former Soviet. Since very few Bolshevik deputies had been elected before October, the Socialist Revolutionaries were in control of the congress. Inessa employed a tactic she now had developed to perfection: she called together a few kindred souls and led them out of the congress hall.[33] Perhaps as an extension of this work, Armand then went to Petrograd where she attended the First Extraordinary Congress of Peasant Deputies which opened on 10/23 November 1917.[34] Bolsheviks with any knowledge of peasant matters were scarce and thus Inessa, on the basis of this limited experience at two congresses, was drafted to work on peasant affairs for the Central Committee in Petrograd.[35] Little is known about the precise nature of this work, which lasted for two months, except that it was sufficiently important for Lenin to issue instructions that she be given a pass to attend meetings of the Council of People's Commissars at the Smolny Institute.[36]

In late January 1918 Armand returned to Moscow, possibly because of her growing involvement with the Left Communist opposition to Lenin's pending Brest-Litovsk peace with Germany. In her 'autobiography' she acknowledged that 'I joined the Left Communists over the question of the Brest peace but was on their right wing and very clearly opposed to a break with the party.'[37] The first manifestation of her opposition came at the Fourth Congress of Soviets, which met in Moscow from 14 to 16 March 1918, where she abstained from voting on the ratification of the peace treaty and joined other Left Communists in issuing a declaration that 'this treaty should not be ratified. On the contrary, it is necessary to substitute for it an appeal for the sacred

---

31 Institute for the Study of the USSR, *Who Was Who in the USSR* (Metuchen, N.J., 1972), p. 29.
32 *Ocherki istorii Moskovskoi organizatsii KPSS* (Moscow, 1966), p. 276.
33 Krupskaia in Krupskaia (ed.), *Pamiati*, p. 23.
34 D. I. Grazkin, 'Glubokoe znanie zhizni trudiashchikhsia', *Vosp. o V. I. Lenine*, vol. III, pp. 92–3.
35 Podliashuk, p. 220.   36 *Biog. khr.*, vol. V, p. 198.
37 Cited in Podliashuk, pp. 194–5.

defence of the socialist revolution.'[38] Her name also appeared on the
masthead of two issues of *Kommunist*, the organ of the Moscow Oblast
Bureau and the mouthpiece of the Left Communists, though there is no
indication that she contributed any articles to the journal.[39] 'The largest
and most powerful Bolshevik opposition in the history of Soviet Russia'[40] died out in June and July 1918 with the beginning of the Civil
War and the introduction of War Communism.

Even though Armand's affiliation with the Left Communists was her
most overt defiance of Lenin, it certainly was not the first time she
disagreed with him nor was it inconsistent with her previous ideological
orientation. Many of the Left Communists had been her friends in Baugy
or elsewhere in Switzerland during the war – Bukharin, Piatakov,
Radek, Safarov, Usievich, Ravich; others had been colleagues in the
Moscow organization – N. Osinskii, G. I. Bokii, Iakovleva, Bubnov.[41]
Indeed, the Moscow Committee and especially the Moscow Oblast
Bureau were the strongholds of the movement. The ideas which she had
shared with the Baugy Group during the war and the grounds for
disagreeing with Lenin over the defence of the fatherland were consistent with her opposing the Brest peace as a sell-out of proletarian
internationalism. In 1916 she argued that 'the worker has no
fatherland' and that there were no just wars which pitted workers
against one another. In 1917 she was a strong advocate of fraternization in the trenches, of taking advantage of the situation on the
eastern front to begin the march toward world revolution and a 'proletarian peace'. She talked about a workers' militia in Russia and an
'international army of the proletariat' in Europe.[42] Like other Left
Communists, she saw world revolution as inevitable and felt it was the
duty of the Russian proletariat to join the European proletariat in
waging revolutionary war. To sign the Brest peace was a short-term
expediency and a long-term surrender to world imperialism which now
was in a position to crush the new Soviet state.

In other areas as well the Left Communists were more orthodox than
Lenin and opposed his ideological concessions for the sake of political
survival. They opposed his adoption in early 1918 of the Socialist

---

[38] Quoted in *Istoriia KPSS*, vol. III, pt. 1, p. 556.
[39] For her involvement with the Left Communists, see also V1. Sorin, *Partiia i Oppozitsiia: iz istorii oppozitsionnykh techenii*, vol. I: *Fraktsiia levykh kommunistov* (Moscow, 1925).
[40] Cohen, p. 63.
[41] See Ronnie Kowalski, 'The Left Communist Movement in 1918: A Preliminary Analysis of Regional Strength', *Sbornik* of the Study Group on the Russian Revolution, no. 12 (1986), pp. 52–3, for a list of the leading Left Communists.
[42] 'Protokoly pervoi (Moskovskoi) oblastnoi konferentsii ... ', p. 164.

Revolutionary programme of land socialization and the resulting division of the land into small unproductive units.[43] It would be interesting to know if Inessa Armand, who was involved in formulating peasant policy at the time, left her work with the Central Committee because of disagreements with this programme and whether it influenced her decision to join the Left Communists. After the Brest peace was implemented in March 1918, many Left Communists started to criticize Lenin's new economic policies which called for an abandonment of worker control and a reduction in the nationalization of industry in favour of more labour discipline and cooperation with bourgeois managers. Throughout 1917 Armand had been a strong advocate of worker control. Her continued defence of these utopian policies may explain the presence of her name in *Kommunist*'s masthead on 27 April and 16 May after defeat on Brest-Litovsk had been acknowledged. It may also explain her appointment in April 1918 by the Moscow Guberniia Soviet as chair of the Guberniia Economic Council (Sovnarkhoz). In other places, most notably in and around Moscow, the *sovnarkhozi* had become bastions of Left Communist support.[44] Thus, rather than resigning her state positions in protest against Brest-Litovsk, as other Left Communists such as Aleksandra Kollontai had done, Inessa Armand may have taken up her appointment so as to have some influence on economic decision making.

The Moscow Guberniia Economic Council was one of thirty-eight guberniia *sovnarkhozi* set up under the general authority of the Supreme Economic Council (VSNKh) between 23 December 1917 and May 1918. The Supreme Council 'was originally conceived as the lynch-pin of the entire economic life of the country'.[45] Its mandate was to 'work out the general norms and plans for regulating the economic life of the country, coordinate and unify the activities of the central and local regulatory institutions'.[46]

One of the many problems facing VSNKh was that the 'local regulatory institutions', i.e., the guberniia *sovnarkhozi*, were set up by their respective soviets and considered themselves answerable to these soviets. This meant, among other things, that local economic needs and

---

[43] For Left Communist agrarian policy, see Ronald I. Kowalski, 'The Transition to Socialism: The Programme of the Left Communist Movement of 1918', unpublished paper presented to the Soviet Industrialization Seminar (March 1985), pp. 7–11.

[44] Samuel A. Oppenheim, 'The Supreme Economic Council, 1917–21', *Soviet Studies*, vol. XXV, no. 1 (July 1973), pp. 6, 12–13; Kowalski, 'The Left Communist Movement', p. 31.

[45] Oppenheim, 'Supreme Economic Council', p. 19.   [46] Cited in *ibid.*, p. 4.

particularly a logical desire to hoard local resources often took priority over central planning and control.[47] A further complication was the frequent appointment by local soviets of Left Communists such as Inessa Armand to guberniia *sovnarkhozi* where they could both perpetuate the principles of workers' control over those of labour discipline and also engage in 'wildcat' nationalizations 'more for reasons of politics than economics'.[48] These problems became less acute when the government committed itself to sweeping nationalization in June 1918 and to the militarization of labour following the outbreak of the Civil War in July.

The choice of Inessa Armand to chair the Moscow Guberniia Sovnarkhoz may have been influenced by her political orientation or by the fact that as a sitting member on the Presidium of the Guberniia Soviet she could be counted on to keep local interests foremost. She certainly was not chosen because of her economic training or business acumen since she was totally lacking in either. Perhaps like Aleksei Rykov, a Bolshevik of similar background who took over as chairperson of VSNKh in April 1918, she was picked because it was thought her integrity and her lack of expertise would lead her to be a good coordinator.[49] While she continued to be engaged in other endeavours during 1918 – arranging conferences for working women, participating in the French Section of the Russian Communist Party, teaching at various party schools and sitting on the All-Russian Central Executive Committee (VTsIK) – her principal activity from April 1918 until the end of January 1919 was to coordinate the work of the Moscow Guberniia Economic Council.

This was a difficult assignment. On most *sovnarkhozi* there were representatives from the workers' control movement, trade unions, local industry and the guberniia soviets – each with conflicting interests.[50] At the first plenary meeting of Moscow Guberniia Sovnarkhoz on 25 April 1918 Armand noted that their tasks would be to 'regulate' and 'organize' the economic life of the guberniia as well as serving as the contact between local economic units and higher economic organs.[51] These tasks were complicated by the enormity of the economic problems facing any body seeking to 'regulate' the economy of a large region of Russia in the summer and fall of 1918. Productivity had been disrupted

---

[47] The problem of 'localism' is discussed in more detail in Buchanan, pp. 94–101, and in Thomas F. Remington, *Building Socialism in Bolshevik Russia: Ideology and Industrial Organization, 1917–1921* (Pittsburgh, 1984), pp. 60–72.
[48] Oppenheim, 'Supreme Economic Council', p. 13.   [49] *Ibid.*, p. 7.
[50] Buchanan, p. 95.
[51] L. I. Davydova, 'Inessa Armand – pervyi predsedatel' Mosgubsovnarkhoza', *Istoricheskii arkhiv*, 1959, no. 5, p. 250.

by two revolutions in 1917 and now by Civil War and foreign military intervention; 25 per cent of the industrial labour force had left Moscow; there was a shortage of food in the cities aggravated by a shortage of agricultural machinery in the countryside; and there was a lack of fuel especially after the beginning of the Civil War and the consumption of tsarist reserves. Fuel consumption in Moscow during 1918 was 56 per cent of what it had been in 1916 and this in turn reduced drastically industrial production[52] even in an area blessed with abundant wood and peat. A shortage of fuel and of raw materials, particularly cotton, caused 20.1 per cent of Moscow's industries to be idle by the end of August 1918.[53]

Armand's immediate goals for her *sovnarkhoz* were realistic and largely organizational or informational in nature. There was a need, she told the plenary session on 25 April, to create economic councils in all the districts of the guberniia and to establish special sections for the five main industries of the region. At a meeting of the *sovnarkhoz* presidium later that month she suggested arranging periodic conferences, inspections and training sessions at the factory level.[54] According to her Soviet biographer, she personally visited many of the factories in Moscow Guberniia and worked to recruit experienced people, even bourgeois specialists and managers, who could train new Soviet economic cadres.[55]

After eight months, Inessa could report modest success in reaching these objectives.[56] Lower-level *sovnarkhozi* had been created in almost all districts under her jurisdiction; special sections had been set up for four of the five targeted industries in the guberniia; all industrial operations had been inspected; an inventory of the economic resources of the guberniia had been completed; in accordance with the June 1918 decrees, most bourgeois industrial holdings had been nationalized; and progress had been made in regulating the supply and financial aspects

---

[52] Richard Sakwa, 'The Commune State in Moscow in 1918', *Slavic Review*, vol. XLVI, nos. 3/4 (Fall/Winter 1987), pp. 432–3; Oppenheim, 'Supreme Economic Council', pp. 17–20.

[53] Richard Sakwa, *Soviet Communists in Power: A Study of Moscow during the Civil War, 1918–21* (London, 1988), p. 45.

[54] Davydova, 'Inessa Armand', p. 250.   [55] Podliashuk, pp. 224–5.

[56] Armand published two reports in January 1919: a detailed one on the work of the Moscow Guberniia Sovnarkhoz entitled 'Moskovskii Gubernskii Sovet Narodnogo Khoziaistva i ego rabota', in *Sotsialisticheskoe stroitel'stvo*, no. 2 (18 January 1919), pp. 50–5; and a general one on the work of the Supreme Economic Council entitled 'God raboty Soveta' which was originally published in French in *La IIIe Internationale* (Moscow), 12 January 1919, and reproduced with material omitted in Armand, *Stat'i*, pp. 46–9. This summary is based on these two reports.

of industrial production. But, as she admitted, 'we are still a long way from regulating everything'.[57] She noted the practical necessity of re-drawing administrative and geographic borders to reflect economic reality; the need to resolve jurisdictional disputes with neighbouring *sovnarkhozi*; the perennial problem of trying to mesh the concurrent horizontal and vertical organization of Soviet industry; and the reluctance of trade unions to second experienced organizers to work for the new regulatory agencies. She failed, however, to mention the key statistic: productivity in Moscow Guberniia in 1918 was down by almost 39 per cent in comparison to 1917. In the crucial textile industry, production stood at 40 per cent of pre-war levels in 1918 and declined to 21.7 per cent in 1919.[58] Perhaps this failure was inevitable given the dislocation caused by the Civil War, fuel shortages, wholesale nationalization, and an attempt to effect a radical transformation of an economy without first having sufficient human and material resources. Inessa Armand left her position as chair of the Moscow Guberniia Economic Council in late January 1919 at about the time that the powers of all *sovnarkhozi* were being reduced in favour of a momentarily stronger Supreme Council.[59] One suspects that she turned her attention to other, more familiar matters with a certain sense of relief.

Throughout her nine months as *sovnarkhoz* chairperson she continued to be active in pedagogical work. In the spring of 1918 the Moscow Oblast Bureau established a School for Soviet and Party Workers. Inessa, on the basis of her experience at Longjumeau and at the 1917 Moscow party school, was given the job of setting up the curriculum of the new school and overseeing its first term of operation. Twenty-one courses – starting with the principles of dialectical materialism and ending with the art of public speaking – were offered in the former residence of the Moscow textile magnate P. L. Riabushinskii. Inessa herself lectured the fifty enrolled students on the 'Woman Question' and on the 'History of the Workers' Movement in Western Europe'. In the second term, the school joined forces with another programme run by the Soviet's Central Executive Committee for instructors and agitators. Within a year this amalgamated school was superseded by the Sverdlov Communist University at which Armand also on occasion taught.[60]

---

[57] Armand, 'Moskovskii Gubernskii Sovet ... ', p. 50.
[58] Derived from table in Sakwa, p. 46. Richard Sakwa's discussion of the general problems of the Moscow-area *sovnarkhozi* (pp. 49–53) makes it clear that Armand was not unique either in the difficulties which she encountered or in her lack of measurable results.
[59] Buchanan, p. 282.   [60] Podliashuk, pp. 218–19.

As an active member of the presidium of the Moscow Guberniia Soviet of Workers and Soldiers Deputies in 1918 and 1919, Armand was often delegated to serve as the guberniia's representative to the All-Russian Central Executive Committee (VTsIK).[61] This position near the apex of the state hierarchy brought with it certain perquisites. On 16 December 1918 Lenin wrote to the commandant of the Kremlin, P. D. Mal'kov, asking him to provide Inessa as a member of VTsIK with accommodations suitable for four persons.[62] He also arranged later on for her apartment to be connected to the closed-circuit Kremlin telephone system.[63] These efforts on her behalf allowed her to escape the 'desperately cramped' quarters in the Hotel National which she shared with her daughter Varvara throughout most of 1918.[64]

The first year of the revolution had greatly affected the lives of the Armand family, as it did those of most Russian citizens. Varvara, who was studying art and sculpture in a school where students paid no fees and chose their own teachers, was the only one of Inessa's children still living with her.[65] Varvara's older sister Inna, the first of the Armand children to join the party in April 1917, had been secretary of a party youth group in Moscow until the summer of 1918 when she volunteered to do political work in a Red Army unit in Astrakhan.[66] Fedor, probably much to his mother's relief, was also in the Red Army serving as a pilot-observer and then as acting commander of the 38th Air Squadron.[67] Alexander, after serving in the army through most of the war, left Moscow in the fall of 1918 for Mogilev to help set up schools and do 'enlightenment work' for the new regime. The baby of the family, Andre, was in a 'model school' and, much to Inessa's displeasure, was forced by the Commissariat of Education to board at the school with the rest of the students. Even her former husband Alexander had left Moscow, giving up the apartment on Denezhnyi Lane to live in his country home in Aleshino, five kilometres from their old estate at Eldigino. Inessa mentioned to Inna in late September that he was in the process of equipping a textile mill which he would manage, perhaps as

---

[61] Krupskaia in Krupskaia (ed.), *Pamiati*, p. 23.   [62] *Biog. khr.*, vol. VI, p. 317.

[63] Fischer, p. 487.

[64] Letter to Inna Armand (between 3 October and 6 November 1918), in Armand, *Stat'i*, p. 254. See also Marcel Body, 'Les groupes communistes français de Russie, 1918–1921', in Jacques Freymond (ed.), *Contributions à l'histoire du Comintern* (Geneva, 1965), p. 44.

[65] Letter to Inna Armand (between 3 October and 6 November 1918), in Armand, *Stat'i*, p. 254.

[66] Lenin, *PSS*, vol. LII, p. 465.

[67] Institute for the Study of the USSR, *Who Was Who*, p. 29.

one of the bourgeois specialists the *sovnarkhozi* were now employing.[68] Several months later, in early February 1919, Inessa herself left Moscow and her various duties there to be part of an ill-fated Red Cross Mission to France.

[68] Information on the two Alexanders and Andre is contained in Inessa's letter to Inna (after 15 September 1918), in Armand, *Stat'i*, p. 253.

CHAPTER 11

FRENCH FIASCO

On 12 January 1919 Inessa Armand had been named by the Commissariat of Foreign Affairs (Narkomindel) as one of the three members of a 'Red Cross Mission' the Soviet government proposed sending to France. The stated purpose of the mission was to assist in the repatriation of the 45,000 Russian soldiers who had fought in France during the First World War.[1] Now that the war was over, they were of no military value to the French and most wanted to return home. From the Soviet point of view, these troops would be extremely useful to the Red Army in the Civil War and, conversely, it was obviously desirable that they not end up fighting in the White Russian armies. Overland routes for their return were out of the question, not only because France lacked the rolling stock needed to send so many troops by rail, but also because Switzerland and Germany refused to allow passage after breaking off relations with Soviet Russia in November 1918.[2] Since this meant that the soldiers would have to go by sea, the Narkomindel wanted to make sure the route chosen was the Baltic rather than either the White or the Black Sea whose ports were in anti-Bolshevik hands. The Commissariat of Foreign Affairs argued that a Russian Red Cross delegation was needed in France to assist in making these transportation arrangements and to determine that all those who wanted to return were given an opportunity to do so.[3] From the French point of view, the exchange would facilitate the return of some 100 French citizens held as hostages by the Soviet government after the French military intervention in Archangel during August 1918.

Both sides realized, however, that the Red Cross Mission had unstated and perhaps more important objectives as well. It could be used as a 'cover' for other activities such as ascertaining the mood of the French

---

[1] Richard K. Debo, 'The Manuilskii Mission: An Early Soviet Effort to Negotiate with France, August 1918–April 1919', *The International History Review*, vol. VIII, no. 2 (May 1986), p. 220. Soviet estimates of the number of Russian soldiers in France vary from 35,000 (*Dokumenty vneshnei politiki SSSR*, vol. II [Moscow, 1958], p. 27n [hereafter *DVP*]) to 60,000 (Podliashuk, p. 237).

[2] Debo, 'Manuilskii Mission', p. 220.   [3] *DVP*, vol. II, pp. 112–13.

workers, telling them the 'truth about Soviet Russia',[4] making contact with radical elements in the French Socialist Party, undermining at home French interventionary efforts in Russia, and perhaps even fomenting the start of world revolution in France. Similar Soviet Red Cross missions were used as fronts for political and revolutionary activity in several other European countries; indeed, in January 1919 four members of a Red Cross delegation to Poland had been killed and another arrested in Hungary on suspicion of carrying out illegal operations.[5] Richard Debo has recently suggested that the 'real aim' of the Red Cross Mission was neither humanitarian nor revolutionary but rather 'to open peace negotiations with the government of France' so as to end both French intervention and also Soviet isolation.[6] The French government, however, was upset with the cancellation of tsarist debts and convinced that the Soviet regime would soon be toppled. It therefore had no interest in regularizing relations or in taking any steps toward a negotiated peace before the conclusion of the Paris peace conferences.

At first glance it would seem as if the two hidden objectives of the Soviet Red Cross Mission – to foment revolution and to regularize relations – were contradictory and self-defeating. In practice, it was one of the first examples of the duality of early Soviet foreign policy wherein one agency sought to use illegal measures to undermine the same government from which another Soviet agency was seeking concessions by diplomatic means. In this instance, the French government was well aware of and opposed to both objectives. It could frustrate the mission on both scores simply by denying it an 'official' character and isolating it from all contact with French and Russian citizens.

The fact that the Soviet government had more than just humanitarian purposes in mind was evident in its selection of the personnel for the Red Cross Mission. All three were 'old French hands' and trusted party members; two were high in the Soviet hierarchy and had considerably more political influence than was needed to arrange a simple exchange of interned soldiers for hostages. The head of the delegation was D. Z. Manuil'skii. Manuil'skii, who was 36 years old, had joined the Social

---

[4] Podliashuk, p. 233.
[5] Branko Lazitch and Milorad M. Drachkovitch, *Lenin and the Comintern*, vol. I (Stanford, 1972), p. 132; *DVP*, vol. II, p. 34.
[6] Debo, 'Manuilskii Mission', p. 215. The Red Cross Mission was virtually ignored by Western scholars before the appearance of Richard Debo's article. Information which he found in the archives of the French Foreign Ministry confirms and supplements previously published Soviet documents (see *DVP*, vol. II, pp. 27–160). The following discussion of the Red Cross Mission owes much to his careful investigation.

Democratic Party in 1903, become an Otzovist or left Bolshevik after the 1905 Revolution, and a follower of Trotskii during the war. He returned to Russia on the second 'sealed train' in May 1917 and, as a member of Trotskii's *Mezhraionka*, joined the Bolsheviks in August of that year. After the October Revolution he became the Soviet negotiator with Ukraine, a member of the Central Committee from 1923 to 1952, and the secretary of the Comintern from 1926 until its dissolution. According to the French ambassador to Sweden, Manuil'skii was 'one of the most dangerous soviet leaders, because he is intelligent and flexible'.[7] Armand had first met Manuil'skii while on her underground mission to St Petersburg in 1912 and she subsequently had dealings with him in Paris in 1914 and again in 1916. Inessa also knew the second member of the mission, Jacques Davtian, who had worked with her in the Brussels Social Democratic group in 1909 to 1910 and had been one of her subordinates in the Moscow Guberniia Sovarkhoz in 1918. He later held a succession of ambassadorial posts in Lithuania, Iran, Greece, and Poland.[8]

Armand was a logical third member of the delegation. Like the other two, she was fluent in French and had lived in Paris intermittently from September 1910 to April 1916 where she had come to know many of the leaders and factions of the French Socialist Party. Like Manuil'skii, she was considered one of Soviet Russia's leading experts on France. She also had been involved for much of 1918 in the work of the French Section of the Russian Communist Party – a unique new body which suddenly found itself in need of an agent with a legal cover in France.

In the spring of 1918 a series of foreign communist groups had been formed in Soviet Russia out of prisoners of war and *émigré* residents to support the October Revolution and to spread revolution to their native lands. In May these groups, most of which were made up of eastern European nationals, had united under Bela Kun to form the Federation of Foreign Groups which in turn was affiliated with the Central Committee of the Russian Communist Party. After allied intervention in northern Russia in August 1918, a short-lived Anglo-French Communist Group had been formed. At its second meeting on 4 September Inessa Armand had suggested the establishment of a special French Section of the Russian Communist Party that could organize the French-speaking proletariat in Russia, agitate among the French interventionary forces,

---

[7] Cited in Debo, 'Manuilskii Mission', p. 226. On Manuil'skii, see also *ibid.*, p. 224, and Branko Lazitch, *Biographical Dictionary of the Comintern*, 2nd edn (Stanford, 1986), p. 295.   [8] Podliashuk, p. 236; Debo, 'Manuilskii Mission', p. 224.

and inform the workers of France, Belgium and Switzerland about the goals of the October Revolution. The group, which never had more than a score of members, was diverse in its composition. In addition to French-speaking Russians like Armand who had lived in France and had an interest in French affairs, it included a number of French communists. Some, such as Jeanne Labourbe, had been in Russia for many years while others, like Boris Souvarine, had been attracted by the success of the October Revolution. One of the key members of the Section was Captain Jacques Sadoul, a former member of the French Military Mission in Moscow. The group had no officers other than Labourbe who served as secretary and Armand who functioned as a liaison with the Central Committee.[9]

One of the major activities of the French Section was the publication of a four-page, French-language newspaper, *La IIIe Internationale*. Co-edited by Armand and Sadoul, this paper first came out on 20 October 1918 and continued to publish one issue a week until 1 March 1919. Its 10,000 copies were distributed among French-speaking residents of Moscow, where possible among French troops engaged in the Russian Civil War, and in small numbers among workers in francophone countries of western Europe. The editors sought to publish articles which illuminated Soviet peace overtures, the need to protect the new Soviet state, and the accomplishments of that state.[10] While Armand is alleged to have written 'many articles' for the paper which she co-edited,[11] only one of these appears in her collected works.[12] Another, 'Etouffront-ils bolchevisme?', was subsequently adapted for publication as a leaflet and widely circulated among French troops on the southern front.[13] The composition and circulation of these leaflets, and the publication of an underground French newspaper *Le Communiste* in Odessa, was principally the work of a new Board of Foreign Propagandists created in part out of members of the French Section who could provide language skills lacking in party units near the front. Armand was fortunate that

---

[9] On the formation and composition of the French Section, see L. M. Zak, 'Deiatel'nost' Frantsuzskoi kommunisticheskoi gruppy RKP(b) v 1918–1919 godakh', *Voprosy istorii*, 1960, no. 2, pp. 153–5; Kriegel, p. 266. See also the memoirs of another former member of the French Military Mission who joined the Section, Marcel Body, 'Les groupes communistes français', pp. 39–44.

[10] On *La IIIe Internationale*, see Zak, pp. 156–8; Kriegel, p. 265.

[11] Karavashkova, p. 56.

[12] I. Armand, 'God raboty Soveta', in Armand, *Stat'i*, pp. 46–9. I have been unable to locate a copy of *La IIIe Internationale* in Western libraries.

[13] The leaflet is found in L. M. Zak, 'Kommunisticheskie listovki i vozzvaniia k soldatam antanty', *Istoricheskii arkhiv*, 1958, no. 1, pp. 32–4, under the title 'Podaviat li oni bol'shevizm?'.

her other activities kept her from being seconded to the Board of Foreign Propagandists. One of those who was sent, Jeanne Labourbe, was captured and shot in Odessa on 1 March 1919 while Inessa was in France.[14]

Because of the Civil War and the allied naval blockade, the French Section found it difficult to establish contact with revolutionary elements in France, to get their newspaper into the hands of French workers, and to obtain news about unrest in France. An ideal solution to some of these problems would be to have one of the Section's members sent to France under the protection of a diplomatic passport. This thinking was undoubtedly a contributing factor in the decision to include Inessa Armand in the Red Cross Mission.

Even though the negotiations over the exchange had been going on since August 1918 through the Danish consul in Moscow, it was not until 9 January 1919 that an agreement in principle was reached to exchange 1150 Russian soldiers and 57 civilians for 26 French military personnel and 42 civilians. It was agreed that the steamship *Megallas Hellas* would bring the Russians to Riga or another Baltic port and return with some of the French hostages and the Red Cross Mission. Once the mission reported that all of the remaining Russians in France were free to return, then the second contingent of French would be released.[15] The French accepted the Red Cross Mission with reluctance. One official at the Quai d'Orsay felt 'that the presence in France of delegates from the Russian Red Cross would not be without inconvenience and it would be desirable to avoid it ... [but] henceforth we also would have in the persons of the three Russian delegates certain interesting hostages'.[16] On 29 January the French finally decided to guarantee the personal immunity of the delegates but noted that they 'will be expelled if they use the guise of a humanitarian mission as a cover for carrying out acts of propaganda'.[17]

Manuil'skii and Davtian welcomed the delay as it gave them an opportunity to purchase new clothes appropriate to their diplomatic status. Much to their dismay, Inessa – who had always been neatly, almostly stylishly, dressed before the revolution – announced that Parisian fashions were a waste of the peoples' money and that she

---

[14] Zak, 'Deiatel'nost' Frantsuzskoi kommunisticheskoi gruppy', pp. 160–1; Zak, 'Kommunisticheskie listovki', p. 27; Body, 'Les groupes communistes français', pp. 44–5.
[15] *DVP*, vol. II, p. 27.
[16] Jules Laroche, as cited in Debo, 'Manuilskii Mission', p. 223.
[17] *DVP*, vol. II, pp. 53–4.

would wear the same drab clothing that had sufficed since 1917. Davtian told Vinogradskaia that he and Manuil'skii feared this sartorial disparity would lead the French to think that Soviet men dressed well but forced their wives to wear rags.[18] His concern proved groundless since they were to be seen by very few French citizens.

Armand finally picked up her diplomatic passport, one of the first issued by the Soviet state, on 4 February 1919 and crossed the Finnish border four days later with the other members of the mission. Because of ice in the Baltic, which had prevented the *Megallas Hellas* from proceeding beyond Copenhagen, the return trip was slow and necessitated a change of vessels. Upon reaching Dunkerque on 22 February, the delegation was taken under heavy escort to the nearby resort of Malo-les-Bains where they were accommodated first in a hastily evacuated hotel and then in a private villa.[19] Much to their displeasure, they found they were under virtual house arrest. The day after their arrival the French confiscated the 1.5 million rubles and 49,000 Swiss francs they had brought with them supposedly to help Russian soldiers wanting to return home.[20] To underline the unofficial character of the mission, the French denied them the right to receive diplomatic mail, to send telegrams or coded messages to Moscow, to hire secretaries or translators, or to establish their headquarters in Paris as planned.[21] Instead, Lt. Col. Wehrlen, the Russian-speaking officer in charge of their safety, was told to enforce an earlier decision that 'all contact between the delegates and certain French or Russian circles was to be avoided at any price'.[22] Wehrlen made sure that they received no unauthorized visitors and made no unescorted excursions.

This 'internment' frustrated all three objectives of the mission: they could not visit centres where Russian soldiers were being kept, they could not contact French radicals, and they could not spread Russian peace plans or engage in official discussions with the French government. Dunkerque might have been a pleasant place in the summer to recuperate from a particularly hard Russian winter but in February and March the English Channel resort was raw and inhospitable. About the

---

[18] Vinogradskaia, p. 220.
[19] An early Soviet report erroneously identified Malo-les-Bains as 'the island of St Malo' – a mistake which has been repeated by several Western writers. Cf., *The Foreign Policy of Soviet Russia: Report Submitted by the People's Commissariat for Foreign Affairs to the Seventh All-Russian Congress of Soviets* (London, [1920]), pp. 14–15; E. H. Carr, *A History of Soviet Russia: The Bolshevik Revolution, 1917–1923*, vol. III (London, 1961), p. 114.
[20] *Pravda*, 20 May 1919, p. 2.   [21] *DVP*, vol. II, pp. 54 and 115.
[22] Cited in Debo, 'Manuilskii Mission', p. 225.

only entertainment was to listen to Manuil'skii, who had a 'jovial air and [an] inexhaustible stock of stories and jokes',[23] do amusing impersonations of various Soviet leaders.[24] Armand, in particular, appeared to chafe under these restrictions and sought to circumvent them. On one occasion she contrived to grant a short interview to a reporter from *Le Populaire* and on another she stood by the villa window so that a photographer from *Le Petit Parisien* could get a picture of her under guard. She also went out of her way to torment her French escort who reported that she displayed a 'hateful state of mind' and 'an absolute want of intelligence'.[25]

While the delegates had been effectively neutralized in Malo-les-Bains, the French soon realized that their citizens and military personnel still held in Russia would not be repatriated until the Red Cross Mission reported that all Russians in France were free to return to their homeland. Therefore, on 26 March, a compromise was suggested. The mission could communicate with Moscow, it could put notices in the press informing other Russians how to get in touch with the mission, and it could remain in France after the scheduled departure of a second contingent of Russians in early April.[26] Manuil'skii and Davtian were in favour of accepting these concessions; Armand, however, felt they did not go far enough. Sometime after 28 March the Russian mission was allowed to communicate these terms to Moscow along with an account of their frustrations to date and a French commentary on the Russian interpretation of the events of the past five weeks.[27] The ensuing exchange of telegrams between the Commissar of Foreign Affairs, G. V. Chicherin, and the Quai d'Orsay ignored Manuil'skii's request for 'further instructions' and became increasingly polemical and threatening. Finally, on 10 April the French informed Moscow that they considered 'the polemics exhausted' and that the Red Cross Mission would be sent back to Russia with the second contingent of Russian repatriates.[28]

With a forced departure imminent, Inessa Armand apparently made plans to escape Malo-les-Bains. According to the police, her guard was

---

[23] Georges Haupt and Jean-Jacques Marie, *Makers of the Russian Revolution: Biographies of Bolshevik Leaders* (Ithaca, 1974), p. 314. See also Isaac Deutscher, *The Prophet Armed: Trotsky, 1879–1921* (New York, 1954), p. 222.

[24] I. A. Armand, 'Vospominaniia o Vladimire Il'iche Lenine', in *Vosp. o V. I. Lenine*, vol. IV, p. 328.

[25] Cited in Debo, 'Manuilskii Mission', p. 231.   [26] *DVP*, vol. II, pp. 115–16.

[27] *Ibid.*, pp. 115–17.

[28] Cited in Debo, 'Manuilskii Mission', p. 230, which has a more detailed summary of this exchange. See also *DVP*, vol. II, pp. 112–15.

to be overpowered by several well-armed men while she was taking a walk along the beach and she was then to be driven by a high-powered car to Paris so as 'to make a triumphant appearance on May Day'.[29] To frustrate these plans, the police decided to move the three Russians immediately to the *Dumont d'Urville* and to hold them there until the ship was ready to depart for the Baltic. Manuil'skii, who initially feared that their sudden detention was a prelude to suffering the same fate as the murdered Red Cross delegates in Poland, must have been relieved when they finally left French waters three days later with a second group of 1000 Russian soldiers. His problems were not over yet, however. Either because of heavy ice in the Baltic or the perversity of the French, the *Dumont d'Urville* put into Hangö in early May rather than one of the friendlier ports the Russians had suggested. The anti-Bolshevik Finnish government at first refused to allow either the soldiers or the Red Cross Mission to disembark and then threatened them with internment. It took further threats against the French hostages by Chicherin[30] to get the situation resolved and, even so, the Red Cross Mission did not re-enter Russia until 15 May. To show its irritation, the Soviet government then exchanged only three very ill French citizens it had held in captivity.

The Red Cross Mission was a fiasco on all levels. It had played no role in the return of the 2200 troops through the Baltic. The remainder of the more than 40,000 Russian troops in France were sent back by way of Odessa where General Denikin had a chance to enroll or impress them into his White Army.[31] Manuil'skii had no opportunity to popularize Bolshevik peace proposals or to regularize relations with France. On the day his mission was forcibly put on the *Dumont d'Urville*, he took aside the French officer in charge and confided that his primary objective was 'to engage the French government in negotiations that would serve as the beginning of a *rapprochement*'.[32] In return for peace and economic cooperation, he said his government was willing to recognize pre-war tsarist debts owed to France, grant industrial concessions in Russia, and put an end to 'official' propaganda in France. Since the French government was still more interested in the rapid demise of the Soviet regime than in cooperating with it, this last-minute overture was ignored. Inessa Armand, who like many former Left Communists had no sympathy with these attempts to improve relations with bourgeois

---

[29] Debo, 'Manuilskii Mission', p. 231.
[30] See note of 9 May 1919 to the French Foreign Minister in *DVP*, vol. II, p. 160.
[31] *Foreign Policy of Soviet Russia*, p. 15.
[32] Cited in Debo, 'Manuilskii Mission', p. 232.

France, had even less success in contacting radical elements on behalf of the French Section or in fomenting unrest. While she could 'say with some confidence' upon her return to Russia 'that France is already on the eve of revolution',[33] this optimistic conclusion was not a result of her personal observations or of her personal contributions in France. One sign of her failure was the absence of a delegate from France at the First Congress of the Communist International which met in Moscow in March 1919. Ironically, because of their failed mission, she and Manuil'skii also missed out on the formation of the Comintern – a body they both would be deeply involved in for the rest of their lives.

Because the French could not or would not land in a Russian port, Armand also was unable to assist one of her sons when he ran afoul of revolutionary justice. In late April Fedor Armand, still serving as a pilot in the 38th Air Squadron, was arrested by his divisional commander on suspicion of treason. Whether this suspicion had its roots in the Armand name or in Fedor's anti-Bolshevik activities in October 1917 or in events at the front during the Civil War is unknown. Fortunately, his mother had friends in high places. On 3 May 1919, while Inessa was stranded in Hangö harbour, V. I. Lenin cabled the Minsk Military Committee that F. A. Armand, 'who is personally known to me, is trustworthy even if he is a former officer and a non-communist. I ask Red Army comrades not to treat him with suspicion.'[34] As a result of this intervention, Fedor Armand was released and remained in the fledgling Red air force as an instructor until 1926.[35]

[33] E. Blonina [I. F. Armand], 'Perspektivy revoliutsii vo Frantsii', *Kommunisticheskii Internatsional*, no. 3 (1 July 1919), p. 338. See also D. Manuil'skii, 'Kogda budet revoliutsiia vo Frantsii?', *Pravda*, 20 May 1919, p. 1.
[34] Lenin, *PSS*, vol. L, p. 301.
[35] Institute for the Study of the USSR, *Who Was Who*, p. 29.

CHAPTER 12

SOVIET FEMINISM

After Inessa Armand returned to Moscow in mid-May 1919 she turned her attention to party work among Russian women. This activity, which took up almost all of her time during the last sixteen months of her life, represents her chief contribution to Soviet feminism. Unlike in 1918, she concentrated her efforts and her abilities on one objective rather than taking on a myriad of assignments. She no longer permitted herself to be deflected by opposition movements within the party; she gratefully allowed the Moscow Guberniia Sovnarkhoz to be run by someone with more economic training; she welcomed the absorption of the French Section and its propaganda activities into the new Comintern;[1] and she left the running of the party schools to others though she lectured occasionally on topics of interest to her. The period from the summer of 1919 to the summer of 1920 was the most productive and perhaps rewarding of her life. She was doing work she enjoyed, she no longer was anyone's 'Girl Friday', and she could see that the goal of female emancipation was gradually being achieved in part through her own efforts. The work also took its toll. Many influential people did not agree with her objectives and tried to frustrate her efforts; women's liberation was low on the party's list of priorities and rarely received the resources it required; and living conditions in Moscow during 1919–20 were bleak and difficult even for someone in the 'new class'. Inessa worked long hours, smoked incessantly, ate poorly and did not look after her health.[2] Her succumbing to illness at the age of 46 in September 1920 is not altogether surprising.

*   *   *

What may be surprising at first glance is the slowness with which Armand returned to women's work following her arrival in Petrograd

[1] She did, however, serve on the editorial board of *Demain*, a French-language publication published in Moscow but aimed at the French proletariat. One issue of the paper appeared in September 1919 and then for unexplained reasons it ceased publication (Zak, 'Deiatel'nost' Frantsuzskoi kommunisticheskoi gruppy', p. 166); Kriegel, p. 267.

[2] Stal' in Krupskaia (ed.), *Pamiati*, p. 44.

in April 1917. She, after all, had been involved with helping disadvantaged women and with aspects of the woman question since joining the Moscow Society for Improving the Lot of Women almost twenty years earlier. She had gone out of her way to attend prerevolutionary women's conferences – both of the feminist and socialist variety – and she had been the instigator in 1914 of *Rabotnitsa*, the party's first organized attempt to appeal to working women. During the war she had been the Bolsheviks' link with the international socialist women's movement and she had pursued her interest in developing a socialist view of marriage and the family. And yet, when revolution came spontaneously in February 1917, she and almost all of the party leadership, male and female, lost sight of the fact that it was discontented women in bread lines and demonstrating for International Women's Day who helped topple the Romanov dynasty. It is curious that no one seemed to connect rising labour unrest in 1916 and 1917 with increased discontent on the part of the female proletariat which since mobilization made up over a third of Petrograd's industrial labour force and had good reason to hate a war that was devouring their husbands and fathers and sons.

The Bolshevik Party throughout 1917 and the first half of 1918 was preoccupied with more urgent matters – organizing its forces after the February Revolution, protecting itself after the July Days, seizing power from the Provisional Government in October, setting up the machinery of a new government – than appealing to and organizing working women. It also was preoccupied with its long-held preconceptions that women workers were politically backward, conservative and unresponsive to party propaganda. Few were willing to question traditional assumptions that special women's organizations represented separatism and that special policies for women was a feminist deviation. The predominantly male leadership of the party and the labour movement failed to recognize the signs and causes of female unrest in February 1917 and continued to see things in a traditional paternalistic manner.[3] Ironically, only a few of the limited number of women in their midst tried to dissuade them of these out-dated beliefs until the summer of 1918. In the case of Inessa Armand, at least, this acquiescence can be explained both by her personal preoccupations in 1917 and by her acceptance of the logic of her party's political priorities if not of its paternalistic outlook.

[3] For a more detailed discussion of these attitudes, see Barbara Evans Clements, 'The Birth of the New Soviet Woman', in Abbot Gleason, Peter Kenez and Richard Stites (eds.),

One of the few Bolshevik women who tried to get the party to address the female proletariat in 1917 was Vera Slutskaia. Nine years earlier Slutskaia had opposed Kollontai's efforts to organize a workers' delegation to the 1908 Women's Congress and afterward to set up a women's bureau within the Petersburg Committee. On 13 March 1917, however, Slutskaia herself suggested that the Petrograd Committee re-establish *Rabotnitsa* and create a Bureau of Women Workers under the jurisdiction of the committee. The Petrograd Committee shortly thereafter approved the idea of a bureau made up of representatives from the various districts of the city, but insisted that it limit itself to agitational work and that no independent women's organization be created.[4] Even though the Bureau restricted itself to issuing a couple of leaflets, its activity was 'disrupted by the opposition of district party workers [who] considered that carrying out special work among women smelled very much of feminism'.[5]

It is not surprising, therefore, that Kollontai could not get support from the Bolshevik organization in Petrograd or from the Seventh Party Conference in April for a more far-reaching proposal that every party organization create a women's section to coordinate all party work among women. What must have surprised her, however, was that not even the Bolshevik women associated with the pre-revolutionary *Rabotnitsa* – Krupskaia, Samoilova, and a non-committal Armand – would support the scheme. The safer solution they felt was to take up Slutskaia's other suggestion to revive *Rabotnitsa*. The precedent for a paper run by women and aimed at working women had been established three years earlier and it was therefore less likely to run into opposition from party leaders or be seen as a feminist scheme to divide the working class along gender lines at a decisive moment in the history of the class struggle. The first issue of *Rabotnitsa* appeared on 10 May, albeit without the financial support of the Petrograd Committee. For the rest of 1917 it became the *de facto* organizational centre for Bolshevik work among the women of the capital – collecting information, organizing meetings, setting up a school for agitators, trying to popularize Bolshevik positions on women's issues – all the while reiterating that it

---

Bolshevik Culture: Experiment and Order in the Russian Revolution (Bloomington, 1985), pp. 220–37.

4 N. D. Karpetskaia, 'Vovlechenie trudiashchikhsia zhenshchin Petrograda v revoliutsionnoe dvizhenie (mart-iiul' 1917 g.)', *Vestnik Leningradskogo Universiteta*, 1966, no. 8, p. 46.

5 L. Stal', 'Rabotnitsa v Oktiabre', *Proletarskaia revoliutsiia*, 1922, no. 10, p. 299.

was not a separate women's organization and that it was uninterested in feminist causes.[6]

In Moscow the development of Social Democratic work among women took a different course in 1917 and was even less productive. As already noted, Inessa Armand and Varvara Iakovleva managed to put out only two issues of *Zhizn' rabotnitsy* in June and July. In August the Moscow Oblast Bureau approved Iakovleva's suggestion that each local party committee establish a Commission for Agitation and Propaganda among Working Women. The fact that these commissions closely resembled in theory the sections Kollontai had proposed in April may explain why only one commission was created in practice in the Moscow area. What it achieved, other than the calling of a large women's meeting on 15 October and promoting the election of Bolshevik candidates to the Constituent Assembly,[7] is unrecorded in party histories of the period.

The need to prepare for the Constituent Assembly elections also prompted the editors of *Rabotnitsa* in Petrograd to call a Conference of Working Women for 25 October. On that date, however, the party was engaged in more pressing matters around the Winter Palace and the conference was postponed until 12 November when over 500 women – many of them not belonging to the Bolshevik Party – showed up to approve the seizure of power. The conference, at Kollontai's suggestion, also passed resolutions urging all city and guberniia party committees to create Commissions for Agitation and Propaganda among Women, calling for greater recognition of *Rabotnitsa*'s organizational role, and recommending that an All-Russian Congress of Working Women be convened in February to bring together women from across the country.[8] As they were to find out, however, it was one thing for a women's conference to approve a policy; it was something else for the party to carry it out. In this instance, the proposed commissions remained inoperative for another eight months; *Rabotnitsa* was forced to suspend publication in late January 1918 for lack of newsprint; and the First All-Russian Congress of Working Women scheduled for February was indefinitely postponed when Kollontai, Armand, Iakovleva and

---

[6] Drumm, pp. 256–7, 308; Carol Eubanks Hayden, 'The Zhenotdel and the Bolshevik Party', *Russian History*, vol. III, pt. 2 (1976), pp. 52–3; Donald, 'Bolshevik Activity Amongst Working Women', pp. 129–51.

[7] Smidovich, 'Rabota sredi zhenshchin', p. 19; Barulina, 'Iz istorii bor'by . . .', pp. 60–3.

[8] On the conference, see Kudelli, pp. 66–9; Stal', 'Rabotnitsa v Oktiabre', pp. 299–300; Hayden, pp. 120–7; Donald, 'Bolshevik Activity Amongst Working Women', pp. 151–7.

several other of its Left Communist organizers gave all of their attention to opposing the Brest-Litovsk peace treaty.

The Bolshevik policy or non-policy with respect to working women had the predictable result of turning these women away from the party and the institutions it promoted. The party grew dramatically during 1917, but it attracted its new members primarily from men of proletarian origin. Its women members, in contrast, came as before from the *sluzhashchie* and the intelligentsia but in much smaller numbers. As a result, the relative strength of women in the party dropped to 2 per cent of the total membership in 1917.[9] Few women chose to run in elections to the Petrograd Soviet, and fewer still were elected.[10] Women were very poorly represented in trade unions and factory-shop committees. While women workers made up over 33 per cent of the factory workforce, only 4 per cent of the delegates to the First Conference of Factory Committees were women.[11] In some areas, where women made up the majority of the factory workers, elections to factory committees were rigged so that men would be elected.[12] When demobilized soldiers started looking for employment, many factory committees urged that women workers be laid off.[13] Instead of jobs, the revolution gave women political and civil equality and equality with their husbands in marriage. Civic marriage, the right to use one's maiden name, divorce upon demand of one partner, equal rights for children born out of wedlock and the other sweeping social changes brought by the revolution meant more to the female intelligentsia than they did to the female proletariat. As a result of this disinterest by the party and discrimination in the workplace, many women workers used their new right to vote to support the Mensheviks, the Socialist Revolutionaries, and the few feminist groups that remained in 1918. This trend became clearly evident in the elections of new soviets in June 1918 and in the failure of the party to attract new members from among working women during the first half of 1918.[14]

Inessa Armand encountered this apathy and lack of support in early May 1918 when she made a half-hearted attempt to call the All-

[9] Hutton, p. 171. See also a discussion of this trend in Fieseler, 'The Making of Russian Female Social Democrats', pp. 195–6, 210–11.
[10] Smith, p. 192; Drumm, p. 213.   [11] Smith, p. 199.   [12] Bobroff, p. 724.
[13] Drumm, p. 380; Smith, p. 175.
[14] Drumm, pp. 384, 510; Clements, *Bolshevik Feminist*, p. 150. For the failure of the party, trade unions and factory committees to attract women in 1918, see also Elena Blonina [I. F. Armand], 'Rabota sredi zhenshchin proletariata na mestakh', in Armand, *Stat'i*, p. 71.

Russian Congress of Working Women which had already been post-poned from the previous February. Since only 130 delegates showed up, the would-be All-Russian Congress was downgraded to be a Moscow City Conference. Inessa later acknowledged that this shortfall was a direct result of the lack of party ties with women in the factories.[15] The modest gathering did, however, benefit from its organizer's good con-nections. When some of the delegates asked that Lenin be invited, Inessa picked up the phone and in short order produced the Chairman of the Council of People's Commissars who gave an impromptu speech.[16] Armand was less successful a month later when she called the First Moscow Guberniia Conference of Working Women. This time the small group of 57 women who showed up were not honoured by Lenin's presence.

One positive feature of these two rather insignificant conferences was that they made women like Armand and even some of the male leadership of the party aware of the dangers of ignoring the special requirements of women workers. This awareness was heightened by the beginning of the Civil War in the summer of 1918 and the sudden need once again to get non-party women back into the factories and to gain their active support for the new regime. In July Armand reminded the Moscow Committee of the request to set up a Commission for Agitation and Propaganda among Women made by the Petrograd Conference of Working Women in November 1917. After eight months of ignoring this recommendation, it was put into effect and a commission of fifteen members was set up.[17] A month later, in August 1918, the Petrograd Committee established a similar body but called it a bureau rather than a commission.[18] Armand also suddenly found modest support in a

---

[15] Elena Blonina [I. F. Armand], 'Moskovskaia bespartiinaia konferentsiia rabotnits', *Pravda*, 25 September 1919, in Armand, *Stat'i*, p. 51.

[16] Skovno, 'Samoe dorogoe', p. 21. Inessa's daughter Inna (who Lenin called 'Inessa Little') once tried the same approach to get the Bolshevik leader to speak at a Komsomol conference. After being refused entrance to the Kremlin, she and three colleagues went to her mother's apartment and used the closed-circuit telephone. Announcing that she was Inessa Armand, she was put through to Lenin and immediately asked:

'Vladimir Ilyich, a delegation of our youth conference instructed me and my comrades to ask you...'
'Who is speaking?' Lenin enquired.
'Inessa Little.'
'Little but shrewd,' Lenin exclaimed before saying he was too busy.
Quoted in Fischer, pp. 487–8.

[17] E. Goreva in Artiukhina *et al.* (eds.), *Zhenshchiny v revoliutsii*, p. 150.

[18] Bette Daneman Stavrakis, 'Women and the Communist Party of the Soviet Union, 1918–35' (unpublished Ph.D. dissertation, Western Reserve University, 1961), p. 96.

previously disinterested party leadership for the twice-postponed All-Russian Congress of Working Women.

Both the Moscow Conference in May and the Moscow Guberniia Conference in June had endorsed the calling of a national congress[19] and had elected Armand and Kollontai to a commission charged with making the necessary preparations. In late September the two women received invaluable assistance from Iakov Sverdlov, head of the party's Secretariat, who was able to secure the approval of the Central Committee for the proposed congress over the opposition of Zinoviev and Radek.[20] The organizing commission was given additional staff, a modest budget and a very cramped Moscow office in which to plan the congress. Under the continued leadership of Kollontai and Armand, it drew up an agenda, drafted resolutions, made local arrangements and sent agitators into the provinces to drum up delegates.[21]

In retrospect, the organization of the congress was haphazard and inexpert – perhaps as a result of the other duties which took much of Armand's and Kollontai's time, perhaps because of a lack of cooperation from government agencies whose assistance they needed. The congress originally was to have opened on 6 November[22] but at the last moment it had to be postponed once again to the 16th because its organizers had apparently overlooked the fact that an All-Russian Congress of Soviets was to convene in Moscow on the 7th. Moreover, their counterparts in Petrograd had been unable to arrange for the election of delegates by the earlier date.[23] Word of the postponement failed to reach many of the provincial delegates who arrived early and had to be accommodated until the 16th. On the basis of the limited turnout at the spring women's conferences, Armand and Kollontai expected about 300 delegates to show up in November. Much to their surprise, 1147 women appeared which meant a new congress hall had to be found, more accommodation secured, additional baby-sitting services arranged. Insufficient attention had been given to feeding such a large group and on the first day the organizers had a near revolt on their hands when no food whatsoever was provided. Ultimately, Kollontai, with the continued assistance of Sverdlov, found some soup and porridge. The next

---

[19] Smidovich, 'Rabota sredi zhenshchin', p. 19. [20] Farnsworth, *Kollontai*, p. 138.
[21] On the preparations for the congress, see A. Kollontai, 'Kak my sozvali pervyi Vseross-iiskii S″ezd rabotnits i krest'ianok', *Kommunistka*, 1923, no. 11, pp. 4–6; Clements, *Bolshevik Feminist*, pp. 152–3; Farnsworth, *Kollontai*, pp. 138–40.
[22] See letter to Inna Armand (after 3 October 1918), in Armand, *Stat'i*, p. 255.
[23] E. Kogan-Pismanik, 'Soldatki Revoliutsii', in Artiukhina *et al.* (eds.), *Zhenshchiny v revoliutsii*, p. 188.

morning the hungry delegates were given herring, a piece of bread, tea and ersatz coffee for breakfast.[24]

Despite all these difficulties, Armand and Kollontai must have derived a sense of satisfaction and accomplishment when they sat on the presidium and looked out over more than 1000 working women assembled in the Great Hall of Columns where the Moscow City Duma had once met. They had come a long way from the bourgeois Women's Congress they both had attended almost ten years earlier when the workers' group numbered only forty-five delegates. The apathy of the previous spring seemed to have dissipated and it was symbolic of at least modest male support that Sverdlov officially opened the congress. Later Lenin and Bukharin also addressed the delegates. The socialist women's movement, which had been strangely quiescent in Russia since the February Revolution, came back to life at the November 1918 congress.

The delegates began by repeating the old formula that female workers had the same interests as male workers and did not seek separate solutions to their problems. They then proceeded to pass a series of resolutions that seemed to argue to the contrary. Armand gave two of the major reports. In one of these – on 'Women Workers in the Home and the Workplace' – she brought up a major theme for future work and also touched some sensitive nerves. She condemned the traditional double burden whereby women spent long hours under capitalist slavery in the factory and then returned home to household slavery of cooking, cleaning and child-rearing. She noted that the revolution had destroyed the capitalist economic system and the 'bourgeois-capitalist family'. The time had now come to replace the household economy and free women as housewives so that they could participate in party, soviet and other public activity. This could be done, she said, by setting up communal nurseries, kindergartens, laundries and kitchens financed by the state.[25] This was moving too fast for many of the delegates who feared that 'collective upbringing' would deprive them of their role as mothers. The retort heard from the audience, 'We won't give up our children',[26] should not have surprised a woman who did not like to see her youngest son forced to live in a state-run boarding school.

On the fifth and last day of the congress Samoilova introduced a resolution 'On the Organizational Question' which called on the Central

24 V. Nikolaeva, 'Po ukazaniiam Il'icha', in *ibid.*, p. 209; Kollontai, 'Kak my sozvali...', pp. 7–8.
25 See Armand's account of the congress in 'Polozhenie rabotnitsy v Sovetskoi Rossii', *Stat'i*, pp. 117–18.
26 Quoted in Podliashuk, p. 253.

Committee to establish under its aegis a special commission for agitation and propaganda among working women and for similar commissions to be set up subordinate to local party organizations. This resolution represented a compromise. In earlier discussions, Armand had argued that an autonomous Women's Bureau on the German model, such as Kollontai had always wanted, would be seen by the party leadership as a feminist and a separatist body.[27] It was better, she felt, to use the precedent of a subordinate commission already established by the Moscow organization in 1917 and revived in 1918 and then to expand its activities once higher approval had been obtained. This pragmatic approach was accepted by the Women's Congress in November and by the Central Committee in December. Inessa Armand was named chairperson of the new Central Commission for Agitation and Propaganda among Working Women[28] assisted by Kollontai and Samoilova. She said that similar commissions, which were to be set up by lower party bodies, had a two-fold objective: to raise the political consciousness of women through meetings, schools and propaganda circles which would attract the best of these women to party membership; and to involve women in the building of a new society through fostering their participation in local soviets, factory committees, and trade unions. She urged local commissions to assist in the setting up of the communal facilities which the congress had endorsed as ways of emancipating women from household drudgery.[29]

Armand and Samoilova also developed an idea which Inessa had first proposed before the Women's Congress: that the delegates to the congress should hold meetings upon their return home to explain the significance of decisions reached to other women. The Central Commission took this one step further and suggested that women entering soviet or trade-union work should periodically report back to local meetings on their experiences thereby increasing general female awareness and attracting others to public activity. This practice eventually evolved into 'delegates' meetings' and became one of the principal organizational devices used by Zhenotdel during the 1920s.

It is difficult to gauge the success and the impact of the commissions established as a result of the 1918 Women's Congress. While they received for the first time the official support of the hierarchy of the

---

[27] Clements, *Bolshevik Feminist*, pp. 153 and 156.
[28] Artiukhina, *Zhenshchiny v revoliutsii*, p. 33. According to Kudelli (p. 60), the Central Committee first offered the job to Samoilova who declined the position.
[29] Elena Blonina [I. F. Armand], 'Rabota sredi zhenshchin proletariata na mestakh', in *Stat'i*, pp. 71–2.

Communist Party, they continued to run into opposition from local party officials who often failed to supply financial or organizational assistance.[30] Many could not see the value of wasting resources on raising the political consciousness of backward women when counter-revolutionary armies threatened on three fronts and starvation was facing workers in the cities. There also were leadership problems. Armand, in addition to her new work on the Central Commission, was expected to run the Moscow Guberniia Sovnarkhoz and to co-edit *La IIIe Internationale*. Then, in early February 1919, she was asked to suspend her work with women, just when it seemed on the verge of producing results, and to go to France as a delegate of the Russian Red Cross. It was left to Kollontai to defend recent advances in work among women at the Eighth Party Congress in March 1919 and then she too left Moscow to serve as a propagandist for five months on the southern front.

In August 1919, several months after Armand's return from Malo-les-Bains but while Kollontai was still in Ukraine, the Central Committee decided to replace the Central Commission for Agitation and Propaganda among Working Women with a new Women's Section of the Central Committee (Zhenotdel) and to make Inessa Armand its first director.

*   *   *

Zhenotdel has been called 'one of the most ambitious attempts to emancipate women ever undertaken by a government'.[31] Unlike the localized women's bureaux and commissions for agitation and propaganda which flared up spontaneously and often died out just as rapidly, Zhenotdel lasted until 1930, covered the entire country and ultimately affected the lives of most women in the Soviet Union. In light of its longevity and impact, it is surprising that the origins of Zhenotdel – who organized it, and for what reasons – are so indistinct.[32]

In September 1919 the Central Committee of the Russian Communist Party passed a decree 'On Work Among Women Workers' in which it 'reaffirmed the importance of, and the need for, work among women proletarians and makes it binding upon all Party committees to set up

---

[30] Clements, *Bolshevik Feminist*, p. 158; Smidovich, 'Rabota sredi zhenshchin', p. 20.

[31] Clements, 'Baba and Bolshevik', p. 165.

[32] Little detailed attention was given to Zhenotdel by Soviet scholars. The best available studies are by Western writers – most notably Barbara Clements, Bette Stavrakis and Richard Stites. Carol Hayden's thesis on Zhenotdel pays little attention to Armand and is at variance with other evidence in its interpretation of the body's early years.

departments [*otdels* or sections] for work *exclusively* among women'.[33] By this decision a central Zhenotdel was created as a section within the Central Committee as well as subordinate women's sections connected to party committees at the guberniia and district (*uezd*) levels throughout the country. Despite the superficial similarity between Zhenotdel and the German Women's Bureau – long the ideal advocated by Aleksandra Kollontai and a few of her radical followers – the Women's Section did not result 'from the persistent and rather unpopular efforts of a small group of women communists committed to the liberation of their sex'[34] nor was Kollontai 'almost single-handedly responsible for the organization of Zhenotdel'.[35] The sporadic agitation for a women's bureau died down following the November 1918 Congress of Working Women while Kollontai herself spent the five months preceding the decision to set up Zhenotdel in Ukraine occupied with other matters.

A more plausible explanation for the establishment of Zhenotdel was that it was a product of organizational housecleaning by the Central Committee itself. It was recognized that the various bodies that had grown up on an *ad hoc* basis since the revolution – Commissions for Agitation and Propaganda among Women set up by some party units, women's bureaux created by conferences of non-party working women, women's sections established by a few trade unions – were cumbersome, uneven in their coverage, and repetitious in their functions.[36] The decree replaced these bodies with a much more centralized structure. The new sections, unlike the earlier commissions, were directly responsible to the Central Zhenotdel as well as being connected to their local party units. Zhenotdel was one of nine sections within the Central Committee and thus subject in turn to central party supervision. Unlike the women's commissions, Zhenotdel could issue decrees that carried the authority of the Central Committee.[37] In many respects it resembled another of the Central Committee's sections, the Evsektsiia or Jewish Section. As Gail Lapidus has pointed out, 'in composition and goals, both organizations breached the sexual, ethnic, and organizational unity of

---

[33] Quoted in Yemelyanova, p. 24 (emphasis added).
[34] As claimed by Beatrice Farnsworth, 'Communist Feminism: Its Synthesis and Demise', in Carol R. Berkin and Clara M. Lavett (eds.), *Women, War, and Revolution* (New York, 1980), p. 147.
[35] As claimed by Hayden, p. 110.
[36] See Armand's report to the First All-Russian Meeting of Zhenotdel Guberniia Organizers, 15–17 October 1919, in *Pravda*, 24 October 1919, and *Stat'i*, p. 59.
[37] Robert H. McNeal, 'The Early Decrees of Zhenotdel', in Tova Yedlin (ed.), *Women in Eastern Europe and the Soviet Union* (New York, 1980), p. 76.

the Party in an effort to reach and mobilize an otherwise inaccessible constituency'.[38]

A second reason for the establishment of Zhenotdel was precisely to 'mobilize' a constituency which may have been 'inaccessible' but only because the party had given a very low priority in the past to organizing working women. In the summer and fall of 1919, with the Soviet state threatened on all sides by White Russian armies supported and supplied by allied interventionary forces, there was a desperate need to get women back into the factories so as to free male workers for military duty. Women, if properly mobilized, could also fill auxiliary positions in support of the Red Army. At the very least, in time of crisis the party wanted the passive support of a group which earlier had been written off as inert, illiterate, superstitious and fearful of change.[39] In July 1919 the Central Committee acknowledged that work among women was one of the weakest areas of party activity.[40] It was hoped that Zhenotdel would succeed where the decentralized, poorly supported women's commissions had failed in mobilizing women in defence of the state.

It was also expected that Zhenotdel would do a better job in informing Russian women of the rights – political, civil, economic – which the revolution had brought them. All too often illiteracy and the paternalistic structure of society had kept women in ignorance of change. This did not mean that the Central Committee set up Zhenotdel 'to implement a program of sexual equality'[41] or that it was intended as a way for the female masses to pressure the state and influence its policies. It was created as a transmission belt but a transmission belt downwards only, a way of conveying the party's objectives and instructions to a hitherto 'inaccessible constituency'. It was meant to be the party's communicator to and organizer of working women, not the representative of women to the government. Perhaps in time it came to be seen by some of its leaders as an instrument of female liberation but this was not the intent of its creators.

Who precisely created it is impossible to determine from the available evidence. Lenin must have been in support of the idea. In 1920 he told Clara Zetkin that

The Party must have bodies ... whose particular duty is to arouse the masses of women workers, to bring them into contact with the Party, and to keep them under its influence ... We need appropriate bodies to carry on work amongst

---

[38] Lapidus, p. 72.   [39] Stavrakis, p. 131.   [40] Hayden, p. 140.
[41] As suggested by Hayden, p. iv.

them, special methods of agitation and [special] forms of organization. This is not feminism; it is practical revolutionary expediency.[42]

This was also a change from his thinking in 1914 and in 1917. Very possibly Inessa Armand helped to influence his acceptance of greater organizational work among women workers. Krupskaia noted that at this time Inessa was a far more frequent visitor to their apartment than she had been in 1918 and that the three of them often discussed work among women employed in factories and in the countryside.[43] According to Smidovich, it was the Moscow Commission for Agitation and Propaganda among Women under Armand's direction which called the organizational shortcomings of the commissions to the attention of the Central Committee and pressured for the creation of a more centralized system of women's sections.[44]

Despite the fact that Aleksandra Kollontai had been the chief advocate of a Zhenotdel-type structure since 1908, it is not surprising that the party chose Armand to head up the new body rather than her more renowned rival. Kollontai had indeed been 'the central figure in the Russian socialist women's movement since 1905'.[45] While she may have come to women's work somewhat later than Armand, her involvement was much more sustained between 1905 and 1914 when Inessa was involved as an underground propagandist or in helping to build a 'party of the new type' abroad. Kollontai, unlike Armand, had made her mark as a theoretician on women's issues and was recognized by the Second International as Russia's spokesperson in this area. In 1917 she proved herself to be a gifted orator, was elected to the Central Committee, and named the first People's Commissar of Welfare. Under her influence, much of the regime's revolutionary social legislation affecting women had been passed if not necessarily implemented.

Despite Kollontai's standing in the women's movement, the party leadership had many reasons for preferring Armand to be the first head of Zhenotdel. She was far less flamboyant, mercurial and unpredictable than Kollontai. She also was less independent politically. While Armand may not have always been the loyal Leninist some have claimed, she at least had been a good Bolshevik since 1910 if not 1904. Kollontai, on the other hand, had been a Menshevik before 1915 and, unlike her fellow Left Communist, she had resigned her state positions in protest against the Treaty of Brest-Litovsk. As Angelica Balabanoff recalled,

---

[42] Zetkin, p. 15.   [43] Krupskaia in Kon (ed.), p. 66; Krupskaya, *Lenin*, p. 539.
[44] Smidovich, 'Rabota sredi zhenshchin', p. 20.   [45] Farnsworth, *Kollontai*, p. 178.

Kollontai was a 'frequent source of both personal and political annoyance to the Party leaders'.[46]

Another and more important factor in the party's decision was the fact that Armand was not as radical on the woman question. To be sure, she had advocated carrying out agitation and propaganda among working women since 1914 and she welcomed the destruction of the bourgeois family after 1917. She did not, however, write about a new revolutionary morality or talk about the sexual liberation of women at a time when Lenin was preaching sexual restraint. She also had not been accused, as Kollontai was by Krupskaia and Vinogradskaia, of undermining the nuclear family.[47] In time, Armand came to believe that women were best organized by other women working within their own organization. But she was more circumspect in making this argument than Kollontai and more willing to accept in 1917 and 1918 a compromise solution when she realized her male colleagues were frightened by the separatist prospects of a German-type Women's Bureau which Kollontai advocated. As one contemporary noted, 'Inessa's leadership of work among women was a guarantee that this work would not deviate into some special "women's" movement or degenerate into Soviet feminism.'[48] She took over Zhenotdel as a party assignment – to be sure, an assignment which interested her and fitted her qualifications – but nevertheless as an assignment just as she had taken over the Moscow Guberniia Sovnarkhoz or had joined the Red Cross Mission to France.

Armand had other characteristics which the party leadership appreciated. She may not have been as charismatic as Kollontai, but she was a better politician. Unlike Kollontai, who often missed Central Committee meetings, she was diligent in carrying out her party work and she paid more attention to organizational detail.[49] Moreover, she had been the 'architect' of the 1918 commissions out of which Zhenotdel emerged[50] and she was the creator of the delegates' meetings which soon became synonymous with Zhenotdel's operations. She also had the advantage of being in Moscow when the Central Committee made its decision, rather than isolated in Ukraine, and she had Lenin's ear. It is too simple, however, to attribute the appointment solely to Lenin's patronage. It is nevertheless understandable that Kollontai may have thought favouritism was a factor; that she did not appreciate the logic of

[46] Balabanoff, *My Life*, p. 277.   [47] Hutton, pp. 117–18.
[48] Vinogradskaia in Krupskaia (ed.), *Pamiati*, p. 64.
[49] Stavrakis, p. 110.
[50] Barbara Evans Clements, 'Kollontai's Contribution to the Workers' Opposition', *Russian History*, vol. II, pt. 2 (1975), p. 193.

Armand's appointment from the party's point of view; and that it rankled[51] and contributed to a difficult working relationship between the two women over the course of the next year. It did not help this relationship that Kollontai was initially given an 'insultingly minor job'[52] and almost impossible task of organizing peasant women while Armand set about organizing the central office of Zhenotdel in Moscow.

Headquarters of the Central Zhenotdel, or 'Tsentro-Baba' as it often was derisively referred to, was a flat at 5 Vozdvizhenka near the Kremlin. As director, Armand served as the contact with other bodies dealing with women – the maternity and infancy sections of the Commissariat of Health, the Commissariat of Education, the Komsomol and the Commission for the Struggle against Prostitution – as well as representing Zhenotdel in discussions with the Central Committee.[53] She had a paid staff of twenty-two to assist her in organizing courses for guberniia instructors, publishing women's literature, and setting overall policy for lower-level *otdels*. The guberniia zhenotdels were primarily administrative units made up of three full-time workers who supervised the work of the *uezd* sections within their region and met every six months with the Central Zhenotdel. The actual organizational and instructional work was done at the *uezd* level by instructors who worked closely with local party and soviet organizations in their own area.[54]

From the very beginning, one of the most difficult tasks was recruiting women to serve in Zhenotdel. Even with the assistance of N. N. Krestinskii, a powerful member of the Politburo and Orgburo who had taken over many of Sverdlov's appointment duties in the party Secretariat, Armand found it hard to get women to work in the central or regional zhenotdels. She was able to staff a few of the guberniia posts with veterans of the women's movement – Smidovich in Moscow, Samoilova in Ukraine, S. I. Deriabina in the Urals – but she soon discovered most women with pre-revolutionary experience considered these positions too unimportant or too feminist.[55] Stasova had no interest in women's work and Vinogradskaia, who had been helping out at the front, was unhappy when re-assigned to less-exciting Zhenotdel work and appealed to Armand to let her do something else.[56] Some

---

[51] Farnsworth, *Kollontai*, p. 179.   [52] Clements, *Bolshevik Feminist*, p. 163.
[53] Richard Stites, 'Zhenotdel: Bolshevism and Russian Women, 1917–1930', *Russian History*, vol. III, pt. 2 (1976), p. 182.
[54] For more detail on the structure of Zhenotdel, see Stavrakis, pp. 127–30.
[55] Clements, 'Baba and Bolshevik', p. 177; Farnsworth, in Birken and Lavett (eds.), p. 148.
[56] Vinogradskaia, p. 199.

long-time male party members refused to allow their wives to take up Zhenotdel work[57] which might disrupt patriarchal home relations. As a result, during its first year at least, most of the new sections were led by young and inexperienced women.[58]

The initial purpose of Zhenotdel had been to mobilize Russian women for the war effort. This was made clear at the First All-Russian Meeting of Guberniia Organizers on 15 October 1919 which defined the tasks of the organization as:

1 attracting women to the defence of Russia, both in the factories and at the front;
2 promoting labour conscription and economic reconstruction;
3 providing political education on a wide variety of economic and social problems.[59]

If men were needed at the front, then women must be encouraged to take their places in the factories.[60] Some women responded to the repeated political exhortations of Zhenotdel's propagandists; others went to work out of economic necessity. The results of this campaign could be seen in Petrograd where women, who had made up 38.5 per cent of the industrial labour force at the start of the Civil War, comprised 42.2 per cent of the work force in 1920.[61]

Considerable attention was also given to getting women to take over auxiliary positions in support of the Red Army. Commissions were set up through Zhenotdel to aid sick and wounded soldiers. Working women were encouraged to volunteer a free day's labour on Saturday or Sunday. On these *subbotniki* they would make bandages, bathe soldiers in hospitals, and sew military clothing.[62] Zhenotdel propagandists were also used to give crash courses in nursing so that the trainees could assist in field hospitals. On occasion women were encouraged to go beyond auxiliary work by serving in the Red Army itself. As Armand noted, the revolution had destroyed the myth that only men could be involved in armed struggle.[63] By the end of the Civil War,

---

[57] Lapidus, p. 69.
[58] S. T. Liubimova, 'Iz istorii deiatel'nosti Zhenotdelov', *Vosprosy istorii KPSS*, 1969, no. 9, p. 70.
[59] Stavrakis, p. 102.
[60] See Armand's report on this meeting in *Pravda*, 24 October 1919, and in *Stat'i*, p. 58.
[61] Hayden, 'Zhenotdel and the Bolshevik Party', p. 155.
[62] Elena Blonina [I. F. Armand], 'Rabotnitsy i krest'ianki zabotiatsia Krasnoi Armii', in *Pravda*, 8 February 1920, and *Stat'i*, p. 88.
[63] E. Blonina (t. Inessa) [I. F. Armand], 'Zadachi rabotnits v Sovetskoi Rossii', in *Stat'i*, p. 68.

1850 women had been killed, captured or wounded while fighting at the front.[64]

As the Civil War came to an end in 1920, Zhenotdel gave more attention to improving the quality of work done in the factories, to promoting better labour discipline among women workers, and to justifying labour conscription in light of the destruction caused by six years of war and civil war. At the Second All-Russian Meeting of Zhenotdel Guberniia Organizers on 28 March 1920 Armand stressed that the chief task now was to attract women to the 'fight on the labour front' and to convince them not only to practice but also to defend labour discipline and labour conscription against accusations that these programmes represented 'a new slavery law'.[65] Once the immediate danger of the Civil War was over, Zhenotdel sought to mobilize women in other areas as well. They were urged to participate more actively in the work of their local soviet.[66] Perhaps as a result of this agitation, the number of women in the Petrograd Soviet climbed from three in 1917, to 27 in June 1918, to 307 in July 1919, to 400 in 1920.[67] Women were reminded of the importance of taking part in the work of trade unions, especially those enrolling non-industrial workers where Menshevik influence was often greatest.[68] Zhenotdel also sought to mobilize women for the party. Special 'Party Weeks' were held to convince women that belonging to the party would not take time away from their families.[69]

One of the chief means Zhenotdel used to mobilize women and to increase their political consciousness was through delegates' meetings and ultimately through the apprenticeship programme which grew out of them. Armand felt that these meetings represented 'the principal core of our work' during her brief tenure as director of the Women's Section.[70] Krupskaia estimated that 10,000,000 Soviet women passed through these 'schools of communism'[71] before delegates' meetings were abolished in 1935 – five years after the demise of Zhenotdel itself.

Identifying women to attend delegates' meetings was the first task. Zhenotdel leaders were well aware of the habit of Russian factory

[64] Hayden, p. 147.
[65] See her report to that meeting in Armand, *Stat'i*, pp. 125–6.
[66] See *ibid.*, pp. 64 and 133.   [67] Drumm, pp. 605–6; Armand, *Stat'i*, p. 133.
[68] Armand, *Stat'i*, p. 131.
[69] Elena Blonina [I. F. Armand], 'Kommunisticheskaia partiia i rabotnitsa', in *Pravda*, 9 October 1919, and *Stat'i*, pp. 53–6.
[70] Report to Second Meeting of Zhenotdel Guberniia Organizers, in Armand, *Stat'i*, p. 124.
[71] Stavrakis, p. 199; Armand, *Stat'i*, p. 138.

workers electing men rather than women as their representatives to various committees and extra-factory meetings on the grounds that male workers were more literate, more class conscious, and did not have household responsibilities.[72] This practice simply perpetuated the image and the reality of female backwardness. To get around it, Zhenotdel or party officials at first selected more outward going non-party women as delegates (delegatki) to attend these meetings. In time, the delegates were elected by their female peers on a ratio which varied from one delegate for every ten workers to one for every fifty workers. They would attend meetings after work with up to seventy other delegates several times a month. At these meetings they heard reports by Zhenotdel instructors on political issues, on the work of local soviets, and on practical matters such as ways of establishing crèches in factories where women worked. The delegates also attended literacy classes and they participated in mobilization campaigns organized by Zhenotdel. They themselves were urged to participate more actively in the work of their local soviets, trade unions and party organizations. After three to six months of this activity the delegate would return to full-time work in her factory, report on her experiences to a meeting of fellow female workers, and participate in the election of a new delegate. Through this recurring process Zhenotdel sought to increase the class consciousness and civic awareness of working women. Inevitably, through association with other women and through discussion of issues of interest to women, they became more conscious of their gender and of the woman question in its new Soviet context. This indirect result of delegates' meetings was probably Armand's most lasting contribution to Soviet feminism. It was a source of considerable pride to her that she could report in March 1920 that these meetings were functioning in all but two guberniias.[73]

A logical outgrowth of the delegates' meetings as they were practiced during Armand's brief period as director of Zhenotdel was the system of apprentices or probationers which went into operation in 1921. Under this scheme, delegates would be temporarily seconded from their factory employment to a local soviet, cooperative or government office to observe its operation and to gain first-hand experience in administrative procedures. After three to six months, upon completion of their term as

[72] V. A. Moirova, 'Women's Delegates' Meetings and their Role in the Work of the Party among Working and Peasant Women', in Work Among Women (London, 1924), p. 19.
[73] Report to the Second Meeting of Zhenotdel Guberniia Organizers, in Armand, Stat'i, p. 124. On the structure and work of the delegates' meetings, see also Stavrakis, pp. 133–9, 198–204; Armand, Stat'i, pp. 119–20, 136–8; Artiukhina, Zhenshchiny v revoliutsii, pp. 33–4.

probationers, they too were to report back to their factory colleagues on their experiences.[74]

If women were to spend their days in factories, their evenings at delegates' meetings and their weekends on *subbotniki*, then they needed relief from household and child-rearing duties. At the November 1918 Women's Congress Inessa Armand had stressed the need for communal services to take over many of these individual duties. This was an area where theory and practice seemed to coalesce very nicely. 'Petty housework crushes, strangles, stultifies and degrades' the woman, wrote Lenin. It 'chains her to the kitchen and to the nursery and wastes her labor on barbarously unproductive, petty, nerve-racking, stultifying and crushing drudgery.'[75] Inessa Armand agreed but for once used more theory and fewer adjectives to make her point. 'Until the old forms of the family, domestic life, education and child-rearing are abolished', she wrote in 1919, 'it is impossible to obliterate exploitation and enslavement, it is impossible to create the new person, impossible to build socialism.'[76] She argued that the restructuring of the family and of social relations, through the help of the state, would allow women to take part on an equal basis with men in public life.[77]

This restructuring involved the setting up of crèches in factories to take care of babies while women worked and canteens to provide free light meals. Factory settlements also built communal kitchens and dining rooms to relieve women of cooking duties at home. At one point in 1921, 93 per cent of the residents of Moscow ate in public dining halls.[78] Communal laundries were established in larger towns and nurseries and kindergartens were created to care for pre-school children. Some 1500 mother and child-care centres were set up in 1919 and 1920 to provide medical advice, maternity care, baby food and homes for parentless children.[79]

Zhenotdel played an important role in popularizing and administering these communal services. The central and regional offices pressured for the establishment of laundries, nurseries and communal kitchens; *delegatki* and later the probationers helped to staff the day care and

---

[74] For more on the probationers' scheme, see Moirova in *Work Among Women*, pp. 21–4; Yemelyanova, pp. 26–7; Stavrakis, pp. 153–7.

[75] Quoted in Engel, 'Women in Russia', p. 787.

[76] E. Blonina (t. Inessa) [I. F. Armand], 'Zadachi rabotnits v Sovetskoi Rossii', in Armand, *Stat'i*, p. 69.

[77] Elena Blonina [I. F. Armand], 'Usloviia polnogo osvobozhdeniia rabotnits i krest'ianok', in *Kommunistka*, 1920, nos. 1/2, and *Stat'i*, p. 106.

[78] Alix Holt, 'Marxism and Women's Oppression: Bolshevik Theory and Practice in the 1920s', in Yedlin (ed.), p. 92.

[79] Yemelyanova, p. 49.

medical centres; and through general meetings with other women and a wide variety of literature they sought to get working women to use these facilities. On occasion, *delegatki* would make a point of enrolling their own children in nurseries and kindergartens in order to overcome popular suspicions of the new facilities.[80] Inessa Armand referred to the communal services as examples of 'propaganda of the deed'.[81] They would show conservative women the benefits of socialist rule, help break down the restrictive bourgeois family structure, and bring more women into economic and civic life. Armand used the case of a nursery as an example of the type of evolution she hoped would take place. The first step was to get uninvolved women to enroll their children in the nursery and to take part in its running. Local Zhenotdel instructors would then help them hold meetings to discuss child-care matters and, in time, broader political and economic questions as well. Ultimately, these women with their increased political consciousness would be attracted to trade unions and party meetings.[82]

Armand realized this process of breaking down the traditional forms of the bourgeois family was going to take time[83] but she did not envisage the degree of resistance these communal institutions would encounter. Communal laundries never caught on. Women, while not fond of washing, were even less pleased with lost or torn clothing. Communal kitchens and dining rooms also decreased in popularity. Many women did not want to give up their kitchen functions and from the state's point of view food was hard and expensive to procure in bulk during a period of near-famine.[84] At times, local soviet offices responsible for housing were reluctant to give up space to Zhenotdel for nurseries when living accommodation was scarce.[85] Of all the communal services created during the early years of Zhenotdel, the medical and child-care facilities proved the most popular and lasted the longest, largely because they fulfilled practical as well as theoretical objectives of the state. It is noteworthy that they, like the other communal facilities, were staffed almost entirely by women doing traditional and low-paying 'women's work'. The state agencies thought this was natural and the anomaly apparently never was questioned by the Zhenotdel leadership. Nor did any of the early Soviet feminists ever suggest that

[80] *Ibid.*, p. 50.
[81] Elena Blonina [I. F. Armand], 'Polozhenie rabotnitsy v Sovetskoi Rossii', in *Kommunisticheskii Internatsional*, 1920, no. 9, and in *Stat'i*, p. 119.
[82] See Elena Blonina [I. F. Armand], 'Rabota sredi zhenshchin proletariata na mestakh', in Armand, *Stat'i*, pp. 72–3.
[83] See, for example, Armand, *Stat'i*, pp. 69, 85–7. [84] Stavrakis, p. 70.
[85] Vinogradskaia, p. 224.

one way the traditional bourgeois family could be restructured and the lot of Russian women made easier would be by having husbands share in housekeeping and child-rearing duties.

Besides fostering 'propaganda of the deed', Inessa felt very strongly that Zhenotdel should be engaged in 'propaganda of the word'. Through articles, brochures and newspapers she believed Zhenotdel could overcome traditional resistance to change which its new communal facilities were encountering as well as mobilizing women for socialist construction.

Following the demise of *Rabotnitsa* in January 1918, the Bolshevik women's movement did not have its own paper or journal for two and a half years. Instead, it had to make do with special 'women's pages' in the regular party press. The first of these was a weekly page in Petrograd's *Krasnaia gazeta* entitled 'Rabotnitsa' which began appearing in the fall of 1918.[86] On 2 April 1919 *Pravda* initiated a more regular 'Women Workers' Page' (*Stranichka rabotnitsy*). The initiative for the 'Women Workers' Page' came from Samoilova but after Armand's return from France she took over the editing of it.[87] By the summer of 1920, forty-seven guberniia and thirty-eight district papers had 'Stranichki rabotnitsy'[88] – most of them written or edited by local Zhenotdel personnel. The purpose of these pages was to get poorly educated women interested in reading a daily newspaper. The articles were written in a simple and comprehensible style and tended to deal 'with the needs and problems in the life and work of the working woman'.[89]

Inessa Armand threw herself wholeheartedly into this work. Between September 1919 and February 1920 she published at least twelve articles in *Pravda*, many of them on its 'Stranichka rabotnitsy'.[90] At their best, these articles are upbeat, enthusiastic and optimistic about the future of Russian women. Read out of context seventy years later, however, some seem pedantic, patronizing and cold. While they are addressed to women's issues, they are not written from a specifically woman's perspective. Armand does not seem to have empathized with her audience, to have understood the hardships of daily existence in early Soviet Russia, or to have been very much interested in working

[86] Drumm, p. 545.
[87] R. Kovnator, 'The Press as a Means of Organizing the Proletarian Women', in *Work Among Women*, p. 39; Podliashuk, 'Pravda i zhizn'', p. 59.
[88] Podliashuk (p. 245) also claims Armand played a major role in creating 'Stranichki krest'ianki' in a series of rural papers.
[89] Kovnator in *Work Among Women*, p. 39.
[90] Armand, *Stat'i*, pp. 49–65, 70–2, 86–91.

251

women *per se*. In the early articles, especially, she was much more concerned with mobilizing women and with raising their political consciousness than she was in defending their interests. Other Zhenotdel writers apparently shared these journalistic shortcomings[91] since most 'women's pages' were discontinued when Kollontai took over as Zhenotdel's director after Inessa's death.[92]

In the spring of 1920 Armand became involved in preparations for a new monthly publication solely under Zhenotdel's jurisdiction. This journal, entitled *Kommunistka*, was aimed at women organizers, instructors and more literate working women. With this audience in mind, most of its articles were more theoretical, methodological and organizational than those found on the 'women's pages'. In the pre-war *Rabotnitsa* tradition, some fiction was also included. While its initial editorial board listed such party luminaries as Bukharin and Kollontai, Krupskaia acknowledged that Armand 'was the soul of the journal'.[93] She arranged the editorial meetings, selected the articles, did the editorial work and wrote five articles herself.[94] The first double issue of 30,000 copies came out in time for the International Conference of Communist Women in late July 1920. She took care of editing numbers 3 and 4 before leaving for a vacation in the Caucasus. And the fifth issue, which appeared in October 1920, carried her obituary. Of all the women's publications put out by the party before and after the revolution, *Kommunistka* was the only one to deal with the broader aspects of female emancipation and the need to alter the relationship between the sexes if lasting change was to be effected.

In addition to 'women's pages' and *Kommunistka*, Zhenotdel during its early years also published brochures and pamphlets – many of them of a very popular nature. During the first half of 1921 alone, its literary section turned out 400,000 copies of 51 different publications.[95] Armand wrote four brochures during the last year of her life. Typical of Zhenotdel's popular genre was her *Pochemu ia stala zashchitnitsei Sovetskoi vlasti?*: sixteen pages long, printed in large and often bold type on cheap paper, and in a small enough format to be put in a pocket. It was written in a conversational, colloquial style in an attempt at answering topical questions of the day confronting a woman worker. What it lacked in theory and sophistication, it made up for in idealism, optimism and naiveté.

91 Clements, 'Birth of the New Soviet Woman', p. 224.
92 Stites, 'Zhenotdel', p. 179. *Rabotnitsa* was brought back as a popular women's journal under Zhenotdel's direction in 1923.
93 N.K. [Krupskaia], 'Inessa Armand', p. 20.   94 Armand, *Stat'i*, pp. 91–113.
95 Ross, p. 179.

In 1919 Inessa Armand had been concerned with getting women back into the factories and convincing them to take part in trade union, soviet and party work. In 1920 she shifted Zhenotdel's emphasis to urging women to seek leadership positions in these bodies. She noted that Soviet power had 'thrown all doors open to women' and had put women on an equal legal footing with men. This did not mean, however, that women had in fact achieved full equality in all areas. She pointed out that 'extremely few' women had been drawn into the management of industrial production, into factory committees or trade-union boards, and virtually none were found in *sovnarkhozi*. As an example, she cited the textile industry where women made up over half of the work force but had less than 9 per cent of the representatives at a recent Congress of Textile Trade Unions.[96] The same was true in the soviets where few women served as deputies and fewer still were on executive committees.[97] Low representation at the middle echelons meant that women were greatly under-represented at the apex of state power – at the all-Russian congresses of soviets and of the party.[98] As a consequence of not being involved in political decision-making and economic management, she felt that the stereotype of female backwardness was perpetuated, discriminatory policies went unchallenged, and the interests of women were ignored.

Armand sought to correct this situation through what a later generation would call an affirmative action programme. First of all, women had to be encouraged to seek leadership positions through publicizing forthcoming elections in Zhenotdel publications and urging women to run at delegates' meetings. It meant breaking down traditional self-images of female subordination and inferiority. Secondly, Zhenotdel sought to remove one of the causes of this sense of inferiority – a lack of education – by convincing women to attend trade-union schools and making sure they were accepted on an equal basis with men in these schools.[99] This training would further qualify women for positions on trade-union boards or as delegates to trade-union congresses. The third stage in Armand's affirmative action programme was the most difficult: to erase male prejudice against being led by women or working as equals with them in management or leadership positions.[100] In time this might be done through the traditional means of agitation and

---

96 Elena Blonina [I. F. Armand], 'Rabotnitsa i organizatsiia proizvodstva', *Kommunistka*, 1920, nos. 1/2, and in *Stat'i*, pp. 92–3.
97 Armand, *Stat'i*, p. 133.
98 Elena Blonina [I. F. Armand], 'Usloviia polnogo osvobozhdeniia rabotnits i krest'ianok', *Kommunistka*, 1920, nos. 3/4, and in *Stat'i*, p. 107.
99 Armand, *Stat'i*, pp. 93, 129.   100 *Ibid.*, p. 107.

propaganda – if indeed men bothered to read Zhenotdel literature. A more innovative way of breaking down male prejudice and introducing women into management positions was through Zhenotdel's apprenticeship or probationer programme whereby women were selected by delegates' meetings and seconded by their normal place of employment to work for short periods in soviet committees, *sovnarkhozi* and trade-union bodies. There they would serve side by side with men, gain valuable experience and confidence,[101] and function as watchdogs or advocates of female equality. Upon returning to their factories, they would be in a position to encourage others to follow in their footsteps or seek election to these higher bodies themselves. Robert McNeal has called this affirmative action programme 'the centerpiece of the Zhenotdel feminist activity'.[102] While parts of it were not implemented until after Armand's death, her successor credited Inessa with its conception.[103] It is doubtful whether she would have been happy with its end results.

Male prejudice was one of the major obstacles Zhenotdel encountered in all of its early programmes.[104] Many men – both party and non-party – objected to working under female direction and they opposed their wives assuming responsibilities that would take them away from the family. This attitude manifested itself in ridicule of Zhenotdel's work and derisive jokes about Babotdel and *babkomy* and Tsentro-Baba. Lenin, who was finally coming to realize the importance of work among women, recognized that 'it is still true to say of many of our comrades, "scratch a Communist and find a Philistine." Of course, you must scratch the sensitive spot, their mentality as regards woman.'[105]

This mentality contributed to another on-going problem for Zhenotdel: its relations with trade unions and the Communist Party. Russian trade unions had long been male bastions where women workers were under-represented and unappreciated. Many unions did not like cooperating with Zhenotdel on various mobilization drives or providing facilities for women's meetings. There was a general feeling that Zhenotdel should not infringe on the prerogatives of trade unions to organize workers – both male and female – and that perhaps the best solution

---

101 Lenin, in a condescending way, recognized this when he acknowledged that 'by taking part in administration, women will learn quickly and will catch up with men'. Quoted in Yemelyanova, p. 7.
102 McNeal in Yedlin (ed.), p. 79.   103 *Ibid.*
104 See Elena Blonina [I. F. Armand], 'Usloviia polnogo osvobozhdeniia rabotnits i krest'ianok', *Kommunistka*, 1920, nos. 3/4, and in *Stat'i*, p. 110.
105 Quoted in Zetkin, p. 19.

254

was to abolish the women's sections.[106] Local party attitudes toward Zhenotdel varied from hostility to indifference. Some *apparatchiki* saw women's organizers as unwanted interlopers and competitors who duplicated their own efforts. Others were quite content to relegate all work with women to the *otdels* and then to forget about it. If women's work appeared on party agendas at all, it was usually the last item and was never really integrated into local party operations.[107] Because of this attitude, the work of the women's sections was increasingly isolated from general party activity on the lower levels thus inadvertently perpetuating the separatism which male party leaders had always feared. The disinterest and distrust of parallel party bodies also contributed to Zhenotdel's lack of funds, shortage of places to meet and, especially, to the scarcity of trained organizers and instructors. Armand came to the conclusion that if the party would not second experienced personnel, then Zhenotdel would have to recruit new and untried female communists who would either be sent off to party schools (where 10 per cent of the places were reserved for Zhenotdel personnel[108]) or given crash courses in agitation and propaganda by the sections themselves.[109]

Yet another problem which Zhenotdel never really succeeded in overcoming was its lack of appeal to peasant women. Traditional patriarchal attitudes were even stronger in the villages than they were in urban areas. No women attended the Congress of Poor Peasants in November 1918 because the men organizing it felt they would be discussing 'serious matters' and might perhaps 'curse'.[110] In 1919 only 3 of 160 volost soviets had women members.[111] Husbands and mothers often objected to young peasant women attending political meetings. According to Armand, traditionalists in one village threatened to drown a woman who became a communist and a propagandist.[112] Armand's solution was to try to attract peasant women to delegates' meetings, to urge city women to make trips out into the villages on Sundays to agitate their more backward rural sisters, and to try to organize

[106] Clements, *Bolshevik Feminist*, p. 170.
[107] Stavrakis, pp. 105 and 109; Holt in Yedlin (ed.), p. 105.
[108] Liubimova, 'Iz istorii deiatel'nosti Zhenotdelov', p. 72.
[109] See Armand's report to the Second All-Russian Meeting of Zhenotdel Guberniia Organizers, in Armand, *Stat'i*, pp. 134–5.
[110] Cited in Drumm, pp. 565–6.
[111] Orlando Figes, 'The Village and *Volost* Soviet Elections of 1919', *Soviet Studies*, vol. XL, no. 1 (January 1988), p. 38.
[112] Elena Blonina [I. F. Armand], 'Volostnoe delegatskoe sobranie krest'ianok', *Pravda*, 8 February 1920, and in *Stat'i*, p. 95.

women's sections in the countryside.[113] In March 1920, however, she had to admit that Zhenotdel was doing almost no systematic work among peasant women and that this was an area of great weakness.[114]

When the Second All-Russian Meeting of Zhenotdel Guberniia Organizers convened on 28 March 1920, Armand was pleased to report that 68 delegates from 48 guberniias were present. In contrast to the first meeting in 1919, when only 27 guberniias were represented, now women's sections and delegates' meetings existed in almost all guberniias and *uezds*.[115] After discussing some of the problems mentioned above, the meeting tried to put Zhenotdel's house in order by reducing the vertical isolation that was hindering its work. Guberniia *otdels* were told to meet more frequently with *uezd* sections and *uezd otdels* were instructed to be more systematic in coordinating the work of volost and district sections.[116] Debate at the Ninth Party Congress immediately after this meeting was more candid. It was noted that Zhenotdel's work was progressing unevenly and unsystematically and that very little work was being done among the peasantry, largely because of a lack of organizers.[117] The congress sought to reduce the horizontal isolation which existed between party work and women's sections by ordering all guberniia and *uezd* party committees to create *otdels* where they did not already exist and to strengthen existing ties by assigning qualified party workers to women's sections as organizers.[118] On 30 April 1920 the Orgburo turned its attention to expanding and strengthening the Central Zhenotdel. Two sub-sections were created – one for organization and instruction and the other for agitation and propaganda – which were to coordinate and advise lower *otdels* on work in these fields. To make overall policy, a Zhenotdel plenum was set up consisting of the leaders of the Central Zhenotdel, the Moscow, Petrograd and Ukrainian sections, and representatives from the Komsomol and peasant sections. The director of Zhenotdel was also delegated to attend meetings of the Central Committee and the Orgburo in a consultative capacity.[119]

*   *   *

[113] Armand, *Stat'i*, pp. 61 and 97.
[114] See report to Second All-Russian Meeting of Zhenotdel Guberniia Organizers, in Armand, *Stat'i*, p. 130.
[115] *Ibid.*, p. 124; Liubimova, 'Iz istorii deiatel'nosti Zhenotdelov', p. 71.
[116] Armand, *Stat'i*, pp. 134–5.
[117] Institut marksizma-leninizma pri TsK KPSS, *Deviatyi s"ezd RKP(b), mart-aprel' 1920 goda: Protokoly* (Moscow, 1960), pp. 334–6.
[118] *Ibid.*, pp. 430–1.
[119] Liubimova, 'Iz istorii deiatel'nosti Zhenotdelov', pp. 70–1; Yemelyanova, pp. 24–6; Stavrakis, p. 104.

Besides implementing these much-needed organizational reforms, running Zhenotdel's central office, arranging for the publication of *Kommunistka* and later organizing the First International Conference of Communist Women, Armand also took an active part in the work of the Moscow Women's Section. Much of the leadership of the women's movement fell to her alone, especially after Kollontai suffered a heart attack in November 1919 and was convalescing until the following March. Armand spent her working days, which often stretched to fourteen or sixteen hours, both at the central headquarters on Vozdvizhenka and also in the cold reading room of the Rumiantsev Museum where she often fled to escape the chatter of her fellow workers.[120] The long hours, poor food and difficult working conditions began to affect her health. In February 1920 Vinogradskaia visited Armand's new apartment at 9 Neglinnaia five blocks from the Kremlin and close to the Bolshoi Theatre. She was shocked to find her friend sick and alone. 'The room was terribly cold, it was unheated, everything was neglected. Everywhere one could see only dust.' Inessa had neglected her clothing, her voice was hoarse and she 'coughed and shook from the cold' but lacked matches to heat water for tea.[121] In mid-February Lenin learned of her illness. Because her phone as usual was out of order, he sent her a series of get-well notes urging her to take better care of herself, telling her about the state of Krupskaia's current ailments, and declaring 'it is sheer madness to go out with a temperature of 38 to 39 degrees [100–102F]! I insist that you do not go out.'[122] She apparently did not heed his advice for her condition deteriorated in March when he wrote to her again.

Dear Friend,

So, the doctor says pneumonia. You have to be *extra*-careful. You must have your daughter phone me every day (12–4). Write *frankly*, what do you need? Do you have wood? Who makes the fire? *Do you have food? Who prepares it?* Who makes you compresses?

You are evading my questions – that is not good. Answer immediately on this sheet, answer *all my points*.

Get well!

Your Lenin

Is the telephone repaired yet?[123]

---

[120] Vinogradskaia in Krupskaia (ed.), *Pamiati*, p. 63. [121] *Ibid.*, pp. 61–2.

[122] *Leninskii sbornik*, vol. XXXV, p. 109.

[123] *Izvestiia*, no. 96 (22 April 1962), p. 1 (emphasis in the original). See also three other brief notes of this period recently published in 'Novye dokumenty V. I. Lenina', *Izvestiia TsK KPSS*, 1989, no. 1, pp. 215–16.

Very soon after she recovered, Inessa became involved in the final preparations for the First International Conference of Communist Women scheduled to meet concurrently with the Second Congress of the Comintern in late July 1920. The previous December the Executive Committee of the Communist International (ECCI) had asked the Politburo that Armand's services be made available to it.[124] It was a difficult assignment. Armand acknowledged that Zhenotdel had virtually no direct contact with socialist and communist women's movements abroad.[125] Moreover, Kollontai's continued illness and Krupskaia's work with the Commissariat of Education deprived her of the assistance of the two other Russian women with experience in the international women's movement. As a result, according to Vinogradskaia, Inessa 'took on herself all the work of preparing, organizing and conducting the conference'.[126] She drew up the agenda, drafted the resolutions, wrote a background brochure for the delegates,[127] and made the local arrangements. She found, however, that the Comintern on the international level, like the Communist Party on the national level, was reluctant to provide the financial and organizational support needed to create an effective women's organization. No attempt was made to solicit women delegates in Europe specifically for the First Conference of Communist Women. Instead, after the Comintern Congress convened on 19 July in Petrograd, those delegates who happened to be women were urged to go to Moscow on the 30th to meet as a special section to discuss the international organization of working women. After four days of debate they were to return to Petrograd to present their report to the concluding plenary sessions of the Communist International.

Not surprisingly, this attempt at getting two conferences for the price of one resulted in a small and undistinguished gathering in Moscow. Kollontai, Krupskaia, Balabanoff and Zetkin – who along with Lenin were elected to an honorary presidium[128] – were conspicuous by their absence. The twenty-one delegates who did attend the opening ceremonies in the Bolshoi Theatre were outnumbered by the women factory workers observing the proceedings from the surrounding balconies and

---

[124] *Biog. khr.*, vol. VII, p. 103.
[125] See report to Second All-Russian Meeting of Zhenotdel Guberniia Organizers, in Armand, *Stat'i*, p. 138.
[126] *Otchet o Pervoi Mezhdunarodnoi Konferentsii Kommunistok* (Moscow, 1921), p. 3.
[127] Elena Blonina [I. F. Armand], *Rabotnitsy i Internatsionale* (Moscow, 1920); abridged version in Armand, *Stat'i*, pp. 139–76.
[128] *Otchet o Pervoi Mezhdunarodnoi Konferentsii Kommunistok*, p. 21.

stalls.[129] Many of the delegates had not been members of women's organizations in the nineteen countries they represented and had no real interest in the woman question.[130] Some were openly suspicious of the feminist implications of the gathering they were attending. Perhaps for this reason, most of the discussion was limited to organizational matters and to methods of appealing to working women.

Inessa Armand was the dominant figure at the conference. She sat on its presidium, chaired its formal sessions in the Kremlin, and introduced the major resolutions. She did not always get her way, however. In her 'Theses on the Development of Work Among Women of All Countries' Armand repeated the familiar cliché that the Second International had done little to further women's liberation. This brought a sharp rebuttal from the German delegation which defended Clara Zetkin's pioneering work within the International and succeeded in getting a more moderate resolution passed.[131] Armand also met some opposition to her efforts at imposing the Russian experience and form of organization on the international women's movement. The proper approach, she said, was not to have a separate communist women's organization as in England and Sweden or to defer all work among women until after the socialist revolution as the French wanted to do but rather to follow the Russian example of having agencies within the Communist Party devoted exclusively to carrying out agitation and propaganda among women. She also stressed that delegates' meetings could serve as a useful way of mobilizing women for party causes and of increasing class consciousness in non-communist countries. Some delegates failed to see the reason for imposing a single organizational form on all countries, many of which had different conditions than those prevailing in post-revolutionary Russia, while others felt endorsing special work among women was a feminist deviation despite the Russian experience.[132] On this point, the Bolshevik view prevailed and foreign communist parties

---

129 Vinogradskaia, p. 226; Elizabeth Waters, 'In the Shadow of Comintern: The Communist Women's Movement, 1920–43', in Sonia Kruks, Rayna Rapp and Marilyn B. Young (eds.), *Promissory Notes: Women in the Transition to Socialism* (New York, 1989), p. 29.
130 Krupskaia in Krupskaia (ed.), *Pamiati*, pp. 32–3.
131 Elena Blonina [I. F. Armand], 'Osnovnoi vopros poriadka dnia mezhdunarodnoi konferentsii', *Kommunistka*, 1920, nos. 3/4, and in *Stat'i*, pp. 112–13.
132 Armand's report to the congress is in *Otchet o Pervoi Mezhdunarodnoi Konferentsii Kommunistok*, pp. 82–7; her appraisal of the meetings was published in *Kommunistka*, 1920, nos. 3/4, and in *Stat'i*, pp. 110–14. Some of her ideas were also set forth on the eve of the conference in *Kommunistka*, 1920, nos. 1/2, in *Stat'i*, pp. 98–103. For a more lengthy discussion of the conference, see Waters, 'In the Shadow of the Comintern', pp. 30–9.

13. Inessa Armand near the time of her death in 1920.

were told by the Executive Committee of the Comintern to establish their own zhenotdels and their own delegates' meetings. The ECCI also approved the establishment of an International Women's Secretariat that would unify the communist women's movement under the Comintern's watchful eye.[133]

From the party's point of view, Armand's success in appealing to Russian women without challenging the unitary party and in harnessing European women to the Russian model made her a logical candidate to head up the new international Secretariat. This climax to her revolutionary and feminist career was not to be. After seeing the Women's Conference through to a reasonably successful conclusion on 2 August, Armand returned to Petrograd to promote its resolutions at the Comintern Congress and in the ECCI. 'By the end of the Congress', Krupskaia wrote, 'Inessa was on her last legs.'[134] At Lenin's insistence, she took leave of her work with Zhenotdel and *Kommunistka* and left the Secretariat to others while she went off on a much-needed vacation in the Caucasus.

[133] E. H. Carr, *A History of Soviet Russia: Socialism in One Country, 1924–1926*, vol. III (London, 1964), p. 977.

[134] Krupskaia in Krupskaia (ed.), *Pamiati*, p. 33. See also Vinogradskaia, p. 226. For a photograph of Armand taken about this time, see Plate 13.

CHAPTER 13

DEATH IN THE CAUCASUS

On the eve of the First International Conference of Communist Women Lenin wrote Inessa Armand his last and most poignant letter. He expressed his sorrow that she was frustrated and tired with her work in Zhenotdel and especially in her relations with Aleksandra Kollontai. Like others, he was concerned about the effect long hours of work and the stress of her many activities was having on her health and offered to help her make arrangements for a vacation. In the past, when she needed a rest, she had gone to Pushkino. Lenin reported that he had recently been out in the region and everywhere heard favourable comments about the Armand family.[1] What he did not mention was that the Armand estates were no longer a suitable place for peaceful recuperation. I. V. Got'e, a longtime family friend and head librarian at the Rumiantsev Museum, had visited the elder Armands in September 1919. He recorded in his diary the sorrowful effects of the revolution on their way of life: 'God, what horror in Pushkino! In the garden [of the Armand estate] they are cutting down trees for firewood and calves are grazing in the flower beds ... The lanes are uncared for, the gate in the park stands wide open. I left with a heavy feeling.'[2] Conditions had not improved by August 1920 when he returned to arrange for the transfer of Evgenii Armand's books which Inessa had perused in her youth.

Such horror and neglect there, where life once burgeoned! E. E.'s house has been turned into a club; everything has been pilfered, is falling down and leaking; Ad.E.'s house is serving as a nursery, and not a single object has remained in the rooms. The old women have been stuffed into an old people's home and are sadly living out their lives among the ruins of the past. The

---

[1] *Leninskii sbornik*, vol. XXXVII, p. 233, wherein this letter is said to have been written 'before 17 August 1920'. *Biog. khr.*, vol. IX, p. 134, is more accurate in dating it 'before 28 July'.

[2] Got'e, p. 300.

garden is overgrown, there are tall weeds everywhere, and the gazebos have been wrecked. Horror and abomination.[3]

Lenin suggested other alternatives for a holiday. Inessa could, of course, return to her native France but he did not think that this was a very good idea.

They will arrest [you] and not let [you] out for a long time ... It is necessary to be very careful. Would it not be better to go to Norway (many people know English there) or Holland or Germany as a French, Russian (or even Canadian) subject?

He closed his letter with yet another suggestion:

If a sanatorium [abroad] doesn't appeal to you, why not go south? To Sergo [Ordzhonikidze] in the Caucasus? Sergo could arrange for rest, sun, and a good job for sure. He is *the boss* there. Think about it.[4]

She did think about it and came to the conclusion that a holiday was a good idea especially since her sixteen-year-old son Andre was also ill and once again needed medical attention.[5] She decided not to go abroad but to follow Lenin's last suggestion of seeking sun and rest at the mineral spa of Kislovodsk on the northern slopes of the Caucasus. Lenin greased the wheels of the bureaucracy for her. He gave her a letter addressed to the administrator of health resorts and sanatoria in the Caucasus asking that the official 'do everything possible to provide the best accommodation and treatment for the bearer, comrade Inessa Fedorovna Armand and her sick son. Please afford these party comrades, who are personally known to me, complete trust and assistance.'[6] He also wrote to Ordzhonikidze, the head of the Revolutionary Council in the Caucasus, asking him not to forget a promise he had made earlier in Moscow to take care of arrangements in Kislovodsk for Inessa and to establish personal contact with her so that she could if necessary be evacuated quickly 'in view of the dangerous situation in the Kuban'.[7] Not satisfied, he cabled Ordzhonikidze two days later: 'don't forget you promised to arrange for treatment for Inessa Armand and her sick son who left here on 18 August'.[8]

Inessa and Andre arrived in Kislovodsk, after an arduous four-day

---

[3] *Ibid.*, p. 376. I assume that 'E. E.' is Evgenii Evgen'evich Armand and not his brother Emil who is not otherwise mentioned in the diary. 'Ad. E.' is probably the third brother – Adolf Evgen'evich Armand.
[4] *Leninskii sbornik*, vol. XXXVII, p. 233 (emphasis in the original).
[5] Stal' in Krupskaia (ed.), *Pamiati*, p. 45.
[6] Letter of 17 August 1920, in Lenin, *PSS*, vol. LI, p. 261.
[7] Letter of 18 August 1920 in *ibid.*, p. 262.
[8] Telegram of 20 August 1920 in *ibid.*, p. 265.

train trip, on 22 August. Conditions there were not what she had expected. The sanatorium turned out to be an expropriated dacha lacking in health equipment and sometimes in food. Despite Lenin's intercession, no accommodation was available for her in the crowded main building. The room that friends found for her was without a light or even proper bedding.[9] Liudmila Stal', who was in Kislovodsk with her ailing husband, felt that her old friend looked tired, worn out and emaciated when she arrived.[10] 'At first, I slept night and day', Inessa wrote to her daughter Inna three weeks later.

Now, to the contrary, I sleep quite poorly. I sunbathe and take [mineral] baths, but the sun here is not very hot – it is no match for the Crimean sun and the weather is so indifferent: frequent storms and yesterday it was quite cold. In general, I cannot say I am enamoured with Kislovodsk. And now I am already beginning to get bored.[11]

Even after recovering her health, she avoided contact with other people at the sanatorium preferring instead to spend her days reading on a nearby hillside while Andre occupied himself playing croquet with the other guests.[12]

Lenin did not help matters by wiring Ordzhonikidze again on 2 September: 'Please add fullest details about the progress of the fight against banditry and about arrangements you made in Kislovodsk for Soviet functionaries about whom I spoke to you here personally.'[13] Ordzhonikidze belatedly ordered local party officials to visit the health spa to make sure its influential guest was safe and content. When asked what she needed, Inessa replied that she would like a pillow and promptly was given three.[14] The authorities were even more concerned by a White Russian military detachment under General Fostikov in the hills around Kislovodsk. At night sounds of artillery could be heard in the distance and the district Military Committee would frequently sound the alarm forcing the patients to grab the rifles they had been issued and run to assigned posts in the darkness.

Faced with the prospect that a close friend of Lenin's might be in harm's way, the local Red Army commander Davydov and Stepanov-Nazarov from the Tersk Oblast Committee decided that Inessa should be evacuated to a safer location. She protested about this special treatment arguing that truly sick people, children and other women should be

---

[9] Vinogradskaia in Krupskaia (ed.), *Pamiati*, p. 66; Vinogradskaia, pp. 228–9.
[10] Stal' in Krupskaia (ed.), *Pamiati*, p. 45.
[11] Armand, *Stat'i*, p. 257.
[12] Stal' and Kotov in Krupskaia (ed.), *Pamiati*, pp. 45 and 76.
[13] Lenin, *PSS*, vol. LI, p. 273.　　[14] Vinogradskaia, p. 230.

removed first. Nazarov, reacting to continued pressure from Moscow and from regional officials, threatened to use force unless she complied. Vinogradskaia and several other friends tried to convince Inessa and her son to join them in returning to Moscow. Again she protested claiming rather obstinately that they had used up only half of their two-month holiday and would be of more use to the party after they were fully rested. Despite an improvement in the military situation around Kislovodsk with the defeat and subsequent retreat of General Fostikov in mid-September, Nazarov decided to close the entire health spa for the season and to evacuate the more important patients whether they liked it or not. On the eve of their departure, Inessa was persuaded to play the piano for the other guests after dinner. For several very moving hours she worked her way through her classical repertoire for the last time to the surprise of Vinogradskaia who never realized her colleague possessed such ability.[15]

The forced evacuation of Kislovodsk turned out to be poorly planned, chaotic and far more dangerous than continued residence at the sanatorium. On 16 or 17 September, Inessa, Andre and a number of the other patients including two pregnant women climbed on board a special railway car attached to a military train under the command of Davydov. Their first destination, Vladikavkaz on the Georgian Military Highway, was reached safely despite several running gun battles with anti-Bolshevik irregulars along the route. Accommodation proved hard to find in Vladikavkaz – a town crowded with cossacks and Georgian refugees – which had recently experienced several cases of cholera. Ordzhonikidze, who Inessa had known at Longjumeau and who was clearly concerned with her growing irritation, visited her in the town which now bears his name and offered to put a car at her disposal so that she might explore the Military Highway and surrounding region. She objected again to this special treatment and insisted instead that some decision be made on their ultimate destination. Since Vladikavkaz, where they had been forced to spend two days in their railway car, was obviously unsuitable, it was decided to retrace their steps to the picturesque resort of Nal'chik. Their train had travelled only 35 kilometres before renewed fighting forced them to stop in Beslan. Beslan turned out to be even dirtier than Vladikavkaz, had no accommodation for unexpected visitors, inadequate toilet facilities and little food. For the next

---

[15] Vinogradskaia in Krupskaia (ed.), *Pamiati*, p. 67. Other personal accounts of Armand's last days in Kislovodsk can be found in *ibid.*, especially Stal', p. 46; Kotov, pp. 76–8; I. S. Ruzheinikov, 'Poslednie dni tovarishcha Inessy Armand', pp. 81–2; Evsei Rikhterman, 'Pamiati Inessy Armand', pp. 90–1. See also Vinogradskaia, pp. 229–31.

two days they continued to live in their railway carriage and existed on raw fruit and locally grown melons. They finally arrived in Nal'chik – only 85 kilometres as the crow flies from Kislovodsk – in the evening of 21 September after spending five or six days covering 385 kilometres through disease-ridden and battle-scarred territory.[16] Inessa decided, following a quick inspection of the town, that the party would have to spend yet another night in their railway car. That evening she went to a meeting of the Nal'chik Executive Committee, perhaps intent on using her influence to secure more permanent accommodation for the wandering band from Kislovodsk. She returned to the station around 10 pm where, during the course of the night, she began to vomit and have convulsions. Dr I. S. Ruzheinikov, who had been travelling with the group since Kislovodsk, felt that her weakened constitution had not been able to withstand possibly contaminated food eaten in Beslan. He arranged for her to be admitted to the local hospital the next morning. By mid-day, her symptoms were such that he had no alternative but to move her into the cholera ward. Thirty-six hours later, in the early morning hours of 24 September, Inessa Armand died at the age of 46, just one of over 12,000 Russian citizens to perish of cholera during the first nine months of 1920.[17] For the next eight days her wasted body lay in the Nal'chik mortuary until a zinc-lined coffin could be secured from Vladikavkaz.

*   *   *

It is no wonder that when the coffin finally arrived in Moscow early in the morning of 11 October Lenin was on hand to greet it and that, at the funeral the next day, he was distraught. Inessa Armand had been a close family friend for more than a decade; she had been his special protégée and invaluable 'Girl Friday'; she had served as a scapegoat for abuse he should have taken before the revolution; and she had exhausted herself working for his party and the state after 1917. Her death, while on a vacation at a sanatorium, was 'incomprehensible' to him.[18] As he waited for the train carrying her body to arrive at the

---

[16] The best accounts of this trip are by Kotov and Ruzheinikov in Krupskaia (ed.), *Pamiati*, pp. 79, 82–3.

[17] *Pravda*, 11 September 1920. One rumour, which was passed on to me without denial by a member of the Armand family in Moscow, is that Inessa in despair over personal problems ended her life with poison rather than dying of cholera (letter to the author from Egor Nazarenko, 20 December 1990). For what I consider to be more reliable eye-witness accounts, on which the above description of her death is based, see Kotov and Ruzheinikov in Krupskaia (ed.), *Pamiati*, pp. 79–80, 84–6.

[18] Vinogradskaia, p. 233.

Kazan Station he could not help but reflect that it was he who had urged her to go to the Caucasus and that his constant reminders to subordinates in the area had resulted in her unnecessary evacuation from Kislovodsk. This intervention – plus wartime confusion, transportation breakdowns, local inefficiency and the prevalence of typhus and cholera in the Caucasus – had obviously contributed to her needless death.

The long walk through the deserted streets of Moscow behind her horse-drawn hearse was a form of penance for the Bolshevik leader. He turned down an offer of a ride, preferring instead to trudge along with Krupskaia, Inessa's children and a few of her friends from Zhenotdel.[19] When they reached the House of Unions, where her body was to lie in state, he must have remembered the triumphant day less than two years earlier when he had addressed over one thousand working women attending the All-Russian Women's Congress Inessa had helped arrange in the same building. Now her coffin lay in an adjoining room – the same room where Sverdlov had lain nineteen months earlier and where Lenin himself was to rest a little more than three years later – under a prophetic banner proclaiming that 'the leaders may die but the cause lives on'.[20]

It was appropriate at noon the next day, as her coffin was carried out for the final trip to Red Square, that the Bolshoi Theatre Orchestra should play the music from Chopin, Mozart and Beethoven which she had loved so much. It was also fitting that the cortège should be followed by her children, family, friends and 'an endless stream of women workers',[21] who had come to honour one of their few defenders in the Soviet hierarchy. Lenin, hatless but bundled in a heavy coat despite the pleasant fall weather, met the entourage with Krupskaia as it entered Red Square and approached the 'Red Graveyard' between the Nicholas and Spassky Towers of the Kremlin.

The final homages to Inessa Armand were less appropriate and less fitting. Whether by design or by accident, the seven persons chosen to speak over her grave were neither particularly close friends of the deceased nor did they give an accurate picture of her relatively short life. No one spoke about her work as a teacher of peasant children at Eldigino or as a protector of prostitutes in the Moscow Society for Improving the Lot of Women. None of her associates from the Moscow underground spoke about her activity as a propagandist before and after the 1905 Revolution, none of her friends from Mezen talked about

[19] *Izvestiia*, 12 October 1920, p. 4.   [20] *Pravda*, 12 October 1920, p. 1.
[21] *Izvestiia*, 13 October 1920, p. 2.

her fortitude in the far north, none of the Paris *émigrés* recalled her role in building a 'party of the new type', and none of the Baugy Group recounted her ideological differences with Lenin. No foreign communist spoke about her role in undermining the Second International and in fostering the growth of militant socialism in the land of her birth. To those who knew Inessa well, the orations of the three principal speakers must have seemed hollow. V. I. Nevskii spoke on behalf of the Central Committee which rarely gave more than token support to enterprises such as *Rabotnitsa* and Zhenotdel she thought were important. Polidorov praised her work as head of the Moscow Guberniia Sovnarkhoz – work which she was woefully unprepared to do and was delighted to leave. Aleksandra Kollontai gave an 'impassioned'[22] but perhaps insincere speech about her longtime rival in the Russian women's movement with whom she had recently quarrelled. Inessa herself probably would have been happiest with the last four speakers – all relatively insignificant women representing Zhenotdel and related women's groups in the Far East and the Caucasus who had come to honour one of their own.[23]

After the lowering of the coffin into the flower-bestrewn ground and the singing of the 'Internationale', Lenin and Krupskaia embraced Inessa's children and then returned to the Kremlin where the Bolshevik leader presided over a scheduled meeting of the Council of People's Commissars.[24] He and especially his wife, however, did not forget about their 'closest friend'[25] and her family. Inna Armand later wrote that she had a chance to see Lenin quite often since, 'after my mother's death in 1920, Vladimir Il'ich and Nadezhda Konstantinovna became the guardians of my sister, my youngest brother and me'.[26] It was a new role for the childless couple and one which they seemed to enjoy.

Even before Inessa's funeral, Lenin had instructed his secretary L. A. Fotieva to find out what had happened to Andre whom he feared might have become stranded in the Caucasus.[27] In November and December 1920 he often visited Inna and Andre at the Chaika rest home outside Moscow. According to Inna, he offered moral support and sympathy as well as giving Andre chess problems to solve and suggesting to them (as he had to their mother four years earlier) that they take up skiing 'so as

---

[22] *Ibid.*
[23] For summaries of these funeral orations, see the appendix to Krupskaia's *Pamiati*, pp. 105–7.
[24] *Biog. khr.*, vol. IX, p. 361.   [25] Vinogradskaia, p. 232.
[26] I. A. Armand, in *Vosp. o V. I. Lenine*, vol. IV, p. 321.
[27] *Biog. khr.*, vol. IX, p. 346.

to build up their strength'.[28] During 1921 the girls in particular were frequent visitors to the Ul'ianovs' apartment. Indeed, Boris Souvarine, who worked with Inna at the time in Moscow, recalled that 'she used to live in the Kremlin in Lenin's home, where she was the object of great affection'.[29] Inna spent that summer at Lenin's private retreat in Gorki studying for her university entrance examinations. Krupskaia once introduced Inna's sister Varvara to Louise Bryant as 'my niece. She is usually with me. I love her and want you to know her.'[30] In February 1921 Lenin and Krupskaia paid a surprise late night visit to the hostel where Varvara was living while studying at the Higher Art-Technical Institute. In the ensuing debate with the students about the virtues of revolutionary culture, Vladimir Il'ich predictably tried to defend realistic painting and classical literature. Lenin enjoyed arguing with the students but he could not bring himself to partake in the spartan midnight meal which Varvara's friends offered their illustrious guests.[31]

Perhaps as a result of this visit, Lenin decided that Varvara could use a change of scenery and of vocation. On 11 July 1921 he wrote to F. A. Rothstein, the Soviet ambassador to Iran, stating that he had dispatched Varvara and Alexander Armand to Teheran in the expectation that he might find something useful for them to do.[32] A month later, he wrote again, confessing that he was 'very anxious' about Varvara and expressing the hope that Rothstein 'would be able to devote some little time' to Inessa's children.[33] In December 1921 Lenin cabled Rothstein about Varvara suggesting that if necessary she be sent back to Moscow but to make sure she brought warm clothing with her.[34] Varvara, who was in poor health in 1923 and 1924, returned to her art studies, finally graduating from the institute in 1927. After seven years' employment in a textile factory, she became an instructor of graphics and then a decorative artist. Following the Second World War, she was named an 'Honoured Artist of the RSFSR' and in 1977 a retrospective

---

28 I. A. Armand, in *Vosp. o V. I. Lenine*, vol. IV, p. 322.
29 Boris Souvarine, 'Comments on the Massacre', in M. M. Drachkovitch and Branko Lazitch (eds.), *The Comintern: Historical Highlights – Essays, Recollections, Documents* (New York, 1966), p. 181.
30 *The Liberator*, November 1921, as cited in McNeal, *Bride of the Revolution*, p. 211. Bryant, while not mentioning the 'niece' by name, refers to her as 'a pretty girl of eighteen'. McNeal concludes, correctly I believe, that this was Varvara who Krupskaia on other occasions referred to as 'my beloved daughter'. In 1964 the editors of *Novyi mir* stretched credulity by identifying the young 'niece' as Lenin's 43-year-old sister Mariia.
31 I. A. Armand, in *Vosp. o V. I. Lenine*, vol. IV, pp. 324–6.
32 Lenin, *PSS*, vol. LIII, pp. 21–2.
33 *Ibid.*, p. 119.   34 *Ibid.*, vol. LIV, p. 67.

exhibit of her work was held in Moscow.[35] A decade later, she died at the age of 86, the last of Inessa's surviving children.

Inna, like her mother and her sister, was the recipient of Lenin's benevolent intervention. On 6 September 1922 he learned from Krupskaia that Inna was ill. This prompted a letter from the head of the Soviet state to the doctor in charge of the rest home where she was staying in the Crimea insisting that she be given sufficient food and medical attention and that he be informed of her condition. This, and a follow-up enquiry on 17 September,[36] cost Inna 'a lot of discomfort' as she was forced by the frightened doctor to stay in bed a week after she had recovered.[37] One of Lenin's last acts before he was incapacitated by a stroke was to enquire if the temperamental phone in the Armand apartment where Inna was now staying was finally in working order.[38]

Inna, like Varvara, remained in close contact with Krupskaia throughout the 1920s and 1930s. The two women corresponded often about Lenin's failing health, about plans for his funeral in January 1924, and about the birth of Inna's first child (who was named after her grandmother).[39] Inna had married Hugo Eberlein, a German communist whom she met while working in the secretariat of the Comintern in 1921. In 1923 she was appointed to the Soviet trade delegation in Berlin and later to the Soviet embassy in Germany where she remained until 1931. From 1933 until her retirement in 1961, Inna Armand worked in the Institute of Marxism-Leninism editing Lenin's *Sochineniia* and in the Foreign Languages Publishing House. More than any of the other children, Inna was devoted to preserving the memory of her mother. In addition to several reminiscences, she published a year before her death in 1971 a revealing collection of Inessa's letters to her children and relatives.[40] Inna's influential contacts could not save her husband. In 1928 Eberlein fell from power in the German Communist Party and in 1933 he fled to Moscow. Four years later he was arrested

---

[35] V. A. Armand, *Vystavka proizvedenii: Zhivopis, Grafiki, Gobeleny, Kovry* (Moscow, 1977). Biographical information on Varvara Armand is in Lenin, *PSS*, vol. LII, p. 465. For a photograph of Varvara with Krupskaia, taken in 1932, see McNeal, *Bride of the Revolution*, pp. 54–5. See *Novyi mir*, 1967, no. 4, pp. 200–3, for some of her correspondence with Krupskaia.

[36] *Biog. khr.*, vol. XII, p. 373; *Leninskii sbornik*, vol. XL, p. 101.

[37] I. A. Armand, in *Vosp. o V. I. Lenine*, vol. IV, pp. 327–8.

[38] *Biog. khr.*, vol. XII, p. 448.

[39] Some of this correspondence is reproduced in 'O zhizni i deiatel'nosti V. I. Lenina', *Izvestiia TsK KPSS*, 1989, no. 4, pp. 179–85. See also Nina Tumarkin, *Lenin Lives! The Lenin Cult in Soviet Russia* (Cambridge, Mass., 1983), p. 177.

[40] 'Pis'ma Inessy Armand', *Novyi mir*, 1970, no. 6, pp. 196–218. Biographical information on Inna can be found in her obituary (*New York Times*, 9 July 1971, p. 34) and in Lenin, *PSS*, vol. LII, p. 465.

during the purges. Through subterfuge he managed to escape being handed over to the Gestapo in 1941 but died in a Soviet prison three years later.[41]

Less information is available about the subsequent lives of Inessa's three sons. Fedor, who supported the Provisional Government in October 1917 and was suspected of treason in April 1919, remained in the Soviet Air Force as an instructor until 1926. He was then transferred to the reserve for medical reasons and for the next decade was involved with sports organizations in Moscow. He died either from the delayed effects of his war wounds or from tuberculosis in 1936.[42] Fedor was the only one of Inessa's children who did not join the Communist Party. His younger brother Andre became a member in 1944 shortly before being killed at the front as a member of the Moscow militia. Prior to the war he had been a mechanic and an engineer in automobile works in Gorki and in Moscow.[43]

Inessa's eldest son, Alexander Alexandrovich, was the least affected by Lenin's attention. After service in the Imperial Army and then in the Red Army, he worked as a secretary of the Soviet trade mission in Teheran during 1921 and 1922. In 1928 he joined the All-Union Thermotechnical Institute where he quickly rose through the bureaucratic ranks to become the head of a research department in the Commissariat of Heavy Industry. In 1937 he wrote an obsequious article praising his late commissar (and his mother's friend) Sergo Ordzhonikidze as well as Stalin and Stakhanovism and demanding the rooting out of bourgeois prejudices and the remnants of Trotskyism from scientific institutes. He died in 1967.[44] No information is available about the fate of Inessa's long-suffering husband Alexander Armand other than that he lived in the Soviet Union until the time of his death near Moscow at the age of 70 in 1943.[45]

Lenin and Krupskaia also did their best to keep alive the memory of Inessa herself. On 24 April 1921 the Bolshevik leader wrote to Kamenev as chairperson of the Moscow Soviet to enquire about the erecting of a permanent memorial to Armand in Red Square and the planting of flowers around her grave. He noted that her children wanted

---

[41] Lazitch, p. 107–8.
[42] Biographical information on Fedor will be found in Institute for the Study of the USSR, *Who Was Who*, p. 29, and in Lenin, *PSS*, vol. LII, p. 465.
[43] Lenin, *PSS*, vol. LIII, p. 464.
[44] A. A. Armand, 'Zavety Sergo', *Zavodskaia laboratoriia*, vol. VI, no. 2 (1937), pp. 139–40. For biographical information, see Lenin, *PSS*, vol. LII, pp. 464–5.
[45] Podliashuk, p. 34. Wolfe claims that Alexander 'entered "agriculture", working in a kolhoz until his death' (Wolfe, 'Lenin and Inessa Armand', p. 114).

to place a small plaque or gravestone at the site but did not know the proper public or private agency to contact concerning the inscription.[46] Long after Lenin's own death, arrangements in the 'Red Graveyard' were standardized and Inessa was given a simple granite gravestone, which she has to share today with John Reed and two early Soviet martyrs – I. V. Rusakov and S. M. Pekalov – in the second row behind the marble mausoleum. During the early 1920s, Krupskaia wrote several commemorative articles about her friend and in 1926 fulfilled a pledge made by the Central Zhenotdel at the time of Inessa's death by editing a collection of fourteen essays about her life and work entitled *Pamiati Inessy Armand*. Some of these were contributed by former colleagues in the party such as Kamenev and Safarov; others by friends from the women's movement like Stal' and Vinogradskaia. The warmest and longest was written by Krupskaia herself. Notable by their absence were entries by Zinoviev, his wife Zinaida Lilina, members of the Baugy Group, Dmitri Manuil'skii and Aleksandra Kollontai.

After Lenin's death and particularly during the 1930s, the reputation of Inessa Armand, like that of many of the contributors to her memorial volume, went into eclipse. Until the early 1960s, little mention was made by Soviet writers of her role in the pre-revolutionary party, of her friendship with Lenin, or of her contributions to the women's movement after 1917. This silence is in part explained by elements of her biography. Party historians had no desire to acknowledge that children of the propertied and privileged classes were attracted to Russian Social Democracy and contributed both personally and financially to the ultimate success of the Bolshevik Party. Inessa came from the manor house in Pushkino, she lived in comfort in the Arbat, and she vacationed in Switzerland. If such people had a social consciousness, it was not supposed to extend beyond participating in the Moscow Society for Improving the Lot of Women. If Soviet historians had their choice, the party coffers would have been filled with the kopeks of nameless proletarians rather than with the rubles of industrialists named Morozov and Armand. Moreover, Inessa Armand was an Old Bolshevik, *par excellence*. While she had paid her dues in the Moscow underground and in Mezen, she also spent almost a decade in western Europe. She was educated, cultured, at home in four languages and uncomfortable with the *apparatchiki* of the new regime. She was one of those 'herrings with ideas' – an intellectual

---

[46] *Biog. khr.*, vol. X, p. 348; Lenin, *PSS*, vol. LII, p. 166.

communist woman – for whom Stalin had no use whatsoever.[47] Many of Inessa's Old Bolshevik friends at Longjumeau, her travelling companions on the 'sealed train', and her associates among the Left Communists later ended up in the Gulag.

Inessa's relationship with Lenin also contributed to her eclipse under Stalin. To the manufacturers of the myth of the omnipotent and puritanical *vozhd*, it was embarrassing to have to explain why he used the *ty* form of address with an attractive woman who was not his wife, why he took time out from revolutionary planning to write to this woman several times a week on the eve of the war and during the year before the February Revolution, or why he showed her uncommon signs of favour ranging from teaching assignments at Longjumeau to vacations in the Caucasus. It was equally difficult to explain why the once 'most perfect of men' needed constant linguistic assistance from a female subordinate, went down on bended knee to get her to do his dirty work for him, and repeatedly apologized for arrogant, rude or patronizing behaviour unbecoming in an idealized leader. It was much easier to forget that the relationship ever existed, to suppress the offending correspondence, and to ignore completely one of the parties involved.

A third and perhaps paramount reason for the demise of Inessa Armand's reputation was her work on behalf of Soviet women in 1919 and 1920. During the years of the Civil War, through the actions of women such as Armand, Kollontai and Samoilova, the legal and economic position of Soviet women vastly improved. The old cliché that the answer to the woman question would be found in the triumph of socialism seemed to be becoming a reality. In fact, many of the gains were more apparent than real and even these were reversed once the male leaders of the party could concentrate on domestic affairs in the decade after the threat of civil war receded. By 1930 the party leaders wanted to forget about communal kitchens, the 'new morality', affirmative action programmes, and special organizations such as Zhenotdel and the International Women's Secretariat. Under Stalin, the paternalism and disinterest in women's issues which characterized the Social Democratic Party before 1914 returned. It is no wonder then that agit-prop officials no longer had much use for the reputation of the woman who was largely responsible for securing these transitory gains.

---

[47] Beatrice Farnsworth, citing Svetlana Allilueva, in 'Bolshevism, the Woman Question, and Aleksandra Kollontai', *American Historical Review*, vol. LXXXI, no. 2 (April 1976), p. 313.

Inessa would not have been happy with the fate of her legacy to Soviet women. The crèches, communal dining rooms and communal laundries which she had promoted to ease the household burden on women and to get them out into economic and civic life proved too expensive to be maintained by the state during the 1920s. With the advent of NEP, labour conscription came to an end and many women factory workers were laid off. Owners and managers felt that women were less skilled, that maternity benefits and new laws designed to protect the female organism were too expensive, and that therefore the largely unorganized women workers were the most expendable part of the labour force. Many Soviet women were thus forced back into the home and into economic dependence of marriage. Liberal divorce laws were meaningless when women could not support themselves outside of marriage. This return to the conventional nuclear family with the woman being responsible for child rearing, cooking and housework appealed to the patriarchal male party leaders. Soviet women were now to pay for the fact that their early leaders tried to liberate them through state edict rather than through stressing male involvement in a restructured household. As Beatrice Farnsworth has noted, 'the withering away of the family' became just another 'socialist myth'.[48] Instead of fostering Kollontai's 'new morality', Soviet leaders in 1939 resurrected Inessa Armand long enough to publish Lenin's letters to her condemning any notion of 'free love'.

One of the reasons the gains of the immediate post-revolutionary period could be rolled back so easily was the failure of Armand's affirmative action programme to take root. While the percentage of women involved in the work of the city soviets had increased to 18.2 per cent by 1926, only 8.2 per cent of the delegates to the 1927 All-Russian Congress of Soviets were women and only two women – Krupskaia and Klavdiia Nikolaeva – ever sat in the Presidium of the Soviet's Central Executive Committee before the war. Although 26 per cent of trade-union members in 1924 were women, women made up a mere 4 per cent of the Trade Union Central Committee in that year. The situation was even worse in the party apparatus. In the youth groups, where women comprised 15 per cent of the Komsomol membership in 1924, they held only 3 per cent of the congress seats. While slightly less than 9 per cent of the regular party membership in 1924 were women,

[48] *Ibid.*, p. 308.

only 3 per cent of the guberniia committee members and 1 per cent of the delegates to the Twelfth Party Congress were females. From 1922 to 1934, only three women (Krupskaia, Nikolaeva, and A. V. Artiukhina) were full members of the party's Central Committee and none belonged to the Politburo.[49]

This meant that decisions affecting women were made by a party and state apparatus overwhelmingly dominated by men whose attitudes towards feminist aspirations and organizations were little changed from the paternalistic ideas held by the pre-revolutionary Social Democratic leadership. One of the organizations to suffer was Zhenotdel. Now that the mobilization of women was no longer a priority and the validity of early radical social legislation was being questioned, the Women's Sections found themselves in a precarious situation made only worse by the loss of their three strong and independent leaders – Armand in 1920, Samoilova who died of cholera in 1921, and Kollontai who was fired as Zhenotdel's director in February 1922 for her role in the Workers' Opposition. Their successors lacked the influence to stop the gradual erosion of the organization's powers. Between March 1921 and March 1922, the central Zhenotdel staff was cut from 42 to 23.[50] At the same time lower-level Zhenotdel operatives were transferred by party officials to other activities and male agit-prop functionaries moved in to take over much of the organizational work among Russian women.[51] After 1923 *Kommunistka* no longer discussed theoretical aspects of the woman question and became simply the bulletin board for a women's auxiliary. The hopes of some Bolshevik women, and belatedly even of Armand, that Zhenotdel might serve as a voice for women, as an advocate for their special needs, and as a generator of new ideas[52] had died long before the organization itself was closed down by Stalin in 1930 on the fatuous grounds that its work had been accomplished.

The same fate befell Inessa's last organizational creation – the International Women's Secretariat. In 1923 the Executive Committee of the Comintern took over the right to elect the Secretariat from the periodic International Conferences of Communist Women. In 1924 the headquarters of the Secretariat was moved from Germany to Moscow and

---

[49] These statistics are found in Bette Stavrakis' pioneering dissertation, pp. 206–48.
[50] *Ibid.*, p. 110.
[51] Clements, 'Kollontai's Contribution to the Workers Opposition', p. 203.
[52] Clements, *Bolshevik Feminist*, p. 166.

two years later the organization was abolished by the ECCI for being too independent in its operations.[53]

*   *   *

Inessa Armand, who witnessed the birth of the Soviet state, was belatedly rediscovered during the last quarter century of that state's existence by the myth-makers of the Institute of Marxism-Leninism. The woman to whom Lenin wrote more than 139 letters, but whose name was rarely mentioned in Stalinist textbooks, suddenly, in the Brezhnev era, became Lenin's loyal protégée recruited to the revolutionary cause by a reading of his inspired works. She was now portrayed as a dedicated mother who faithfully served the party and in the end gave her life for the new state. Even under the influence of *glasnost'*, little was said about the revolutionary milieu of the Armand household in Push-kino, about Inessa's work with women's groups before and after the revolution, or about her attempts to gain intellectual independence from Lenin and to be her own person. In 1977 the house she lived in briefly in Eldigino was opened as a museum and the school she helped to establish on her husband's estate was renamed in her honour, as were a street in Pushkino and an ocean-going freighter.[54]

It would have been more fitting had Armand been rediscovered by the embryonic Soviet feminist movement which itself began to revive under Gorbachev. Soviet society in the 1980s, even more than in her time or now in the West, was characterized by sex-role stratification, a lack of male involvement in housework and child rearing, the exclusion of women from decision-making positions but not from the majority of low-paying jobs, and by a male leadership defining the restrictive nature of the 'womanly mission' and the acceptable limits of female emancipation.[55] Elena Zelinskaia, one of Leningrad's few female political activists, could have been reading from a speech of Inessa Armand to Zhenotdel in 1920 when she told a meeting at the Kennan Institute in 1990 'that women in the Soviet Union are so overburdened with daily needs, such as acquiring food, they have very little experience' in bodies

---

[53] For accounts of the International Women's Secretariat, see Carr, *Socialism in One Country*, vol. III, pp. 976–86, and Waters, 'In the Shadow of the Comintern', pp. 43–50.

[54] Abramov, p. 124; Rusakov and Solov'ev, 'Stanovlius' bol'shevichkoi', p. 77; Pod-liashuk, inside endcover.

[55] Mikhail Gorbachev, *Perestroika: New Thinking for Our Country and the World* (New York, 1987), p. 117. For an excellent description of the situation of Soviet women in the 1980s, see Barbara Holland (ed.), *Soviet Sisterhood: British Feminists on Women in the USSR* (London, 1985).

such as the Leningrad City Soviet (where they made up only 6 per cent of the delegates) or in the short-lived Congress of People's Deputies because patriarchal voters continued to cross out the names of female candidates.[56]

While Armand never advocated that women form pluralistic pressure groups in a socialist society or pursue the more extreme forms of Kollontai's 'new morality', she persistently fought for female equality in the home and in the workplace and for female participation in leadership bodies. She also recognized that women are best organized by other women addressing issues of interest to all women. She realized that woman's female nature was significant in determining her oppression and must be reflected in her eventual liberation. Throughout the last six years of her life, Inessa Armand promoted a sense of female collectivity which is at the heart of her feminism and also is totally alien to the organizational precepts of Bolshevism. Unfortunately, she did not live long enough to realize or to resolve this contradiction. Perhaps in the more liberal and pluralistic Commonwealth of Independent States which is presently emerging, Russian feminists – in their inevitable search for organizational identity and for equality in the home and the workplace – will look for the origins of their movement and discover that someone had trod the same path more than seventy years ago.

[56] 'Inside Leningrad Politics', *Meeting Report* of the Kennan Institute for Advanced Russian Studies, vol. VII, no. 16 (14 May 1990).

BIBLIOGRAPHY

ARCHIVAL MATERIALS

Archives de l'Université Nouvelle de Bruxelles, Free University of Brussels, Brussels

Bern Staatsarchiv, BB4. 1. 946. Akten der Polizei-Direktion. 1914. Bern, Switzerland

Okhrana Archives, Hoover Institution on War, Revolution and Peace, Stanford, California

WORKS BY INESSA ARMAND

Armand, I. F. *Stat'i, rechi, pis'ma*. Moscow, 1975. (Contains 49 letters to relatives and friends written between 1903 and 1920 as well as 39 articles and brochures. Articles not included in this collection are listed below.)

'Moskovskii Gubernskii Sovet Narodnogo Khoziaistva i ego rabota', *Sotsialisticheskoe stroitel'stvo*, no. 2 (18 January 1919), pp. 49–55

'Otchet sekretaria KZO Inessy Armand ob itogakh trekhmesiachnoi deiatel'nosti Zagranichnoi organizatsii RSDRP', in *Istoricheskii arkhiv*, 1961, no. 2, pp. 112–14

'Perspektivy revoliutsii vo Frantsii', *Kommunisticheskii Internatsional*, no. 3 (1 July 1919), pp. 333–8.

'Podaviat li oni bol'shevizm?', in *Istoricheskii arkhiv*, 1958, no. 1, pp. 32–4 (different version in *La IIIe Internationale*, 12 January 1919)

'Pis'mo iz Stokgol'ma', *La Sentinelle* (La Chaux-de-Fonds), no. 93 (23 April 1917), in N. Krutikova, *Na krutom povorote* (Moscow, 1965), pp. 82–3

Pochemu ia stala zashchitnitsei Sovetskoi vlasti? Moscow, 1919

'Pis'ma Inessy Armand', *Novyi mir*, 1970, no. 6, pp. 196–218. (Contains more complete versions of twenty-six letters written to family and friends between 1903 and 1909 as well as two letters to A. E. Armand written in 1899 which are not included in *Stat'i, rechi, pis'ma*.)

Vinogradov, S. (ed.), *Sokrovishcha dushevnoi krasoty*. Moscow, 1984, pp. 7–46. (Selection of letters from *Stat'i, rechi, pis'ma*.)

278

DISSERTATIONS AND OTHER UNPUBLISHED MATERIAL

Bernstein, Laurie. 'Sonia's Daughters: Prostitution and Society in Russia'. Ph.D. dissertation, University of California, Berkeley, 1987

Bobroff, Anne Louise. 'Working Women, Bonding Patterns, and the Politics of Daily Life: Russia at the End of the Old Regime'. Ph.D. dissertation, University of Michigan, 1982

Buchanan, Herbert Ray. 'Soviet Economic Policy for the Transition Period: The Supreme Council of the National Economy, 1917–20'. Ph.D. dissertation, Indiana University, 1972

Burch, Robert Jean. 'Social Unrest in Imperial Russia: The Student Movement at Moscow University, 1887–1905'. Ph.D. dissertation, University of Washington, 1972

Drumm, Robert E. 'The Bolshevik Party and the Organization and Emancipation of Working Women, 1914–1921: or, A History of the Petrograd Experiment'. Ph.D. dissertation, Columbia University, 1977

Gately, M. O. 'The Development of the Russian Cotton Textile Industry in the Pre-Revolutionary Years, 1861–1913'. Ph.D. dissertation, University of Kansas, 1968

Goldberg, Rochelle Lois. 'The Russian Women's Movement: 1859–1917'. Ph.D. dissertation, University of Rochester, 1976

Hanchett, Walter C. 'Moscow in the Late Nineteenth Century: A Study in Municipal Self-Government'. Ph.D. dissertation, University of Chicago, 1964

Hayden, Carol Eubanks. 'Feminism and Bolshevism: The *Zhenotdel* and the Politics of Women's Emancipation in Russia, 1917–1930'. Ph.D. dissertation, University of California, Berkeley, 1979

Honeycutt, Karen. 'Clara Zetkin: A Left-wing Socialist and Feminist in Wilhelmian Germany'. Ph.D. dissertation, Columbia University, 1975

Hutton, Marcelline J. 'Russian and Soviet Women, 1897–1939: Dreams, Struggles, and Nightmares'. Ph.D. dissertation, University of Iowa, 1986

Hyer, Janet. 'Pre-revolutionary *Rabotnitsa*: A Study of Bolshevik Policy towards Working Women'. MA thesis, Carleton University, 1985

Knight, Amy W. 'The Participation of Women in the Revolutionary Movement in Russia, 1890–1914'. Ph.D. dissertation, University of London, 1977

Kowalski, Ronald I. 'The Transition to Socialism: The Programme of the Left Communist Movement of 1918'. Paper presented to the Soviet Industrialization Project Seminar, March 1985.

McNeal, Robert H. 'The Birth of the Myth of the Individual Hero in the USSR: The Red Square Memorials' (1987)

Pelchat, Bianca D. 'Vladimir Burtsev: Wilful Warrior in Dubious Battle'. MA research essay, Carleton University, 1988

Ross, Dale. 'The Role of the Women of Petrograd in War, Revolution and Counter-Revolution, 1914–1921'. Ph.D. dissertation, Rutgers University, 1973

Scott, Mark Chapin. 'Her Brother's Keeper: The Evolution of Women Bolsheviks'. Ph.D. dissertation, University of Kansas, 1980

Stavrakis, Bette Daneman. 'Women and the Communist Party of the Soviet Union, 1918–35'. Ph.D. dissertation, Western Reserve University, 1961

West, J. L. 'The Moscow Progressists: Russian Industrialists in Liberal Politics, 1905–1914'. Ph.D. dissertation, Princeton University, 1975

Yedlin, Tova. 'The First Legal Bolshevik Journal for Women: *Rabotnitsa*, February–June 1914: A Profile' (1986)

BOOKS AND ARTICLES

Abramov, A. *U kremlevskoi steny*, 5th edn. Moscow, 1983

Adamovich, E. 'Vosstanovlenie podpol'noi bol'shevistskoi organizatsii v Khar'kove v 1911–12 gg.', *Letopis' revoliutsii*, 1924, no. 1 (6), pp. 137–70

Andreeva, M. F. *Perepiska, vospominaniia, stat'i, dokumenty*. Moscow, 1968

Armand, A. A. 'Zavety Sergo', *Zavodskaia laboratoriia*, vol. VI, no. 2 (1937), pp. 139–40

Armand, Inna. 'Inessa Armand' in E. D. Stasova (ed.), *Slavnye bol'shevichki*. Moscow, 1958, pp. 75–88

Armand, V. 'Zhivaia nit' (Iz vospominanii i perepiski s N. K. Krupskoi)', *Novyi mir*, 1967, no. 4, pp. 178–203

Artiukhina A. V. *et al.* (eds.). *Zhenshchiny v revoliutsii*. Moscow, 1959 (see articles by E. Goreva, E. Kogan-Pismanik, V. Nikolaeva, L. Stal')

Astrov, N. I. *Vospominaniia*. Paris: YMCA Press, 1940

Atkinson, D., Alexander Dallin and G. W. Lapidus (eds.). *Women in Russia*. Stanford: Stanford University Press, 1977 (see articles by Rose L. Glickman, A. G. Meyer, Richard Stites)

Bailes, Kendall. 'Alexandra Kollontai et la nouvelle morale', *Cahiers du Monde Russe et Soviétique*, vol. VI, no. 4 (October-December 1965), pp. 471–96

Balabanoff, Angelica. *Impressions of Lenin*. Ann Arbor: University of Michigan Press, 1964

My Life as a Rebel. London: Hamilton, 1938

Barulina, A. T. 'Iz istorii bor'by partiinykh organizatsii Petrograda i Moskvy za zhenskie proletarskie massy v 1917 godu (iiul'-oktiabr')', *Vestnik Moskovskogo Universiteta*, series IX: *Istoriia*, 1962, no. 5, pp. 57–69

Beliavskii, M. T. and V. V. Sorokin. 'Neizvestnye stranitsy zhizni soratnikov V. I. Lenina', *Vestnik Moskovskogo Universiteta*, series VIII: *Istoriia*, 1979, no. 6, pp. 51–6

Bergman, Jay. *Vera Zasulich: A Biography*. Stanford: Stanford University Press, 1983

Beucler, Andre and G. Alexinsky. *Les Amours secrétes de Lénine*. Paris: Éditions Bandinière, 1937

Blackwell, William L. 'The Old Believers and the Rise of Private Industrial Enterprise in Early Nineteenth-Century Moscow', in William L. Blackwell (ed.), *Russian Economic Development from Peter the Great to Stalin*. New York: New Viewpoints, 1974, pp. 139–58

Blizhe vsekh: Lenin i iunye internatsionalisty (sbornik dokumentov i materialov). Moscow, 1968

Bobroff, Anne. 'The Bolsheviks and Working Women, 1905–1920', *Soviet Studies*, vol. XXVI, no. 4 (October 1974), pp. 540–67

Bochkaryova, Y. and S. Lyubimova. *Women of a New World*. Moscow, 1969

Body, Marcel. 'Alexandra Kollontai', *Preuves* (Paris), vol. II, no. 14 (April 1952), pp. 12–24

'Les groupes communistes français de Russie, 1918–1921', in Jacques Freymond (ed.), *Contributions à l'histoire du Comintern*. Geneva: Librairie Droz, 1965, pp. 39–65

'Bol'sheviki na briussel'skom soveshchanii 1914 g.: dokumenty Instituta marksizma-leninizma pri TsK KPSS', *Istoricheskii arkhiv*, 1959, no. 4, pp. 9–38

Bonnell, Victoria E. *Roots of Rebellion: Workers' Politics and Organizations in St. Petersburg and Moscow, 1900–1914*. Berkeley: University of California Press, 1983

Borets za raskreposhchenie rabotnitsy: K. N. Samoilova. Moscow, 1925

Bratskaia mogila: Biograficheskii slovar' umershikh i pogibshikh chlenov Moskovskoi organizatsii RKP, 2 vols. Moscow, 1922–23 (see articles by L. Stal' in vol. I and S. M. Zubrovich in vol. II)

Breslav, B. A. 'O V. I. Lenine (Beglye vospominaniia)', *Katorga i ssylka*, 1934, no. 1, pp. 127–79

Buryshkin, P. A. *Moskva kupecheskaia*. New York: Chekhov Publishing House, 1954

Carr, E. H. *A History of Soviet Russia*, 8 vols. London: Macmillan, 1960–64

Clark, Ronald W. *Lenin: The Man Behind the Mask*. London: Faber, 1988

Clements, Barbara Evans. 'Baba and Bolshevik: Russian Women and Revolutionary Change', *Soviet Union/Union Soviétique*, vol. XII, pt. 2 (1985), pp. 161–84

'The Birth of the New Soviet Woman', in Abbott Gleason, Peter Kenez and Richard Stites (eds.), *Bolshevik Culture: Experiment and Order in the Russian Revolution*. Bloomington: Indiana University Press, 1985, pp. 220–37

Bolshevik Feminist: The Life of Aleksandra Kollontai. Bloomington: Indiana University Press, 1979

'Kollontai's Contribution to the Workers' Opposition', *Russian History*, vol. II, pt. 2 (1975), pp. 191–206

Cohen, Stephen F. *Bukharin and the Russian Revolution: A Political Biography, 1888–1938*. New York: Knopf, 1973

Colquhoun, Keith. 'Lenin's Dearest Friend', *Observer Magazine*, 13 April 1975, pp. 33–4

Davydova, L. I. 'Inessa Armand – pervyi predsedatel' Mosgubsovnarkhoza', *Istoricheskii arkhiv*, 1959, no. 5, p. 250

Debo, Richard K. 'The Manuilskii Mission: An Early Soviet Effort to Negotiate with France, August 1918-April 1919', *The International History Review*, vol. VIII, no. 2 (May 1986), pp. 214–35

Degot, V. *Pod znamenem Bol'shevizma: zapiski podpol'shchika*. Moscow, 1927

Deiateli SSSR i Oktiabr'skoi Revoliutsii (avtobiografii i biografii), 3 vols. Moscow, 1925–28

'Delo o pokushenie 16-ti lits na zhizn' generala Trepova v 1905 godu', *Byloe* (St Petersburg), 1907, no. 10 (22), pp. 271–307

Despy-Meyer, Andrée. *Inventaire des archives de l'Université Nouvelle de Bruxelles (1894–1919)*. Brussels: Université Libre de Bruxelles, 1973

Deutscher, Tamara (ed.). *Not by Politics Alone ...: The Other Lenin*. London: George Allen and Unwin, 1973

Dokumenty vneshnei politiki SSSR, vol. II. Moscow, 1958

Dolinov, G. 'Inessa Armand', *Rabotnitsa i Krest'ianka*, no. 9 (May 1941), p. 18

Donald, M. 'Bolshevik Activity Amongst the Working Women of Petrograd in 1917', *International Review of Social History*, vol. XXVII, no. 2 (1982), pp. 129–60

Drachkovitch, M. M. and Branko Lazitch (eds.). *The Comintern: Historical Highlights – Essays, Recollections, Documents*. New York: Praeger, 1966 (see essays by Branko Lazitch and Boris Souvarine)

Druzhinin, N. M. 'O trekh uchastnitsakh revoliutsionnoi bor'by', *Voprosy istorii*, 1983, no. 1, pp. 85–9

Dudgeon, Ruth A. 'The Forgotten Minority: Women Students in Imperial Russia, 1872–1917', *Russian History*, vol. IX, pt. 1 (1982), pp. 1–26

Dunayevskaya, Raya. *Rosa Luxemburg, Women's Liberation and Marx's Philosophy of Revolution*. Atlantic Highlands, N.J.: Humanities Press, 1982

Edmondson, Linda Harriet. *Feminism in Russia, 1900–1917*. Stanford: Stanford University Press, 1984

'Russian Feminists and the First All-Russian Congress of Women', *Russian History*, vol. III, pt. 2 (1976), pp. 123–49

Elizarova, A. 'Zhurnal "Rabotnitsa" 1914 g.', *Iz epokhi 'Zvezdy' i 'Pravdy', 1911–1914*, vol. III (Moscow, 1923), pp. 63–78

Elwood, R. C. 'How Complete is Lenin's *Polnoe Sobranie Sochinenii?*', *Slavic Review*, vol. XXXVIII, no. 1 (March 1979), pp. 97–105

'Lenin and the Brussels "Unity" Conference of July 1914', *Russian Review*, vol. XXXIX, no. 1 (January 1980), pp. 32–49.

'Lenin and the Social Democratic Schools for Underground Party Workers, 1909–11', *Political Science Quarterly*, vol. LXXXI, no. 3 (September 1966), pp. 370–91

'Lenin's Correspondence with Inessa Armand', *Slavonic and East European Review*, vol. LXV, no. 2 (April 1987), pp. 218–35.

Emmons, Terence. 'The Beseda Circle, 1899–1905', *Slavic Review*, vol. XXXII, no. 3 (September 1973), pp. 461–90

Engel, Barbara Alpern. 'Mothers and Daughters: Family Patterns and the Female Intelligentsia', in David L. Ransel (ed.), *The Family in Imperial*

Russia: New Lines of Historical Research (Urbana: University of Illinois Press, 1978), pp. 44–59.

'Women in Russia and the Soviet Union', *Signs*, vol. XII, no. 4 (summer 1987), pp. 781–96

Farnsworth, Beatrice. *Alexandra Kollontai: Socialism, Feminism and the Russian Revolution.* Stanford: Stanford University Press, 1980

'Bolshevism, the Woman Question, and Aleksandra Kollontai', *American Historical Review*, vol. LXXXI, no. 2 (April 1976), pp. 292–316

'Communist Feminism: Its Synthesis and Demise', in Carol R. Berkin and Clara M. Lavett (eds.), *Women, War, and Revolution.* New York: Holmes and Meier, 1980, pp. 145–63

Fel'dman, I. 'Inessa Armand – revoliutsionerka i mat', *Doshkol'noe vospitanie*, 1966, no. 4, pp. 72–9

Fieseler, Beate. 'The Making of Russian Female Social Democrats, 1890–1917', *International Review of Social History*, vol. XXXIV, no. 2 (1989), pp. 193–226

Figes, Orlando. 'The Village and *Volost* Soviet Elections of 1919', *Soviet Studies*, vol. XL, no. 1 (January 1988), pp. 21–45

Filippova, L. D. 'Iz istorii zhenskogo obrazovaniia v Rossii', *Voprosy istorii*, 1963, no. 2, pp. 209–18

Fischer, Louis. *The Life of Lenin.* New York: Harper and Row, 1964

The Foreign Policy of Soviet Russia: Report Submitted by the People's Commissariat for Foreign Affairs to the Seventh All-Russian Congress of Soviets. London: n.p. [1920]

Fréville, Jean. *Lénine à Paris.* Paris: Éditions Sociales, 1968.

'Portrait d'Inessa Armand, révolutionnaire', *La nouvelle critique*, nos. 87–8 (1957), pp. 87–96

Une grande figure de la Révolution russe: Inessa Armand. Paris: Éditions Sociales, 1957 (see also review by L. M. Egorova in *Istoriia SSSR*, 1958, no. 4, pp. 187–9)

Gankin, Olga H. and H. H. Fisher. *The Bolsheviks and the World War: The Origins of the Third International.* Stanford: Stanford University Press, 1940

Gautschi, W. *Lenin als Emigrant in der Schweiz.* Zurich: Benziger, 1973

Glickman, Rose L. *Russian Factory Women: Workplace and Society, 1880–1914.* Berkeley: University of California Press, 1984

Got'e, I. V. *Time of Troubles: The Diary of Iurii Vladimirovich Got'e (Moscow, July 8, 1917 to July 23, 1922),* trans. and ed. by Terence Emmons. Princeton: Princeton University Press, 1988

Grechnev-Chernov, A. S. 'Vospominaniia o V. I. Lenine', in *O Vladimire Il'iche Lenine.* Moscow, 1963

Grishina, Z. V. 'Pervyi vserossiiskii zhenskii s"ezd', *Vestnik Moskovskogo Universiteta*, series IX: *Istoriia*, 1976, no. 5, pp. 55–67

Gross, Babette. *Willi Münzenberg: A Political Biography,* trans. by Marian Jackson. East Lansing: Michigan State University Press, 1974

Haimson, Leopold H. *The Making of Three Russian Revolutionaries: Voices from the Menshevik Past*. Cambridge: Cambridge University Press, 1987

Haupt, Georges. *Aspects of International Socialism, 1871–1914: Essays by Georges Haupt*. Cambridge: Cambridge University Press, 1987

Haupt, Georges and Jean-Jacques Marie. *Makers of the Russian Revolution: Biographies of Bolshevik Leaders*. Ithaca: Cornell University Press, 1974

Hayden, Carol Eubanks. 'The Zhenotdel and the Bolshevik Party', *Russian History*, vol. III, pt. 2 (1976), pp. 150–73

Holland, Barbara (ed.). *Soviet Sisterhood: British Feminists on Women in the USSR*. London: Fourth Estate, 1985

Iakovlev, N. 'Aprel'sko-maiskie dni 1912 goda v Peterburge', *Krasnaia letopis'*, 1925, no. 3 (14), pp. 224–49

Iakushina, A. P. 'Iz istorii deiatel'nosti Komiteta zagranichnoi organizatsii RSDRP (1911–1914 gg.)', *Voprosy istorii KPSS*, 1966, no. 4, pp. 72–80

'Materialy po istorii Komiteta zagranichnoi organizatsii RSDRP', *Voprosy istorii KPSS*, 1961, no. 1, pp. 167–74

'Parizhskoe soveshchanie bol'shevikov', *Voprosy istorii KPSS*, 1964, no. 12, pp. 39–49

Lenin i Zagranichnaia organizatsiia RSDRP, 1905–1917. Moscow, 1972

Institut marksizma-leninizma pri TsK KPSS. *Vladimir Il'ich Lenin: biograficheskaia khronika*, 12 vols. Moscow, 1970–82.

Deviatyi s"ezd RKP(b), mart-aprel' 1920 goda: Protokoly. Moscow, 1960

Istoriia kommunisticheskoi partii sovetskogo soiuza, 8 vols. Moscow, 1964–70

Kommunisticheskaia partiia sovetskogo soiuza v rezoliutsiiakh i resheniiakh s"ezdov, konferentsii i plenumov TsK, 8th edn, vol. I. Moscow, 1970

Revoliutsionerki Rossii: Vospominaniia i ocherki o revoliutsionnoi deiatel'nosti rossiiskikh bol'shevichek. Moscow, 1983 (see memoirs of Iu. Ia. Zhukova/ Ts. V. Zorina and E. I. Pismanik)

Sed'maia (Aprel'skaia) Vserossiiskaia konferentsiia RSDRP (bol'shevikov), Petrogradskaia obshchegorodskaia konferentsiia RSDRP (Bol'shevikov). Aprel' 1917 goda: Protokoly. Moscow, 1958

Shestoi s"ezd RSDRP (bol'shevikov), avgust 1917 goda: Protokoly. Moscow, 1958

Vos'maia konferentsiia RKP(b). Dekabr' 1919 goda: Protokoly. Moscow, 1961

Istoriia Moskvy: kratkii ocherk, 3rd edn. Moscow, 1978

I. Iurenev, *Bor'ba za edinstvo partii*. Petrograd, 1917

Iz epokhi 'Zvezdy' i 'Pravdy', vol. III. Moscow, 1923

'Iz istorii bor'by Bol'shevikov za proletarskii internatsionalizm v mezhdunarodnom zhenskom sotsialisticheskom dvizhenii (1915 g.)', *Novaia i noveishaia istoriia*, 1959, no. 4, pp. 108–14

Johnson, Richard J. 'Zagranichnaia Agentura: The Tsarist Political Police in Europe', *Journal of Contemporary History*, vol. VII, no. 1 (January 1972), pp. 221–42

'K istorii izdaniia zhurnala "Rabotnitsa"', *Istoricheskii arkhiv*, 1955, no. 4, pp. 25–53

'K istorii prazdnovaniia Mezhdunarodnogo zhenskogo dnia v Rossii', *Krasnyi arkhiv*, 1938, no. 2 (87), pp. 3–18

Karavashkova, S. V. *Publitsistka A. M. Kollontai, I. F. Armand, L. N. Stal', A. I. Ul'ianovoi-Elizarovoi v bor'be za ukreplenie mezhdunarodnogo rabochego dvizheniia.* Moscow, 1973

Karpetskaia N. D. 'Vovlechenie trudiashchikhsia zhenshchin Petrograda v revoliutsionnoe dvizhenie (mart-iiul' 1917 g.)', *Vestnik Leningradskogo Universiteta*, 1966, no. 8, pp. 45–53

Karpinskii, V. 'Vladimir Il'ich za granitsei v 1914–1917 gg.', *Zapiski Instituta Lenina*, vol. II. Moscow, 1927, pp. 71–111

Kassow, Samuel D. *Students, Professors and the State in Tsarist Russia.* Berkeley: University of California Press, 1989

Kharitonov, M. 'Iz vospominanii', *Zapiski Instituta Lenina*, vol. II. Moscow, 1927, pp. 112–47

Khoniavko, I. P. 'V podpol'e i v emigratsii (1911–1917 gg.)' *Proletarskaia revoliutsiia*, 1923, no. 4 (16), pp. 159–75

Kobetskij, Aleksandra. 'Der Hvor Lenin Boede', *Fakta om Sovjetunionen* (Copenhagen), 1964, no. 8, pp. 19–21

Kollontai, A. 'Avtobiograficheskii ocherk', *Proletarskaia revoliutsiia*, 1921, no. 3, pp. 261–302

A Great Love, trans. by Cathy Porter. New York: Norton, 1981

'Kak my sozvali pervyi Vserossiiskii S"ezd rabotnits i krest'ianok', *Kommunistka*, 1923, no. 11, pp. 3–8

Women Workers Struggle for Their Rights, with introduction by Sheila Rowbotham. London, 1971

Kowalski, Ronnie. 'The Left Communist Movement in 1918: A Preliminary Analysis of Regional Strength', *Sbornik* of the Study Group on the Russian Revolution, no. 12 (1986), pp. 27–63

Kriegel, Annie. *Aux Origines du Communisme Français, 1914–1920*, 2 vols. Paris: Mouton, 1964

'Sur les rapports de Lénine avec le mouvement Zimmerwaldien Français', *Cahiers du Monde Russe et Soviétique*, vol. III, no. 2 (April–May 1962), pp. 299–306

Krupskaia, N. K. (ed.), *Pamiati Inessy Armand*. Moscow, 1926 (see contributions by N. K. Krupskaia, L. B. Kamenev, L. Stal', E. Rivlina, P. Vinogradskaia, E. Vlasova, G. Kotov, I. S. Ruzheinikov, E. Rikhterman, V. L. Malakhovskii, G. Safarov)

'Inessa Armand', in F. Kon (ed.). *Pamiati pogibshikh vozhdei*. Moscow, 1927, pp. 63–6

'Inessa Armand', *Kommunistka*, 1920, no. 5, pp. 17–20

'Plamennye bortsy za sotsializm', *Sputnik kommunista v derevne*, 1938, no. 4, pp. 16–19

Krupskaya, N. K. *Reminiscences of Lenin.* Moscow, 1959

Krutikova, N. *Na krutom povorote.* Moscow, 1965

Kudelli, P. K. N. *Samoilova–Gromova ('Natasha'), 1876–1921 gg. (biografiia)*. Leningrad, 1925

Lapidus, Gail Warshofsky. *Women in Soviet Society: Equality, Development and Social Change*. Berkeley: University of California Press, 1978

Lazitch, Branko. *Biographical Dictionary of the Comintern*, 2nd edn. Stanford: Hoover Institution Press, 1986

Lenin, V. I. *Polnoe sobranie sochinenii*, 55 vols. Moscow, 1958–65

Leninskii sbornik, 40 vols. Moscow, 1924–85

Lenin v Moskve: mesta prebyvaniia, daty i sobytiia. Moscow, 1959

Levi, E. 'Moskovskaia bol'shevistskaia organizatsiia ot fevralia do iiul'skikh dnei', in *Ocherki po istorii Oktiabr'skoi revoliutsii v Moskve*. Moscow, 1927, pp. 33–83

'Moskovskaia organizatsiia bol'shevikov v iiule 1917 goda', *Proletarskaia revoliutsiia*, 1929, nos. 2/3, pp. 123–51

Levidova, S. M. and S. A. Pavlotskaia. *Nadezhda Konstantinovna Krupskaia*. Leningrad, 1962

Lezheva, L. and G. Rusakov (eds.). *Pamiatnik bortsam proletarskoi revoliutsii pogibshem 1917–1921 gg.*, 3rd edn. Moscow, 1925

Lifshits, S. I. *Partiinye universitety podpol'ia*. Moscow, 1929

Liubimova, S. T. 'Iz istorii deiatel'nosti Zhenotdelov', *Voprosy istorii KPSS*, 1969, no. 9, pp. 68–77

Liudvinskaia, T. F. 'V gody emigratsii (1914–1917)', *Istoricheskii arkhiv*, 1962, no. 4, pp. 144–62

Loginov, V. T. *Leninskaia 'Pravda', 1912–1914 gg.* Moscow, 1972

Margarian, A. E. 'Novoe ob Inesse Armand', *Voprosy istorii*, 1962, no. 3, pp. 213–15

McKay, John. *Pioneers for Profit: Foreign Entrepreneurship and Russian Industrialization, 1885–1913*. Chicago: University of Chicago Press, 1970

McKean, Robert C. *St Petersburg between the Revolutions: Workers and Revolutionaries, June 1907–February 1917*. New Haven: Yale University Press, 1990

McNeal, Robert H. *Bride of the Revolution: Krupskaya and Lenin*. Ann Arbor: University of Michigan Press, 1972

'Lenin and "Lise de K . . . "': A Fabrication', *Slavic Review*, vol. XXVIII, no. 3 (September 1969), pp. 471–4

'Women in the Russian Radical Movement', *Journal of Social History*, vol. V, no. 2 (Winter 1971–2), pp. 143–63

Men'shikov, L. P. *Okhrana i revoliutsiia*, vol. I. Moscow, 1923

Miliutina, N. *Nakanune pervoi revoliutsii v Moskve*. Moscow, 1926

Miuntsenberg, V. [Willi Münzenberg]. *S Libknekhtom i Leninym: piatnadtsat' let v proletarskom iunosheskom dvizhenii*. Moscow, 1930

Morison, J. D. 'Political Characteristics of the Student Movement in the Russian Revolution of 1905', in F-X. Coquin and C. Gervois-Francelle (eds.), *1905: La Première Révolution Russe*. Paris: Sorbonne, 1986, pp. 63–75

Mukhamedzhanov, M. M. 'V. I. Lenin i mezhdunarodnaia sotsialisticheskaia molodezh v gody pervoi mirovoi voiny', *Novaia i noveishaia istoriia*, 1967, no. 2, pp. 3–13

Mullaney, Marie Marmo. 'Gender and the Socialist Revolutionary Role, 1871–1921: A General Theory of the Female Revolutionary Personality', *Historical Reflections/Réflexions historiques*, vol. XI, no. 1 (Summer 1984), pp. 99–151

Revolutionary Women. New York: Praeger, 1983

Najdus, Walentyna. *Lenin wsród przyjaciól i znajomych w Polsce 1912–1914*. Warsaw, 1977

Nation, R. Craig. *War on War: Lenin, the Zimmerwald Left, and the Origins of Communist Internationalism*. Durham: Duke University Press, 1989

Neiman, Iu. 'Inessa Armand', *Smena*, 1941, no. 5, pp. 11–13

Nevskii, V. I. (ed.). *Deiateli revoliutsionnogo dvizheniia v Rossii: Bio-bibliograficheskii slovar'*, vol. V. *Sotsial-demokraty, 1880–1904*, vyp. 1. Moscow, 1931

Novikov, M. M. *Ot Moskvy do N'iu Iorka*. New York: Chekhov Publishing House, 1952

'Novye dokumenty ob Inesse Armand', *Istoricheskii arkhiv*, 1961, no. 3, pp. 281–2

'Novye dokumenty V. I. Lenina', *Izvestiia TsK KPSS*, 1989, no. 1, pp. 213–17

'Novyi pod"em rabochego dvizheniia (1910–1914)', *Krasnyi arkhiv*, 1934, no. 62, pp. 223–48

Ocherki istorii Moskovskoi organizatsii KPSS. Moscow, 1966

Odell, Ralph M. *Cotton Goods in Russia*. Washington: Government Printing Office, 1912

'O mezhdunarodnoi zhenskoi sotsialisticheskoi konferentsii v 1915 g.', *Istoricheskii arkhiv*, 1960, no. 3, pp. 106–25

Oppenheim, Samuel A. 'The Supreme Economic Council, 1917–1921', *Soviet Studies*, vol. XXV, no. 1 (July 1973), pp. 3–27

Otchet o Pervoi Mezhdunarodnoi Konferentsii Kommunistok. Moscow, 1921

'Otchet pervoi partiinoi shkoly v Lonzhiumo', *Istoricheskii arkhiv*, 1962, no. 5, pp. 36–54

Ovcharova, A. V. and K. V. Shakhnazarova, 'Briussel'skoe "ob"edinitel'noe" soveshchanie (iiul' 1914 g.)', *Voprosy istorii KPSS*, 1959, no. 5, pp. 152–63

Owen, Thomas C. *Capitalism and Politics in Russia: A Social History of Moscow Merchants, 1855–1905*. Cambridge: Cambridge University Press, 1981

'O zhizni i deiatel'nosti V. I. Lenina', *Izvestiia TsK KPSS*, 1989, no. 4, pp. 169–85

Pak, B. I. 'Savva Timofeevich Morozov', *Soviet Studies in History*, vol. XX (Winter 1981–2), pp. 74–95

Pazhitnov, K. A. *Ocherki istorii tekstil'noi promyshlennosti dorevoliutsionnoi Rossii: sherstianaia promyshlennost'*. Moscow, 1955

Pearson, Michael. *The Sealed Train*. London: Macmillan, 1975

Peregudova, Z. L. and V. V. Khmeleva. 'Dokumenty ob Inesse Armand', *Sovetskie arkhivy*, 1967, no. 6, pp. 104–6

'Perepiska TsK RSDRP s mestnymi partiinymi organizatsiiami v gody novogo revoliutsionnogo pod"ema', *Istoricheskii arkhiv*, 1957, no. 1, pp. 3–45

Petrovskii, G. I. 'Zhizn', polnaia blagorodstva i predannosti idee kommunizma', in A. M. Arsenev *et al.* (eds.), *Vospominaniia o Nadezhde Konstantinovne Krupskoi*. Moscow, 1966, pp. 81–6

Pianzola, Maurice. *Lénine en Suisse*. Geneva: Éditions Librairie Rousseau, 1952

Pinchuk, L. R. 'Moim detiam – vmesto zaveshchaniia', *Vospitanie shkol'nikov*, 1985, no. 3, pp. 62–8

Pintner, Walter M. 'The Burden of Defense in Imperial Russia, 1725–1914', *Russian Review*, vol. XLIII, no. 3 (July 1984), pp. 231–59

'Pis'ma V. I. Lenina Inesse Armand', *Bol'shevik*, 1939, no. 13, pp. 58–61

Podliashuk, P. 'Pravda i zhizn' – za nas!', in V. Vavilina (ed.), *Vsegda s vami: Sbornik posviashchennyi 50-letiiu zhurnala 'Rabotnitsa'*. Moscow, 1964

'Prekrasnaia zhizn' (I. F. Armand)', in L. P. Zhak and A. Itkina (eds.). *Zhenshchiny russkoi revoliutsii*. Moscow, 1968, pp. 28–44

Tovarishch Inessa: dokumental'naia povest', 4th edn. Moscow, 1984

Pogodin, S. 'Komandirovka', *Sovetskie profsoiuzy*, 1986, no. 17, p. 16

Popova, E. 'Moskovskaia okruzhnaia organizatsiia v 1917 godu', in *Ocherki po istorii Oktiabr'skoi revoliutsii v Moskve*. Moscow, 1927, pp. 316–84

Portal, Roger. 'Muscovite Industrialists: The Cotton Sector (1861–1914)', in William L. Blackwell (ed.), *Russian Economic Development from Peter the Great to Stalin*. New York: New Viewpoints, 1974, pp. 161–96

Porter, Cathy. *Alexandra Kollontai: A Biography*. London: Virago, 1980

Possony, Stefan T. *Lenin: The Compulsive Revolutionary*. Chicago: Regnery, 1964

'Protokoly pervoi (Moskovskoi) oblastnoi konferentsii tsentral'no-promyshlennogo raiona RSDRP(b) proiskhodivshei v g. Moskve [2–4 mai] 19–21 aprel'ia 1917 g.', *Proletarskaia revoliutsiia*, 1929, no. 10, pp. 129–206

'Protokoly VI (Prazhskoi) vserossiiskoi konferentsii RSDRP', *Voprosy istorii KPSS*, 1988, no. 7, pp. 31–57

'Protokoly zasedanii Moskovskogo oblastnogo biuro (mai–iiun' 1917 g.)', *Proletarskaia revoliutsiia*, 1927, no. 4, pp. 235–80

Put' k Oktiabriu: sbornik statei, vospominanii i dokumentov, 4 vols. Moscow, 1923–25 (see articles by M. Petrova in vol. I, A. Shestakov and P. P. Bulanov in vol. II, F. O. Kriukov in vol. III, N. P. and P. P. Bulanov in vol. IV)

Raskol'nikov, F. *Kronshtadt i Piter v 1917 g*. Moscow, 1925

Ravich, O. 'Iz vospominanii o Vladimire Il'iche', *Proletarskaia revoliutsiia*, 1929, nos. 8/9, pp. 96–106

'Mezhdunarodnaia zhenskaia sotsialisticheskaia konferentsiia 1915 goda', *Proletarskaia revoliutsiia*, 1925, no. 10 (45), pp. 165–77

Remington, Thomas F. *Building Socialism in Bolshevik Russia: Ideology and Industrial Organization, 1917–1921*. Pittsburgh: University of Pittsburgh Press, 1984

Rieber, Alfred J. *Merchants and Entrepreneurs in Imperial Russia*. Chapel Hill: University of North Carolina Press, 1982

Rosenthal, B. G. 'Love on the Tractor: Women in the Russian Revolution and After', in Claudia Koonz and Renate Bridenthal (eds.), *Becoming Visible: Women in European History*. Boston: Houghton Mifflin, 1977, pp. 370–99

Ruckman, JoAnn. *Moscow Business Elite: A Social and Cultural Portrait of Two Generations, 1840–1905*. DeKalb: Northern Illinois University Press, 1984

Rusakov, Iu. and V. Solov'ev. 'Stanovlius' bol'shevichkoi ...', *V mire knig*, 1978, no. 8, pp. 77–80

Safarov, G. 'Nasha Piterskaia organizatsiia pered vyborami v IV Dumu', in *Iz epokhi 'Zvezdy' i 'Pravdy'*, vol. III. Moscow, 1923, pp. 126–8

Sakwa, Richard. 'The Commune State in Moscow in 1918', *Slavic Review*, vol. XLVI, nos. 3/4 (Fall/Winter 1987), pp. 429–49

Soviet Communists in Power: A Study of Moscow during the Civil War, 1918–21. London: Macmillan, 1988

Salisbury, Harrison E. *Black Night, White Snow: Russia's Revolutions, 1905–1917*. Garden City, N.Y.: Doubleday, 1978

Sanders, Joseph L. *The Moscow Uprising of December 1905: A Background Study*. New York: Garland, 1987

Sanov, Vladimir. 'Mezenskaia ballada', *Sever*, 1971, no. 12, pp. 82–96

Scherrer, Jutta. 'Un "philosophe-ouvrier" russe: N. E. Vilonov', *Mouvement social*, no. 111 (1980), pp. 165–87

Senn, Alfred Erich. 'The Bolshevik Conference in Bern, 1915', *Slavic Review*, vol. XXV, no. 4 (December 1966), pp. 676–8

Nicholas Rubakin: A Life for Books. Newtonville, Mass.: Oriental Research Partners, 1977

'Russian Emigré Funds in Switzerland, 1916: An Okhrana Report', *International Review of Social History*, vol. XIII (1968), pp. 76–84

The Russian Revolution in Switzerland, 1914–1917. Madison: University of Wisconsin Press, 1971

Serditova, S. N. *Bol'sheviki v bor'be za zhenskie proletarskie massy*. Moscow, 1959

Shapovalov, A. S. *V izgnanii (sredi bel'giiskikh i frantsuzskikh rabochikh)*. Moscow, 1927

Shaumian, S. S. 'V. I. Lenin i briussel'skoe "ob"edinitel'noe" soveshchanie', *Istoriia SSSR*, 1966, no. 2, pp. 27–43

Shklovskii, G. L. 'Iz moikh vospominanii', *Zapiski Instituta Lenina*, vol. I. Moscow, 1927, pp. 105–22

'Vladimir Il'ich nakanune konferentsii', *Proletarskaia revoliutsiia*, 1925, no. 5 (40), pp. 134–49

'Vospominaniia uchastnikov Bernskoi konferentsii', *Proletarskaia revoliutsiia*, 1925, no. 5 (40), pp. 182–93

Shub, David. *Lenin: A Biography*, rev. edn. London: Penguin, 1966

Singer, Ladislaus. *Korrekturen zu Lenin*. Stuttgart: Seewald, 1980

Skovno, R. A. 'Samoe dorogoe v zhizni', *Nash Il'ich: Sbornik vospominanii starykh Bol'shevikov zamoskvorech'ia o vstrechakh s V. I. Leninym*. Moscow, 1960, pp. 17–24

Smidovich, S. 'Rabota sredi zhenshchin v Moskve i Moskovskoi gubernii', *Kommunistka*, 1923, no. 11, pp. 19–21

Smith, S. A. *Red Petrograd: Revolution in the Factories, 1917–18*. Cambridge: Cambridge University Press, 1983

Solzhenitsyn, Alexander. *Lenin in Zurich*. New York: Farrar, Straus, Giroux, 1976

Sorin, Vl. *Partiia i Oppozitsiia: iz istorii oppozitsionnykh techenii*, vol. I; *Fraktsiia levykh kommunistov*. Moscow, 1925

Stal', L. 'Rabota Parizhskoi Sektsii Bol'shevikov sredi frantsuzskikh rabotnits v 1914–1916 gg.', *Bor'ba klassov*, 1934, no. 9, pp. 17–24

'Rabotnitsa v Oktiabre', *Proletarskaia revoliutsiia*, 1922, no. 10, pp. 299–301

Stites, Richard. 'Kollontai, Inessa, and Krupskaia: A Review of Recent Literature', *Canadian-American Slavic Studies*, vol. IX, no. 1 (Spring 1975), pp. 84–92

'Prostitution and Society in Pre-Revolutionary Russia', *Jahrbucher für Geschichte Osteuropas*, vol. XXXI, no. 3 (1983), pp. 348–65

The Women's Liberation Movement in Russia: Feminism, Nihilism, and Bolshevism, 1860–1930. Princeton: Princeton University Press, 1977

'Zhenotdel: Bolshevism and Russian Women, 1917–1930', *Russian History*, vol. III, pt. 2 (1976), pp. 174–93

Suliashvili, D. 'Vstrechi s Leninym v emigratsii', *Neva*, 1957, no. 2, pp. 135–44

Swain, G. R. 'The Bolsheviks' Prague Conference Revisited', *Revolutionary Russia*, vol. II, no. 1 (June 1989), pp. 134–41

Russian Social Democracy and the Legal Labour Movement, 1906–14. London: Macmillan, 1983

Syromiatnikova, M. 'Bernskaia konferentsiia zagranichnykh organizatsii RSDRP v 1915 g.', *Proletarskaia revoliutsiia*, 1925, no. 5 (40), pp. 150–78

Tarasenko, K. 'Inessa Armand (1874–1920)', *Agitator*, 1974, no. 9, pp. 47–9

Torez, Moris [Maurice Thorez]. 'Oktiabr' ukazal nam put'', *Voprosy istorii KPSS*, 1957, no. 3, pp. 84–96

Trotsky, Leon. *My Life: An Attempt at an Autobiography*. New York: Pathfinder Press, 1970

Tsiavlovskii, M. A. (ed.), *Bol'sheviki: dokumenty po istorii bol'shevizma s 1903 po 1916 g. byvsh. Moskovskago Okhrannago Otdeleniia*. Moscow, 1918

Tugan-Baranovsky, M. I. *The Russian Factory in the Nineteenth Century*, trans. by Arthur and C. S. Levin. Homewood, Ill.: Richard Irwin, 1970

Ulam, Adam B. *The Bolsheviks: The Intellectual and Political History of the Triumph of Communism in Russia*. New York: Macmillan, 1965

Urakadze, G. *Vospominaniia Gruzinskogo sotsial-demokrata*. Stanford: Hoover Institution Press, 1968

Valentinov, N. *Vstrechi s Leninym*. New York: Chekhov Publishing House, 1953

Vinogradskaia, P. S. *Sobytiia i pamiatnye vstrechi*. Moscow, 1968

Voitinskaia, O. 'Leninskie pis'ma k Inesse Armand', *Pod znamenem marksizma*, 1939, no. 11, pp. 72–85

Volodarskaia, A. M. *Lenin i partiia v godu nazrevaniia revoliutsionnogo krizisa, 1913–1914*. Moscow, 1960

Vospitanniki Moskovskogo universiteta – Bol'sheviki oktiabr'skogo prizyva. Moscow, 1977

Vospominaniia o Vladimire Il'iche Lenine, 5 vols. Moscow, 1969–70 (see entries by I. S. Ganetskii and T. F. Liudvinskaia in vol. II; D. I. Grazkin in vol. III; I. A. Armand in vol. IV)

Warth, Robert D. 'Armand, Inessa Fedorovna', in *The Modern Encyclopedia of Russian and Soviet History*, vol. II (1976), pp. 94–5

Waters, Elizabeth. 'In the Shadow of the Kremlin: The Communist Women's Movement, 1920–43', in Sonia Kruks, Rayna Rapp and Marilyn B. Young (eds.), *Promissory Notes: Women in the Transition to Socialism*. New York: Monthly Review Press, 1989, pp. 29–59

Williams, Robert C. *The Other Bolsheviks: Lenin and His Critics, 1904–1914*. Bloomington: Indiana University Press, 1986

Wohl, Robert. *French Communism in the Making, 1914–1924*. Stanford: Stanford University Press, 1966

Wolfe, Bertram D. 'Lenin and Inessa Armand', *Slavic Review*, vol. XXII, no. 1 (March 1963), pp. 96–114

Three Who Made a Revolution: A Biographical History. Boston: Dell, 1948

Work Among Women. London: Communist Party of Great Britain, 1924 (see articles by R. Kovnator and V. A. Moirova)

Yedlin, Tova (ed.). *Women in Eastern Europe and the Soviet Union*. New York: Praeger, 1980 (see contributions by Barbara Clements, Alix Holt, Robert McNeal and Richard Stites)

Yemelyanova, Yelena. *Revolution in Woman's Life*. Moscow, 1985

Zak, L. M. 'Deiatel'nost' Frantsuzskoi kommunisticheskoi gruppy RKP(b) v 1918–1919 godakh', *Voprosy istorii*, 1960, no. 2, pp. 152–66

'Kommunisticheskie listovki i vozzvaniia k soldatam antanty', *Istoricheskii arkhiv*, 1958, no. 1, pp. 26–40

Zetkin, Clara. *Lenin on the Woman Question*. New York, 1934

NEWSPAPERS

Izvestiia, Moscow
Kommunist, Geneva (1915)
Kommunist, Moscow (1918)
Pravda, St Petersburg (1912–14)
Pravda, Moscow (1918–)
Rabotnitsa, St Petersburg
Revoliutsionnaia Rossiia, Geneva
Russkie vedomosti, Moscow
Sbornik Sotsial-demokrata, Geneva
Sotsial-demokrat, Paris and Geneva
Le Temps, Paris

INDEX